THE VIRTUOSI

OTHER BOOKS BY HAROLD C. SCHONBERG

The Guide to Long-Playing Records: Chamber and Solo Instrument Music

The Collector's Chopin and Schumann

The Great Pianists

The Great Conductors

The Lives of the Great Composers

Grandmasters of Chess

Facing the Music

HAROLD C. SCHONBERG

THE VIRTUOSI

Classical Music's Legendary Performers from Paganini to Pavarotti

VINTAGE BOOKS
A DIVISION OF RANDOM HOUSE
NEW YORK

ORIGINALLY PUBLISHED IN HARDCOVER AS *The Glorious Ones*

This book is dedicated to those great performers of past and present who, on the stage or through recordings, have exhilarated and inspired me through the decades.

FIRST VINTAGE BOOKS EDITION, October 1988

 Published in the United States by Random House, Inc., New York, and simultaneously in Canada by Random House of Canada Limited, Toronto. Originally published, in hardcover, as *The Glorious Ones* by Times Books, a division of Random House, Inc., New York, in 1985.

Library of Congress Cataloging-in-Publication Data
Schonberg, Harold C.
The virtuosi.
Reprint. Originally published: The glorious ones.
New York: Times Books, 1985.
Bibliography: p.
Includes index.
1. Musicians—Biography. I. Title.
ML394.S393 1985 780'.92'2 [B] 88-40022
ISBN 0-394-75532-4 (pbk.)

Owing to limitations of space, all acknowledgements of permission to reproduce illustrations will be found on page 510.

Manufactured in the United States of America
10 9 8 7 6 5 4 3 2 1

Contents

Preface

MARION BAUER, one of my music teachers, once said something I never forgot: "If you are interested in a subject and do not know as much about it as you would like to, write a book about it. By the time you have finished the research, you might even be an authority on the subject."

Over lunch one day Jonathan Segal, my editor at Times Books, brought up the subject of a Sunday piece I had written in 1980 about the unprecedented fees that top musicians were charging. Fascinating, he said. Did the classical superstars always make that kind of money? And, he continued, who *were* the superstars back in 1900? In the 1850's? In the early nineteenth century? How far back can one go to find superstars? How did they live? How did they get around? Did they have managers to negotiate for them? What made them superstars? Were the great stars always as good as their reputations or were other musicians perhaps better who never became the idols of the public? What was money worth before World War I? In the nineteenth century? Why not write a book about it?

I remembered Miss Bauer's words.

The idea of a book on the lives and times of the great performers, the most highly paid artists, the ones who set the standards by which all others are measured—the superstars of music, if you will—was intriguing. Indeed, it was irresistible. In several previous books I had touched on the subject but never fully explored it. Nor was there any such book in the field.

As one who has made a lifelong study of performance practice, I knew the major figures and rattled off some names to Segal. But some of the questions he asked stumped me. The field of performance practice has many imponderables that lie outside music proper. Musicians flourish at a particular time and in a particular kind of society. To get a full idea of what they represented, the society itself must be studied. Music has something to do with ideas, and the prevalent intellectual, musical, and audience esthetic of any particular time has to be taken into account. Modern prejudices can make performances in a previous age hard to understand.

In any age there has been a handful of performers who have set standards and captivated the public. There is no great mystery about their success. With very few exceptions they have been more naturally gifted than their colleagues, and they also have a kind of personality that comes right over the footlights to the point where people will tear down the doors to attend their performances. Somehow—and *that* is a mystery—they manage to bring music to life—and, even more important for their success, convince the public—in a way that colleagues perhaps possessed of a better mind and more scrupulous musicianship cannot match. In 1910 certainly no professional pianist in his right mind would have maintained that Paderewski played the piano better than, say, Leopold Godowsky or Josef Hofmann. Compared to them, Paderewski was all but a cripple. But it was Paderewski who captured the public imagination, and whose name still is a symbol for the heights of piano playing. He was one of the exceptions—a superstar whose magnetism was much greater than his ability. By and large, however, superstars have combined charisma with ability to a supernal degree.

Almost from the beginning there have been two performing approaches to music—the Dionysian and the Apollonian. In the largely Dionysian nineteenth century, there still were such Apollonian musicians as Julius Stockhausen, Clara Schumann, and Joseph Joachim. Each eschewed empty virtuosity and applied themselves selflessly to what they considered "pure" music, the music of the great masters. And in some cases they even became superstars. Joachim certainly was one.

In other cases, performers have started out as great musicians and ended up merely as entertainers. When Adelina Patti broke upon the European scene shortly after mid-century, she conquered everybody, including the composers whose music she sang—and some of them were very tough critics. Toward the end of her life she was little more than a trained monkey, making her endless farewell tours, singing *Home, Sweet Home* and other such tidbits again and again, collecting unheard-of fees. But the late Patti should not be confused with the sublime singer who in her prime set a new standard for the vocal art.

The point is that a musician does not become a superstar without having contributed significantly to the development of the art. Superstars do certain things better than anybody else and, in the process, collect an enthusiastic, adoring international audience. It may be that the art of Paganini and Liszt had its meretricious aspects. It is also unarguable that the course of violin and piano playing was forever changed once they came before the public. Every age has many stars but few superstars.

Musical superstars seem to have some things in common. A surprisingly large number came from musical or theatrical families and were exposed to music from babyhood. Their talent showed up early, and most of them made their first public appearances at an alarmingly early age. From the beginning most of them seemed to have a kind of personality and projection that, coupled to their markedly superior talent, immediately set them apart from their colleagues. They had that mysterious Factor X, the ingredient that enabled them to generate frenzy in an audience. They were paid accordingly, becoming extremely rich, vain, pampered, and spoiled. They became international stars, and their names still ring through the ages: Caruso; Jenny Lind, "the Swedish Nightingale"; Adelina Patti, "the Queen of Song"; Paderewski; Heifetz; Toscanini. They remain in the popular mind as the exemplars of their art.

It is inevitable that among singers the high-voiced ones attract most adoration, get the most publicity, and make the most money. There have been superstar basses—Luigi Lablache and Feodor Chaliapin are two outstanding examples—but they are greatly in the minority. There are, of course, obvious reasons for the persistent admiration of the high-voiced singer (though who was it who said that the higher the voice, the lower the intelligence?). Some reasons are physiological: the more penetrating quality and greater brilliance of high voices, the empathy they create when they reach for a note *in alt,* the greater technical and musical opportunities given to them by nineteenth-century composers (which means the bulwark of the active repertory). That is one reason so many mezzo-sopranos attempt to become sopranos. *That* way lies superstardom and riches. This inalienable fact was pointed out by the London *Times* as early as 1856: "It is notorious that a prima donna in modern times can only claim the highest rank and emoluments if she has a soprano voice. A contralto may be a prima donna, but not *assoluta*."

Music is a mystery. It is a potent art, and obviously has a great deal of meaning, but has anybody satisfactorily defined it? Books have been written on the meaning of meaning in music. Music is pitched sound, rhythmically organized for expressive purposes. But it needs intermediaries to make it come to life. By itself, music is merely a series of black notes on a printed page. Somebody has to take those notes and follow the directions of the composer, as much as those admittedly vague and unsatisfactory symbols allow. If this sounds like a pointless truism, it is a truism generally ignored by so many of today's critics and musicologists, who seem to regard music as a Platonic ideal—an Idea, bloodless, bound up in form and content, the written note sanctified, all adding up to some kind of objective patterns in sound. If they had their way, one feels, they would abolish the performer. Unfortunately for them the performer cannot be abolished. Ultimately those wonderfully abstract patterns of the composer have to be translated for the listener, and that is where the performer steps in.

At any given time a few performers manage to translate the notes in a more transcendental, exciting manner than any of their colleagues. They do so in their own manner and, usually, according to the dictates of their age. Every age has its own way of making music, and every age thinks *its* way is the only true way. Today, for instance, young musicians tend to sneer at the Romantic way of making music, not realizing that they really have as little idea of nineteenth-century performance practice as a typical nineteenth-century artist had about style in Bach and Mozart. Nineteenth-century performance practice was not the an anarchy today's musicians seem to think it was. Recordings made by the better artists born in the nineteenth century reveal an aristocratic and even surprisingly classical approach, delivered with much more flair and even technical expertise than almost anybody today can duplicate. This is not an unconsidered statement. Many dozens of nineteenth-century artists, born as early as 1819, can be heard on recordings; and a large number of them, singers especially, put equivalent contemporary artists to shame.

There is another side to that coin, however. When they were singing or performing the music of their own time, nineteenth-century artists had a confidence, authority, and delivery that have vanished from the earth. But the nineteenth century was nowhere near as historical-minded as today, and when those musicians performed music of the past, including Beethoven, they did bring Romantic mannerisms to their interpretations. By and large, modern musicians have—or firmly believe they have—a much greater understanding of, and respect for, early music than their forbears ever did. Even older musicians, brought up in an older tradition, can also change with the age, imperceptibly and often without realizing it until something happens to bring their past to life. Then, all of a sudden, *their* traditions seem outdated. This fact was noted by Georg Solti, who studied Mozart's *Zauberflöte* in 1936 at Salzburg under Toscanini. Solti played the glockenspiel in the Toscanini-led performance. "I was in love with that performance," he told an interviewer many years later. "A great man stood before me and I believed every bar of *The Magic Flute,* every bar without hesitation. I lived on that memory up to a year and a half ago when somebody said to me there is a tape of that performance. I got it and listened to it. It is not to believe. There is not one tempo which is right. There is nothing which I would consider right for my picture of *The Magic Flute* today. You see, this was about 35 years ago and it's changed so much. I laughed. It was a joke." (It is true that even in his own day Toscanini's ideas about Haydn and Mozart were considered out of line. Solti hastened to add that he still considers Toscanini incomparable in many other aspects of the repertory.)

Yet nagging questions remain, and I wish I could be as sure of the answers as some of my colleagues are. Or even as sure as that justly eminent conductor, Sir Georg Solti, is about the Toscanini performance. The fact that his opinion has changed in accordance with the dictates of a more modern age does not necessarily mean that the Toscanini approach was all wrong. It merely illustrates a shift in the musical esthetic; and it could well be—indeed, it probably *will* be—that fifty years from now Solti's Beethoven and the Beethoven of most of today's admired interpreters will be held up to the kind of scorn that the Toscanini *Zauberflöte* evokes in Solti.

Take the case, mentioned above, of the typical nineteenth-century musician in relation to the music of early Beethoven and his predecessors. There can be no doubt that modern interpreters build their performances on a much more secure musicological basis than their predecessors did. We not only know more about ornamentation in classic and baroque music than Liszt did; we also could well know more about it than Bach himself did. But the more that performance practice of early music is studied, the more it seems that there were no set rules. What is more, the pre-Beethoven composers never seemed to concern themselves with the form and structure so *de rigueur* in today's circles. When they wrote about their music, they were constantly harping on its *Af-*

fekt, its emotional significance, and not on the way the music was put together. When we study handbooks about performance written in the late eighteenth or early nineteenth century, we find the constant use of expressive devices commonly supposed to belong to the Romantic period. When we look at first editions of Haydn and Mozart we often find the performer granted, on the printed page, a kind of freedom and actual Romanticism that no modern urtext shows. ("Urtext" is a big word in today's musical circles. It is supposed to be an "authentic" edition, purged of later editorial emendations, stating exactly what the composer desired and no more. In reality the concept of an urtext is a myth.) So can it be that the derided Romantic way of playing, say, an early Beethoven sonata, is closer to Beethoven than today's more astringent style? Can it be that we are making the naughtiest of esthetic errors, and that is to judge the work of a previous age by our own esthetic—an esthetic removed from the original by some two hundred years and more?

Modern thought distrusts the concept of the virtuoso, the performer as hero. Where Franz Liszt frankly admitted that he was the servant of the public, today's musicians unanimously say that they are the servant of the composer. Yet that noble modern statement is a dubious half-truth. If it is axiomatic that the performer must bring the music to life, it also follows that only through the mind, fingers, voice, and heart of the executant can the nobility of his calling be exercised. A performer is no good at all if he does not express himself as much as he expresses his concept of the composer's meaning. If ever there was a symbiotic relationship, this is it. But today, by and large, artists are literal-minded and careful, and there is a dreadful unanimity of approach. Performers seem much too worried about the text and not enough about its message.

The stars and superstars of the past, on the other hand, were never literalists. They accepted, as the composers also did, the fact, which today tends to be ignored, that re-creation is the mark of the artist; and composers were always happy to work closely with the ones they trusted, as Mendelssohn did with Ferdinand David and Brahms with Joseph Joachim and, as a matter of fact, as Mozart, Rossini, Bellini, and Donizetti did with some of the singers of their day.

In the study of performers and performance practice through history, there are many unexplored areas. How were the stars of the past "handled"? Did managers take care of their affairs? Nobody knows much about the setup. There has never been a book on the history of concert managers, some of whom, such as Max Maretzek, James Mapleson, Hermann Wolff, and Sol Hurok, were fabulous characters.

When it comes to money and its relative value through the centuries, most scholars hastily avoid the subject. What would a thaler have meant to Mozart or to Brahms? When Maria Malibran received £66 a performance in 1829, what did that mean in terms of modern money and spending power? Even so experienced a researcher as Alan Walker, in his biography of Franz Liszt, threw up his hands and said that nobody can make sense of the subject. As a matter of fact, however, it is not that hopeless, and in the following pages an attempt will be made to clarify the problem.

Another area that never has been satisfactorily explored is the nature of the musical child prodigy (and prodigies in general). There is next to no literature on the subject. It is a fascinating topic that, one should have thought, psychologists, physiologists, behaviorists, and educators would have studied in detail. But no. Yet certain children (and not only in music) are born with an order of ear, memory, reflex, synthesis, intelligence, and instinct that far separates them from normal children. These children are the ones who are going to become the great performers (it is hard to think of an outstanding pianist or violinist who started after six years of age), mathematicians, physicists, chess players, linguists, and polymaths. Whence came this incredible order of ability at so early an age?

This book will not pretend to be an encyclopedia. At any period there could be a dozen claimants to superstar position, and it would take a mighty tome to include everybody. Faced with the impossibility of writing a book on all superstars, I have opted for a book on *some* superstars. There will be complaints about the omission of certain favorites, but at least those in the following pages are among the most potent that music has to show. The choices are admittedly arbitrary, based (in admittedly haphazard proportions) on musical quality, degree of international celebrity, and lasting contributions to the art (sometimes purely technical, sometimes musical, and a combination of the two in the greatest figures).

I would like to thank my editor, Jonathan Segal, for his understanding and expertise; my wife, Helene, for her support and patience; Haidi Kuhn-Segal, my indefatigable photo researcher and photographer; Bea Friedland of Da Capo Press for her generosity in supplying me with many reprints in the superb Da Capo series; Gregor Benko, who lent me some pictures from his vast collection; Rocco Galatioto, for his invaluable work in the photo lab; and my Northstar Advantage, the personal computer on which this book was written.

THE VIRTUOSI

1 *The Castrati*

LUNGS OF MEN, VOICES OF WOMEN

VOCALLY the eighteenth century was the age of the castrato singer, those *evirati* with the lungs of men and voices of women. At least two of them—Farinelli, born Carlo Broschi, and Gasparo Pacchierotti—were, arguably, the greatest singers the world has ever known, and among the highest paid. Every generation claims that the art of singing is on the road to perdition. Every age might be right. It could well be that singing has been in decline ever since the castrati, those ungainly, spoiled, vain capons, trod the stage and were chased by women all over Europe.

Yes, chased by women. They were castrated males, but they were anything but eunuchs. Europe resounded with the love affairs of these first musical superstars. Many were grotesque: tall, strangely proportioned (barrel chest, skinny legs), often with secondary sexual characteristics including female breasts and femalelike hips and buttocks. But the top castrato singers were internationally famous, fabulously rich, friends with royalty of state and church. As such they attracted women, especially high-bred women on the lookout for something exotic and titillating—and they could not impregnate the women who had affairs with them. Their personal lives give the lie to the old joke about castrati being gentlemen cut out to be bachelors.

Some, like Domenico Cecchi, had homosexual affairs. Giovanni Francesco Grossi was a known lady-killer. Gaetano Guadagni had mistress after mistress. The famous Gaetano Majorano, known as Caffarelli, narrowly escaped death at the hands of a jealous husband in Rome. Luigi Marchesi got involved in a great scandal in London when a lady left her husband and children to live with him. Gasparo Pacchierotti had an affair in Naples with the Marchesa Santa Marca, and her lover made plans to have the singer assassinated. Giusto Ferdinando Tenducci, Mozart's friend, eloped with a girl of good family in 1766 and ended up in jail when her furious parents and relatives prosecuted him. Giovanni Battista Velluti (1781–1861), the last important castrato, chased women all over Europe and in Russia lived for a while with a grand duchess.

And the money they made! They came into full flower in the early 1700's, and from the beginning were the despair of opera-house managers. Luigi Riccoboni, in a survey of European theaters made in 1738, wrote that the fees of a Farinelli (he also mentioned Faustina and Cuzzoni, the first two really important women singers in history) were so prodigious that they "have ruined all the presenters of opera in Venice and drained the heaviest purses in Italy." In order to pay them the impresarios had to cut down on scenery and the orchestra and "other expensive machinery." In Naples, Senesino got 3,693 ducats (about $6,500) for a performance (the composer got 200 ducats). In England, Caffarelli got 1,000 guineas (about $6,000) and expenses for the season. Angus Heriot, in his book on the castrati, estimated that Caffarelli cleared some £5,000. Farinelli commanded 2,000 guineas for the season and probably ended up with twice as much as Caffarelli. They spent it, too, living not like any old members of the nobility but like dukes and princes. With money from his enormous fortune Caffarelli built himself a fine palace and purchased a dukedom for his nephew. The other great castrati could and did live as lavishly if they had Caffarelli's tastes. But a few, although as rich, were less ostentatious.

In the period from 1700 to 1750 in England, the castrati made incredible sums. To give an idea, in 1737 Samuel Johnson came to London from Lichfield. He dined "very well" for eightpence. "I had a cut of meat for sixpence, and bread for a penny, and gave the waiter a penny." Johnson told a friend that "thirty pounds a year was enough to enable a man to live there [in London] without being contemptible." In 1763 he was telling Boswell that "If you wish only to support nature"—that is, live at a bare subsistence level—"Sir William Pitt fixes your allowance at three pounds a year; but as times are so much altered, let us call it six pounds. This sum will fill your belly, shelter you from the weather, and even get you a strong lasting coat, supposing it to be made of a good bull's hide." In those days, we learn from Sterne's *Tristram Shandy,* a gentleman could make do on £100 a year, a sum that would provide him with a home, a servant, and a cook. An income of £200 a year made a man very well off indeed; see Boswell's footnote about the finances of the Langton family in reference to Johnson's letter of May 10, 1766. And here, at about the same time, was Caffarelli pocketing £5,000 for a few months of singing.

The castrati were unparalleled vocal technicians, and the world has not seen their like since. The Abbé Raguenot in 1709 gave an idea of what they sounded like. He said that nobody could come near them. "No man or woman in the world can boast of a voice like theirs; they are clear, they are moving, and affect the soul itself." The castrato voice could melt the listener in pianissimo passages and even at low volume soar over a full orchestra. "These pipes of theirs resemble the nightingale; their long-winded throats draw you so to speak out of your depth and make you lose your breath; they will execute passages of I know not how many bars together, they will have echoes on the same passages and swellings of a prodigious length, and then with a chuckle in the throat exactly like that of a nightingale they'll conclude with cadences of an equal length, and all this in the same breath."

Castration of males can be traced back to the early Egyptians. In medieval times castrati started singing in the church, because women singers were forbidden there. Had not St. Paul written *Mulier taceat in ecclesia?* In the sixteenth century Pope Paul IV (1555–59) banished all women's voices from St. Peter's. Boys and castrati were used, and by 1650 castrati were common in the church and on the stage. Early in the eighteenth century they became virtually synonymous with Italian opera, and the vogue lasted through the beginning of the nineteenth. So rich and famous were the successful castrati that the sterilization of boys, though forbidden by law, became a minor Italian industry. To poor parents with many children, one boy more or less did not matter; and if he were castrated, sent to singing school, and became a success, the family's monetary problems were forever solved.

The operation itself seems to have been relatively painless. As described by the late Dr. Meyer M. Melicow in the *Bulletin of the New York Academy of Medicine* (October 1983), the boy, age five to seven, would be put into a hot bath and given a potent drink. The jugular veins were compressed, and when he became groggy the gonads were compressed and rubbed until they were no longer palpable. Or, if testicles were already present, they were snipped out with a knife. The article has some graphic illustrations, circa 1500, of the actual operation. It was Dr. Melicow's opinion that whereas complete castration could kill the sexual impulse, the type of operation practiced on these young boys did not prohibit the male manufacture of testosterone. In his own words: "Numerous cells elaborating testosterone line the interior of the capsule of the testis and, if they survived and functioned, then it was possible for some castrati singers to have heterosexual relationships."

The boys who were sent to singing school did not have an easy life. They got up at dawn and were at their music and other studies until going to bed. Year after year they had to work on technique, exercises in front of a mirror, counterpoint and composition, ornamentation, harpsichord playing, and also studies relating to general culture, manners, and deportment. They worked under such famous teachers as Nicola Porpora, Francesco Pistocchi, and Antonio Bernacchi. When they were ready to appear some of them had voices that could span three octaves and more (up to high F in full voice in a few cases), could swell and diminish on a note, could trill on intervals from half notes to thirds, had breath control that enabled them to spin out a phrase apparently forever, and were masters of coloratura. Baldassare Ferri was said to be able to sing in one breath two chromatic octaves, ascending and descending, trilling on each note. What is more, these singers were so well trained that they could, and did, sing for three and four decades without showing any signs of strain.

The most famous of them all was Carlo Broschi (1705–82), known to the world as Farinelli. He also led the most interesting life of any of the castrati. Born in Andria, Apulia, of a noble family, he had a brother, Riccardo, who became a well-known composer. Nobody knows the circumstances of his castration. Members of the nobility—even the minor nobility, as the Broschi family was—did not normally castrate their children. It has been advanced that perhaps young Carlo either had an accident or had to be operated upon for reasons of health. Or perhaps, it has been conjectured, family reverses made it necessary for the father to "sell" the boy into a school for castrati. But at first he was taught by his father and brother; then he worked with Porpora. He made his debut at the age of fifteen in Naples, sang throughout Italy and then Europe. In 1734 he arrived in London, having been engaged by the Opera of the Nobility, a company set up against Handel's. (As early as 1728 Handel had heard him in Italy, had wanted him for his opera company, and was loud in his praises. It was not to be. Farinelli never sang in a Handel opera.) He took London totally by storm, in the process taking business away from Handel. "Signor Farinelli," reported the Abbé Prévost, "who came to England with the highest expectations, has the satisfaction of seeing them fulfilled by generosity and favor as extraordinary as his own talents. The others were loved: this man is idolized, adored; it is a

Farinelli and Pacchierotti were probably the two greatest singers the world has ever known. Pacchierotti's name was variously spelled in the free and easy days of eighteenth-century orthography.

consuming passion." It was agreed that Handel, said Prévost, "was the Orpheus of his age," but at his performances "he is admired, but at a distance, for he is often alone; a spell draws the crowd to Farinelli's."

Farinelli impressed not only as the supreme singer of the age but also as a gentleman who could move with grace in the highest social circles. He appears to have been a genuinely sweet, unaffected man who had no enemies. From London he went to Paris and spent a few years alternating between the two cities. In 1737 he left the stage because he had been summoned to the court of Philip V of Spain. Farinelli remained in the Spanish court for twenty-two years, until 1759.

The story is bizarre. Philip was suffering from what in those days was called melancholia. Among the forms it took was an aversion to bathing, shaving, or changing his clothes or bed linen. His queen, Elisabeth Farnese, thought that music would soothe him, so she got the most famous singer in the world to take his mind off the things that were bothering him. Farinelli and Philip hit it off, and the two became inseparable to the point where Farinelli in effect was the ruler of Spain. There was something Da Vincian in Farinelli's Spanish activities. He directed the royal chapel, redesigned the opera house, imported Hungarian horses, worked with engineers to redirect the course of the Tagus River, staged and produced Italian operas (but did not sing in them), helped the king in matters of state. He had one other duty: for ten years Farinelli sang the same four songs to his king every night. His salary was £3,000 a year. When Philip died in 1746, Farinelli worked with Ferdinand VI in much the same way. But Charles III succeeded Ferdinand in 1759, and Farinelli, after receiving a large pension, was asked to leave Spain. He retired to his villa in Bologna, surrounded by mementos, a fine art collection, and a variety of musical instruments. He was a legend, and was constantly receiving famous guests.

Charles Burney, the English author, traveler, and music historian, never heard Farinelli sing, but did visit him in Bologna and wrote about the meeting—and about Farinelli in general—in his

General History of Music and *The Present State of Music.* From the inquisitive, nosy Burney come many of the Farinelli anecdotes that help flesh out this mythical figure. With lip-smacking relish Burney recites Farinelli's patrons: "two emperors, one empress, three kings of Spain, two princes of Asturias, a king of Sardinia, a prince of Savoy, a king of Naples, a princess of Asturias, two queens of Spain, and Pope Benedict the XIVth." Farinelli talked about himself, and Burney also got information from the composer Padre Martini. There was the story of the trumpet player, for example:

> During the run of an opera, there was a struggle every night between him and a famous player on the trumpet, in a song accompanied by that instrument: this, at first, seemed amicable and merely sportive, till the audience began to interest themselves in the contest, and to take different sides: after severally swelling out a note, in which each manifested the power of his lungs, and tried to rival the other in brilliancy and force, they had both a swell and a shake [trill] together, by thirds, which was continued so long, while the audience eagerly awaited the event, that both seemed to be exhausted; and, in fact, the trumpeter, wholly spent, gave it up, thinking, however, his antagonist as much tired as himself, and that it would be a drawn battle; when Farinelli with a smile on his countenance, shewing he had only been sporting with him all this time, broke out all at once in the same breath, with fresh vigour, and not only swelled and shook the note, but ran the most rapid and difficult divisions, and was at last silenced only by the acclamations of the audience. From that period may be dated that superiority which he ever maintained over his contemporaries.

Castrati had the lungs of an Indonesian pearl diver. Some of them were timed at sixty-second phrases without pausing for breath.

Also from Burney, as related to him by Farinelli himself, we have the pleasant story about Senesino, one of the mainstays of Handel's opera company, who was Farinelli's predecessor as the foremost castrato of the day. Both were in London at the same time and had never appeared together, much less heard each other. Suddenly they were put together in the same cast. "Senesino had the part of a furious tyrant to represent, and Farinelli that of an unfortunate hero in chains: but in the course of the first song, he so softened the heart of the enraged tyrant, that Senesino, forgetting his stage-character, ran up to Farinelli and embraced him in his own." That was the performance at which a lady in the audience cried out, "One God, one Farinelli!" From Burney, too, comes the story of Farinelli and the talented young castrato Gioacchino Conti, who heard Farinelli at a rehearsal, broke into tears, and fainted away.

Burney in 1770 was but echoing the opinion of the 1730's when he wrote that in Farinelli the excellence of every great singer was brought together in one man. "In his voice, strength, sweetness, and compass; and in his style, the tender, the graceful, and the rapid. Indeed, he possessed such powers as never met before, or since, in any one human being; powers that were irresistible, and which must have subdued every hearer; the learned and the ignorant, the friend and the foe."

If Burney never heard Farinelli, Johann Joachim Quantz, the great flute player and composer, did, and his analysis can be taken with respect. Quantz heard Farinelli as early as 1726, in Naples. He reported that the singer had "a penetrating, well-rounded, luscious, clear and even soprano whose range at that time was from the low A to the D above high C. In later years it was extended several tones below without the loss of the high notes. The result was that in many operas there would usually be an adagio for him in the contralto range, and another in the soprano. His intonation was pure, his trill beautiful, his lung capacity extraordinary and his throat very flexible, so that he could sing the most distant intervals in fast tempo and with the greatest ease and accuracy. . . . In arbitrary embellishment of an adagio he was very inventive. The fire of youth, his great talent, universal applause and an accomplished throat led him from time to time to excessive display." It should be noted that in those days some singers achieved fame as interpreters of "adagios"—slow melodies in which a soaring line and sentiment were emphasized. Others of a more virtuosic nature were considered best in allegros featuring rapidity, agility, and vocal pyrotechnics. It was felt that very few singers were equally at home in adagio and allegro.

Farinelli's vocal compass eventually extended to a high E, but normally he did not use high notes, which were really a Romantic invention. In his *General History* Burney prints some of Farinelli's cadenzas and embellishments. There is a good deal of fantastic passagework and trills, but nothing over a high A or B. Perhaps Farinelli occasionally inserted higher notes while improvising a cadenza. Singers had a great deal of leeway in those days. One thing we do know: Farinelli, like the other castrati, was not much of an actor. But who expected singers to act in those days? Many of them would have been insulted at the mere notion. Carl Zelter, a fine German musician (he was the teacher of Mendelssohn), once asked the noted soprano Gertrud Mara why she did not try to get more of herself into a role. He told her that connoisseurs censured her for her lack of action in passionate parts. Mara bridled. "What!" she exploded. "Am I to sing with my hands and legs? I am a singer, and what I cannot do with my voice, I will not do at all."

Opera was spectacle and singing rather than drama. Plots were stilted, based on mythological subjects and not exactly full of action. The prevailing musical form was the da capo aria, in which the singer sang the first part pretty much as written and then, on the return (da capo—from the beginning) showed what could be done in the way of ornament and embellishment. Some da capo arias seem to go on forever. Handel may have poured his heart and soul into the music he created for his characters, but the singers of the day wanted only to sing the emotions rather than act them. Farinelli and the other castrati scarcely moved on stage, except perhaps to have a conversation with friends in the boxes while other singers were holding forth. Nor did the audience apparently care much for the subtleties of the music. Society came to see each other. They would talk, eat, play cards, pausing only when a favorite singer had an aria, come very late, leave very early. In the pit

Eighteenth-century opera was a noisy affair. The audience would eat, talk, play cards, and gossip, coming to some sort of attention only when a favorite singer advanced to the footlights. Even the singers would talk to friends in the boxes during a performance. Pictured here is Covent Garden early in the nineteenth century.

were the servants, hackneymen, some gay young blades, all talking noisily or shouting during a performance. This was true all over Europe except in the court theaters when the reigning royalty was present. Sometimes there would be some unscheduled excitement on stage. That once happened in London, when Cuzzoni and Faustina had at each other.

Francesca Cuzzoni (1698–1770) and Faustine Bordoni (1700–81), called Faustina, were probably the first two female superstars in operatic history. Both must have been spectacular singing machines. Cuzzoni was a soprano, Faustina a mezzo. Cuzzoni came from a peasant family, Faustina's parents were patricians. Cuzzoni excelled in adagio, Faustina in allegro. Cuzzoni was dumpy, ill-favored, sloppy in her dress, greedy for money (she earned enormous sums), loud-mouthed. Faustina was pretty, had a good figure and good manners. She too was a top money-maker. In London Cuzzoni was supported by the Countess of Pembroke and her coterie. Faustina's backers were the Countess of Burlington and Lady Delawar. The two factions detested each other, and so did the two singers in question. They both were singing in Handel's opera company, both created quite a few roles, and their antics amused all London. Cuzzoni loudly announced that she would not sing if Faustina received more money. Handel solved the problem by paying them equal amounts, £2,000 each. They would not talk to each other. Handel had a great deal of trouble from the opinionated, egoistic Cuzzoni, and once threatened her with bodily harm if she would not sing the way he wanted.

On June 6, 1727, in Buononcini's *Astianatte* the two ladies appeared together on the stage, and it was one of the wilder nights in operatic history. Perhaps the story became embellished over the years, but it was an evening in which temperaments clashed, hair was pulled during the performance, and the audience got into the act. Handel, to get rid of Cuzzoni, let it be known that he was paying Faustina a higher salary—one guinea more. Cuzzoni kept her promise and retired, going to Vienna. Always improvident, spending more than she made, she ended up impoverished, a button-maker in Bologna. Faustina, on the other hand, saved her

The first two female superstar opera singers, Faustina (above) and Cuzzoni, hated each other. In 1727 they came to blows on the stage in London while appearing together in a Buonconcini opera.

money, married the important composer Johann Adolph Hasse, sang in his operas, and lived happily ever after. John Gay, in his *Beggar's Opera* of 1728, satirized the two singers as Polly and Lucy.

The most perfect castrato singer, next to Farinelli, was Gasparo Pacchierotti (1740–1821). Trained at St. Mark's in Venice, he remained there for several years as a soloist, then moved to Venice, Palermo, and Naples. In 1775 he was engaged at the ducal theater in Milan, also sang all over Italy, and went to London in 1778. His house was the King's Theatre, and he immediately became a favorite, moving in the best circles. He may have been ungainly and anything but handsome; but he also had a beautiful soprano voice, flawlessly produced. One of his friends was the eccentric William Beckford, who followed him to Lucca in 1780. Pacchierotti was a busy singer, relatively as busy as the globe-trotting singers of today, constantly in a stagecoach going from city to city all over Italy, then departing for Paris and London. He sang at the opening of La Scala in 1778 and the opening of the Teatro La Fenice in 1792. In 1791 he took part in Haydn's first London concerts, singing a cantata—*Arianna a Nasso*—with the composer at the clavier. Fortunate were those who heard it. He eventually retired to Padua, a very rich man, a friend of Stendhal, Rossini, Goldoni, and other notables. Like Farinelli, he seemed to have no enemies, though it must be said that some of his love affairs got him into trouble.

All who heard him were struck by the sweetness of the voice and its incredible technique. Burney raved: "My pleasure was such as I had never experienced before," and went on to describe the glories of the singing in great detail: "A great compass of voice downwards, with an ascent up to B flat and sometimes to C *in alt,* with an unbounded fancy, and a power not only of executing the most refined and difficult passages of other singers, but of inventing new embellishments, which, as far as my musical reading and experience extended, had never then been on paper, made him, during his long residence here, a new singer to me every time I heard him. . . . A more perfect shake on short notice, and in every degree of velocity, I never heard . . . a variety of new graces and ornaments. . . ."

With a voice covering three octaves, Pacchierotti could take on any role. Apparently he was one of those singers who had the power to move the listener as well as stun him with brilliance. Stendhal reported that when Pacchierotti sang in Forlì on one occasion, the orchestra players could not continue because of the tears in their eyes. The Earl of Mount-Edgcumbe was fascinated by the versatility of the singer. Edgcumbe had a lifetime passion for opera and singing, was one of the earliest opera buffs to commit his memories to paper, and is a prime source on early singers. From what he says—and generally he was reliable—Pacchierotti was as great a musician as he was a singer; he could read anything at sight, he never indulged in display for its own sake, his taste was impeccable, his variety inexhaustible. And his trill! It was ". . . the very best that could be heard in every form in which that grace can be executed: whether taken from above or below, between whole or semitones, fast or slow, it was always open, equal and distinct, giving the greatest brilliance to his cadences." Edgcumbe called him "the most perfect singer it ever fell my lot to hear."

He, Farinelli, and the other castrati led directly into the bel canto school. Rossini, who had grown up with their kind of unmatched sound in his ears, expected something similar from his own singers. He was not interested in high notes; indeed, he hated them. Instead he wanted flexibility, beauty of texture and of phrase. He wanted tasteful ornamentation, to him the index of a singer's musicianship. Singers from Monteverdi to Wagner and middle-period Verdi were expected to embellish upon the ideas of the composer. There were those—Farinelli himself, in his early days—who took excess advantage of the opportunity. In the mid-eighteenth century Gluck tried to reform opera and curb the excesses of the spoiled virtuosi of the French opera; and, around the same time, the music-loving, flute-playing Frederick the Great insisted that his musicians play exactly what was written and no more. Informed opinion believed Gluck and Frederick to be out of line with the way things should be done. As Burney put it, when he heard about Frederick's innovation, "This, when compositions are good, and a singer is licentious, may be an excellent method, but it certainly shuts out all taste and refinement." In any case singers for the next hundred years or so—despite the efforts of Gluck and Frederick, of Mozart and Rossini and other composers who took a dim view of the "licentiousness" of the prima donna temperament—remained the rulers of the opera houses.

A faint idea of what the castrati may have sounded like can be found in the recordings of Alessandro Moreschi, made in 1902 and 1904. Moreschi (1858–1922) was, as far as is known, the last active castrato and the only one who ever made records. A member of the Vatican choir, he was probably not a very good singer to begin with. Certainly his interpretations are disfigured by vulgar stylisms. Yet through the old records and the out-of-tune singing comes a soprano sound of considerable size, with a range up to a comfortable B natural. And there is something haunting in the texture of the voice. It is sweet in sound, does have a "throw," and is curiously appealing despite the sobs and other devices that Moreschi thought were expressive. Obviously it is a pale echo of the real thing, but it does give a faint idea of the characteristics so fully described by the contemporaries of Farinelli and Pacchierotti.

2 *Angelica Catalani*

PYROTECHNICS AND GREED

IT is a peculiar fact that until the emergence of the bel canto tenors after 1810, very few male singers made much of an impression on the public or in the operatic world. At least their names are not familiar to anybody today except a few specialists, whereas every opera buff resonates to the names of Rubini, Duprez, Mario, and the other bel canto heroes. The castrati were altos or sopranos, and one would think that somewhere along the line a true male singer, tenor or bass, would capture the public imagination. But no. For some reason composers in those days did not write much for tenors, and such a role as Tamino in Mozart's *Zauberflöte* is exceptional for the eighteenth century. They wrote for low-voiced men, and some of them must have been excellent singers, judging from the difficulty of the vocal parts in operas of the period. But no male singer of the period is more than a footnote to history, and that includes even John Braham, the great British tenor.

Many women, however, had splendid international careers

before the full flowering of bel canto opera, and the greatest of them all was Angelica Catalani, who has come down in history as perhaps the most phenomenal female vocal virtuoso who ever trod the stage, and also as perhaps the greediest singer who ever lived. She also is remembered as the prototype of the worst kind of nineteenth-century *prima donna assoluta*—brilliantly talented but a law unto herself.

Faustina and Cuzzoni in Handel's time were the two ladies who first showed the world what a prima donna was all about—the irreplaceable prima donna, the supreme singer with ego, temperament, *amour propre,* and demands for huge fees. Those two great ladies had followers who solidified the rules, adding to the accomplishments of the two originators. One new accomplishment was the increasing tendency of the prima donna to marry into nobility. In England, Anastasia Robinson captured the Earl of Peterborough, and the bewitching Lavinia Fenton, the star of Gay's *Beggar's Opera,* married the Duke of Bolton. Or, if the new generation of prima donnas did not marry a noble, they frequently lived with one. Sophie Arnauld, Gluck's great interpreter and the idol of the French lyric stage, was a remarkable woman. She was pretty, vivacious, extremely bright, and moved in the company of Voltaire, Diderot, Beaumarchais, and Benjamin Franklin. For years she had a liaison with the Count de Lauraguais and bore him three children. When the count finally left her and married into his proper station, Arnauld sent to the new countess everything she had received from the count—including the three children. The countess returned everything to Arnauld—except the children.

Songbirds began to appear—sopranos who could fly high above the staff. Burney encountered Anna De Amicis in 1762—"exquisitely polished and sweet"—and wrote that she was the first female singer to introduce staccato passages and the first he ever heard sing an E flat above high C. It is well to remember that pitch then was about a halftone lower than it is today. Only a short time later Mozart, very impressed, notated Lucrezia Agujari in a C above high C (that would have been in his pitch; today it would be a high B); and if Mozart notated it, one can be assured that it was accurate. Burney heard Agujari and was not happy. High notes, he wrote, gave him more pain than pleasure. "Such notes become a Canary-bird; but they are not human." But if Burney was disturbed, the public doted on Agujari, who was getting a fee of £100 for singing just two songs. The German soprano Gertrud Mara also was one of the early canaries, a bravura singer who went up to F above high C. A strong-minded woman, she led one of the more tempestuous lives. She had rickets as a child and never fully recovered. She started as a violinist, turned to singing, and spent some years at the court of Frederick the Great, where she fell in love with a cellist, Johann Baptist Mara. Frederick opposed the marriage and had the couple jailed when they tried to escape. Then he allowed them to marry on the condition that they remain permanently in Berlin. In 1779 they escaped, and she sang under the name of Mara, with an important career in Paris and London. Soon she left her husband and took up with a flutist. They gave concerts together and settled in Moscow. Mara left him, too, and died in poverty in what is now Tallinn.

Into the world on May 10, 1780, in the small Italian city of Sinigaglia, came Angelica Catalani, who became the vocal phenomenon of her day and, some experts think, of all time. Not much is known about her early training. Her father was a bass in the cathedral choir, and presumably she got some instruction from him. Educated in a convent, she had minimal musical background prior to her debut, at the age of seventeen, at La Fenice in an opera by Mayr. Some believe she patterned her style after the great castrati, Pacchierotti in particular. Certain it is that, blessed with a natural voice and an easy manner of production, she had all the characteristics of the castrati: unlimited breath and technique, an arched projection, complete command in coloratura, and tremendous volume. What she did not have was taste. She thrilled the public, but the more sober musicians of the time were distressed by the inferior music she sang and by her lack of emotional involvement.

She sang in Italy and began to tour Europe. She was especially popular in Lisbon, where she is supposed to have received as

Angelica Catalani, whose vocal brilliance was exceeded only by her cupidity. More than any soprano of her day, she could "warble with native melody."

much as £3,000 ($15,000) for a concert. Such a fee would be very high even today. In those days it broke all records. It was in Lisbon, in 1804, that she married a French officer, Paul Valabrèque, who from then on managed her affairs. There is no biography of Catalani, and information about her is scant. One necessarily falls back on a few, familiar sources, all of which declare Catalani to have been money-mad. Yet one wonders if it were not her husband who pushed her into the spectacular fees she was soon to receive. Little is known about him, but some early writers on Catalani say that he gambled away a good part of her earnings. It seems a valid supposition that he wanted big money even more than she did. In that case, they must have made a happy couple, and it does seem that the marriage was a success. There never was a hint of scandal in Catalani's private life, while there was in that of many other singers of the day. It also should be said that she had her generous side. She gave many concerts for charities, and the proceeds that went to the sick and poor have been estimated to be as much as £80,000.

She made her London debut in 1806. London, then the wealthiest city in the world, paid favorite artists large fees, but Catalani's prices were unheard of. For her first London season she received £2,000. So great was her success that the following season she demanded, and got, more than twice that; and in 1808, from January 2 to August 2 at the King's Theatre, she was engaged to sing twice a week at £5,250 and also got two benefit performances at which all the proceeds went to her. She sang operas by Paisiello, Nasolini, Piccini, Paer, and Pucitta. Most of these were wretched works. But in 1812 she took Mozart into her repertory, singing Susanna in *Le Nozze di Figaro* in its first London performances. To British audiences she was vocal perfection. When she sang in Oxford in 1807 the reviewer of the *Journal* was ecstatic and wrote an article that gives an idea of the literary style of the period: "The Music Room was graced by Madame Catalani. This elegant Syren seems to have poured forth all the treasures of sweet sounds, with peculiar fascination, into the bosom of Isis; for never at the Opera, or in any of her Concerts, did she display more science, or warble with more native melody than here."

She also sang at salons and charity events, was a famous exponent of the Handel oratorios, made tours of the provinces, and would depart from England each season with tremendous sums, sometimes as much as £50,000. (That is H. Sutherland Edwards's estimate; it does seem high, even for Catalani.) The London newspapers discussed her finances, part admiringly, part furiously. Robert Elkin, in his *The Old Concert Halls of London,* quotes one writer: "Madame Catalani is to receive 500 guineas for performing three times at the Ladies' Concert, in Argyle-street. Her engagement, for the season, at the Opera, will produce her seven thousand pounds.—Quere [Question]. Is the lady to pay any Income Tax,—or, by putting her money into the British Funds, is it to be exempt as the property of a foreigner?" In 1826 the tax would have been around 3 percent.

So high were her fees that, to show any profit, the London impresarios were forced to raise subscription prices, from 150 to 300 guineas for a box. Lord Mount-Edgcumbe was outraged. "Thus she has permanently injured the establishment; for the price once raised, has never been lowered, or at most in a very trifling degree; and it is become quite impossible for persons of moderate incomes to afford so unreasonable a sum for a mere entertainment," he wrote in his *Musical Reminiscences.* Mount-Edgcumbe goes on for page after page, describing the degeneration caused by Catalani's inordinate demands.

She was the international queen of opera for two decades and expected to be treated as a queen. Patti or Melba later in the century had nothing on her when it came to temperament, and to tantrums when expected homage was not paid. In his *The Great Singers,* Henry Pleasants tells of an event in Munich when, "taken to task for occupying a seat in church reserved for the royal family, she cancelled her concert, swearing never to set foot in Munich again, and required that a rug be laid from the hotel door to her carriage, throwing her own shawl in her path as a final act of defiance as she flounced out." When she sang in London in 1826 she and her husband worked out a contract that is reproduced in H. Sutherland Edwards's *The Prima Donna.* Among the conditions: Mme. Catalani shall choose and direct the operas in which she is going to sing; she will have her choice of performers; she will take orders from nobody; she will have two benefits, to be divided with the manager; and, Item 10,

> Madame Catalani, in return for the conditions above mentioned, shall receive the half-part of the amount of all the receipts which shall be made in the course of the season, including the subscription to the boxes, the amount of those sold separately, the monies received at the doors of the theatre, and of the concert room; in short, the half-part of the general receipts of the theatre for the season.

Catalani was equally popular in Paris. In 1806 Napoleon gave her 5,000 francs for an appearance before him, plus a pension of 1,200 francs and the use of the opera house for two concerts that brought her 49,000 francs. In 1814 she was asked to take over the direction of the Thèâtre-Italien at the Salle Favart. There she specialized in operas by Marcos Antônio Portogallo and Vincenzo Pucitta composed especially for her. So great was her drawing power that everybody came to hear her, but it could not have been very good opera. The miserable music was made even more so by Catalani's constant introduction of cadenzas, interpolated arias, and display pieces. In private life she was a handsome woman with a good deal of personality, but on the stage she did little more than stand and sing. Nor was her manager-husband going to lay out any money for important supporting singers or a large orchestra. All that was needed for successful (i.e., profitable) opera, he said, was *"ma femme et trois ou quatre poupées, voilà tout ce qu'il faut."* So that is what Paris got—Catalani and a few puppets.

This went on until 1817, when she largely abandoned opera for European tours that took her from Lisbon to St. Petersburg. She billed herself as the *Prima Cantatrice del Mondo* (others called her "the trilling gypsy"), was decorated by every monarch in Eu-

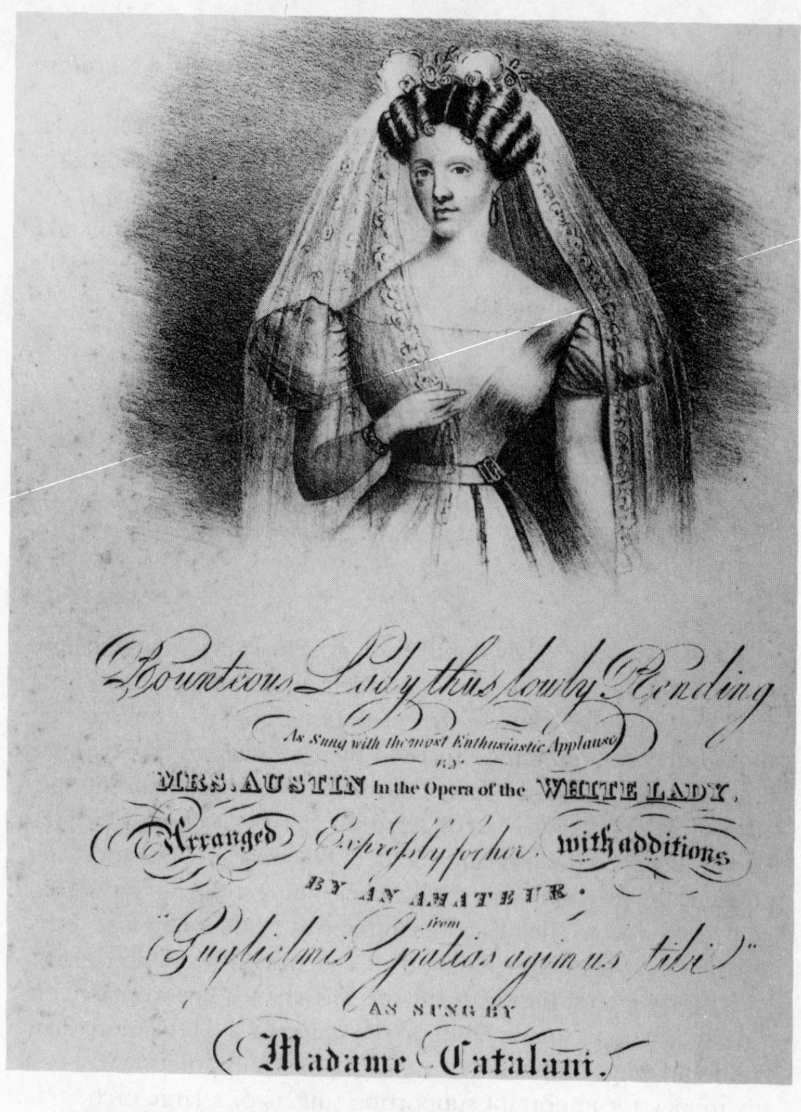

"Bounteous lady, thus lowly bending . . ." Publishers all over the world, including Thomas Birch in New York, rushed into print the songs that Catalani sang. This one was arranged from a work by Pietro Carlo Guglielmi, the son of a famous composer. From 1809 to 1811 Guglielmi lived in London, where Catalani was a great favorite.

rope, and found Russia especially generous. There she made £15,000 in four months, exclusive of rich presents from the czar, czarina, and assorted nobility. In Warsaw the ten-year-old Chopin played for her and Catalani gave the boy an engraved gold watch that he treasured for the rest of his life. She returned to England in 1824, sang for four seasons, and retired in 1828. She died of cholera in Paris during the epidemic there in 1849. Chopin was desolate when he heard of her death. They had remained on close terms.

Was Angelica Catalani worth the huge fees she charged? As an artist, no. As a singer there may never have been anybody like her. All, including her detractors, were forced to admit that this kind of female singing machine had never previously appeared on earth. Some writers lumped together all living singers to make one Catalani. Thus Jacques Godefroi, a pupil of Paisiello, went on record as saying, "This organ of so rare a beauty might be compared for splendor to the voice of Banti; for expression, to that of Grassini; for sweet energy, to that of Pasta, uniting the delicious flexibility of Sontag to the three registers of Malibran." Of Catalani as a technician, "her groups, roulades, triplets and *mordenti* were of admirable perfection; her well articulated execution lost nothing of its purity in the most rapid and difficult passages. . . . Her beautiful notes rose above and dominated the ensemble of the voices and instruments; nor could Beethoven, Rossini or any other musical Lucifer have covered this divine voice with the tumult of an orchestra." Apparently she sang so effortlessly that there was never any perceptible deterioration in her technique. When she returned to London in 1824 after an absence of over ten years, experienced critics such as Mount-Edgcumbe marveled that she sounded the same. Constant reference was also made to the size of Catalani's voice. Thomas Busby, a knowledgeable musician, said that one had to hear her from a distance to enjoy her fully, and Queen Charlotte said she needed cotton wool in her ears when Catalani sang.

It was not only a big voice, but it also had a very wide range, from low A to high G. Connoisseurs marveled at the agility of this extraordinary instrument. The famous French critic Castil-Blaze said that whenever it came to music that had difficulties of execution, Catalani could look the world in the eye and exclaim *"Sono Regina!"* She had no rival, according to Castil-Blaze. "I never heard anything like it. She excelled in chromatic passages, ascending and descending, of extreme rapidity. Her execution, marvellous in audacity, made talents of the first order pale before it; and instrumentalists no longer dared figure by her side."

Virtually the only adverse comments about Catalani's voice *qua* voice came from Ludwig Spohr, one of the better musicians in Europe, who heard her in Milan in 1815 at the Fiorento Theatre, "the prices of admission being seven-fold the usual ones." Catalani must have had formidable presence. Italian audiences could be unruly, but when she came on stage "a deathlike silence permeated the whole house." Spohr found her "cold and pretentious," and noted that she did not salute the court or the public. She loosened up after storms of applause. On the whole Spohr was impressed, much as he hated the inferior music she sang, but he found her transition notes—around E and F in most sopranos, where chest voice passes to head voice—weak. He found no "soul" in her singing and decided that she was an unbelievable technician and nothing more.

In this view, Spohr was stating the informed opinion about Catalani as an interpreter, and it was echoed by Paganini who, eight years later, went to one of her concerts in Milan. Paganini made the trip from Pavia to Milan just to hear her, and in a letter to a friend reported that he had been bored. "Her powerful, flexible voice is a most beautiful organ, but she lacks the grand line and musical philosophy." Technically there was nothing she could not do. Loud, medium, or soft passages all were produced "with great sweetness, and from this springs all the magical effects." Paganini concluded by saying that she would have more soul had she been trained by such celebrated masters as Crescentini, Pacchierotti, "and our celebrated Serra." Giovanni Serra was a composer and conductor of the day.

Spohr is the only one who mentions awkwardness around the

transition notes or, as the Italians call it, the *passaggio*. Everybody else raved about her encompassing technique. Stendhal wrote that Catalani could "mimic and outrival the mechanical dexterity of a violin." He tartly adds that "It is true, however, that God somehow forgot to place a heart within reasonable proximity of this divine larynx." Nevertheless Catalani's "prodigiously beautiful voice fills the soul with a kind of astonished wonder, as though it beheld a miracle." Stendhal's dream was of a singer with the Catalani sound and technique, and the Pasta passion and drama.

But given Catalani's kind of musical approach, one that was incapable of growth, Stendhal's dream was not to be. Mount-Edgcumbe went so far as to call Catalani's taste "vicious." To him, her excessive ornamentation spoiled every simple song. She was happy only in music where "she can indulge in *ad libitum* passages with a luxuriance and redundancy no other singer ever possessed, or if possessing ever practiced, and which she carries to a fanatical excess. She is fond of singing variations on some known simple air, and latterly has pushed this taste to the very height of absurdity, by singing, even without words, variations composed for the fiddle."

Could Catalani have been the first singer in history to come up with the vocalise—a song without words, using only vowel sounds? The variations that so bothered Mount-Edgcumbe were composed by the virtuoso violinist Pierre Rode. "Absolute nonsense," fulminated the peer. "A lamentable misapplication of that finest of instruments, the human voice, and of the delightful faculty of song." Catalani prepared another vocalise, adapted from a violin piece by Giacomo Ferrari. She had both of them in her permanent repertory and would also insert them into whatever operas she sang.

Catalani was the culmination of a particular line, one that ended with the appearance of such tremendous all-around artists as Malibran, Pasta, Grisi, and Sontag. Those singers associated themselves with important composers and worked closely with them. They were creatures of the stage. They created important roles. They had professional relationships with their colleagues.

But Catalani, an anachronism even in her own day, was only a vocalist. She sang mostly in second-rate operas, she indulged in tasteless acrobatics, and she was an example of the rattle-headed singer out only to amaze the public and collect gigantic fees. Her ego was such, from all accounts, that she never once thought of sharing the stage with an artist of comparable stature. She represented exactly the kind of singer that the German composer and theorist Moritz Hauptmann fulminated against early in the nineteenth century, writing that "they stand in the same relation to genuine artists as harlots to virgins. . . . They live on artistic misconduct."

3 *A Digression on Travel, the Industrial Revolution, and Related Matters*

THE reign of the castrati, ending in the first quarter of the nineteenth century, coincided with some of the more convulsive changes in history—among them the ideas of the Enlightenment, the American Revolution, the Industrial Revolution, the rise of the middle class, the Napoleonic wars, the linkage of European cities first by stagecoach and then by rail. To most musicians, dominated and driven as they always have been by a special talent to the exclusion of almost everything else, the vast reorientation of thought and life did not matter much. Great musicians tend to be complete egoists, interested primarily in their vocal cords, fingers, and whatever else goes into making them the unique configurations they are.

But one thing did interest them very much, and that was travel. Whereas most of society stayed put their entire lives, seldom venturing away from the farm or city where they had been born, the top musicians were in demand all over Europe, and had to go from city to city. In the eighteenth century this was no easy task, and it required considerable planning. It also involved a large amount of physical discomfort and even risk.

Ever since railroads started linking far-flung points, mankind has taken ease and rapidity of travel for granted. The eighteenth century did not. Travel was hazardous. In the first half of the century, Europe and even England were an unchartered wilderness. Early in the Christian era the Romans had built an extraordinary road system through Europe, and some of those roads are still in use. But after the breakup of the Roman Empire the roads were allowed to disintegrate, and in medieval times they had largely disappeared. Even in the great cities there was no road system, and in London conditions were so bad that goods had to be carried on the backs of porters. Travel between cities was hard. The roads were generally too poor for coaches or any other wheeled traffic, and it was necessary to go on horseback. In the early 1700's a traveler who went from London to Canterbury was not much better off than Chaucer's pilgrims. Daniel Defoe, around 1700, complained bitterly: "Supposing one takes the North Road by St. Alban's; after Dunstable the road disappears into deep clay, surprisingly soft, perfectly dreadful." At that time it took a week to get from London to York, two weeks from London to Edinburgh. In Europe a traveler would try to book some kind of transportation on a ship from seaport town to seaport town when feasible, and then arrange for land travel on horseback unless he was lucky enough to be near one of the few roads that could accommodate a coach.

Not until the seventeenth century did coaches begin to appear, but experienced travelers avoided them. They had no springs or windows, many of them were open to the elements, and riding in them was an invitation to neuralgia and pneumonia. In Germany, passengers had to travel in post wagons, and Thomas Nugent, in a book published in 1766, describes them as "little better than common carts, with seats made for the passengers without any covering. . . . They go but a slow pace, not much above three miles an hour." England had similar vehicles in the early 1700's; they were called "hell carts." Greater comfort was introduced in the middle of the seventeenth century.

If reliable means of travel outside the big cities was still a thing of the future, cities themselves at least were forced to develop mass transport systems. The first important one started in Paris, when the great mathematician and philosopher Blaise Pascal inaugurated his *Carrosses à Cinq Sous* in 1662. London soon followed suit.

But outside those two cities the roads were still primitive, and remained so until the end of the eighteenth century. Even in England, the richest and most progressive country in the world, travel was very difficult until about the 1750's. A traveler from London to Coventry had to pass through about a hundred different parishes, and it was up to the parish to maintain its roads. Some did, most didn't. The coach to Coventry would encounter quagmires in which it would sink to its axles. Another hazard of early coach travel was the passengers themselves. Early travel books and guides warned about traveling companions who might be infected with a venereal disease. Those with sensitive noses would find themselves traveling with a marvelous assortment of body odors. John Dryden, in a letter to his cousin in 1696, wrote feelingly about his trip from Titchmarch to London:

> My journey to London was yet more unpleasant than my abode at Titchmarch; for the coach was crowded up with an old woman, fatter than any of my hostesses on the road. Her weight made the horses travel very heavily; but to give them a breathing time she would often stop us, and plead some necessity of nature, and tell us we were all flesh and blood. . . . When I was rid of her, I came to London and kept my house for three weeks together.

In more primitive reaches of Europe, travel was arduous in the extreme. As late as 1793 it took ten days to get from St. Petersburg to Moscow (night travel was, of course, impossible). Travelers often would be at the mercy of drunken drivers, and

A contemporary drawing illustrating a frightening aspect of stagecoach travel. This depicts the descent of the St. Gothard, with an abyss at the left, the horses at full gallop, and terrified passengers holding on for dear life. Coaches were known to overturn.

overturned coaches were a common occurrence. A trip from Rome to Florence took eleven days; one hired a *vetturino* from its owner and contracted for food and accommodation en route. Italy was famous for its disgusting inns, and the British author Tobias Smollett, who made the Grand Tour in the 1760's, indignantly said that a common prisoner in a London jail "is more cleanly and commodiously lodged than we were in many places on this road." Most inns outside the big cities anywhere in Europe had lice, forced patrons to sleep two or more in a bed (experienced travelers carried their own bedding), did not have sanitary conveniences, and served rotten food and polluted water. In Sterne's *Sentimental Journey* (1768) the pleasures of travel in France are set forth: "We were toasted, roasted, grill'd, stew'd, and carbonaded on one side or another all the way—and being all done enough in the day we were ate up at night by bugs, and other unswept-out vermin, the legal inhabitants (if length of possession gives right) of every inn we lay at."

Thus the early musical superstars—all singers, and in demand from St. Petersburg to Paris and London—had to do a great deal of thinking and planning before undertaking a tour. As early as the days of Faustina and Cuzzoni singers were on the road; they would work out a tour that took them from, say, Naples to Milan to Vienna to Berlin to St. Petersburg. From there they would embark on a ship to London, then make their way to Paris. They could afford their own horses and coaches. They engaged guides, had an armed escort to discourage highwaymen (they traveled with their costumes and jewels, and returned home with many more), and had their servants in a coach behind them. They became experts in money affairs. Every duchy, state, province, and town had its own currency, and the travelers had to know all about pistoles, genovins, ducats, soldi, pichioli, louis d'ors, sequins, shillings, pounds, sols, rubles, guineas, thalers, and the many other kinds of money.

Travel could be worth it once one arrived at his destination, especially if the destination was Paris. Then as now, Paris was the culinary capital of the world, and it is impossible to resist quoting from the irresistible reminiscences of Augustus von Kotzebue, the famous German dramatist who visited that city and talked about it in one of his books, published in 1804. He made the *tour gastronomique* of the city. His favorite restaurant was Very's in the Palais Royal, and he discusses the menu. The diner was faced with nine different soups, followed by seven sorts of meat pies. "Those that do not like pies may have oysters, at 10 sous, or 5 pence English, per dozen." There were twenty-five hors d'oeuvres. There was beef, "dressed in fourteen different ways; and likewise beefsteaks and roast beef." Then, "after laying a solid foundation," the menu offered "thirty-one entrées of wild and tame fowls, and twenty-eight of veal and mutton." This plethora could be confusing. "What foreigner, for instance, would at first know what is meant by *mayonnaise de poulet,* a *galantine de volaille,* a *côtelette à la minute,* or even an *épigramme d'agneau*?" If fish were preferred, there were twenty-eight kinds. "There is likewise an abundance of roast and fifteen different sorts are to be had, the dearest of which are fat Normandy capons, red partridges, and snipes." Side dishes accompanied all main courses. "They are very numerous and tempt the appetite under forty-eight different forms." Kotzebue also tells his readers not to forget the vegetables. And, "There are eggs and pancakes dressed in different ways, jellies and creams, macaronies and truffles in champagne, champignons and craws [crayfish], cherries and apricots." If the really serious eater still has room left, "thirty-one articles of dessert will afford him an opportunity of filling it up." If the diner was not fond of sweets, there were plenty of cheeses to choose from. The wine card listed twenty-two reds and seventeen whites, seven kinds of liqueurs, and coffee. The price for all this was 8 shillings ($1.50). Of course, Kotzebue says, most restaurants in Paris were considerably cheaper.

By 1820, France and England at least had comfortable, fast-moving stagecoaches. A generation of engineers, most prominent of whom were John Loudon McAdam (better known as Macadam) and Thomas Telford, had shown how to build roads that had proper drainage and a hard top that would accommodate the

A Hogarth engraving entitled "The Stage Coach; or Country Inn Yard." Coaches like this represented the first rapid and safe means of public transport. Nobody ever claimed that they were very comfortable. But Mendelssohn found the run from Glasgow to Liverpool exhilarating.

heaviest vehicle. It was the golden age of the stagecoach, with vehicles that could take up to thirty passengers and, with relays of horses, travel at eleven miles an hour, all running on a strict schedule on turnpikes free of highwaymen. Touring musicians loved it, and when Felix Mendelssohn was in Scotland in 1829 he wrote a letter to his family describing the stagecoach experience. He was tremendously impressed with "the furious English speed":

> We flew away from Glasgow on top of the mail, past steaming meadows and smoking chimneys. . . . Sitting on top of the stage and madly careering along ravines, past lakes, uphill, downhill, wrapped in cloaks and umbrellas up, we could see nothing but railings, heaps of stones or ditches, and but rarely catch a glimpse of hills or lakes. . . . In the evening a thick fog, the stage running madly in the darkness. Through the fog we see lamps gleaming all about the horizon, the smoke of many factories envelop us on all sides; gentlemen on horseback ride past; one coach-horn blows in B flat, another in D, others follow in the distance—and here we are in Liverpool.

But the stagecoach was soon doomed to extinction. The Industrial Revolution brought the railway into being. Beginning around 1730 a series of inventions and events changed the face of the earth and its way of thinking.

The Industrial Revolution started in England and was built on steam and cheap—one might well say slave—labor. There were some key breakthroughs. John Kay invented the flying shuttle in 1733. This revolutionized the weaving industry and led to the invention by James Hargreaves of the spinning jenny in 1768, by means of which individual operators could work multiple spindles, as many as a hundred. The sewing machine was invented. The century saw the iron industry revolutionized; the Bessemer converter came into being, and by 1780 coke furnaces were all over England. Invention stimulated invention. James Watt took out a patent on a steam engine in 1769, and that was the most significant invention of all. It led to the invention of the factory and then the railway, which was first used to haul coal and iron.

The age of fast travel started with the Stockton and Darlington Railway, authorized by Parliament in 1821. It was a line with three branches, thirty-eight miles long, and it opened on September 27, 1825. Top speed was fifteen miles an hour, and many were frightened. Could the human frame stand such outlandish demands on the body? Would not eyes pop out and blood vessels burst? Articles were written about the dire results that could be expected. Medical men said that train travel would lead to dyspepsia, dysentery, Saint Vitus's dance, hysteria, epilepsy, inflammation of the retina, and miscarriages. But the public, disregarding this fine and thoughtful advice, enthusiastically adopted train travel. In 1830 the Liverpool & Manchester Railway opened, with high-speed locomotives, up to forty-four miles an hour. Within three decades the major cities of Europe, from Lisbon to St. Petersburg and Moscow, were linked by fast trains.

One of the first impressions of train travel ever written by a musician came from Ignaz Moscheles in 1831. Moscheles was one of the leading piano virtuosos of his time, an important composer and a teacher among whose pupils was Mendelssohn. He was a sweet, unselfish man, universally admired; he was on good terms with everybody in the musical world, and his memoirs are important source material for European music in the first half of the century. In 1830 he was on a concert tour in the north of England. This is his report:

> On the 18th I went by rail from Manchester to Liverpool; the fare was five shillings. At 1:30 I mounted one of the omnibuses, which carried all passengers gratis to the great building called "the station." Eight to ten carriages, each about as long as an omnibus, are joined closely to one another; each carriage contains twelve places with seats like comfortable arm-chairs; at a given signal every traveller takes his place, which is marked with the number of his ticket, and the railway guards lock the carriages. Then, and not before, the engine is attached to the foremost carriage; the motion, although one seems to fly, is hardly perceptible, and the traveller is amazed when he looks out of the window and observes at what incredible speed the train approaches the distant object

The very first passenger train—the Liverpool & Manchester Railway as it looked when opened in 1829. Two years later, when the pianist Ignaz Moscheles described the novel experience, the cars were closed-in and he could peer out a window.

> and suddenly whirls by it. Words cannot describe the impression made on me by this steam excursion on the first railway made in England [Stockton and Darlington had been used mostly for hauling freight], and the transports I felt with an invention that seemed to me little short of magic.

Concurrent with all this new technology was an extraordinary leap in world population, to the factory owners an agreeable source of cheap labor. It has been estimated that in 1751 the population of the United Kingdom was about 10 million. In 1801 it was 16 million and by 1831, 24 million. Convulsive social changes took place. The artisan began to disappear, to be replaced by the factory worker and machine-made goods. There was a movement from country to city. The Luddites destroyed machinery in a vain attempt to hold back the new movement. There was a sudden need for capital, the opening of new local and international markets, the emergence of the middle class, the creation of great banks and money exchanges.

And slums, slave labor, and child labor developed. Karl Marx, who studied the phenomena in England, *knew* that the downtrodden masses would revolt. He had some indications to back him up. In 1819 the knitters in Leicestershire went on strike, demanding more money. Their top pay was 9 shillings ($1.75) a week. At that, they were better off than the knitters in Nottingham, who for a 14–16-hour working day got only 7 shillings a week. Trade unions were illegal until 1826. Women and children worked in sweatshops under appalling conditions. Children were put into factories before they were six years old. They lived in dormitories, worked fifteen hours a day, and were even used to drag coal cars. Even Parliament was worried about this, and in 1802 a law was passed regulating working hours of pauper children to twelve hours a day. Who said there were no Christians in Parliament? The law also specified that their dormitories had to be washed at least two times a year. Not until 1847 was a law passed that limited the working day to ten hours. And that was passed over the opposition of the conservative middle class which, like the aristocracy, believed the social order to have been set up by divine command. There was a famous hymn of the day:

> The rich man in his castle,
> The poor man at his gate.
> God made them high and lowly
> And ordered their estate.

This exactly echoed the sentiments of the rich. As Samuel Smiles wrote in 1859, in his popular *Self Help,* "That there should be a class of men who live by their daily labors in every state is the ordinance of God, and doubtless it is a wise and righteous one." The church knew what side to be on, and was the defender of the status quo. In the eighteenth century the church still owned a good part of the land in Europe and drew enormous revenues from it. The top prelates were fantastically wealthy. Not so the lower orders of the clergy, and in England a country vicar was lucky if he got £50 a year.

Nor was the middle class going to favor anything that threatened profits. Large fortunes were being made, and even a workman from the lower classes could partake if he had imagination and determination. At mid-century the great French historian Hippolyte Taine marveled at the new social order that England had created. In his *Notes on England,* he described a typical middle-class head of a family as one thrown early on his own resources who could marry a woman without a fortune, have plenty of children, spend up to the limit of his income, work prodigiously, and instill the work ethic in his children, "always producing and always acquiring." Some members of the middle class achieved great wealth through merchandising, industry, or banking. They wanted nothing more than to join the aristocracy. Often their children married into it.

If the rich English middle class could seldom become aristocrats, they could and did become gentry. In the British social structure the gentry, or "squirearchy," stood just below the nobility. As defined in the *Cambridge Economic History of Europe,* the gentry was "an amorphous group, without legal definition or status, that had no equivalent on the Continent." Some of the gentry had noble antecedents. Others had made their fortunes in trade, the professions, or government service, and had purchased estates in the country. Some were scions of old country families; still others were farmers or yeomen who had amassed wealth. The gentry, whatever their differences in background, had two things in common—they owned land that gave them an income, and they were the local dignitaries: lords of the manor, justices of the peace, or county sheriffs. With the peers, they practiced primogeniture and were the true rulers of provincial England.

The new middle class prompted significant growth in culture and education. Believing as they did in self-improvement, they demanded good schools for their children, and they supported culture. In the previous century the church and the aristocracy held the reins of power. Now the middle class started to move in. The middle class also developed cultural interests, and it was profitable to cater to their taste. Professors of music taught their children to play the piano, flute, and harp. Magazines addressed to the self-improvement of the middle class were avidly read. The middle class also read the novels of Defoe, Fielding, Smollett, and Richardson, identifying with the new realism. Hogarth and Rowlandson chronicled the adventures of the new class. Newspapers paid more attention to cultural matters and engaged critics to explain the arcane arts to their readers. Where concertgoing used to be primarily for aristocrats, now it was the middle class that thronged the concert halls. The "business" of music came into being, with managers, impresarios, publicists, critics, what today is called "media hype," and all of the paraphernalia associated with selling music and artists.

More and more, as the century went on, programs began to reflect the conservative tastes of the middle class. Alfred Dörffel, in his history of the Leipzig Gewandhaus concerts, shows how music of the past gradually usurped music of the present in that city, and his statistics are representative of those in metropolitan centers everywhere. From 1781 to 1785, only 13 percent of the Gewandhaus programs contained music by dead composers. From 1820 to 1825, it was 23 percent; from 1828 to 1834, 39 percent; from 1837 to 1847, 48 percent; and from 1865 to 1879, an enormous 70 percent. Leipzig always was a conservative center, but Vienna was even more so. During the period of the Viennese Concert Spirituel, between 1819 and 1848, half the music consisted of works by dead composers, mostly Handel, Haydn, and Mozart. After 1830 the ratio was 70 percent dead to 30 percent modern.

With the railways making travel easy, musicians now could plan much more extended concert engagements, and all over Europe and the United States concert halls and opera houses began to be built to take care of the ever-increasing middle-class taste for culture.

It seems to be an article of received opinion that early concert halls were of small size. Of course concerts given in salons could not take care of much more than 200 people, depending on the size of the room in the great house at which the concert was given. The piano firm of Pleyel had in its building a concert hall in which Chopin and other notables played. It could seat about 300. In the case of the czar's palace in St. Petersburg, the salon was of monstrous size, easily accommodating some 3,000. But on the whole, the concert halls put up in the first third of the nineteenth century were much larger than has generally been realized, and the same could be said of earlier halls. As early as 1772 the Pantheon in Oxford Street could present concerts to 1,600 listeners. The Crown and Anchor Tavern in the Strand, rebuilt in 1790, had a concert hall that could accommodate 2,500 people. When Haydn came to London in 1791 his concerts were given at the Haymarket (also known as the King's Theatre, His Majesty's Theatre, and Her Majesty's Theatre, depending on who was on the throne), and the awed composer wrote home saying that "it holds 4,000 persons." Actually its seating capacity was 3,300, which made it bigger than most concert halls today. Haydn also appeared at the Hanover Square Rooms, which normally seated 800; but at his 1792 benefit, 1,500 people crowded into the area. London had other big theaters at which musical events were given. The Drury Lane Theatre, built in 1812, could seat 2,600; and Exeter Hall, built in 1831, seated 3,000. The rebuilt Crosby Hall, in 1850, also held 3,000. For smaller events there were the Argyll Rooms, put up in 1820 and seating 800. Crystal Palace in the 1850's could accommodate over 17,000, but was used only for special musical events, such as the great Handel choral festivals. London's most famous concert hall, St. James's, was built in 1858 and held 2,127. The opera house at Covent Garden, opened in 1808, was unusually large for its time; it held 2,800. When the new Covent Garden opera house opened in 1858, it was more in line with the other major opera houses throughout Europe, seating 2,117.

Through the years Paris used several houses for its Opéra and other opera companies. All were in the 1,700–2,000-seat range. Vienna's major concert hall at the turn of the nineteenth century was the Burgtheater, seating 1,800. The largest concert hall in Vienna, the Winterreitschule, held well over 2,000. If an entry in the April 5, 1859 issue of *Dwight's Journal of Music* is to be believed, the opera house in Berlin, built in 1741, seated 3,500 to 4,000. In New York, pre–Civil War theaters used for musical events included Niblo's Garden (seating 1,750), the Astor Place Opera House (1,800), the Tabernacle (2,800), the Academy of Music (4,800), and Castle Garden, which was something of a counterpart to London's Crystal Palace (7,000). Immediately after the Civil War, in 1866, the new Steinway Hall on East Fourteenth Street was opened, with a 2,500 seating capacity. Chicago in 1814 erected the Metropolitan Hall (2,000). The Boston Theater, 1854, had almost 3,000 seats; the Philadelphia Academy of Music, opened in 1857, seated 2,984. Even then America was the apostle of the Bigger and the Better.

By mid-century concerts had a family resemblance to today's affairs, though the programs differed considerably. They were longer, by far, than today's, and resembled variety programs. The featured artist would appear only in a few groups before and after intermission, and the rest of the program would be filled by guest artists (often locals) heard in a few vocal, harp, violin, or flute

New York's huge Castle Garden in the 1850's. At this performance of Lucia *the soprano is Henrietta Sontag. Note the position of the conductor, who stands facing the orchestra and audience with his back to the prompter's box. The conductor was probably the well-known impresario Max Maretzek. Was he left-handed?*

solos, and by two or three orchestral numbers. Not until 1839 did a pianist defy convention and give a recital unsupported by assisting artists. But Franz Liszt's innovation was not followed up by many pianists, and it took even longer for the solo song recital as we know it today to come into being. Julius Stockhausen, a baritone, seems to have been the pioneer there; he was the first, as far as is known, to sing the big Schubert song cycles as a unit, which he first did in 1856, introducing *Die schöne Müllerin* to the Viennese. With the arrival of the steamship, it was also possible for an artist to undertake world tours, and one of the earliest ones—perhaps the earliest—was a well-known violinist named Miska Hauser. He went as far as Tahiti and gave a concert in the Sandwich Islands to a perfectly uncomprehending audience of natives. Hauser appears to have been amused by his reception: "So unapplauded I have never played before any public on the earth."

Thus the history of concert-giving as we know it today is very recent, though there had been concerts of one kind or another since the Middle Ages. When word gets around that a superior musical intelligence is coupled to an unforgettable technique, the public responds, sometimes actually breaking down the doors to get in. As Marc Pincherle pointed out in *The World of the Virtuoso,* "In the seventeenth century Frescobaldi's organ attracted tens of thousands of listeners to St. Peter's in Rome." Thus the cathedral became, in effect, a concert hall. In France there were "musical academies" as early as 1570, and in 1725 the famous *Concert Spirituel* was founded. What is believed to have been the very first public concert in England was organized by the music-loving Samuel Pepys in 1644. John Banister in 1672 was advertising paid public concerts "performed by excellent masters, beginning precisely at 4 of the clock in the afternoon." For a shilling, the customer could stay as long as he liked, smoke to his heart's content, and drink all the ale he wanted. Georg Philipp Telemann in Hamburg and Johann Sebastian Bach in Leipzig were active in public concerts in the 1730's. In the British colonies, concerts were being given in Boston as early as 1731. The nobility all over Europe had its own theaters, the most lavish of which probably were those of the Esterházy family, for whom Haydn was the Kapellmeister.

With the expansion of the symphony orchestra and the emergence of the star conductor, the symphonic concert became a staple of concert life. All of a sudden men began waving little sticks in front of bewildered orchestra musicians. The pioneers were Ludwig Spohr, Carl Maria von Weber, Mendelssohn, and François Habeneck. Mendelssohn was the one who stabilized the symphony concert once and for all. He took over the Leipzig Gewandhaus concerts in 1835 and conducted programs similar in format to the ones heard today. He even presented historical concerts at which the music of Bach, Handel, Haydn, and Mozart was exhumed.

Until about mid-century, touring artists did most of their own managerial work, arranging for the hall, paying for the assisting orchestra and guest artists, and doing their own publicity. But the most successful ones at that time already were engaging secretaries and managers to take such onerous work off their shoulders. There were, however, impresarios even before the turn of the century, men like Johann Peter Salomon in London and Philipp Jacob Martin in Vienna, who put together subscription concerts and engaged prominent soloists. The definitive book on the financial, managerial, and administrative setup of the concert and opera business remains to be written.

For the first third of the nineteenth century, the history of performance was bound up with the original bel canto singers. There were superb pianists and violinists at the time, but the original bel canto singers were the musical heroines and heroes of the time, the ones who attracted most public interest and were paid the highest sums. Not until Paganini came out of Italy to bedazzle Europe was their supremacy threatened. They were a remarkable breed, and they set the course of singing for the first half of the century—and even later, if Adelina Patti is considered a bel canto singer. Unfortunately for posterity all of them except Patti died before the cylinder or early phonograph era. But they were so popular, their work so minutely discussed and analyzed by some of the finest musical minds in Europe, that it is possible to get a very good idea of how they sounded and what they represented.

4 *Giuditta Pasta, Maria Malibran, Henrietta Sontag, and Giulia Grisi*

BEL CANTO

IF Angelica Catalani was an aberration, her successors were the ones who established the role of the opera singer for most of the nineteenth century. Giuditta Pasta, Maria Malibran, Giulia Grisi, and Henrietta Sontag, the four fabled women of the bel canto period, were the prototypes of singers very much with us to this day. Pasta and her colleagues—unlike Catalani, the castrati, and most of the eighteenth-century singers—were the first singers associated with operas that have remained staples of the repertory—the operas of Rossini, Bellini, and Donizetti. They were the first to benefit by the detailed attention of qualified newspaper and magazine critics, and as a result much more is known about their work and personal lives than about their predecessors'. They were constantly in the public eye, from the United States (where reports about them were eagerly read) to the Russian court.

Rossini, Bellini, and Donizetti wrote bel canto operas. "Bel canto" means, merely, beautiful singing. It was a carryover from the castrato style. The composers and the public expected singers to produce a beautiful sound, to sing in tune with a perfect legato, to have unbroken registers and a complete technique, to be able to melt the listener with a flowing cantilena and arouse him with transcendental pyrotechnics. Above all, singers were supposed to have "taste." Bravura was fine, but not at the expense of the musical line. It was expected that all singers embellish the composer's music. How they did that showed their taste, their musicality. If they departed from all the amenities *à la* Catalani, if their effects were vulgar and devoid of feeling, their taste was derided. Unfortunately for the cause of art, the public could not get enough of some singers who carried bravura ornamentation to excess.

Composers gave their singers a great deal of leeway. Singers could, for instance, transpose anything into a tessitura comfortable for their voice. Castil-Blaze noted that Mme. Righetti sang *Una voce poco fa* in F, Persiani and other sopranos in G, and "We have all heard the principal arias in *Il Barbiere di Siviglia* in all the keys in which they were *not* written." Malibran and Viardot would transpose down as much as a third. Cadenzas would be inserted more or less at will, and many singers, including some of the great ones, abused the privilege.

The ideal, not always met, was for the voice to be used as an expressive instrument. And the accent here is on "instrument." Judging from records made by singers who were born as early as the 1830's and 40's, the early nineteenth-century voice was probably produced in a "white" manner, something on the Melba or Calvé order, with none of the vibrato that came in with the verismo composers late in the century. The singing could be warm, the acting even passionate, but the emphasis was always on pure vocalism.

Opera in the first quarter of the nineteenth century resembled the movie theater of the 1920's and 30's. It was built around stars, and nobody thought of High Culture on going to the opera. It was entertainment, and the popular composers, among whom Rossini was the favorite, supplied a commodity. The music may have been nice, the *mise en scène* often elaborate, but it was on the singers that all attention was focused. And with newspapers starting to come out all over the place pretty much as they are today, gossip about opera singers occupied a prominent place.

One thing that has never changed about any opera house is the intrigue that goes on within its doors. In the 1840's the London papers, as alert to a juicy story then as now, would report about the various feuds among the singers. Madame G. protests against playing in the same opera as Signor H.; Signor D. gives notice that he will be ill if Madame K. is permitted to sing at his performance; Signora L. must have Signor M. and nobody else. All these charming newspaper tidbits are related in the 1840's by the impresario Benjamin Lumley in his *Reminiscences of the Opera;* and Lumley quotes one verbatim: "Ronconi and Frezzolini are at loggerheads, and won't meet at rehearsals. Grisi refuses to allow anybody else the use of her Pollione [in Bellini's *Norma*]. Poor Moltini has unconsciously offended Persiani, by singing so well last Thursday, when she could not. Madame Ronconi vows. . . ." A few hundred more words follow.

The singer was the Law, and that did not seem to bother composers too much, especially the Italians. The bel canto composers wrote formula operas, going from city to city, turning out a complete product in about two weeks. They casually lifted from their previous works, rewrote arias to suit the particular needs of singers, directed the first three performances, and then moved on. "I always knew Rossini was a lazy man," joked Donizetti when he heard that Rossini had composed *Il Barbiere di Siviglia* in thirteen days. Donizetti had turned out *L'Elisir d'Amore* in eight. The serious German composers could not get over it. Mendelssohn, traveling in Italy, wrote about Donizetti's speed. He writes an opera "in ten days. It may be hissed, to be sure, but that doesn't matter, as it is paid for all the same, and then he can go about having a good time." If Donizetti feels his reputation slipping, then, says Mendelssohn, he works really hard on an opera, spending as much as three weeks on it. "Then he can afford to amuse himself once more, and once more write trash."

Chronologically, the first of the great female bel canto quartet

Giuditta Pasta, seen here as Desdemona in Rossini's Otello. *She conquered the operatic world despite a flawed voice.*

was Giuditta Pasta (1797–1865). Ironically, she was the one least representative of the bel canto ideal, having a flawed voice. But to become as famous and admired as she was, she must have had something very special.

Pasta was born in Milan as Giuditta Negri, studied there, married an indifferent tenor named Pasta, and made her debut in 1815 in Milan. The next year saw her in Paris where, apparently, she and her husband were two of the *poupées* in Catalani's Paris season. The following year she appeared in London, where she sang with her husband. They came as a package and received £400 for the season. In those days she sang as a mezzo and nobody paid much attention. Soon her husband stopped singing and devoted himself to taking care of her affairs. Her first real success came in Paris in 1821, when she appeared in the first performances there of Rossini's *Otello*. She had met Rossini and worked with him on his operas. Paris went wild, and London promptly put out bids for the new star.

She returned to London in 1824, singing at the King's Theatre in a company that included several of Europe's greatest singers—among them Catalani, Isabella Colbran (Rossini's wife), Ronzi de Begnis, and Maria Caradori. Pasta arrived in London late in the season and conquered the city with her Paris vehicle, *Otello*. This time she did not sing for a pittance of £400. For her London appearances she had signed for £14,000. Her fees already were starting to get into the Catalani class, and she immediately purchased a villa on Lake Como. The following season she demanded £2,500 a month, and the impresario could not turn her down. She was a regular visitor to London. In her 1828 season London audiences were lucky enough to get her, Malibran, and Sontag. Later in the century some said that the 1828 London season had never been equaled in any opera house at any time.

In Italy she worked with Bellini and Donizetti, creating for them several major roles, among them Amina in Bellini's *Sonnambula* and Anna in Donizetti's *Anna Bolena*. Most important of all, she sang the title role in the world premiere of Bellini's *Norma* at La Scala in 1831. Her voice started to go at a relatively early age;

she did not have much more than fifteen really good years before the public—from about 1820 to 1835. She sang in St. Petersburg in 1840, Berlin in 1841, and made a few appearances, to everybody's embarrassment, in London in 1850. She had returned because she was without money; she had lost a good deal of her enormous fortune in Vienna when the bank of Guymuller failed. Nothing of her voice was left. But when the great contralto Pauline Viardot—one of the most brilliant, interesting, and generous women of the nineteenth century—heard Pasta's last appearance, she broke into tears and made a famous remark: "It is like the *Last Supper* of Da Vinci at Milan—a wreck of a picture. But the picture is the greatest in the world."

Pasta's voice went so early because she never had been a natural singer. She also abused it by overwork. In an *Opera News* article, Kenneth Stern wrote that Pasta maintained a terrifically busy schedule, often singing every day for months at a time. Basically she was a pushed-up mezzo, and that could not have helped her voice. Not that there was much distinction in the 1820's and 30's between a mezzo and a soprano. A female singer was supposed to sing everything, and most of them did. But Pasta's voice was never able to respond the way she should have liked it to. Pierre Scudo, the critic of the *Revue des Deux Mondes,* wrote that "her thick, muffled, mezzo-soprano voice was with great difficulty rendered supple, and Mme. Pasta never was completely mistress of this rebellious organ." Like all singers, she had her little tricks. The *Orchestra* of London said that her voice was hard to describe; it was hard and unyielding, yet expressive. "It is a curious fact that she could not sing an ascending scale. All her florid passages were on down scales." Nevertheless, whatever her vocal failings, she was a supreme, dependable artist, and it was not for nothing that Bellini called her "a sure anchor in any shipwreck."

What Pasta did, she did by sheer determination. Of all the bel canto singers she was by far the most erratic vocally. As the English critic Henry Fothergill Chorley noted, she could sing out of tune, she did not have an equalized scale, "but in depth and reality of expression" she rose above all other singers. And so if her voice

Maria Malibran, who lived life to the full and died at the age of twenty-eight after falling off a horse.

never had the natural beauty of some of her competitors, she compensated by brains, musicianship, intensity, and stage presence. In that, as so many have noted, she was the Maria Callas of her day. Pasta probably was the first of the great sopranos to try to act on the operatic stage, and she was considered the foremost dramatic singer of her time, "as gigantic in her excellences as she was in her defects." In England she was called "the Siddons of the opera," and in Paris she impressed the famous actor François-Joseph Talma. "One turn of her beautiful head," he said, "one glance of her eye, one light motion of her hand, is with her sufficient to express a passion." Her style of operatic acting—which she started—carried over through most of the century. Emotions were broadly portrayed: hand with palm outward over the eyes to express despair, and other movements that today would be considered highly stylistic or exaggerated. As late as the 1950's Zinka Milanov at the Metropolitan Opera represented this kind of dramatic schooling. But in Pasta's day it must have been revolutionary.

She had the power to move her listeners, and the London *Musical World* could not have been far off when, in her obituary, the magazine noted that Pasta "gave a character and expression to her tones that touched upon the most varied chords of the human heart." Pasta must have been a thrilling figure on stage even though she was a rather dumpy, unglamorous woman, with one leg shorter than the other. Stendhal, always enthusiastic in his likes and dislikes, adored her, and the nouns and adjectives flew from his pen in close order drill when he was discussing her: perfect intelligence, moderation, good taste, vocal range from low A to high D, as fluent in the soprano range as she was in the contralto, burning energy, smooth transition from chest to head to falsetto, restrained in her ornamentation. To Stendhal she was the perfect singer, and he said as much in purple prose: "Where can I find words adequate to describe the visions of celestial beauty which spread before us in dazzling glory when Madame Pasta sings, or the strange glimpses into the secrets of sublime and fantastic passions which her art affords us?" Loudly protesting that he cannot find the words, Stendhal goes on to find them. He was also impressed with Pasta's earning power, mentioning that for a season at the Thèâtre-Italien she got $9,000, far above that of any other singer. In two performances she made almost as much as the combined salaries of the conductor and the entire orchestra for the full season. Their total income was $20,000. Pasta made even more for her 1831 London season, getting $17,500.

Pasta's biggest rival was Maria Malibran (1808–36), who made as much money, achieved even more fame, was a much more handsome woman, led a much more interesting life—and died at the age of twenty-eight. In one respect the two ladies had something in common, and that was an intractable voice. Malibran, like Pasta, was a mezzo-soprano who conquered her vocal limitations by sheer force of determination. The French litterateur Ernest Legouvé described it as "pathetic and powerful," but also "harsh and rebellious." It "resembled the most precious of metals, gold; but it had to be torn from the bosom of the earth." Legouvé heard Malibran working on the coloratura passages in *Il Barbiere di Siviglia*. Several times she stopped and addressed her own voice. "I *will* make you obey me." Legouvé says that Malibran never stopped attempting the impossible: "Her life was spent in endeavoring to go up as high as Sontag and as low as [Rosamunda] Pisaroni." Henrietta Sontag was very much on the minds of all female singers in Europe; they envied her incredible ease and purity. When Malibran first heard her, in 1828 at the Théâtre-Italien, she went into a depression. "Why does she sing so divinely?" Malibran wailed. The two singers avoided each other. Later they appeared together at a musicale, sang a duet, and became friends.

Maria Malibran, who was born in Paris, came from a musical family. Her father, Manuel García, was a Spanish tenor and composer, and the teacher of his children, among whom were Manuel and Pauline as well as Maria. Manuel became a baritone, but is more famous as the best-known voice teacher of his time. He died in 1906 at the age of 101. Pauline, the youngest of the García children, was the brainiest—a superb pianist, composer, teacher, linguist, intellectual, the mistress of Turgenev, and a famous contralto who was associated with the music of Gluck and Meyerbeer. She too had an intractable voice—it seemed to run in the family—and she won her audiences by temperament and musicianship rather than with pure singing.

Maria was on the stage at the age of six, in Naples, in an opera by Paer. She made her London debut in 1825 as Rosina in *Il Barbiere di Siviglia,* after which she was engaged by the management at £500 for the remaining six weeks of the season. The family then traveled to New York, where García and his company, at the Park Theatre, staged the first Italian opera season the city had ever encountered. He had assembled a strong company. Maria, then seventeen years old, was given such leading roles as Rosina in *Il Barbiere.* In all, she was the prima donna in eight operas. Papa was still yelling at his daughter, as he had when she was a baby, actually striking her when she was not able to reach the high notes he was teaching her. He was a hard taskmaster. Later Maria was to say that "If my father had not been so severe with me, I should never have been any good. I was lazy and stubborn." But the fact remains that Maria got away from the family as fast as she could. In New York she met and married a merchant, Eugène Malibran, who at forty-five was considerably older than she was. He was supposed to be wealthy. Perhaps he may have been when he married Maria in 1826, but he promptly went bankrupt. The following year Maria returned to Europe without her husband.

She started singing in Paris and was promptly compared to Pasta. Connoisseurs said that Malibran had the better voice and that Pasta was the better actress. Rossini offered her a four-year exclusive contract at 100,000 francs a year. She turned it down, but did sing for him at the Théâtre-Italien. Once Rossini, reminiscing about the great singers he had heard, said that Pasta was remarkable "but Malibran was unique." After Paris she went to England in 1829, where she received $8,000 for a three-month season. She started to get unprecedented fees wherever she sang. For example, her 1833 London season netted her $16,000 for forty performances, plus $10,000 for two benefits, plus large sums for concert and salon appearances. The director of the Trieste Opera paid her $800 a performance, throwing in a set of diamonds at the end of the engagement. In Italy she was adored. She had the courage to sing Norma at La Scala, which up to then had been Pasta's role. After the second performance the audience removed the horses from her carriage and dragged her in triumph back to her hotel. When Bellini heard her Norma he is reputed to have said, "I believed myself in Paradise." So great were her Italian successes that the Duke of Visconti, the manager of La Scala, offered her a contract for 125 performances, spread over two and a half years, for $90,000. She started an affair in 1830 with the Belgian violin virtuoso Charles de Bériot, and that caused a bit of a scandal. Some of her straitlaced friends refused to talk to her. Maria gave concerts with de Bériot, bore him two children, and finally married him in 1836. First, of course, she had to get an annulment from Malibran, who had to be bought off.

In April 1836 she fell from a horse and was dragged along the road. According to the English conductor Jules Benedict, who knew her very well, she told everybody not to tell her husband about the accident, because he had forbidden her to ride horseback. She felt poor and had headaches, but continued her engagements: in Brussels, and in England at the Manchester Festival. In Manchester she sang several times. On the way to the hall for what was to be her last appearance, she fainted, revived and went on stage, finished the performance and had to be carried out of the hall, was put to bed, and lingered for nine days until she died. Dr. Aaron Kellner, chief pathologist of New York Hospital, conjectures that death resulted from a brain hemorrhage or a ruptured spleen. De Bériot fled Manchester while Malibran was still in her coffin. Malibran's physician explained this bizarre behavior by saying it was due to the violinist's excitable nature; that "his grief had been too great for him to remain." More cynical observers believed that de Bériot had rushed to London to secure the estate before Maria's relatives could get their hands on it.

Malibran's initial disregard of her injury was characteristic of the way she went through life. She drove herself hard—at her music, at sports, dancing, entertaining. According to Moscheles,

Charles de Bériot, Malibran's lover and then husband. He was one of the most famous violinists of his time.

she sang at least three performances a week, she was repeatedly engaged for morning and evening concerts, and accepted all sorts of invitations to fashionable breakfasts, *fêtes champêtres,* and private parties. "To attend three parties on the same evening was a matter of constant occurrence." She was supposed to be just a little too fond of the bottle. She could never sit still and was always in motion. "She was mad," her sister Pauline recollected. "She could never keep still for a minute." Castil-Blaze observed her with admiration: "She starts for Sinigaglia, during the heat of July, in men's clothes, takes her seat on the box of the carriage, drives the horses; scorched by the sun of Italy, covered with dust, she arrives, jumps into the sea, swims like a dolphin and then goes to her hotel to dress." She had to have things her way. When she sang at La Fenice in 1835 she refused to ride in the gondolas. The black paint depressed her; she said it was like going to her own funeral. So she purchased her personal gondola and had it decorated: scarlet and gold interior, blue curtains, the boat painted dove gray, and a costume for her gondoliers consisting of blue trousers, scarlet jackets with black velvet sleeves, and yellow hats. Then she was satisfied. She also was a trifle calculating. "When I go by thus, everybody knows it." Malibran, who loved fame and money so much, well knew the value of self-advertising.

She was physically attractive and knew how to emphasize her best features. Legouvé first saw her at one of her Paris concerts, where she accompanied herself on the piano. "The way her hair was dressed astonished people by its simplicity: no curls, no skillfully devised and towering fabric; smooth, flat plaits showing the form of the head; a somewhat large mouth; a rather short nose but such a beautiful oval face; such a purely designed neck and shoulders that beauty of feature was replaced by purity of outline; and, lastly, eyes such as never had been seen since Talma." Malibran sang the *Willow Song* from *Otello*. "At the twentieth bar," wrote Legouvé, "the public was conquered; at the end of the first strophe they were inebriated; at the end of the piece they were mad." She made captives of all with whom she came into contact. Few women before the public have had such magnetism, and

Moscheles said that even in private life Malibran had "magic power to lead us captives, body and soul."

Her voice spanned three octaves, up to the high D, and she could sing soprano as well as contralto roles. She was a fine musician, an expert pianist, and a fast study. Her friend, the Countess de Merlin, wrote that Malibran could study a role in the morning and play it through by memory in the evening. In 1830 a director of the Théâtre-Italien wrote: "We absolutely must have her, and at whatever cost, for she will do us three jobs—dramatic soprano, buffo and contralto; and as for talent . . . she is unequalled in all the world." Doing everything prodigally, as she always did, Malibran was bigger than life in every respect. She was the musical antithesis of Pasta, who always sang everything much the same way once she had mastered a role. Legouvé made a good point when he suggested that Malibran represented the New Art; that where Pasta "was the daughter of Sophocles, of Corneille and of Racine, Malibran was the daughter of Shakespeare, Victor Hugo and Alfred de Musset." Malibran always gave the feeling of improvisation and never seemed to sing anything twice the same way. "If obliged to repeat a cadenza, as is generally the case," reported Moscheles, "she improvises new passages more beautiful and original than the first, unsurpassable as they seemed." Pierre Scudo wrote that "to nobody else has it been given to unite, with so much brilliance and spontaneity, the tragic passion and the buffo verve." He decided that Malibran perhaps was the greatest singer who ever lived.

Her acting thrilled most everybody and disturbed a few. George Sand was an admirer: "She made me weep, shudder—in a word, suffer, as if I had been witnessing a real-life scene. This woman is the foremost genius of Europe." But others thought her acting overemotional. Delacroix was disturbed by her realism; and Mendelssohn, the apostle of gentility, thought it unfortunate that she should "so often exaggerate and so often border on the ridiculous and disagreeable." In 1830 a London critic complained about her "too-frequent indulgences in a certain terror-stricken attitude, the head greatly projected, the back a-hump, and the shoulders crouching upwards."

If she was free and passionate in her acting, she also was free about her treatment of the music. She was accused of overornamentation and of inserting trills ad lib (her trill on the high C must have been glorious). To show off her voice she had no hesitation in changing the vocal line or inserting showpieces into a score. She was one of Bellini's favorite singers, but that did not prevent her from inserting into his *I Capuletti ed i Montecchi* excerpts from operas by Mercadante, Filippo Celli, and others. There were fewer complaints about this kind of vandalism as she grew older. At her best she obviously must have been one of the supreme singers of history, and the kind of woman whose friendship adorned all who knew her. It is nice to remember her in the last year of her life, as reported by her friend and admirer Ignaz Moscheles, who was her host on June 12, 1836:

> She came at three o'clock; with her were Thalberg, Benedict and Klingemann. We dined early, and immediately afterwards, Malibran sat down to the piano and "sang for the children," as she used to call it, the *Rataplan* and some of her father's Spanish songs; for want of a guitar accompaniment she used, while playing, every now and then to mark the rhythm on the board at the back of the keys. . . . At five o'clock we drove to the Zoological Gardens, and pushed our way for an hour with the fashionables. When we had enough of man and beast, we took one more turn in the park, and directly we got home Malibran sat down to the piano and sang for an hour. At last, however, she called out to Thalberg, *"Venez jouer quelque chose, j'ai besoin de me reposer,"* her repose consisting in finishing a most charming landscape in water-colors (an art in which she was self-taught). Thalberg played by heart, and in a most masterly way, several of his studies and fragments of a newly-written rondo, and then my studies, Allegro di Bravura and G minor Concerto. We had supper afterwards; there again it was Malibran who kept us all going. She gave us the richest imitations of Sir George Smart, the singers

> Knyvett, Braham, Phillips and Vaughan, who had sung with her at a concert given by the Duchess of C.; taking off the fat Duchess herself, as she condescendingly patronized "her" artists, and winding up with the cracked voice and nasal tones of Lady——, who inflicted *Home, Sweet Home* on the company. Suddenly her comic vein came to a full stop; then she gave us in the thorough German style the scena from *Freischütz,* with German words, and a whole series of German songs by Mendelssohn, Schubert, Weber and my humble self; lastly, she took a turn with *Don Juan,* being familiar not only with the music of Zerlina, her own part, but knowing by heart every note in the opera, which she could play and sing from beginning to end.

Where Pasta and Malibran combined voice with considerable dramatic power, Henrietta Sontag (1808–54) was content to do it with voice alone, and hers was a voice that was the toast of the civilized world. She never bothered herself about acting—she once told Chopin that acting in opera was too exhausting—and the London *Morning Chronicle,* describing her Rosina, said that "she stood and looked like a young lady waiting to take part in a quadrille." Because she never threw herself into a role, she inevitably was described as "cold." But "cold" singers often are able to achieve great intensity by means of vocal coloring, and Sontag must have had no mean interpretive ability to be so admired by composers as disparate as Beethoven, Rossini, Weber, Berlioz, Chopin, Cherubini, Adam, Boieldieu, Clementi, Moscheles, Auber, and Paer. As a young woman she created the title role of Weber's *Euryanthe* in 1823, and a year later was the soprano soloist in the world premiere of the Beethoven Ninth Symphony. Her repertory was much wider than that of Malibran, Pasta, and Grisi, even if, in the latter part of her life, she dropped the "intellectual" music in favor of the crowd pleasers.

She came from a theatrical family in Koblenz and grew up in the theater. At the age of four she was appearing in plays, at eight she was singing the big *Queen of the Night* aria, at eleven she was in the Prague Conservatory, and at fifteen she made her debut. She had charm, good looks, an extraordinary all-around musical abil-

Henrietta Sontag, the songbird who was representative of pure voice. Her fees were so huge that she almost put Her Majesty's Theatre into bankruptcy.

ity, and a great voice. Naturally she took Vienna by storm when she started to sing there, in 1823. She was put into the German repertory, and her big successes were in *Der Freischütz* and *Die Zauberflöte*. Then she learned many Italian roles. Her only rival in Germany was Wilhelmina Schroeder-Devrient, the star of the Dresden Opera, who had a heavier voice and was especially famous for her Fidelio and also for her numerous love affairs. (She finally married a baron.)

Everybody was in love with the glamorous Sontag, including Count Carlo de Rossi, a diplomat with the Sardinian legation in Vienna. When Sontag moved to Berlin, Rossi managed a transfer to that city. Berlin went Sontag-mad. There were the usual wild demonstrations, including the pleasant custom of the day wherein admirers unhitched the horses from the carriage and pulled the diva back to her hotel. In 1827 Sontag appeared in Paris, with the usual results. The great Catalani heard her there and was impressed, to a point, aphoristically saying something half admiring, half bitchy: *"Elle est absolument la première dans son genre, mais son genre n'est pas le premier."* It was conceded by all that Sontag was inimitable in the lighter side of music, but that she lacked the weight and concentration for such roles as Donna Anna.

When she returned to Germany she received a hysterical reception. The writer Louis Börne took pen in hand. He wrote that he had been doubtful about Sontag-fever until he heard her. Now he too was bewitched:

> They have called her the lovely, the incomparable, the heavenly, the adorable, the celestial maiden, the darling Henrietta, the gracious child, the heroine of song, the daughter of the gods, the dear songstress, the pearl of German opera. To all these epithets I say, Yes, with all my heart. Even the severest judges have given their verdict; her charming person, her playing, her singing, can be compared to everything that is lovely, for such a union of all these gifts of Nature and Art was never found in any other singer.

Henrietta and Rossi became secretly engaged. But the King

of Sardinia would not permit him to marry a woman who not only was of low birth but also put herself on exhibition on the stage. So they secretly got married in 1828. They had no money problems. Sontag by that time was exceedingly rich, and by 1830 had 200,000 thalers (about $150,000) to invest—a considerable fortune. And she had a great jewel collection, given to her by nobility all over Europe. Trouble came from another direction. Sontag became pregnant and malicious tongues wagged. Finally word got out about the marriage. Her great admirer, the King of Prussia, gave as a wedding present to Sontag a patent of nobility with the name von Lauenstein. From Sardinia came word that the marriage would be recognized if Sontag gave up her career.

She could not do so at the time; she had too many commitments. She returned to Paris, where Malibran and Pasta were singing, and the city delighted in the Battle of the Prima Donnas. Then London. Then back to Paris where she and Malibran—by now her friend—sang together in such operas as Rossini's *Tancredi* and *Semiramide*. In 1830 Sontag sang in Russia and then retired. She followed her husband to The Hague, to Buenos Aires (by then there were two children), to St. Petersburg (where she sang in a few operas at the request of Nicholas I), and back to Berlin.

During the various European uprisings in 1848, Sontag lost a great deal of her money. Then Rossi lost his after the Sardinian forces were routed at Novara. Sontag had to resume her career, and in 1848 returned to London, where she received $30,000 for the season plus the proceeds for benefit performances. She was then forty-five, and the consensus was that she sang and looked better than ever. Her voice had retained its brilliance and flexibility, and she could still toss off high E's in full voice all night. Paris took Sontag back to its heart. The critics were ecstatic. Gautier wrote that Sontag's voice still retained its "exquisite beauty and *spirituelle*." The composer Adolphe Adam gallantly refused to believe that the enchanting creature he heard was really the Countess Rossi. No, it had to be her daughter. Moscheles heard her in 1852: "All Leipzig is mad about her; people think and talk about nothing else; they nearly forget to start the railway trains and wind up the church clocks." She sang in London and was received with equal enthusiasm. She also put her impresario, poor Benjamin Lumley, close to bankruptcy. "Great as was her individual success," he sadly wrote, "the fortunes of Her Majesty's Theatre were not much advanced by it. The various sums expended on her and her travelling expeditions were enormous, her own share of remuneration amounting to a total exceeding £20,000."

In 1852 Sontag came to New York for an American tour. Her manager was LeGrand Smith, who had worked for Barnum, studied what Barnum had done for Jenny Lind on *her* American tour, and had everything worked out for his great singer. She was driven to her hotel with cheering crowds lining Broadway. There were receptions, and the publicity apparatus went into high gear. Marietta Alboni (1826–94), the greatest contralto of the nineteenth century (and, most likely, the greatest who ever lived), was also in New York, and the city enjoyed the rivalry. What a contrast the two singers must have afforded—the beautiful, cool, poised Sontag on one side, the exceedingly stout Alboni with her Niagara of sound on the other! Alboni had prodigious fluency and a range from the bass G to a high C, upon which she would trill interminably. Too fat to be much of an actress, she could not stand very long, much less walk. "The elephant that swallowed a nightingale," Rossini said of her. But she was a sheer vocal phenomenon for the *fifty* years that she was before the public.

In addition to giving concerts, Sontag sang a few operatic performances under the aegis of Max Maretzek. She demanded a fortune; but as he later pointed out, Sontag was the greatest prima donna in the world. Jenny Lind had retired and Patti had not yet arrived. Maretzek was content to sign a contract with her in which he would get the first $1,100 of receipts the nights she sang, and the remainder of the box office would be divided equally between the two of them. She sang at the huge Castle Garden in a short season during which she might take the lead in *Lucrezia Borgia* in the afternoon and *Lucia* that same night. Today if a leading singer

Marietta Alboni, by common consent the greatest contralto of the nineteenth century and, very likely, of all time. Rossini, as amused by her size as he was enraptured by her voice, described her as an elephant who had swallowed a nightingale.

at the Metropolitan Opera is asked to sing two nights running, which happens every five years or so, it is considered a miracle, and press agents descend upon newspaper offices demanding page-one stories.

Sontag was impressed by the size of the United States but did not care much for the country. It was too materialistic for her, and she could not understand "these adding-machines of people":

> The businessman sits in his office from morning to night; instead of a heart, one should paint a dollar sign on his chest, and instead of a head and brain, he should be given an arithmetical problem. The people really understand very little about art or science, and only lately has music become fashionable because they now would like to imitate Europeans. . . . As for the women, they wilt between twenty and twenty-five, and when they reach thirty they are old, often looking like thin old spinsters. The girls are extremely pretty up to about nineteen, but are terribly skinny and . . . look like real matchsticks. These young ladies are amazingly selfish and independent; they go unchaperoned in the evening to the theatre and concerts with young men, and enjoy more freedom than any woman in the old world. . . . The young men are tall and lanky, like hop poles, and instead of blood they seem to have milk and water in their veins, which must be why the girls and their parents trust them so much.

The tour took Sontag as far south as New Orleans. From there she went to Mexico, where she contracted cholera and died, on June 17, 1854.

The experienced Scudo once made a smart remark about her voice. He pointed out that voices like Sontag's live long "because they never have experienced the transports which wear out and consume a poor woman as a diamond becomes volatile in the crucible of a chemist." Singers who tear themselves apart at every performance tend to burn out faster than others. Sontag never had that problem, and apparently sang as easily at the end of her career as she did at the beginning. Berlioz, in an analysis of her work after she had resumed her career, felt that she had been a lucky woman,

One of the supreme bel canto sopranos, admired by Rossini and Donizetti, Giulia Grisi was "an irritable and ambitious lady." She was as famous for her acting as for her singing.

for she had never been exposed to the fierce partisanship that surrounded other singers. For,

> She united all the qualities—although not in an equal degree—that all like to find in an artist: sweetness never surpassed, agility almost fabulous, expression, and the most perfect intonation. On she carols, higher and higher, like the "lark at Heaven's gate," so soft, so clear, so wonderfully distinct that, like a silver bell from the altar, it is heard through the pealing organ. But her principal merit, in our eyes, is the absence of "rant"—the substitute for genius—in any shape whatever. She always SINGS, and does not depend on mere strength of lungs—erroneously called "power." She never strains her delicate organ—that sweet instrument susceptible of every shade of expression.

Berlioz previously had discussed Sontag as a singer who "played with notes as an Indian juggler has ever juggled with golden balls; but she also sang music, great and immortal music, as musicians sometimes dream of hearing it sung." How fortunate, Berlioz said, that Sontag was around to show young singers the difference between singing and screaming.

With Malibran gone and Pasta starting to slip vocally, Giulia Grisi (1811–69) became the next great dramatic soprano specializing in Italian roles. She was born in Milan, studied there, and made her debut at La Scala at the age of seventeen. (Her elder sister, Giuditta, also became an important soprano, and a niece, Carlotta, became one of the greatest ballerinas of the century.) For several years Giulia sang all over Italy and in 1832 left, vowing never to return because of a dispute over a contract. In Paris she created the role of Elvira in Bellini's *I Puritani,* and she became strongly associated with the music of that composer. She also was one of Donizetti's sopranos, and she sang some of Verdi's operas up to *Il Trovatore* as well as some by Meyerbeer. She made the usual rounds—St. Petersburg in 1849, the United States in 1854, and many countries in between.

Generally she sang with the tenor Mario, an idolized figure

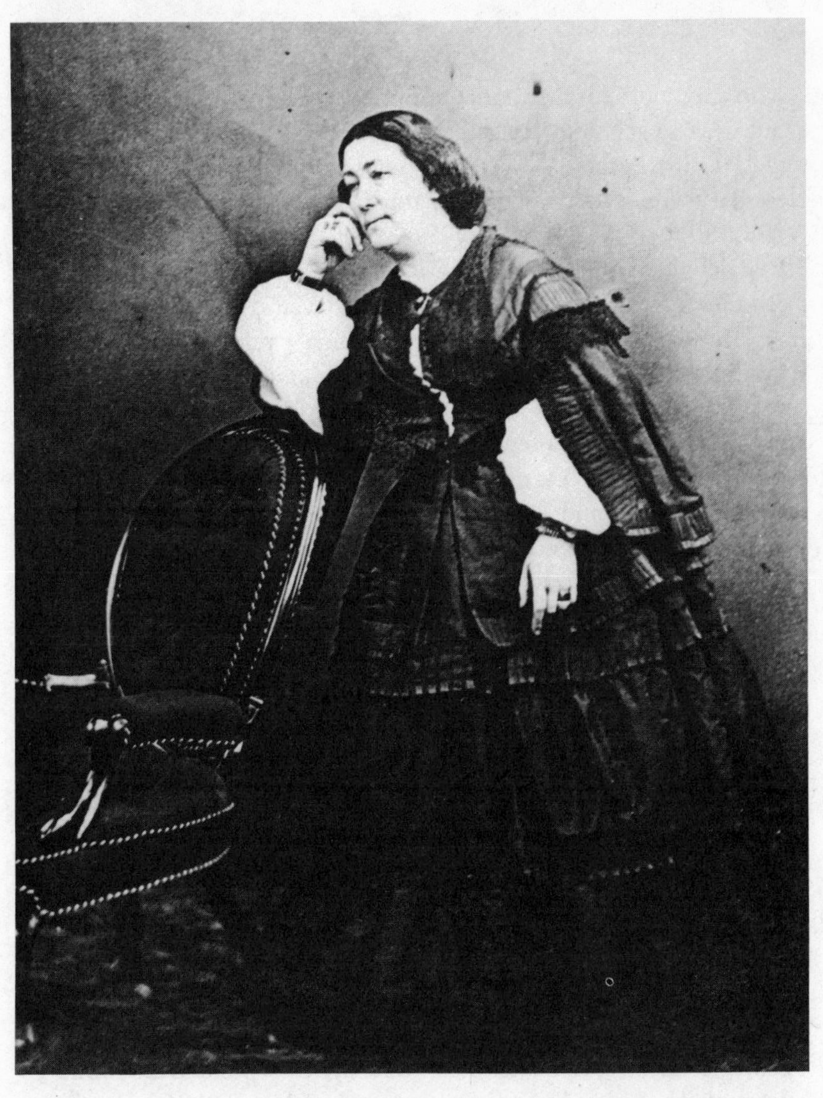

Grisi toward the end of her career, about 1866. She had little voice left and had put on weight. One critic described her as "a stately representation of the Sapphic or Homeric era."

who used only his first name in public. Grisi had married in 1836 but was never able to get a divorce or an annulment. Mario (1810–83) became her lifelong companion. They made a spectacular team, working together for enormous fees (in New York, $95,000 for a season of sixty-three nights). As vocal royalty, they well defended their kingdom. Grisi did not look favorably on singers who might threaten her position, and Mario naturally did what his consort wanted. Thus in 1848, when Pauline Viardot made her first London appearance in *La Sonnambula,* Mario—announced as the tenor—became "indisposed" and poor Pauline had to go on stage with a tenor who had not even had a rehearsal. No wonder Benjamin Lumley, the London impresario, who had to deal with Grisi and meet her incessant demands, called her "an irritable and ambitious lady." She drove him crazy.

In her earlier years Grisi had great singers to work with. The so-called *Puritani* quartet of Grisi, Rubini, Tamburini, and Lablache has probably never been equaled in vocal history. In her younger years Grisi was fiery, a figure of beauty on stage, and a passionate actress blessed with a powerful, perfectly produced voice. Later she put on weight. The New York *Tribune* in 1854 found an elegant way of saying that she was fat: "With more than average fullness of figure, and thus suited to the visual requirements of a large theater . . . Mme. Grisi appears to declaim on the stage like a stately representation of the Sapphic or Homeric era." She could never leave the stage and insisted on singing after her voice was gone, to the distress of her admirers. In Madrid, where she sang in 1859, the audience actually threw potatoes at her. Mario thereupon challenged Señor San Miguel, the director of the Principe Theatre, to a duel. Each was slightly wounded and honor was upheld. In her last appearances in London, in 1866, the former celestial favorite was actually hissed. Finally she realized that her day was over and she retired that year. The *Musical World* was understanding: "Artists like Sontag and Alboni, whose repertories involve no parts which are calculated to fatigue the voice, we can easily understand singing to the end of the chapter. It is another thing to perform such parts as Norma, Lucrezia Borgia, Donna

Anna, Semiramide, Anna Bolena and those belonging to the lofty tragic line, continually." Henry Fothergill Chorley, the critic of the London *Athenaeum,* gave Grisi the highest compliment he could think of: "In our day there has been no woman so beautiful, so liberally endowed with voice, as herself—Catalani excepted."

5 *Giovanni-Battista Rubini, Mario, and Luigi Lablache*

BENGAL ROCKETS, SWEETNESS, AND CANNONADES

THE bel canto composers had their favorite male singers, too, and the most prominent among them were the tenors Giovanni-Battista Rubini (1794–1854) and Mario (1810–83), and the bass Luigi Lablache (1794–1858). Of these three, Rubini had the closest association with them, and he was by far Bellini's favorite tenor, singing in the world premieres of *Il Pirata*, *La Sonnambula*, and *I Puritani*. For Rubini, Donizetti wrote the role of Percy in *Anna Bolena*. All this despite the fact that Rubini was never much of an actor. Generally he would advance to the front of the stage when he was singing—it made no difference whether he was performing a solo or was part of an ensemble—put his hand on his chest, stand motionless, throw back his head, and emit his matchless sound. Nor was he a handsome figure. His face was pitted with smallpox scars and he was a slovenly dresser. He was not well educated, and not a very good musician (a poor reader, he had to learn a role by rote and then rely on his memory). But from all accounts, he owned one of the most spectacular voices in operatic history, and that was his passport to fame, great wealth, and vocal immortality.

There is considerable speculation about the way he and his fellow bel canto tenors managed to achieve their effects. High notes in full voice were not favored by the bel canto composers—Rossini hated loud singing and high notes—and yet Bellini in *I Puritani* gave Rubini an F above high C. It is known that Rubini and others of his generation sang those high notes in falsetto. But exactly what was the mechanism involved, and how did those notes actually sound? Like real singing or an Alpine yodeler?

Most likely the tenors skillfully mixed chest and head voice to produce the facsimile of a real sound. In 1831 the highly regarded tenor Domenico Donzelli, in a letter to Donizetti, described his voice and said that it encompassed one note short of two octaves, up to the high C. He explained that he took chest tones up to the G, "and it is in that range that I can declaim with equal strength and sustain all the force of the declamation. From the upper G to the high C, I can avail myself of the falsetto which, used with artistry and strength, is a resource for ornamentation." The conductor Richard Bonynge has called this a "reinforced falsetto to such an extent that it became so strong a part of the real voice that you didn't know where the change [from chest to head voice] came." Not until 1837 did the tenor Gilbert-Louis Duprez sing the high C from the chest, at which point the *tenore di forza* was off and running. Enrico Tamberlik topped the Duprez C with a C sharp. He visited Rossini once, and the composer asked him to check his C sharp with the concierge.

Rubini was the first tenor in history to achieve international fame. As a child and young man, he was a chorister and violinist in Bergamo and Piedmont. Not much is known about his vocal training. He is said to have made his debut at the age of twelve in a woman's role. His official debut took place in Pavia in 1814, and he was with the San Carlo Opera in Naples for ten years. In 1819 he married a French singer, Mme. Chomel. She was a domineering, jealous woman, and Rubini never dared flirt. It took him a little time to become established. In 1814 he was getting $9 a

Giovanni-Battista Rubini, the first superstar tenor of history. He worked closely with Bellini, who composed several operas with Rubini's voice in mind. Using falsetto, Rubini could ascend to a high F and even above that. Here he is depicted as Arturo in Bellini's I Puritani.

month for his season in Pavia (sixteen years later he was offered $30,000 for an engagement there). But when he came to Paris in 1825 it was as the King of Tenors, and he never relinquished that position.

He appears to have been able to work with his composers without too many outbreaks of temperament, and his relationship with Bellini was always on the most friendly terms. They carefully went through the music together and Bellini listened with great respect to Rubini's suggestions about the entire score—and not only the tenor part. They had their disagreements. Rubini was a florid singer who liked to show off his technique. He demanded many opportunities for ornamentation, and Bellini had to beg him to keep things simple. But Rubini, who exulted in the glory of his voice, did not always obey. Rubini also knew exactly what to give his audiences, and they always came back for more. Bellini in an 1835 letter describes a typical happening during a Rubini performance. The tenor is singing in *I Puritani* at the Théâtre-Italien, and a note is thrown to him on the stage. Voices from the audience: "Read it! Read it!" The orchestra comes to a stop. Rubini picks up the letter and reads it to himself, turns to the audience and says, "*Messieurs, avec plaisir.*" Applause from the entire theater. The letter had asked Rubini to sing, between the acts, an aria from *Il Pirata* that he had sung a month before and, in Bellini's words, "had sung like a god." Rubini sang it, and Bellini says that "there is nothing to say about the effect and the applause."

In London, where he first appeared in 1831, Rubini was equally successful. His fees escalated, and he became by far the richest male singer before the public. He went to St. Petersburg in 1843, where he received a princely salary of £20,000, sang in the Italian Opera, and was named Director of Singing. He retired in 1845. Impresarios all over Europe desperately tried to get him to return to the stage, at his own price, but Rubini had made up his mind. Money meant nothing to him; he had more than he could ever spend, and he was content to stay in his villa and watch the operatic world from a distance.

His voice was thoroughly analyzed by his contemporaries.

He had an even scale from E to a high B, with the falsetto taking it to the high F and even beyond that, if the French critic Léon Escudier is to be believed. Escudier heard him in a performance of Donizetti's *Roberto Devereux*. When Rubini hit high G, "even he himself, after that *tour de force*, appeared astonished at the feat." Escudier also says that it was Rubini who introduced the Italian sob into the life of the tenor. It always produced a great effect for him, "and now there is no singer who does not strive to imitate it." So Rubini has a great deal to answer for. But at his best he must have been a singer capable of melting his listener with the sweetness and flexibility of his voice. When he sang in London, such great artists as Lablache would stand in the wings, entranced. Apparently Rubini could employ his falsetto in such a manner that listeners were tricked into believing that a full voice was used. Chopin, who had one of the best ears in Europe, who adored singing and would tell his students to imitate the voice of a great singer in their cantilena playing, has left a brief description of Rubini in action: "a splendid tenor; takes his notes authentically, not in falsetto, and sometimes sings roulades for two hours altogether (but sometimes embroiders too much) and makes his voice tremble purposely; also he continually trills; which, however, brings him more applause than all else." Another pianist impressed with Rubini was the young Anton Rubinstein, who heard the tenor as a child and never forgot it; he said that the singing produced such an effect "that I strove to imitate the sound of his voice in my playing."

The Rubini obituary in the *Revue des Deux Mondes* in 1854 had something to say about the singer's style, including the "luminous falsetto." When Rubini sang those amazing high notes in falsetto, "the astonished ear followed the singer, in his triumphal ascent, to the highest limits of the tenor register, without perceiving any interruption of continuity in the long spiral of notes." Not only was there no perceptible break from the chest voice to the head notes. Rubini added to that virtue "another no less important—namely, a long breath, the force of which he had learned to economize. Gifted with a broad chest, where his lungs could dilate at their ease, he took a high note, filled it successfully with light and warmth and, when it was completely expanded, threw it forward into the house, where it burst like a Bengal rocket into a thousand colors." It was an effect borrowed from the castrati; and Rubini's singing had other castratolike effects: "simple and double scales, arpeggios, trills taken upon the highest notes, gruppetti, appogiature, and the robust and most ingenious combinations of vocalization, were accomplished with boldness and a rapidity which scarcely gave the astonished ear time enough to appreciate the difficulty." Informed musicians might complain about Rubini's taste, but his audiences, faced with this kind of virtuosity, responded with yells of rapture. It was ever thus.

Rubini's successor was Mario. Born in Cagliari of noble birth, Mario became an officer in the Sardinian army and a member of Mazzini's Young Italy party. Thanks to that association, the young Cavaliere Giovanni Matteo di Candia had to flee Italy, ending up in Paris. His singing up to then had been in places like the officers' mess. In Paris he started serious vocal study, and he was coached by no less than Meyerbeer himself for his debut in *Robert le Diable* in 1838. Meyerbeer, that vastly experienced man of the opera, knew a good voice when he heard it, and his confidence was not misplaced. Mario went on to become the leading tenor of his age. For the next thirty-three years tenors came and went—Duprez, Tamberlik, Bugnoli, Giuglini—but Mario remained supreme. He was a superb technician, and probably no other tenor could execute the florid music of the bel canto composers with equal facility. (The recordings of Fernando De Lucia made in the first decade of the twentieth century give an idea of Mario's singing.) His voice had great sweetness and flexibility, up to a high C and, with a Rubini-like falsetto, four notes above even that. *The New York Times* in 1854 said that those falsetto notes made him sound like a woman.

He was easygoing and genuinely liked, a hard worker and a good colleague (unless Grisi's interests were involved). Colonel Mapleson did not begrudge the high fees—$1,500 a week—he had to pay Mario. Mapleson had him singing four times a week,

Mario, the supreme lyric tenor of his age, as Arturo in Bellini's I Puritani. *He was a Sardinian of noble birth, and his real name was Giovanni Matteo di Candia.*

and the tenor never complained. In addition, he was always ready to spring into the breach when he was needed. Mapleson also says that Mario was generous with money, threw it around recklessly, and was a soft touch who gave at least $200,000 to compatriots seeking aid. Louise Héritte-Viardot, Pauline's daughter, wrote with a certain amount of amusement that Mario was very much "the genuine *grand seigneur*, worthy of the title he held, Marchese di Candia. He had no idea of the value of money and flung it about as though the gold coins were grains of sand. As soon as he came into a shop the prices rose at once, for everybody knew him in those days." One of the few top singers who never could hold on to his money, he ended up in poverty. Short but handsome, a gentleman, a bon vivant, Mario was eternally pursued by the ladies (to Grisi's shrieks of jealousy). A tobacco addict, he was never seen without a cigar in his mouth. During his performances he would leave the stage, when the action permitted, to take a few quick puffs on a cigar kept in readiness for him.

He took over Rubini's roles, adding operas by Verdi, Meyerbeer, Gounod, and others as the century progressed. The great Rossini tenor could also be found singing Manrico in *Il Trovatore* and other such heavy roles. Tenors, like sopranos those days, were supposed to be able to sing everything. Not until the Wagner operas did big-voiced, powerful specialists like Joseph Tichatschek and Ludwig Schnorr von Carolsfeld appear. Mario and Grisi, his longtime companion, sang all over Europe; and he continued to sing after she retired. Not until 1871 did Mario leave the stage, going to Rome to live.

Like Rubini, he succeeded by voice alone (though the two voices had little in common). He was the last genuine bel canto tenor, and as such he never pushed, never strained, always poured forth a sweet, beautifully modulated sequence of sounds. The undisputed leading Italian tenor of his generation, he remained a lyric, and even in such dramatic roles as Manrico he delivered the music with a smooth, mellifluous style, completely different from the stentorian and heavy interpretations of Tamberlik or Giuglini. There might even have been holes in his technique—Chorley, for

Luigi Lablache, the king of bassos, the man with the voice of a cannon, "the very Stentor of vocalists."

Mario in the 1860's, toward the end of his career.

one, believed so, and called Mario an amateur—but even Chorley admitted that his voice had a "persuasive sweetness" that "can never have been exceeded."

When it came to Luigi Lablache, however, nobody ever raised any particle of criticism. In all respects, it was universally conceded, Lablache was perfect. If he ever got a bad review or a negative comment, it has remained unknown. Luigi Lablache was the greatest basso of his time and, one is willing to concede, the greatest who ever lived in the Italian repertory. And Lablache the man was as beloved as Lablache the singer.

He was called the Magnificent, the King of Basses. There was nothing he could not do. He was a famous comic actor who was just as good in serious roles. He was a large, stout man with a large, stout voice. His was a voice of such size that it created sheer wonderment in the world of music. Benjamin Lumley, the London impresario, who did not like most singers, adored Lablache and, like everyone else, could not get over the volume the man could produce. Singing against an entire chorus and full orchestra, said Lumley, the Lablache voice "may be heard as distinctly as a trumpet among violins. He is the very Stentor of vocalists." A correspondent for *Dwight's Journal of Music* wrote that "It is impossible to describe the effect of his magnificent organ in an ensemble; it is a cannon around a rolling fire of musketry—as thunder amid the tempest." The *Musical World* in London went all out, calling Lablache "one of the greatest ornaments of the Italian opera in this or any other age. His voice was perhaps the grandest and most powerful ever heard . . . for volume and quality combined has never been equalled. . . . No strength of band and choir was able to drown the echoes of those immense tones. . . . At sixty years of age, Lablache in many respects sang as powerfully as in his best days." Chorley's voice was added to the universal consensus: "Musical history contains no account of a bass singer so accomplished by art, so popular without measure or drawback. . . . An organ more richly toned or suave than his voice was never given to mortals. . . . The most remarkable man whom I have ever seen in opera." Jenny Lind called him a genius. "And what a voice! Oh, God in heaven! And the most perfect actor you could ever see."

Allied to the vocal strength was physical strength. When he sang Leporello in *Don Giovanni* he would tuck the baritone singing the part of Masetto under his arm and walk off with him. He dominated the stage. When he took even a minor role—and he never felt it beneath his dignity to take minor roles—he would create a figure that dwarfed everybody around him. He did this without apparently trying. "How he filled up the stage—not with his size but with his intellect," a critic wrote. "Every action had its propriety—every movement its meaning—every look its significance. No artist ever took greater liberties with his audience, but in all his freedom and 'gaggings' there was no extravagance or caricature." Everybody admired and even loved him. He moved in the highest society on even terms with everybody. Alexander II of Russia was a friend. So was Queen Victoria, to whom he gave some voice lessons. So were his colleagues. So, even, were the impresarios of Europe.

He was born in Naples, the son of an expatriate French merchant and an Irish lady. At the age of twelve he entered the Naples Conservatory. Stagestruck, he ran away from the conservatory five times to try for an acting career. Finally he was given a singing engagement at about $12 a month. At seventeen he made his official debut in Naples, where he was called upon to sing two performances a day and also morning rehearsals. He bounced from theater to theater, jolly, fat, irrepressible. He married Teresa Pinotti, the daughter of a well-known comic actor. They had thirteen children. In 1817 he sang at La Scala, and he created roles for Bellini and Donizetti. In 1824 he was in Vienna and in 1830 he reached London. There he sang at the King's Theatre (Her Majesty's Theatre, after Victoria became queen) almost every year until 1852. His fees were not in the Sontag or Malibran class—bassos did not move in that exalted financial structure—but he did very well: $10,000 for four months, "with lodgements and one benefit night clear of all expenses." He also sang in Paris in 1830

Lablache and Henrietta Sontag on the cover of a piece of sheet music. The polka, printed by a New York publisher, is an arrangement of music from Donizetti's L'Elisir d'Amore, *and the two singers are in costume as Adina and Dr. Dulcamara.*

and for many years thereafter, creating the role of Don Pasquale in 1843. When he retired in 1860 it was not because his voice was failing him. His health was going. He died in Naples of bronchitis contracted in Russia. In honor of a deathbed request, the Mozart Requiem was sung at his services. Lablache was no stranger to this work. He had sung it in 1827 in Vienna at Beethoven's funeral, and in 1849 at Chopin's. The soloists who came to Naples were old friends and colleagues—Grisi, Alboni, Mario, and Tamburini.

Like many stout men he could be graceful, and in his younger days could whirl around the stage. "Few things are more amusing than to see this Rhodian Colossus caper and flit about the stage with the elasticity of a sylph." When one reads descriptions of his acting, makeup, and costumes, it becomes obvious that Lablache established the buffo acting style that was popular throughout the entire century and continued in recent times through the work of such bassos as Salvatore Baccaloni and Fernando Corena. Toward the end of his life Lablache was too bulky to move around very much, and would get into a chair and seldom move out of it. His vocal range ran two octaves, from E flat to E flat. He handled it like a coloratura, and could do anything that his sopranos could in the way of scales, ornamentation, and improvised cadenzas. During a performance Malibran once tried to throw him off "by introducing ornaments and caprices of extreme difficulty." Malibran had worked on it beforehand. In chess it would be called a prepared variation. The score called for the bass to imitate the soprano, and the mischievous Malibran thought she had trumped any vocal effort Lablache might attempt. "But the trap laid for the vocal Hercules availed only to cause a display of his agility: note after note, trait after trait, shade after shade, did he reproduce in falsetto the fioriture which Malibran had taken such pains to mature." No wonder the public could not get enough of him and bought out every seat when he was announced to sing. "Excellent Lablache! Excellent as an artist and as a man." Thus wrote Benjamin Lumley, and it echoed everybody's opinion.

6 *A Digression on Money*

FROM the very beginning the superstars of music were so popular that they were constantly in the public eye. Their comings and goings were subjects of vast interest; the money they made and the presents they received were immediately reported. We know what Handel paid his famous singers—Nicolini, Senesino, Faustina, Cuzzoni. We have full reports on the earnings of Angelica Catalani, Maria Malibran, Jenny Lind, Adelina Patti, Nellie Melba, Enrico Caruso, and the other headliners. But several elements have been missing from these faithful accounts. Earnings, in books devoted to performers and composers, have been given in the currency of the day, generally without any attempt at translation into modern values. For instance, browsing through Otto Erich Deutsch's *Mozart: A Documentary Biography*, we read that Paisiello in 1784 received the "exceptional" sum of 300 ducats for an opera, or that Wolfgang's salary as Imperial Kammermusikus was 800 florins. That is all. Before the main text of his book, Deutsch has a note on currency, and lists the denominations of Mozart's day: the gulden (or florin), kreutzer, thaler, and so on. But he does not indicate what they were worth, and dodges the matter by saying that "It could only be misleading to attempt to give a modern equivalent for these coins." This leaves the nosy reader—we all are fascinated with money, earnings of great men, spending power—frustrated. Was Mozart's salary high or low? What did 300 ducats or 800 florins mean in 1784? How would that sum translate into modern currency? What was its buying power then? What would its buying power be today?

Alice M. Hanson is one of the few musical researchers to have tried to come to grips with the problem. In the July–October 1983 issue of *Music and Letters,* she made an attempt to list the various currencies in the Vienna of Beethoven's and Schubert's day, giving equivalent values for the British pound and the American dollar. She writes that the problem was complicated by the variety of coins and banknotes in the German and Austrian Empire of the day. The most commonly used currency was the silver florin, also called the gulden; but after the Austrian bankruptcy of 1811, the florin had two unequal standards: the *Conventionsmünze* (CM) and the paper Viennese currency, *Wiener Währung* (WW). One florin WW was worth only two-fifths of the CM florin. In 1820 the British pound was worth 10 CM florins, and Miss Hanson's table of currencies is based on CM values, as is the table below.

Equally important, Miss Hanson studied the city's official statistics to determine the average wages of high and low officials and workers, the rents charged in the city, what food cost, what Beethoven and Schubert really made. It is an area that opens up a huge field for investigation. For instance, we all know that Schubert died penniless. But he led a bohemian life—even a communistic one, in which money for one was money for all—and Miss Hanson notes that Schubert could never hold on to the money he made. "Only four months after his first public concert in 1828, for which he earned 320 florins [$160]—more than many office workers earned in a year—he was described by his friend

Jenger as financially embarrassed." So Schubert's chronic poverty could well have been his own fault, and the same possibility is true of Mozart.

Miss Hanson's method can be extended through every decade of the nineteenth century. An enormous amount of information is waiting to be unearthed. It is available in official records, government reports, and currency tables that came out with regularity during the century. The United States Government Printing Office, the State Department, and such private money-changing companies as Thompson's in *Thompson's Coin Chart Manual of Great Britain,* issued annually, give currency values from the 1850's on. Several books, such as J. Laurence Laughlin's *Money and Prices* (1909), accurately discuss wages and buying power. And many music magazines, especially *Dwight's Journal of Music* in the United States, constantly carried reports from Americans abroad, citing prices and standards of living.

Fortunately there were several stable currencies from 1800 to World War I. The ratios of the pound, dollar, and franc (which replaced the livre in 1803) were very much a constant, varying only a few cents on either side. The pound was worth about $5, the franc about 20 cents. The German thaler held pretty well, too, about 70–75 cents throughout the century.

Following is an alphabetical chart of the important European coins and their value in American currency. Miss Hanson's findings are used, plus information about many other currencies derived from official tables, periodicals, and reports from overseas. A surprisingly large amount of information comes from letters of composers and performers, who were as money-conscious as any bourgeois or banker anywhere; and as they were always negotiating fees in many countries, they were very accurate. Clara Schumann was brought up to appreciate money, and her correspondence with Brahms contains a great deal about finances. A touring pianist like Moscheles, when he wrote home, would often translate his German earnings into pounds, and he can be relied upon for accurate arithmetic.

Alphabetical Table of the Major European Currencies from 1820 to 1914, and Their Worth in American Currency

Carolin (Austrian and German): $4.50; rose to $4.75 in 1910.

Crown (English): $1.15.

Ducat (Austrian and German, but used all over Europe): $1.75 early in century; rose to $2.20 in 1910.

Ducato (Venetian): 65 cents.

Florin, also known as *Gulden* (Austrian and German): 40–50 cents.

Franc (French): 20 cents.

Groschen (Austrian and German): 3 cents.

Guinea (British): $5.25.

Gulden, also known as *Florin* (Austrian and German): 40–50 cents.

Kreutzer (Austrian and German): little under one cent (about ¾ of a cent).

Laubthaler, also known as *Federthaler* (Austrian, c. 1780): $1.00.

Lire (Italian): 13 cents at beginning of century; 19 cents in 1906.

Livre (French): 30 cents.

Louis d'Or (French): $5.50 (c. 1820); $4.50 (in 1910).

Mark (German): 25 cents.

Napoleon (French): $4.00.

Pfennig (Austrian and German): about 40 pfennig to one cent.

Pistole (gold coin used in Austria, last half of eighteenth century): $3.75.

Pound (British): $5.00 (20 shillings and 200 pence to the pound).

Reichsthaler (Austrian): 80 cents.

Ruble (Russian): Varied from 55 cents at mid-century to 73 cents in 1910 and 51 cents in 1912.

Scudi (Italian): $1.00 in 1910.

Souverain (German): $7.00 (c. 1820); $6.50 (in 1910).

Souverain (Milanese): $6.50.

Speciesthaler (Austrian): $1.00.

Thaler (Austrian and German): 70–75 cents.

Now that the relatively stable monetary values of nineteenth-century European currency have been determined, it remains to be seen what that money could buy. Take Mozart and the vexed problem of his finances. Perhaps he was like Schubert, who made respectable sums but never could hold on to them. In his 1785 concert at the Burgtheater, Mozart made 559 gulden (about $225). The musicologist Otto Biba cites Johann Pezzl's *Sketches of Vienna,* published that year, where it is stated that an unmarried middle-class gentleman could live "quite comfortably" on an annual income of 500 or 550 gulden. Mozart made a great deal more than 550 gulden that year, and either he frittered his money away or his standard of living was alarmingly high. Or he had expenses or debts that nobody knows anything about. When Beethoven gave a concert in 1803 he cleared 1,300 gulden. He could have lived on that for two years.

One infallible historian of money matters in the early part of the century was Jane Austen, who herself was of the gentry, wrote novels about girls getting married to eligible bachelors, and never made a mistake when it came to money. At the beginning of *Sense and Sensibility,* published in 1811, we are told that an income of £2,000 a year can nicely maintain a family of the gentry. Says Marianne Dashwood, "A family cannot be maintained on a smaller. I am sure I am not extravagant in my demands. A proper establishment of servants, a carriage, perhaps two, and hunters, cannot be supported on less." In *Pride and Prejudice* (1813), Mr. Bennet, his wife, and the five marriageable girls live handsomely on his income of £2,000. Mrs. Bennet becomes excited about her new neighbor: "A simple man of large fortune; four or five thousand a year." There wasn't a mother in England who wouldn't have thrown her daughter at a man with an income of £4,000. Mr. Darcy, the immensely wealthy hero of *Pride and Prejudice,* had an income of £10,000, out of which he maintained the great house at Pemberley Woods, with its park and woods. The estate measured ten miles around. In those days the gentry and nobility invested in "consolidated annuities," known as consols, which paid between 3 and 4 percent during most of the nineteenth century. Thus Mr. Bennet's estate, to draw £2,000, was worth about £50,000. At around the same time Angelica Catalani would be leaving the British Isles with (so it was reported at the time) the sum of £50,000—which was the size of Mr. Bennet's whole estate—for about six months of work.

But one could live very nicely on an income considerably less than Mr. Bennet's. In 1831, when Paganini came to London for the first time, there was an uproar over the amount of money he was going to make. The *New Monthly Magazine* figured out that Paganini's concert at the King's Theatre would bring in a sum of £3,980 ($19,900) "a sum which if properly invested would give to Signor Paganini and his heirs, etc., forever" the "income of a gentleman." In the meantime the great mass of workers in Europe lived at a poverty level. Paul Mantoux, in his *The Industrial Revolution in the Eighteenth Century,* has a good deal of information about wages and prices, but nowhere is the plight of the poor brought more graphically to life than in Thomas Carter's *Memoirs of a Working Man*. He tells about his childhood, around 1800: "My father's wages were but ten shillings and sixpence per week, and my mother's little school brought from two to three shillings more. With very little besides this scanty income [about $180 a year], they had to provide for the wants of themselves and four children. . . ."

Many writers, incidentally, have worked on the belief that there was no income tax in those days. There was, however. In 1798 Pitt put through Parliament an income tax that began at incomes of £60 a year. Later, in the 1840's, taxation started at £200. It was not onerous, averaging about 3 percent and never over 5 percent. The United States, too, had an income tax in the Civil War period and shortly thereafter. It was 4 percent, and visiting artists just hated to pay it. In 1866 the soprano Carlotta Zucchi was paid $40,000 by the impresario Max Maretzek for his New York season. Twenty-four hours before she was due to embark on her return trip to Europe, she was faced by United States tax collectors, who said she owed the government $1,800. Zucchi put up a good fight. She screamed that she was not a citizen of the United States, had not taken the oath of allegiance, owed nothing to revenue collectors, and would not be "swindled." She finally had to pay up, "in a storm of melodramatic passion," according to the New York correspondent of the London *Musical World*.

Until the middle class started using brains and talent to make money, the great wealth of Europe was largely confined to the aristocrats and higher clergy, some of whom had stupendous amounts of money to indulge themselves. After all, one of the cheapest commodities in Europe was labor. In Poland, Prince Karl Radziwill and Prince Felix Potocki each had over 10,000 retainers. Prince Potemkin in Russia owned 37,000 serfs. The great nobles would have had, in modern terms, millions of dollars a year. While the middle classes could not aspire to that, they suddenly became aware of a standard of living that was within their grasp. They wanted it, and they especially wanted it for their children. Friedrich Wieck, father of the talented Clara, has come down in history as a wretch because he was so adamant in his opposition to her marriage with Robert Schumann; and indeed he did act disgracefully. But one can see his point of view. Who *was* this cigar-smoking young man with a reputation for drinking too much, for skirt-chasing, with vague pretensions as a composer? "Schumann," Wieck wrote, "can operatize, philosophize, be as enthusiastic, idealize, as much as he likes. It remains settled that Clara can never live in poverty or obscurity—but must have over 2,000 thalers a year."

That sum, $1,500, would have bought a great deal at the time, as Schumann himself well knew. Only about ten years previously, in 1829, he had been writing piteous letters to his mother to have his allowance raised from the 360 thalers a year he was receiving. He complained that food was very expensive in Heidelberg. "Every dinner costs me 36 kreutzer or 8 groschen." That would be around 25 cents. In Leipzig a dinner cost 5 groschen, "which makes a tremendous difference in our finances here." But there was a bright side to Heidelberg. "Everything else is pretty cheap here. My rooms are 54 thalers a year; piano hire, 36 thalers."

But Schumann eventually made a decent living, and with Clara's income from piano playing adding considerably to the

Robert and Clara Schumann (above). Her father, Friedrich Wieck, opposed her marriage to the penniless composer. He wanted her to marry a man who could make $1,500 a year. Later in the century Clara advised Johannes Brahms (below) on his investments.

family coffers, they did very well. Seldom in history has there been a case of a great musical talent suffering poverty or living in an attic, his message unknown to the world. Indeed, it is fair to say that a "misunderstood genius" is a contradiction in terms; and if Mozart and Schubert had financial troubles, more and more the evidence is beginning to indicate it was of their own making. By and large the nineteenth-century composers did very well; the successful opera composers made fortunes; the performing stars made much money, and, of course, the superstars made supermoney and did better than anybody else, as they always have done.

Chopin is a case in point of a composer who worked things out for himself exactly as he wanted to. Shortly after his arrival in Paris, in 1831, he became, with Liszt, the most highly paid piano teacher in the city, at 20 francs ($4.00) a lesson. (In Leipzig, only a few years later, Clara Schumann— who, after all, was one of Europe's leading virtuosos—was charging only about $1.00 a lesson. She had wanted to ask for $1.50 but Mendelssohn talked her out of such an outlandish figure.) Chopin also demanded exceptionally high prices for his music, and generally got them. Härtel in Leipzig had to pay 1,000 francs for the Preludes; and Probst in Vienna carried on over Chopin's demands, telling the composer that it was impossible to meet such "frightful" prices. He flatly refused to pay 3,500 francs for a package consisting of the B minor Sonata, the F major Ballade, the C sharp minor Scherzo, two nocturnes, four mazurkas, two polonaises, and an impromptu. Chopin settled for 2,500 on the condition that the money be paid to him immediately. (He must have had a pressing debt or two at the time.)

Other musicians envied the rich Chopin. The young Charles Hallé, an aspiring pianist, came to Paris in 1836 and found that he needed $40 a month to live. He stayed at a hotel where board and lodging came to $20 a month, and his piano rental was $9 a month. He also had to pay for piano lessons, and he could not afford either of the two top teachers, or the ones just under them. So he studied with George Osborne. "Chopin and Liszt charge 20 francs a lesson; Kalkbrenner, as I have heard, only 10 or 12."

Charles Hallé (above), when a young pianist in Paris, was envious of the huge sums that Frederic Chopin (below) was making as a piano teacher. Chopin was getting about four dollars a lesson.

Young Hallé was frankly envious. "You can calculate what a man like Chopin must earn who gives eight or nine lessons every day at 20 francs." Hallé, a superior musician, went on to a distinguished career as pianist, conductor, and teacher. In 1861 he became the first pianist in history to give a cycle of the Beethoven piano sonatas.

Hallé had come from Germany, where prices were considerably lower than in Paris. There, and in Austria, top performers were decently paid, but rank-and-file musicians received a pittance. The Hanson statistics in her *Music and Letters* article show that a leading actress in Austria in the 1830's would be paid $2,500 a year; a leading female opera singer (but not a guest superstar), $2,000; a leading male singer, $1,200; a Kapellmeister, after thirty years, $1,200. But an orchestra player at the opera made only $240 a year, and one at the Burgtheater a miserable $120. House servants could be hired for $30 a year, plus room and board. (At that, they were better off than they had been a few years previously. In 1809 Haydn paid his female servants $10 to $15 a year.)

Prices slowly but surely ascended during the course of the century. In 1858, Alexander Wheelock Thayer, who was to write the definitive biography of Beethoven, returned to Germany to study and sent reports back to *Dwight's Journal of Music*. First-class passage from New York to Bremerhaven cost him $50. Rooms in Berlin were $1.50 to $2.50 a day. Foreigners, Thayer ruefully said, were charged more than the natives. But, said Thayer, you could get good lodgings at $9 to $10 a month if you knew the ropes. Breakfast cost $1 a week, lunch 15 to 20 cents a meal. Most concerts cost 50 cents, and the opera 75 cents (though Thayer sat in the top balcony for 25 cents). Thayer complained that prices had gone up in the two years he had been away. "Rooms that then were rented for five or six thalers a month now cost from seven to ten."

The following year Thayer sent back an even more detailed report. He and his roommate lived in Berlin "in a two-story house, in a woody area, right upon the great Friedrich St., within six or eight minutes of the opera house, on the lower floor. He has the large room and I have the two smaller. Our bills average at this season of the year, for rent, fuel, light, service, coffee in the morning with its etceteras, washing—$12 to $15 a month. Dinners we get out at the hotels or restaurants, at a cost of 15 to 20 cents. Sometimes we feast—and then go up to 25 or even 30." Thayer estimated that one could live comfortably in Berlin at $500 a year. According to E. H. Phelps-Brown and Margaret H. Browne, in their *A Century of Pay,* the average annual wage of a worker on the Continent around 1860 was about $100 a year. In Great Britain it was $180 and in the United States $300. Just about that time the tenor Mario was getting $1,500 a week from the impresario James Mapleson, and the young Adelina Patti was beginning to ask for $600 a performance (a pittance compared to her eventual fee of $5,000).

The average musician in the 1850's made a living, but not a very good one. In the April 16, 1853, issue of his *Journal of Music,* John Sullivan Dwight answered one T. S. Arthur, who complained of high ticket prices and high artists' fees. "The idea of giving a singer five, six or seven hundred dollars a night is preposterous," Arthur had snorted. But, replied Dwight, good opera cannot be cheap. It demanded at least forty musicians a night at $3 to $5. The conductor had to get at least $10 or $20. There had to be a chorus of forty, each chorister getting $2.50. "The four principal singers demand—and justly demand—from $50 to $150 for each performance." The other singers deserved to receive from $10 to $25. Then there were the costs of the opera-house personnel and of advertising. "The rent of the theater is seldom as little as $100 a night." Dwight pointed out that, after all, only a handful of singers in the world could command crazy prices. He mentioned three—Lind, Grisi, and Alboni. Incidentally, the pay for the musicians quoted by Dwight is pretty much in line with what French orchestra players were getting. In 1856 Berlioz rented the 600-seat Salle Herz and paid $160 for an orchestra of 54, which means that the pay for each musician averaged out to about $3.00. If a musician played several times a week he could make out. As late as 1885 very few European workers in any category made more than $9 a week, and it was not that much more twenty-five years later. *A Century of Pay* gives the average annual earnings of workers in 1910 as $250–$300 on the Continent, $350 in the United Kingdom, and $600 in the United States—all for a work-week that ranged from 53 to as many as 78 hours in some lines of work. In that same year, 1910, Caruso was getting $2,000 a performance at the Metropolitan Opera, and he sang many performances during a season.

A few superstars spent so lavishly that they died in poverty. A few were so stingy that they kept almost every cent they ever made. The great tenor Francesco Tamagno was one; he would even wrap up restaurant food and take it home. There even have been a few cases of singers who did not *want* to get rich, spurning money for love. Colonel Mapleson in his memoirs tells the story of a French soprano named Marguerite Chapuy, who had all London talking after her debut at Drury Lane in 1875. Mapleson says she could have had a career rivaling that of Patti. But she fell in love, got married, and never again appeared on the stage, even though Mapleson offered her $1,000 a performance. She explained that her husband did not want her to sing in public, preferring that they live quietly in France on his income of $600 a year.

But most of the musical money-makers not only held on to their earnings, they also knew how to make them grow. One of the canniest musical money managers of the nineteenth century was the redoubtable Clara Schumann, the true child of her thrifty father. She not only invested in securities herself; she also took care of the investments of her close friend Brahms. Like all careful money managers, she invested only in triple-A securities, satisfied with a return of 4 to 6 percent. She wrote to Brahms on May 6, 1867: "I have bought you three Rhineland Railway shares in Cologne for 750 thalers. . . . I should like to have bought 1,000 thalers' worth of securities for you, but I did not know whether you would like me to, as I should have to pay 1,200 thalers for them. They are now standing at 111 and in good times 120 and over, and pay 6½ percent. . . ." The shares did go up, and the happy Clara rejoiced in a dividend increased to 10 percent. She was a good portfolio manager, always looking for a bargain. The Mendelssohn banking family took care of her coupon clipping and closely watched her investments. She was always giving Brahms tips. In 1868 she suggested that he purchase some American government stock of 1861, "issued in 1864 and guaranteed by the Government, which pays good interest of about 6% to 8%."

Investing in American securities was the closest Clara ever came to the United States, but many others did cross the Atlantic. European musicians were convinced that the streets were paved with gold. Starting in 1843 many prominent musicians played or sang in the United States, and the early visitors—Henri Vieuxtemps (one of the great violinists), Ole Bull, Henri Herz, Leopold de Meyer, Marietta Alboni, Angiolina Bosio, Sigismond Thalberg, Alfred Jaëll—returned home with fascinating reports and a lot of money. When Jenny Lind toured the country under the management of P. T. Barnum, she made a fortune. The United States was eager to get the major European artists and paid them accordingly. De Meyer, something of a charlatan as a pianist, was invited back in 1854. His contract called for $60,000 for one year, exclusive of travel and other expenses, and he was required to play only two pieces a night. After the Civil War virtually every European musician of note made American tours, and some of them could have retired and lived lavishly on their earnings.

With rising prices came higher fees for the top musicians. In the 1870's some singers in London were getting $100,000 a year. H. Sutherland Edwards, in his *The Prima Donna* (1888), actually has it in his heart to feel sorry for the poor creatures in many respects. It is expensive to be a star singer, he says. They have great traveling expenses and outlays for costumes. They usually lead charity lists and also donate their services to charity concerts. "Nevertheless, after making due allowance for the prima donna's inevitable expenditure, the fact remains that she is exceedingly well paid. Indeed, no women receive larger incomes except Empresses and Queens." This was true. It should not be forgotten that only the lower classes of women in the nineteenth century worked, and only at menial jobs. And even in those jobs women earned less than men. As late as 1900, spinner girls in American woolen factories got 75 cents an hour; in England they received 50 cents an hour. If there were any women physicians, lawyers, engineers, mathematicians, bankers, and politicians, they were as rare as fingers on a fish. At least the arts were open to them, and a very few women achieved fame as writers and artists. But the only way to really great fame and wealth for a woman came from stage appearances. And it was not only the cash, up in the hundreds of thousands of dollars annually. The favorite singers, the *prime donne assolute,* also had jewel collections, presented to them by admirers, that would and did make the eyeballs of some queens and empresses bulge. Edwards tells about a singer who was asked which of the royalty she had known she best liked. She thought seriously about the question. "Well," she finally said, "the Emperor Alexander [of Russia] gives the best jewelry."

7 *Nicolò Paganini*

SPAWN OF THE DEVIL

THERE really was no precedent for Nicolò Paganini (1782–1840). Until his time, violinists had been nice, quiet, rather retiring creatures, anything but superstars. They gloried in such names as Arcangelo Corelli, Francesco Geminiani, Gaetano Pugnani, Giuseppe Tartini, Pietro Locatelli, and Antonio Vivaldi. Violin playing came out of Italy. So did Nicolò Paganini, but with a difference. He not only changed the entire conception of the violin, and the entire course of violin playing. More important: he set the nineteenth century on its deliriously virtuosic course, establishing the concept of the Artist as Hero, of virtuosity for its own sake as an end in itself. Showman and charlatan, unbelievably brilliant in his playing, he was the first instrumental super-virtuoso. Whatever he was as a musical thinker—and many serious musicians of his time (and of today) refused to take him seriously—he did set a standard of execution that quite possibly has never been equaled. He was the Angelica Catalani of instrumentalists; and modern virtuosity dates from the day when Paganini came out of Italy and threw Europe into a delirium. He suddenly occupied a position previously reserved for only great singers; and it is unnecessary to say that financially he was rewarded accordingly.

Part of his success was an order of technique previously unimagined and hard even to imagine today. There was absolutely no precedent for the effects he introduced—the left-hand and right-hand pizzicato, the double-stop harmonics, the multiple stops, the ricochet bowing, the unheard-of extensions and rapidity of shifting, the fingered octaves, a new use of the glissando, the octave trills, the solos on a single string, the new kinds of bowings. Apparently he had mastered all this when little more than a child. He practiced incessantly when young. Later he never practiced at all and opened his violin case only before a concert. He was an ungainly figure on stage with his cadaverous body, lanky hair, and seemingly awkward way of playing. His elbow was always tucked close to his body and he bowed only from the wrist. During performances he would wave his bow and make faces, playing with his right foot forward and beating time with his left foot. (In private playing, it was noted, there were none of these antics.) To attain some of his effects he used a scordatura tuning that allowed him to execute passages impossible in the original key. In scordatura tuning, which dates back to the sixteenth century, strings are deliberately mistuned. Mozart used it in his great *Sinfonia concertante* in E flat, in which the viola's strings are tuned a semitone high. It is a highly technical subject and hard to explain to non-string players, but scordatura facilitates certain kinds of writing and gives the solo instrument added brilliance.

Another part of Paganini-fever was his awesome personality, one that made his audience shiver when he came on stage. With his awkward, emaciated, spectral figure he looked like something that ought to have been in a shroud, and the Romantics loved every bit of it. Wrote a critic in London's *All the Year Round*: "A vampire in an orchestra is not an every-day sight; and never did man by dress and gesture make more of a ghostly aspect than did he." Paganini carefully cultivated the legends surrounding him. He may not have been well educated, but he was shrewd, knowing

This British caricature gives a good idea of Nicolò Paganini's way of playing: right foot forward, elbow tucked close to the body. Three of the strings of his Guarnerius dangle from the scroll. He is playing one of his fantasias for the G string alone.

the value of publicity and how to exploit it. It helped that he was a mysterious genius surrounded by the most palpitating stories: that he had made a pact with the Devil; that he had been jailed for a long time, during which the strings of his fiddle broke one by one until only the G string remained, and that was how he achieved such facility on the G string; that he had murdered his mistress in a fit of jealous rage; that he had spent years in the galleys. Stendhal swallowed everything hook, line, and sinker, and in his Rossini biography excitedly wrote in great, specific detail, with bulging eyes, about how Paganini had learned his tricks in a dungeon. These stories were taken as gospel. At the beginning Paganini never denied them; he must have been amused and, anyway, such stories were very good for business. They were terrific publicity and sold an awful lot of tickets. Later he tried to set the record straight, but it was too late: he had created his own legend. Folk especially believed in his alliance with the source of all evil. How could he play in this demonic manner if the Devil were not at his elbow? Nobody had ever begun to exploit the resources of the violin in this manner. Obviously he had Outside help.

When the young Franz Liszt heard him, it was a revelation. Liszt made up his mind to do for the piano what Paganini was doing for the violin. But Liszt was not the only one swept off his feet. So was Robert Schumann who, like Liszt, reformed Paganini caprices into piano works. So was Heinrich Heine, brilliant music critic as well as great poet. Mendelssohn raved: ". . . so original, so unique, that it would require an exhaustive analysis to convey an impression of his style." When Friedrich Wieck heard Paganini in Leipzig he responded as much to the musicality as to the virtuosity of the playing: "Never have I heard a singer so moving as an adagio played by Paganini. Never has an artist been who is as great and incomparable as he is in so many genres." Even those who were revolted by his kind of music had to admit that as a performer he stood alone. Thus the fine classical violinist Ludwig Spohr, who found some genius in his music and also found it "childishly tasteless," was amazed by his technique: "His left hand, and his consistently pure intonation, were to me astonishing."

Moritz Hauptmann from Leipzig said that Paganini aroused "aversion" in him; but "in technique and brilliancy, not one of our modern players can approach him." The good, gray Moscheles was swept away at first, and then developed reservations:

> First of all, nothing could exceed my surprise and admiration; his constant and venturesome flights, his newly discovered source of flageolet tones, his gift of fusing and beautifying subjects of the most heterogeneous kind; all these phases of genius so completely bewildered my musical perceptions, that for several days afterwards my head seemed on fire and my brain reeled. . . . Now, however, after hearing him frequently, all this is changed; in every one of his compositions I discover *the same* effects, which betrays a poverty of invention. . . . I long for a little of Spohr's earnestness, Baillot's power, and even Mayseder's piquancy.

As a matter of fact, Moscheles was right. Some of Paganini's music has remained in the repertory, and works like his Caprices for unaccompanied violin, composed in 1820, are as hair-raising as they originally were; but only an addict would claim that the music can stand up against the masterpieces of the repertory or that it has much nourishment. It is music of effect over substance—brilliant and even revolutionary effect, to be sure, but still effect. It represents the exaltation of the violin, and as such may be interesting and even important. But it cannot be taken in massive doses. That said, one Paganini piece has hypnotized composers for generations—the famous Twenty-fourth Caprice. Liszt and Schumann used it for sets of variations. So did Brahms. So did Rachmaninoff. So did Lutoslawski. So did any number of lesser composers.

Paganini still casts a spell. Through the generations his name has remained synonymous with the violin. In recent years medical people have become fascinated with him. Some specialists conjecture that he had a disease of the connective tissue called Marfan's Syndrome, which enabled him to take stretches that a normal left hand could not encompass. But Drs. Richard D. Smith and John

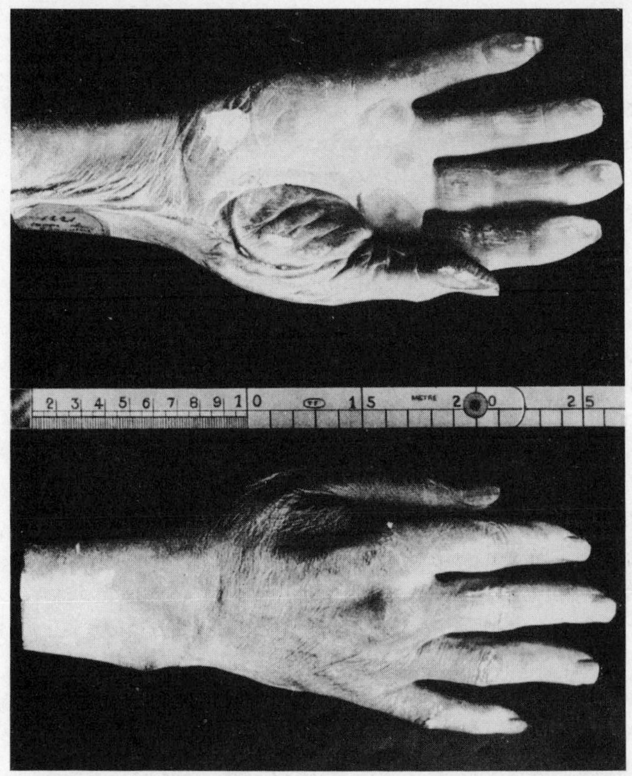

Plaster cast of Paganini's right hand. No cast of his left hand is known to exist. There is a considerable body of medical literature, some of it from Paganini's own day, on the unusual conformation of his hands.

A lithograph of Paganini made in Hamburg, 1830.

W. Worthington, in the March 13, 1967, issue of the *Journal of the American Medical Association,* cited an article in *The Strad* in which measurements taken from a cast of Paganini's hands indicated that they were of normal size. A German violinist, Carl Guhr, is also cited. Guhr wrote about Paganini in the 1830's and said he had a left-hand facility that defied understanding. Paganini could simultaneously finger four C's, D's, or E flats. This requires a phenomenal stretch. How could he do it? By having a thumb of unusual flexibility, it was decided in Paganini's own day. Anatomists who examined Paganini's left hand were startled to see that he could bend his thumb backwards until it touched the little finger. That, plus Paganini's years of practice, gave Dr. Bennati in Paris the answer: "His left hand is not disproportionate in size but he doubles his reach by the extensibility achieved in all the parts." Drs. Smith and Worthington conclude that Paganini had a disease of the connective tissue, but that it was not Marfan's Syndrome. "All the hyperextensibility of the joints point to the Ehlers-Danlos Syndrome. . . . It seems that his extraordinary reach was legitimate and was made possible by abnormal connective tissue."

Ehlers-Danlos was the least of it. No musician who ever lived carried around with him the collection of physical woes that afflicted Paganini. He had measles at four and was critically ill. He had scarlet fever at five and pneumonia at fourteen. As a young man he developed a chronic colitis and a persistent cough that stayed with him his entire life. In 1832 he had a pulmonary hemorrhage in Paris. He suffered from sensitive skin and excessive perspiration, and always had to wear flannel underwear. He had insomnia. He had bad eyes and was forced to wear blue glasses. He had hemorrhoids, rectal stenosis, and rheumatism. He had an abscess in his jaw. He contracted syphilis, and the mercury doses then used caused his skin to take on a peculiar color. It also caused recurrent stomach trouble. Thanks to the syphilis, combined with an infected jaw, he lost all of his teeth. He had trouble with his prostate and needed regular catheterization. That led to bladder infection. In the last years of his life he lost his voice because of tuberculosis of the larynx. He also had tuberculosis of the jaw. He went to every quack in Europe and swallowed every kind of medicine, looking for the magic cure, and some of the medicines made him even sicker. He was especially busy purging himself. Paganini was great on laxatives, some of which almost killed him.

It took Paganini a long time to come out of Italy. He was born in Genoa on October 27, 1782, of poor parents, and received his first lessons from his father. There is no evidence that he ever went to school. When he was seven he started studying with a violinist in the local orchestra. There were other local teachers. At twelve Paganini was playing in public and also composing. In many ways he was self-taught. If any violinist influenced him, it was August Frédéric Durand, a Franco-Polish musician (whose real name was Duranowski) with a big technique. Paganini heard him and was impressed. He was sent to Parma at thirteen for further study. He also became attracted to the guitar and became an expert player on it.

The next step in his life was that of orchestra player. In 1801 he became the first violinist of the orchestra in Lucca. He was a happy-go-lucky young man: wine, women, and song—and syphilis. G.I.C. de Courcy, in her beautifully researched biography (from which all writers on Paganini must necessarily plunder), mentions that Paganini was indeed interested in women, but that he was nowhere near as industrious a lover as legend had it.

He got his great Guarnerius violin between 1802 and 1804. According to Paganini, it had been owned by a businessman who loaned it to him for a concert. When he heard Paganini play he refused to take it back. As money came in, Paganini started collecting violins and owned a fine assortment of Cremonese instruments at his death. Even in the early 1800's they were expensive. The Rev. H. R. Haweis, in *My Musical Life,* has some interesting comments about violin prices. He says that a prince once offered Paganini £80 for one of his Strads, "a large sum at the beginning of the century, even for a Stradivarius. Times have changed, and in these latter days [1888] we think nothing of giving £300 for a genuine instrument of the first class." Times have indeed changed.

In 1982, at an auction in London, the Alard Stradivarius fetched $1.2 million.

Money did not immediately come to Paganini. As a member of the Lucca orchestra he started at 12 scudi (about $15) a month, eventually working his way up to $28. Concertizing on the side brought in some additional money. But the young Paganini was not rolling in wealth.

In his concerts he already, before 1810, was using some of the tricks that so amazed European audiences—playing on two strings or one only and in general dipping into his technical arsenal. After 1810 he was on his own, more a strolling entertainer than a musician. He would amuse his audiences by making the violin sound like a donkey, a rooster, a dog, and they loved it. In a more serious vein he would sometimes play concertos by Rode, Kreutzer, or Viotti. All who heard him were impressed, but they were more impressed with how he played than with what he played. Throughout his life Paganini was associated with junk music. He never played the really great concertos, always falling back on his own showpieces. He never even played his best showpieces; at least, there is no evidence that he ever played his Caprices in public. He gave a concert at La Scala in 1810 and Peter Lichtenthal, the correspondent of the Leipzig *Allgemeine Musikalische Zeitung,* sent back a dazed report:

> . . . an extraordinarily large audience. Everyone wanted to hear this phenomenal wizard and everyone was really staggered. It fairly took one's breath away. In a sense, he is without question the foremost and greatest violinist in the world. His playing is truly *inexplicable*. He performs certain passagework, leaps and double stops that have never been heard before from any violinist, whoever he might be. He plays—with a special fingering of his own—the most difficult passages in two, three and four parts; imitates many wind instruments; plays the chromatic scale right close to the bridge in the highest positions and with a purity of intonation that is sheerly incredible. He performs the most difficult compositions on one string and in the most amazing

manner, while plucking a bass accompaniment on the others, probably as a prank.

But Lichtenthal also made some adverse comments about the cheapness of the music. Nevertheless reports like this whetted Europe's appetite. Music lovers wanted him to come forth so that they could compare him with Spohr or Charles Philippe Lafont, the leading violinists of the time. Paganini was in no rush. Italy loved him and he was beginning to make money. He also did some teaching. The best of his pupils was Camillo Sivori, who became famous, trading on the fact that he was the great Paganini's protégé and rewarding him by saying that Paganini was "probably the worst teacher who ever lived." In 1825 Paganini's son Achille was born. The mother was a singer named Antonia Bianchi, who accompanied Paganini on his tours. (The affair broke up in 1828.) His Italian career came to a climax in 1827, when Pope Leo XII awarded him the Order of the Golden Spur. Now Paganini could call himself "Cavaliere." The next year he started his European travels.

First stop was Vienna, where they believed all that had been written about Paganini's eccentric life, his friendship with the Devil included. What a *frisson* must have gone through Vienna on the announcement that Paganini was coming! Everybody important in Vienna was there for the debut and was bowled over. One critic called Paganini "the greatest instrumentalist the world of music has ever known." Bach and Mozart might have had something to say about that had they been around. The program of Paganini's first concert was representative. The orchestra opened with Beethoven's *Fidelio* Overture. Then came Paganini's B minor Concerto. Bianchi sang an aria by Paer, Paganini played his *Sonata militaire* on the G string, Bianchi sang an aria by Rossini, and Paganini closed the evening with his variations on Rossini's *Non più mesta*. It was not a long program. Some of the musicians may have been amused to notice the care Paganini took to keep his sheet music a secret. From his very first appearances in Italy he

Karikatur auf die Wiener Konzerte

Paganini, as seen by J. P. Lyser, at his debut in Vienna. Many believed Paganini to have been in league with the Devil. How else could he play in so diabolical a manner?

always personally distributed the parts to the various musicians and personally collected them after the concert. Those were the days before copyright laws, and Paganini was not going to let his scores be pirated. Paganini went on to give fourteen concerts in Vienna before going to Prague, where he had two operations on his diseased jawbone and had all his teeth removed. He also played in Prague, where he was too greedy. He quintupled the normal prices, got small audiences, and had to go back to a more reasonable scale.

In most of his concerts Paganini worked with impresarios who took care of the details, hired the hall and orchestra, and provided publicity. The orchestra did not cost much. In Berlin, where Paganini went in 1828, an orchestra of thirty-one players came to $105. Paganini always worked on a percentage of the profits—two-thirds or three-fifths, depending on the event. He played eleven concerts in Berlin (the last five of them given at the Royal Opera) and was able to bank over $20,000 after six weeks in Germany. He also played in Warsaw, where he met the "*giovane pianista*," Frédéric Chopin. Back in Germany, Paganini continued his tour, charging two thalers for the best seats, double the usual price. The young Heinrich Ernst followed Paganini from city to city, hoping to discover his secrets. He claimed to have heard Paganini twenty times. Ernst became one of the leading violin virtuosos of the century. Another violinist who heard him was Carl Guhr, who published a study of his method, mentioning the scordatura tuning, the endless bow, the unorthodox bowings (upbeats with a downbow and so on), the completely different fingerings. Guhr also said that Paganini loved to play Beethoven and Mozart quartets. He never did that in public, of course.

Paganini was in Germany for two years. By this time he had a manager, Paul David Curiol from Frankfurt. Curiol's job was to find engagements, plan the tours, make the hotel reservations—in short, very much what a manager today does. Paganini had made a wise choice. The energetic Curiol made Paganini even richer. For a few months of playing in Germany, Paganini cleared $35,000. In Europe, Paganini was considered a money-mad miser, and in many respects he was. Moscheles, in his memoirs, tells a story about his avarice that is not very nice.

Paris in 1831 was the artistic and intellectual center of the world, and Paganini must have approached the city with a certain amount of trepidation. Louis Désiré Héron, the new manager of the Opéra, immediately engaged Paganini for ten concerts on Wednesdays and Sundays, spread over five weeks. The contract specified that Paganini would get the full proceeds of the Sunday concerts after expenses. For the Wednesday concerts the opera house paid all expenses and received one-third of the receipts up to $4,500, plus one-fourth of anything above that. The price of admission was doubled for all concerts. What an audience assembled on March 9, 1831! Among the celebrities were Gautier, Jules Janin, Delacroix, George Sand, Alfred de Musset, Liszt, Castil-Blaze, de Vigny, Auber, Donizetti, the Rothschilds, Halévy, Heine, and Börne. Paris went crazy. Castil-Blaze unleashed the full force of his style: "This thing is the most astounding, the most surprising, the most marvellous, the most miraculous, the most triumphant, the most unheard-of, the most unique, the most extraordinary, the most incredible, the most unexpected that one can imagine." Berlioz went into deep analysis. "It is past belief," he wrote, "how he discovered in the use of single and double harmonics, in the handling of notes plucked with the left hand, in the forming of arpeggios, in bowings, in passages on three strings—all the more unbelievable in that his predecessors did not so much as give a hint of such effects. Paganini is one of those artists of whom it must be said that they are because they are, not because others were before them." The other critics were equally lavish. Paganini was the toast of Paris—a toast offered in golden cups. He made a fortune.

In England, however, they did not take kindly to the inordinate prices at Paganini's concerts. There was an uproar. Newspapers called it outrageous and demanded a boycott of the concerts. Paganini and his new manager, Pierre Laporte, had to back down, but they still charged a great deal—$5 for orchestra and stall seats, an enormous figure. The London concerts brought in about $50,000. It cannot be said that Paganini provided programs that demanded rigorous listening. The one of August 20, 1831, with an orchestra conducted by Michael Costa, was typical. It opened with Beethoven's First Symphony, followed by an aria from *Il Barbiere* sung by Mlle. du Puy. Paganini appeared, to play his E minor Violin Concerto. Miss Bellchambers sang a Rossini aria, there was an overture by Bernhard Romberg, and then intermission. Next came Dr. Arne's song, *The Soldier Tir'd,* sung by Miss Coveney with trumpet obbligato by Mr. Harper. Paganini came out to play his *Sonata Amorosa Galante, with variations on a theme by Rossini,* "composed expressly and performed on a SINGLE STRING." The Misses Conway and Bellchambers sang a Rossini duet. For Paganini's last appearance on the program he played the *Variations on the National Hymn, God Save the King,* "composed expressly and performed by Signor Paganini with Orchestral Accompaniment." The Beethoven *Prometheus* Overture, which closed the evening, must have come as a dreadful anticlimax. The critics, as in Paris, tried to describe the indescribable. Chorley, the foremost British critic, wrote in the *Athenaeum* that he had not believed the publicity surrounding Paganini, and that he had even said that Charles de Bériot was the better violinist. Now he wished to apologize. "We here retract. . . . Paganini is a solitary man in his art! There is a relation between a unit and a million—none between him and his fellow men." Like Patti and others later on, Paganini started to give farewell concerts. In his first English tour his final appearances were billed, respectively, as his last, the very last, and the absolutely last.

His next few years were occupied in touring. In one of the more bizarre episodes in musical history he asked Berlioz to compose for him a work for viola and orchestra. Paganini played the viola as handsomely as he played the violin, and he owned a Stradivarius viola of which he was very proud. He gave some concerts as a violist. Most likely these were the first viola concerts in history. But to ask Berlioz, of all people! Berlioz was the leader of the avant-garde, and his music and intellectual orientation had nothing in common with Paganini. Berlioz composed a masterpiece, *Harold in Italy*. Paganini looked through it and, of course, discovered that it was not his kind of music. He told Berlioz it did not have enough display in the solo part. Later—whether to salve his conscience or because he sincerely believed in the mission that the French composer was trying to accomplish—he gave Berlioz $4,000, a sum on which one could then live for a long time. Berlioz was able to drop his work as a music critic and concentrate on composition.

Paganini kept playing all over Europe. He purchased, for $45,000, an estate for himself—the Villa Gaione, near Parma—and grew to hate it. He found it very expensive to maintain. He invested in a lavish casino in Paris. It opened in 1837 and promptly went bankrupt, injuring Paganini's pride as well as his pocketbook. In the last years of his life, what with a lost voice and failing health, he played very little and, toward the end, not at all. In 1835 he became administrator and conductor of the ducal theater in Parma. He resigned the following year after a dispute over a reorganization of the theater. His last appearance was at a charity concert in Parma in 1837. He was eccentric to the very end. Charles Hallé became friendly with him. "The striking, awe-inspiring, ghostlike figure of Paganini was to be seen every afternoon in the music shop of Bernard Latte, Passage de l'Opéra, where he sat for an hour, enveloped in a long black cloak, taking notice of nobody, and hardly ever raising his piercing black eyes. He was one of the sights of Paris." He scared Hallé when they met: he had "uncanny" eyes, did not speak, and pointed to the piano when he wanted the young artist to play. One afternoon in Paganini's rooms Hallé played, and there was a long silence. Paganini rose and went to his violin case. Hallé had never heard Paganini play, and he all but had heart failure:

> What then passed in me can hardly be imagined; I was all in a tremble, and my heart thumped as if it would burst my chest; in fact, no young swain going to the first rendezvous with his beloved could possibly feel more violent emotions. Paganini opened the case, took the violin out, and began to tune it carefully

> with his fingers without using the bow; my agitation became almost intolerable. When he was satisfied, and I said to myself, with a lump in my throat, "Now, now, he'll take the bow!" he carefully put the violin back and closed the case. And that is how I heard Paganini.

In the winter of 1839 the dying man went to Nice. He refused to see a priest, and when he died in Nice on May 27, 1840, the bishop denied permission for burial. Had Paganini not dealt with the Devil and refused the last rites of the church? Paganini's coffin was stored in a cellar for several years. Thus his legend lived on. In 1845 he was buried in his villa, and in 1876 the bones were removed to Parma. At his death he owned twenty-two Cremonese instruments. His favorite violin, the Guarnerius that he called "The Cannon," he left to Genoa, where it still reposes in the Palazzo Civico. In 1982, at a concert honoring Paganini's bicentennial, the instrument was brought to New York and played in Carnegie Hall by the Italian violinist Salvatore Accardo. Violin dealers and many violinists were appalled. Suppose the irreplaceable instrument were lost or stolen. Suppose it were damaged. Suppose the plane on which it was being carried went down. Suppose . . .

8 *Franz Liszt*

THE EAGLE OF THE PIANO

HE soared above everybody else, and every pianist in Europe admitted it. His music may not have been liked very much, his personality grated on some, but when he put his ten fingers on the keyboard he was in a class by himself. There was Franz Liszt, and there were all other pianists.

He was a complicated man who lived a complicated life. Though he played the piano from childhood to old age, he was a professional touring pianist for fewer than ten of those years. To the public he represented the Byronic, Romantic ideal. He was incredibly handsome as a young man, he had genius, he had charisma, and he was one of the uncrowned heads of Europe. He flaunted his independence and defiantly drew attention to himself. "To be different from the rest of mankind," Hallé observed, "to know nothing of the usual modes of living, or rather to appear ignorant of them, seemed to be his sole aim." He more or less spanned the century—1811 to 1886—and probably no figure in

European life was more discussed and written about. Only Wagner, two years his junior, received an equal amount of attention, and that was mostly in the period after 1860. Liszt was in action as a child and was written about from the time he was thirteen years old, for he captured the public imagination as no performing musician, not even Paganini, had been able to do.

Everything he did made news, and it was reported all over Europe and America. Even Liszt and apples made news. A correspondent for the New York *Evening Post* in 1861 wrote that Liszt "cherishes a singular animosity against apples, which useful fruit he considers unworthy of being ranked among the edibles of the planet." Journalists paid special attention to the famous Liszt hands, swooning over them, becoming rhapsodic and sentimental. Thus Anne Brewster of the Philadelphia *Evening Bulletin* in 1869: "They are slender, the fingers long, thin; well-kept, good-shaped nails; but the thumb was the wonder. . . . They [the thumbs] are the largest I ever saw, and reach up to the first joint of the forefinger." (As a matter of fact, Liszt did not have a very large hand and could just about stretch a tenth.) For some forty years virtually every issue of *Dwight's Journal of Music* carried something about Liszt. In 1858 *Punch* noted, in a superbly overpunctuated squib, that "There seems to be in the continental papers a grand German confederation to praise Liszt. It is *toujours Liszt*, as with the ghost in *Hamlet*. It is the rule, apparently, with all Teutonic newspapers, if there happens to be a crack, or a small cranny, in their paper, that wants filling up, to dab in, invariably, a bit of Liszt."

But Liszt, after all, gave the papers a great deal to write about. He eloped with a countess. His piano playing drove women crazy, and Heine wrote about Liszt recitals in terms of magnetism, galvanism, electricity, contagion, "musical cantharides and other unmentionable matters." Liszt put on a big act at the piano, and Heine, that sharp observer, was half amused, half respectful: "When he played, for example, a storm on the piano, we saw the lightnings quiver over his own face, his limbs shook as before the storm wind, and his long locks dripped as if it were with the

Franz Liszt, about fifty-five years old. The photograph gives a good idea of his virile good looks; one can see why he was constantly being called the eagle of the piano.

Marie d'Agoult, the countess with whom Liszt eloped and had three children.

splashing rain he represented." For special concerts Liszt got himself decked out with many of his decorations. The Russian critic Vladimir Stasov has left a description of a Liszt concert in St. Petersburg. "Liszt wore a white cravat, and over it the order of the Golden Spur given him by Pius IX. . . . He was further adorned by various other orders suspended by chains from the lapel of his dress coat." (Did they clank while he played?) The Russian intellectuals had been waiting for years for the legendary Liszt, and Stasov and his friends could not contain themselves: "We were like men in love, men possessed. We had never heard anything like it before, never been confronted by such passionate, demonic genius." Heine called Liszt "the mad, beauteous, hateful, enigmatic, fatal and yet withal the very childlike child of his age, the gigantic dwarf, the furious Roland with the Hungarian saber of honor, the harlequin of genius." Liszt was the first male musical matinee idol (whatever Paganini was, he was no matinee idol) and women would follow him on the street the way today's groupies pursue a rock star. This prevailed even when he was approaching old age. Clara Schumann heard him, after a lapse of many years, in 1876. Liszt was sixty-five. Clara had to admit that he was still unique, and he still gave the feeling that "some devilish force" was sweeping him along. She added, primly and disapprovingly, "The women were, of course, mad about him—it was revolting."

To a delighted and awed public, Liszt managed to convey the image of what an ideal pianist should be like, act like, and look like—the kind of pianist normally found only in romantic novels. Liszt was Hungarian-born (though he never could speak his native tongue) and that in itself was romantic. He eloped with a countess and had three children with her, to the scandalized delight of Europe. He later took up with a princess, Carolyne Sayn-Wittgenstein, and tongues wagged about that. He became an abbé. His pupils were all over the world. He spurned money and, after 1847, played only on special occasions, refusing any fee. He had love affairs into old age, and when the cossack Countess Olga Janina (who, as has been pointed out, was neither a cossack nor a countess) waved a pistol at him, all Europe happily reverberated with gossip. He represented the Music of the Future, and the outraged cries of the rear guard helped keep him in the news. Liszt had all the gifts. He never pursued success, Berlioz wryly noted. Success pursued him. His was a unique kind of magnetism, and even those who, like Schumann, had grave reservations about his lifestyle and compositions, paid homage to the magic power he exerted over everybody. "I have never," observed Schumann, "found any artist, except Paganini, to possess in so high degree as Liszt, this power of subjugating, elevating and leading the public." It was *where* Liszt was leading the public that worried Schumann and his conservative Clara.

He had some peers. Mendelssohn was a brilliant pianist but never gave solo concerts, and when he played in public it was to introduce his own music. In his day Mendelssohn was better known as a composer and conductor. Chopin was one of the greatest of all pianists but, unlike Liszt and Paganini, was not for the masses. He gave very few recitals, and those were played in salons and small halls. Hallé hit it exactly on the head when in his comparison of Liszt and Chopin he said that where "Chopin carried you into a dreamland," Liszt was "all sunshine and dazzling splendor, subjugating his hearers with a power that none could withstand." There was Sigismond Thalberg, Liszt's big rival, who exhibited his elegant bag of pianistic tricks and soon disappeared, having none of Liszt's staying power.

It was Liszt who put everything together, and he turned out to be all things to all men. He called himself "the servant of the public" during his touring years, and would play the usual operatic transcriptions and other fluff demanded by audiences of the day. Yet he could, and did, play late Beethoven sonatas, Bach (and not only in his own transcriptions), and his own contemporaries. Liszt had a tremendous ego, but that did not keep him from being the friend and benefactor of many composers. He could tamper horribly with the music of the masters, and next time play the same music with an integrity and flowing line that reduced everybody to tears. We have Berlioz's word for this. Berlioz heard him play the first movement of the *Moonlight* Sonata and "de-

Sigismond Thalberg, Liszt's big rival in the late 1830's.

Cosima, Liszt's daughter. She married Liszt's great pupil Hans von Bülow and then left him for Richard Wagner.

Hans von Bülow, one of the century's major pianists and conductors.

Karl Tausig, perhaps the most gifted of the Liszt pupils. He died in 1871 at the age of thirty.

naturalize" it in every respect—melodically, rhythmically, and emotionally. Not much later he heard Liszt play the piece "with sublime simplicity." Yes, Liszt was a complicated man.

Probably he was the greatest pianist the world has ever known. There was nothing he could not do at the keyboard. "Compared to him we all are children," said his great successor, Anton Rubinstein. Liszt could read anything at sight, could memorize immediately, never forgot anything, could reproduce a complicated piece of music merely on hearing it once, could improvise, and had the entire literature at his fingertips. If he ever had any technical problems, they were never apparent to anybody. When he determined to do for the piano what Paganini had done for the violin, he started to write music of unprecedented complexity and difficulty—more difficult, even, than Chopin's music, which always lay beautifully in the hand. But through all the demands for virtuosity one of the seminal musical minds of the century shone through. Saint-Saëns, Liszt's friend and admirer and no mean pianist himself, had a few words to say about Liszt's contributions. The influence of Liszt on the future generation of pianists, Saint-Saëns wrote in 1893, was incalculable. "I can but compare it with the revolution brought about by Victor Hugo in the mechanism of the French language. . . . This great development of sonority of tone, with the means of obtaining it, which he invented, has become the indispensable condition and foundation of modern execution." Liszt must have had a way of producing a sonority that nobody else was able to duplicate. All professionals for fifty years were talking about the Liszt sound, and Alexander Siloti, who entered Liszt's classes in 1883, tells a story about it. Siloti had heard Rubinstein play the *Moonlight* Sonata and raved to Liszt. Liszt, now seventy-two years old, gave him a peculiar look and sat down at the piano:

> He began to play, and I held my breath as I listened. Rubinstein had played on a beautiful Bechstein in a hall with very good acoustic properties; Liszt was playing in a little carpeted room, in which small space thirty-five to forty people were sitting,

> and the piano was worn out, unequal and discordant. He had played only the opening triplets, however, when I felt as if the room no longer held me, and when, after the first four bars, the G sharp came in the right hand I was completely carried away. Not that he accentuated this G sharp; it was simply that he gave it an entirely new sound which even now, after twenty-seven years, I can hear distinctly. . . . I then realized that I had completely forgotten having listened to Rubinstein two hours before. *As a pianist he no longer existed.* I make this statement deliberately with a full knowledge of what I am saying—and as my readers know my opinion of Rubinstein they may thus gain some faint idea of Liszt as a pianist. . . . I now understood what Anton Rubinstein meant by calling himself a common soldier and Liszt a General, and how true this estimate was.

If Paganini was the first, overpowering influence on Liszt as a performer, he also learned a good deal from Chopin, the elegant, snobbish, introverted Polish genius. The Chopin influence came through mostly in Liszt's compositions, but surely he got from Chopin certain secrets of pedaling, coloration, tonal manipulation, and melodic projection. They had an uneasy friendship. Liszt moved through life as a *grand seigneur* and Chopin envied him his power, his magnetism, his brilliance. Then there was Liszt's friend Berlioz, from whom he got ideas about "orchestrating" on the piano.

Liszt was a child prodigy, as all great pianists and violinists have been. He was born in Raiding, Hungary, on October 22, 1811, was playing very well at seven, started concertizing, and was taken to Vienna to study with Beethoven's pupil, Carl Czerny. Late in life Czerny remembered Liszt as a delicate-looking child who had all kinds of bad pianistic mannerisms, but who also had an awesome talent. Apparently young Liszt was an eager pupil who learned a great deal from Czerny, and he made his debut in 1820, at the age of nine. His father began to take Franz on tour, and in 1823 the boy played in Germany and France to universal acclaim. Then London followed. At the beginning of the tour Liszt was getting $20 a concert; at the end it was as much as $500.

Moscheles heard him in London and immediately put his finger on the boy as the coming pianist; his playing "surpasses in power and mastery of difficulties anything I have ever heard." Liszt started composing and at thirteen wrote a great deal of piano music and his one and only opera. At sixteen, with the death of his father, he was alone and on his own in Paris and that was where he heard Paganini.

The young pianist was not playing much in public at that time. He had enough pupils to live fairly comfortably. He slaved at the keyboard, and he slaved even more after the Paganini experience, experimenting with a new kind of virtuosity and sonority. When his *Paganini* Etudes were published it seems safe to say that no pianist alive except the composer could begin to play them. Their technical problems were too novel and too difficult. Saint-Saëns admitted as much, and said that pianists of the old school were unable to come to grips with this kind of music, for they played by the old methods, "which required perfect immobility of the whole body, the elbows close to the side, and . . . only a limited action of the forearm."

In 1835 Liszt eloped to Switzerland with the Countess d'Agoult, a high-toned lady with intellectual pretensions. They were to have three children before the affair broke up. While Liszt was temporarily out of the public eye, Thalberg conquered Paris. His style consisted of playing operatic paraphrases with themes surrounded by arpeggios, and he seemed to have three hands. "Old Arpeggio," he was fondly called. People at his concerts stood on chairs to see how he did it. Liszt visited Paris, heard Thalberg, and was not impressed. So he engaged the 3,000-seat Opéra and played one of his own operatic paraphrases plus, with orchestra, Weber's *Konzertstück* with great success. Prior to that he had played, for a small and very select audience at the Salle Erard, the Beethoven *Hammerklavier* Sonata. Berlioz, who followed the performance with the music in front of him, was as struck with Liszt's textual fidelity as with his technical mastery in this monumental piece. Paris enjoyed the confrontation between Liszt and Thalberg. The two pianists finally appeared together in the salon of Princess Belgiojoso who, as Alan Walker puts it in his Liszt biography, thus scored the social coup of the season. After the soirée the princess was asked which of the two pianists she preferred. "Thalberg," she said, "is the first pianist in the world. Liszt is the only one."

His romance with d'Agoult coming to an end, Liszt started his years of concert tours. From 1839 to 1847 he was on the road. He played many surefire numbers, including his transcriptions of the Berlioz *Symphonie fantastique,* the *William Tell* Overture and the Beethoven *Pastoral*, his operatic paraphrases, his *Grand galop chromatique* and other crowd pleasers, but an examination of his repertory also shows many masterpieces of the literature, including much Chopin and the less popular Schumann. In Hungary, the native son got a particularly frenzied reception. Liszt was to return there annually for much of the rest of his life.

It was in the first year of his tours that he invented the solo recital. Up to then every musician gave concerts with an assortment of assisting artists. Not Liszt. In 1839, while in Rome, he started playing without a supporting cast. At first he called these events "soliloquies." As he explained to Princess Belgiojoso, "I have ventured to give a series of concerts all by myself, affecting the Louis XIV style, and saying cavalierly to the public, '*le concert, c'est moi.*'" In England, when he played there the following year, his appearances were called "recitals."

Not everybody liked the innovation. Stasov, who reported on Liszt's first appearances in Russia in the spring of 1842, recounts the bewilderment that a pure solo piano recital created. "On April 8 Liszt gave his first concert before an overflow audience of more than three thousand in the Assembly Hall of the Nobility. Everything about this concert was unusual. First of all, Liszt appeared alone on the stage throughout the entire concert: there were no other performers—no orchestra, singers, or any other instrumental soloists whatever." Stasov says that many in the audience thought that Liszt's action was brazen. "What conceit! What vanity! As if to say, 'All you need is me. Listen only to me—you don't need anyone else.'" The program also puzzled the Russians. "Not

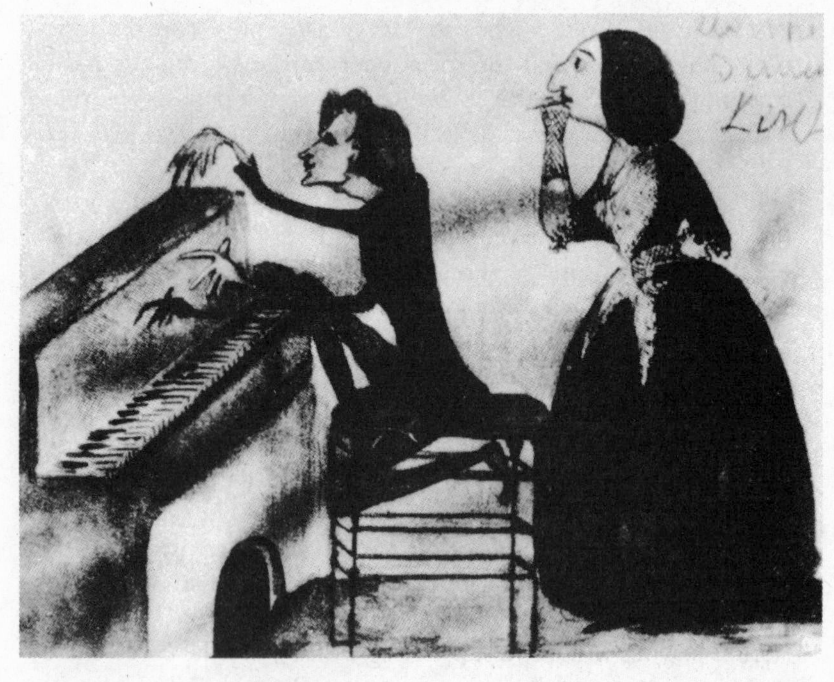

Liszt playing for George Sand. This amusing and skillful caricature was drawn by Maurice, Sand's son.

just piano pieces, his own, his true metier—no, this could not satisfy his boundless conceit—he had to be both an orchestra and human voices." Liszt played transcriptions of songs by Beethoven and Schubert. He also "took large orchestral works, overtures, symphonies—and played them too, all alone, in place of a whole orchestra, without any assistance." (As a matter of fact, there was only one orchestral work on the program—the *William Tell* Overture. The second concert, on April 11, contained the last half of Beethoven's *Pastoral* Symphony in Liszt's arrangement.) "As soon as he finished the overture, and while the hall was still rocking with applause, he moved swiftly to a second piano facing in the opposite direction. Throughout the concert he used these pianos alternatively for each piece, facing first one, then the other half of the hall."

Naturally Liszt was the prime topic of conversation in St. Petersburg. Alexander Serov, the composer and critic, wrote a long imaginary dialogue between Kh ("a major in the transportation service") and N.N. After some talk about Liszt's crazy idea of giving solo recitals, and the great amount of money he made, they get down to Liszt's looks:

> N.N.: . . . Nowadays there are so many starry-eyed addlepates wandering around in a daze of poetic ecstasy—they either don't see the truth or don't want to see it. Would you believe it, I myself have heard a lot of people even admire Liszt's looks, whereas he's really a freak, a scarecrow, with his spindly legs, unkempt hair, and face that looks like a mummy's!
>
> Kh: He must be some beauty.
>
> N.N.: Charming, indeed. And what grotesque manners! Sometimes he even forgets the ordinary proprieties. Imagine, he didn't even take the trouble to look over the hall or the stage before the concert. Now, in mounting the stage, in order to face the royal family, he was supposed to use the steps opposite the imperial box. But did he? No. When the clock struck two, he elbowed his way through the crowd, pushed his way to the platform, bowed low, then glanced at the stage, shook his thick

> hair and, as you might have expected, thanks to his long legs, leaped about four feet onto it.
> Kh: Ha, ha, ha! How charming, how very respectful. How come his breeches didn't burst?

Liszt returned to Russia several times, and ended his career as a concert pianist there with recitals given at Elizavetgrad in 1847. Why did the most magnetic of all pianists, with the world at his feet, abruptly stop playing? Perhaps his creative urge had become overpowering, and Liszt indicated as much in a letter to the St. Petersburg Philharmonic Society, which had invited him back to Russia in 1863 as pianist and conductor. He thanked the gentlemen involved. However,

> if you would be good enough to take into consideration the fact that I long ago refused to din my ten fingers into the public's ears and for fifteen years have persistently refused to participate in any concert whatsoever as a pianist, a role I can no longer recapture save, perhaps, by reminiscence; also that I do not suffer in the least from a craving to personally advance my own works and am content to write with care, reflection and conscientiousness without concerning myself further—then you will not be surprised, gentlemen, that I am not thinking of undertaking any journeys. The fatigue I would have to experience would in no way compensate me for the interruption of my work. . . . How would I now, in Rome, be tempted by the idea of again resuming a responsibility which, I believe, I gave up as honorably as I had once fulfilled it? Batons and pianos will continue to flourish without any difficulty everywhere, quite well without me!

His tours had made him financially independent, despite the fact that he gave much money away. Liszt was a prodigal spender with a complete disdain for money. It was the typical *grand seigneur* attitude. Money would always be there when he needed it. But at the end of his eight or so years of concertizing enough remained to give him an annual income of some $6,000. And he had his salary as Kapellmeister in the ducal court of Weimar. And the great ones of Europe rushed to feed him, house him, and entertain him lavishly. Liszt always lived very well.

Liszt's "impudence" (as he himself put it) in giving solo recitals took a while to become accepted. Most soloists continued to use assisting artists at their "recitals," but a few daring ones dispensed with them. One such was Liszt's pupil Hans von Bülow, and he got roasted in Berlin as late as 1860 for his temerity. The London *Musical World* quoted a German critic, who with heavy Teutonic humor complained that Bülow was "the be-all and the end-all, the alpha and omega, the dinner and the dessert in his own person. He suffered no rival near his music. *'L'état, c'est moi,'* said the Grand Monarque. *'La soirée, c'est moi,'* cries Herr von Bülow. He and he alone, disdaining aid from any one else, was the sole performer."

Liszt demanded respect as an artist, and Europe resounded with stories about the way he handled obnoxious nobles. He lifted his hands from the keyboard at the Russian court when he was disturbed by the noise, and told the emperor that "music itself must stop when Your Majesty speaks," or words to that effect. The Princess Metternich asked him if he had done good business on his tour, and Liszt was insulted. "I make music, Madame, not business." In St. Petersburg a general asked him if he had ever been in the army. "No. Has Your Excellency ever played the piano?" Eduard Hanslick, the brilliant Viennese critic who in an article cited these examples of Liszt's independence, said that such actions made him a hero in the eyes of the young people of Europe, representing as he did "the brave champion of the social equality of the artist." Hanslick's summation was that Liszt "is not only a man of genius and a great artist, but he is one of the most extraordinary men of his time, one of the most remarkable and most attractive incarnations of the modern spirit."

In his years at Weimar, Liszt introduced many new works to Europe, including music by Berlioz, Schumann, Raff, Cornelius, the new French school, and even Verdi. Suddenly the little town became a nexus of the progressive music of the future. That included Wagner's *Lohengrin*, which received its world premiere there in 1850. Wagner eventually was to marry Liszt's daughter Cosima, taking her away from her husband Hans von Bülow, Liszt's first great pupil. Liszt quit his Weimar job in 1858 after the failure of Peter Cornelius's opera *Der Barbier von Bagdad*. He kept the house given to him by the duke, and Weimar was one of his headquarters for the rest of his life. He divided his time among Weimar, Rome (where he received minor orders in 1865), and Budapest, with constant visits to Paris. There was no easing up on his activities, and Hanslick, the witty chronicler of so much of the century's music, poked fun at Liszt in 1866. It amused him that the flamboyantly Byronic pianist had entered the church. Hanslick said that he fully understood why Liszt had retired from the concert stage:

> Was this so unnatural, that an easily excitable, fanciful man, who from his childhood had been tossed from one triumph to another, and in a wildly stirring life had tasted all enjoyments, honors and excitements to excess, should now in his fifty-fifth year feel painfully satiated and unsatisfied? That he should fall from the most intoxicating enjoyment of the world into the opposite extreme of an artistic piety. . . .

Having paid homage to Liszt's switch from the world to the church, from *Zigeuner* to Franciscan, Hanslick deftly and sarcastically inserts the knife. What actually did happen after Liszt became an abbé?

> Liszt, who for some time before his priestly consecration had kept himself concealed behind the Sistine clouds of incense, stepped suddenly and briskly forth into the sinful world. He hastens from Rome to Budapest as king of a music festival prepared for him, conducts there in his ecclesiastical garb his *Saint Elizabeth,* and kindles up the Magyar public by his piano playing. Thereupon he plunges into the artistic vortex of Paris, brings out

his *Festival* Mass with great pomp, and is there reported—so witty is this human life—to have converted a frail sister to virtue by his holy piano playing.

The worldly Liszt played miraculously, the Abbé Liszt plays miracles.

Weimar was where Liszt did the major part of his teaching. Alexander Borodin visited Liszt there in 1877 and wrote an interesting account of the experience. Liszt would generally arrive on April 8. "Here at the same time have come from all corners of the earth the *Lisztianer* and *Lisztianerin,* as Liszt's young couples are called." From every window in Weimar came the sound of pianists working their fingers "with enthusiasm and persistence." Lessons were given every Wednesday and Saturday from 3 to 7 P.M. Those lessons could be tough. Liszt expected homage, and his scared pupils walked on tiptoe. Normally affable, he could fly into rages, and both Bettina Walker and Amy Fay have described some fearsome sessions in which Liszt eviscerated unfortunate players.

In Liszt's studio were a battered upright and a Bechstein grand piano "that has suffered considerably at the hands of Liszt's zealous pupils." Liszt wore the robes of an abbé while he taught, and was a black presence. Borodin heard Liszt play and was impressed:

> In spite of all that I have heard about it, I was struck by the extreme simplicity, sobriety and discipline of his playing and the complete absence of pretentiousness, affectation and any straining for extraneous effect. He adopts moderate tempos, never rushes or gets carried away, and yet in spite of his age, the power, energy, passion, enthusiasm and fire are boundless. His tone is round, full and firm; the clarity, richness and variety of nuance are amazing.

But sometimes the old devil asserted itself, and Borodin noticed that while sight-reading, or playing a new piece, or playing duets, "he will sometimes begin to add things of his own and gradually under his hands will emerge not the same piece but an

Liszt in old age. At the bottom of the photograph are the opening measures of the celebrated Hungarian Rhapsody No. 2.

improvisation on it—one of those brilliant transcriptions that have established his fame as a pianist and composer."

Liszt's Weimar pupils went around the world carrying the message of *Der Meister* wherever they settled and taught. In Russia there were Sophie Menter and Karl Klindworth. In the United States, William Mason, Arthur Friedheim, Rafael Joseffy, and Alexander Siloti. In Portugal, Vianna da Motta. In Germany, Hans von Bülow, Karl Tausig, Karl Klindworth (after his Russian sojourn), Eugen d'Albert, Conrad Ansorge, and Hans von Bronsart. In Austria, Emil von Sauer. In Belgium, Arthur de Greef. In Switzerland, Bernhard Stavenhagen. In Italy, Giovanni Sgambati. In Sweden, Martha Rennert. In France, Marie Jaëll. What a list! Great pianists all, and some are not included because, like Moriz Rosenthal and Alfred Reisenauer, they did not teach very much. Liszt was as important a piano teacher as he was a pianist, and only Theodor Leschetizky in the next generation produced a roster that could match the sharpshooters who emerged from the Liszt atelier. Liszt, incidentally, never took a cent for his lessons. Of his great pupils he was especially fond of Bülow, Tausig, and d'Albert. The remarkable Tausig, who died in 1871 at the age of thirty, could do anything Liszt himself could do, and he was so admired by musicians that he was able to straddle the Wagner and Brahms camps that divided musical Europe. Normally the Wagnerians and Brahmsians did not speak to each other; but Tausig worked with Brahms on some of his piano music, and for Wagner prepared the piano score of *Die Meistersinger*.

Liszt died just before the advent of recording. Edison had invented the phonograph in 1877, but it took well over a decade before cylinders started to be issued commercially; and not until 1895 was the first catalogue of flat discs issued. In the 1880's Edison sent a crew to Europe to get recorded testimonials for his miraculous device, and he netted some great notables, including Tennyson and Gladstone, both of whom were born two years before Liszt. Brahms spoke on a cylinder and recorded a few measures of a Hungarian Dance. There have been persistent rumors of a Liszt cylinder, but if it does indeed exist, nobody has ever come across it. So Liszt remains a legend, whereas the generation of musicians just after him is amply represented on old recordings. One can but envy Saint-Saëns who, in his old age, said of Liszt that "The remembrance of his playing consoles me for no longer being young."

9 *Jenny Lind*

THE MORAL LADY

JENNY LIND was the first singer whose name has remained a household word. Pasta, Malibran, Grisi, and Sontag were glorious singers, and they have not been forgotten, but theirs are names known mostly to opera enthusiasts and well-read music lovers. But Jenny Lind was "the Swedish Nightingale," and her name still means something to people who normally have nothing to do with music. That is especially true in the United States, thanks to her mid-century visit and the hysteria it created under the aegis of P. T. Barnum.

Some of her success was connected with the spirit of the times and her particular outlook. She was the very symbol of the Victorian age—or, at least, several aspects of that remarkable period. She was devout, sincerely devout, and the Victorians responded to that. Whatever their own personal lives might have been, the Victorians paid lip service to morality, and Jenny Lind was a pillar of morality. She could always be counted upon to do all the right things. She would never sing in France because she disapproved of French morality, and she once told John Ruskin that France as a nation was "shut out from the common portion of God's blessing upon men, and deservedly so." She was always going to church. She gave a considerable part of her considerable earnings to charity. Her private life was beyond reproach. Women liked her because she seemed simple and unspoiled, not flamboyant or glamorous, not even pretty, and thus no threat to them or their husbands. The entire conservative establishment adored her. She was on friendly terms with Queen Victoria and was squired by the Duke of Wellington. Another influential establishment figure, the wealthy and prissy genius named Felix Mendelssohn, loudly proclaimed her musical and personal virtues. And when she died in 1887 she was buried in Westminster Abbey, the first woman to be so honored.

And she had a voice.

One sometimes wonders how much of the universal paean of praise stemmed from the Jenny Lind voice and how much was colored by her legend as the symbol of purity and rectitude—Santa Cecilia come to life. There *was* a tendency for critics to read into her singing an element carried over from her personal piety. Thus John Sullivan Dwight, a former minister himself, said that other singers might match Lind vocally, but when she sang *I know that my Redeemer liveth* "it was not mere singing. It was a fervid outpouring of faith, hope and joy, which it would be vain to describe, because we have never had anything in music like it or comparable to it." But then one reads reports from the best musicians and critics of the time, and it is clear that as an artist and vocalist Jenny Lind really was something out of the ordinary. Mendelssohn stated flatly that Lind was "the greatest singer I know, in every style." Robert Schumann said, after hearing her sight-read some of his songs, "I have never before met so clear an understanding of music and text at first sight, and simple, natural and deep comprehension of a work at first reading." Hallé, who later was her piano accompanist for a tour of the provinces, first heard her in Manchester in 1849 and broke into tears when she sang the great *Leise, leise* aria from Weber's *Freischütz*. "Never," he wrote, "have I been moved by any singer as by her and never again shall be, I feel certain." The great violinist Joseph Joachim, who was the spokesman for "pure" (as opposed to exhibitionistic or cheap) music, hailed Lind's singing as "unique. She is by the grace of God!" Moscheles could not find adequate words to describe her: "The language of panegyric is exhausted." Chopin described her as "a typical Swede; not in an ordinary light, but in some sort of Polar dawn. She is enormously effective in *Sonnambula*. She sings with extreme purity and certainty, and her piano notes are steady, and as even as her hair." Opinions like these, uttered by some of the finest musical minds in Europe, cannot be lightly discounted.

Behind it all there remains something of an enigma. To the world, Jenny Lind was the figure of propriety and goodness, and she worked hard to maintain that image. But she was, after all, a diva, and divas are accustomed to having their own way. Joachim, who admired her singing, noted as much at a concert he gave with her in 1854. He was not taken in by her air of "superficial piety." She often, said Joachim, "invokes God when talking of the most ungodly things, such as money and fame. . . . She knows *exactly* what she wants." When she did not have her way she could throw tantrums, as Barnum observed during her American tour. If she did give much to charity, she also knew her own worth and expected to be paid accordingly; and she established a few records in that department. There was something unpleasantly self-righteous about Jenny Lind, and it is interesting to note that although she knew just about everybody of importance in Europe, she had very few real friends. In *The Great Singers,* Henry Pleasants has written a not too flattering psychological study of Lind, supporting his conclusions with some convincing evidence. Pleasants believes that not only was the public taken in by the Jenny Lind legend. She herself also was, and that was a major problem.

Perhaps she remained so enigmatic because of a defense barrier set up in her early years, which were not happy ones. She was born out of wedlock in Stockholm on October 6, 1820, and her parents did not get married until she was fourteen. Her mother was stern and neurotic; it was not a happy relationship. Jenny was a plain-looking girl who may have turned to music and singing as an escape. At the age of ten she was appearing in public, and in 1837 she joined the Royal Theatre in Stockholm as actress and singer at a salary of $300 a year. That year she appeared in ninety-two performances. Soon she learned a large repertory, became a leading singer, was talked about, and her reputation grew. She made her formal debut as Agathe in Weber's *Freischütz* in 1838. Two years later, because of overwork and lack of really proper training, her voice started to go. Off to Paris she went, to work with the most famous teacher in Europe—Manuel García, Maria Malibran's brother. The Royal Theatre hated to see her go and offered her financial inducements to the tune of $750 a year.

The Paris experience must have been traumatic for the shy, provincial, insecure girl. García listened to her and refused to accept her as a pupil. He said that her voice was ruined. Lind later told Mendelssohn it was the worst moment of her life. García ordered her to take a six-week rest, not open her mouth during that period, and then return. She did so. García took her as a beginner, and Lind described his approach to a friend:

> I have to begin again from the beginning, to sing scales up and down slowly and with great care, then to practice the shake [trill]—awfully slowly, and to get rid of the hoarseness if possible. Moreover, he is very careful about the breathing. I trust I have made a happy choice. Anyway, he is the best master, and expensive enough—twenty francs an hour! But what does that signify if only he can teach me to sing.

She stayed with García for ten months, during which time García paid more attention to another pupil, Henrietta Nissen, on whom he pinned great hopes. Nissen never made much of a dent in vocal history, while Lind reached the heights. Of course she had the raw material. But she also had pluck and determination. She returned to the Royal Theatre in 1842 as a finished singer and

Jenny Lind, the very moral lady, about the time of her London debut.

artist, a soprano who was secure up to a high G. In Stockholm and Copenhagen, where she also sang, she took on a variety of new roles. She made friends in Copenhagen with Hans Christian Andersen, who was in love with her and proposed marriage. It is believed that she inspired some of his loveliest tales—"The Ugly Duckling," "The Emperor's Nightingale," and "The Angel."

Her next step was Berlin, where she made her debut as Norma in 1844. She had an immense success. It was not all vocal. People were amazed that this plain-looking young woman could so transform herself on stage, acting with such inner serenity and conviction. Immediately the Prussian Royal Opera offered her a six-month contract for $4,500. It was a quantum jump in salary for her. For a while she toured Germany, creating a furor wherever she appeared. Chorley was in Germany in the late 1840's and took note of the phenomenon. Those were the years, he noted, of the troubles in France, the changes in Papal Italy, the arguments over free trade, and the formation of a German fleet. "But what was this compared in importance to the question whether Jenny Lind had or had not quarrelled with the King of Prussia?" Chorley made a special trip to Frankfurt to hear her. "The day before she was expected," he tartly writes,

> out broke the fatal news that Mdlle. Lind had suddenly thrown up her engagement in consequence of fatigue and illness—that she was gone into Italy to refresh her health—that she was not coming to Frankfurt at all!—Who could doubt, after this, that the Lady must be a great singer? . . . Herr Guhr, who then was the musical director of the Frankfurt Opera, had taken chaise and four, under the cloud of night, in pursuit of Mdlle. Lind, to persuade her to postpone her illness till after she had fulfilled her engagement to the famishing people of Frankfurt. In due time Herr Guhr returned, with cheering news for a public all but maddened by the sudden loss of its idol. Mdlle. Lind was positively coming—not just then, however, but in three weeks' time.—Here was oil upon the waters!—an unhoped-for reprieve!—a piece of consideration and condescension how far

more attractive than the punctuality of any artist, who could only keep her fixed day like any other common creature!

Chorley went to Lind's performances preparing to dislike her intensely. He did come away with a few reservations, but was bowled over, finding in her singing and personality "something eager and deep, and mysterious . . . unquestioned supremacy."

Then, in 1847, Lind received a very flattering offer from London.

Benjamin Lumley, the manager of Her Majesty's Theater, was in trouble. Three of his most popular singers—Grisi, Mario, and the brilliant soprano Fanny Persiani—had deserted him and gone to the new Royal Italian Opera in Covent Garden. He needed a superstar to fill his house and approached Lind, whose reputation in England by then had reached mythic proportions. Lumley went to Germany and chased her from Frankfurt to Stuttgart to Darmstadt, beseeching her to sing at his theater. Lind held out, and when she finally acceded, it was on terms she never before had achieved—a $25,000 contract for the season (April 14–August 20), a home free of charge, a carriage and a pair of servants at her disposal, and an extra $10,000 for a month off her European schedule prior to her London debut. If she was not happy with her reception in England, she would be free to cancel the engagement. Lumley must have been desperate.

As Lumley tells the story, the London season of 1847 started without Lind, although she had been announced. She gave Lumley prostration by not showing up. What happened was that she had previously signed a contract with another manager, Alfred Bunn, for London appearances. In the meantime all London was asking, "Where is Jenny Lind?" Lumley had to drop everything and rush back to Germany to persuade his coy soprano to come. She did. Three days passed while she recuperated from her trip. Finally a date was announced, the opera was Meyerbeer's *Robert le Diable,* and the crowd trying to get into the theater almost caused a riot. "The Jenny Lind Crush," it was called, and it became a feature of all Lind appearances as well as a proverbial expression. Queen Victoria and Prince Albert were in the audience, and Victoria, who loved music and knew a good deal about it, noted in her diary: "She has a most exquisite, powerful and really quite peculiar voice, so round, soft and flexible and her acting is charming and touching and very natural." The evening was a triumph for the new singer, and all subsequent performances were sold out. The Jenny Lind-fever had started, and there had been nothing like it since Sontag's first Berlin appearances. Lumley stood vindicated; and when Bunn sued Lind for breach of contract and won the case, Lumley gladly paid the $12,500 judgment to Bunn. In her first season Lind's operas were *La Sonnambula, La Figlia del Reggimento, Le Nozze di Figaro,* Verdi's *I Masnadieri* (which failed), and *Norma.* Only in *Norma* was there a letdown. Londoners were used to Grisi's fiery interpretation, and it was felt that Lind was too ladylike.

England went wild over Jenny Lind, and the mania lasted as long as she was before the public. She became the vogue of London. The *Musical World* marveled: "Never was such a fuss about any one individual in the world of art. . . . The Catalani fever was nothing to it, the Sontag fever was nothing to it, even the Paganini fever was a fool to it." Jenny Lind souvenirs filled the stores. There were Jenny Lind candies, Jenny Lind dresses, Jenny Lind dinner services. Music was composed in her honor, and young girls played for company the *Jenny Lind* Waltz or the *Jenny Lind* Polka. When she went on tour, crowds would gather at the railway stations to catch glimpses of her as the train whizzed past; or, if the train were resting at a station, her public would press their faces against her compartment window. Crowds would follow her on the street, and some women felt impelled to touch her dress, to her understandably great annoyance. Wilhelm Ganz, who was her accompanist in her 1856 tours, wrote that he had never witnessed such excitement at any of the tours of the other world-renowned artists—"people were simply mad to see her." Another of her accompanists was Hallé, who says much the same thing: "Crowds of people were always waiting at the door of her hotel to get a glimpse of her, and the police often had to be called for her protection." Once, while she was in a carriage, the pressure of the curiosity-seekers against the vehicle was so great that both windows broke, and Hallé got a nasty cut.

For years Lind had been talking about quitting opera, and in 1849 at the age of twenty-nine she did so, making her last stage appearance as Alice in Meyerbeer's *Robert le Diable*. From that point she sang nothing but concerts and oratorio. Perhaps, the way her mind worked, she thought opera had a faint tinge of immorality. Certainly at this stage she did not need the money she had received as an opera singer. At her stage retirement she was extremely rich. A tour of the British provinces in 1848 alone had netted her £10,000.

As a vocalist she deserved her fame. She had almost three octaves at her disposal, and the top register was unusually full and secure. She was a conscientious artist who worked and practiced hard. Her repertory was not negligible; she had sung, since her debut, 677 performances of thirty operas in her twelve years on the stage. By unceasing study, the British composer and conductor Julius Benedict said, she had developed a perfect trill, a perfect blend of registers without a break, and was able to execute the most difficult passages and runs with a full, rich sound. She was at home in all areas—opera, concerts, oratorio. When she wanted to put her voice on display, she had total command of the most incredible coloratura technique, including a trill that must have been unparalleled, perhaps even more brilliant than Patti's. Richard Hoffman, a pianist who appeared on some of her American programs, said it was the finest he had ever heard, "so close and even as to be altogether perfect," and that roulades and cadenzas were "unparalleled in their execution." Sir George Henschel, baritone, pianist, conductor, and wonderful all-around musician, has described the Lind trill:

> I remember once, when we were talking about the technique of singing, her favouring me with a little illustration of her own ways and means, and I shall never forget my wonder when, asking

> me to watch the outside of her throat, she showed me how she used to sing the trill for which she had been so famous. During such a trill, which she continued for an astonishingly long time, increasing, decreasing, and again increasing it, her throat would be visibly quavering with the pulsations of every little succeeding little group of the two notes, exactly like the throat of a warbling canary bird.

But her singing was not all display, and she could melt her listeners with the simplest of means. With her exceptionally wide scale of dynamics she was able to throttle down to the most ethereal of pianissimos. Moscheles called it a "whisper"; yet the sound, "however attenuated, is distinctly audible in the remotest corner of the concert room." Hoffman said that her voice "was not so brilliant as it was deliciously rounded, and of an exquisite musical timbre. It possessed great volume, and what seemed to be an inexhaustible reserve force." Her stage manner, as described by Hoffman, was charming. She would trip on and off "as in an ecstasy of delight, bowing and smiling, taking everybody into her confidence."

Books have been written about Jenny Lind and America. She was invited in 1850 by P. T. Barnum, that American original. The contract they worked out called for Barnum to pay her $150,000, all expenses for herself, a maid, a secretary and a companion, and a carriage and horses. Julius Benedict was to come over as her conductor, he to get $25,000; and Barnum also signed the baritone Giovanni Belletti for $12,500. Lind announced that she wanted the money to found a music school in Stockholm, and that she wanted Barnum to put up $187,500 in advance for herself and the company. The impresario obliged.

Once Barnum had worked out the contractual details and was confident that Lind really would honor them, he set to work on a six-month publicity campaign that paved the way for the most astounding success in the annals of music. The impresario Max Maretzek, who knew the field better than anybody, described in his amusing *Crotchets and Quavers* how Barnum, the Prince of

Jenny Lind's arrival in New York. She had been invited in 1850 by the great showman P. T. Barnum (below), who engineered a media hype hitherto unknown in the United States.

Humbugs, manufactured a reputation for her "by wholesale. It was not merely made by the inch, but was prepared by the cart-load. . . . He exaggerated her virtues *à la Munchausen*; he proclaimed her a ventriloquist, romanced about Victoria's admiration of her excellencies, and fabricated charities by the bushel-full." Could it be—could it possibly be—that Lind's well-advertised American charities were an example of Barnum's hokum? But Maretzek himself was prone to exaggeration.

When she arrived it seemed that Barnum had recruited all New York to greet her. There was a mob scene, a parade up Broadway, serenades, and speeches. Barnum did things with a lavish hand, even supplying a sixty-piece orchestra for Lind and Benedict. Tickets for the first concert were auctioned off. A haberdasher named John M. Genim outbid Dr. Brandredth, a quack who made and sold pills. For the $125 that Genim paid, he achieved instant fame throughout the entire country, and the publicity—as Barnum had predicted—helped Genim thrive mightily in his haberdashery business. All over the country people began to buy Genim hats. Castle Garden, which had 7,000 seats, was sold out for the first concert.

Barnum said that after the unprecedented success of this concert he tore up the old contract and offered Lind a better one. The facts, however, seem to be different. Lind had a good business sense and knew all about impresarios. Careful girl that she was, she had asked an American law firm—Jay and Field—to represent her in America. Even *before* the first concert she had asked for an increase per concert and a share of the receipts over $5,500. It was Lind who, after the first concert, asked for, or probably demanded, a new contract in which she would receive $1,000 every time she sang, with a further stipulation that after Barnum took the next $5,000 for his share, the rest of the receipts were to be divided evenly. She had Barnum over a barrel, and he had to go along.

The program with which Jenny Lind was introduced to America was typical of the day. It started with Weber's *Oberon* Overture. Belletti sang a Rossini aria. Lind came forth to sing

Casta Diva from *Norma.* Richard Hoffman and Benedict played a *Norma* Fantasy for two pianos (presumably the one by Thalberg). Lind and Belletti sang a duet from Rossini's *Il Turco in Italia.* After intermission there was Benedict's overture, *The Crusaders.* Lind sang one of the famous showpieces of her repertory, the aria with two flutes from Meyerbeer's *The Camp of Silesia.* Belletti sang the *Largo al factotum,* Lind sang another of her famous numbers, the *Echo Song,* and there followed *The Welcome to America,* with words written for the occasion by Bayard Taylor and set to music by Benedict. In the remaining concerts of the tour, Lind would close the evening with a song, generally *Home, Sweet Home.*

From New York the company went on the road, and the ninety-five concerts in eight months grossed $712,161.34, of which Lind's share was $176,675. Those, anyway, were Barnum's figures. Lind was reported to have given her fees for many of the concerts to charity. She was besieged by requests for money, and equally besieged by reporters in whatever city she was singing. In Washington, the President and Mrs. Fillmore, and the great figures of Congress, came to pay their respects. Daniel Webster became a close friend.

The country was seized by Lind-fever to the point of hysteria. Some concerts resembled a madhouse. In Boston, Barnum rented the enormous space over the Fitchburg railroad station for two concerts, sold more tickets than the area would hold, and had a riot on his hands. Hoffman, who was supposed to accompany Lind, could not get into the hall. Finally the police let him in, but the aisles were so blocked he could not get to the stage. So he pleaded for help and was raised up and passed over the heads of people. "It was not unlike being tossed in a blanket, but I was a youth of slim proportions and finally reached the footlights, more dead than alive."

On tour Barnum noticed that the angelic Jenny Lind was very money-conscious. She finally broke the contract in June 1851, paying Barnum a forfeit of $25,000. What got into her? Maretzek, for one, had an answer. He firmly believed that she became disgusted with the vulgarity and show-business atmosphere that

Jenny Lind and her husband, the pianist/composer Otto Goldschmidt. They were married in Boston in 1852.

Barnum represented; that she felt like one of the trained monkeys in his circus menageries, an object to be put on show for stupid people to gape at. "Would it be astonishing, that the Swedish Nightingale felt hurt in both her womanly and artistic pride?" She also had made more money than she thought existed. Milton Goldin, in *The Music Merchants,* estimates that by the time the contract was broken Barnum had realized $535,486 for himself and Lind $208,675. In any case it was toward the end of the tour, nerves were frayed, Jenny was tired, and understandable tensions had developed.

By this time Otto Goldschmidt was with the company, and he and Lind managed the tour by themselves, with a noticeable decrease in business. Nine years younger than Jenny, Goldschmidt was a pianist who had first played for her in 1848. They had then fallen in love. Lind thought that Goldschmidt was a great pianist and composer, and was constantly pushing him. She believed he was going to be the next Mendelssohn. Her opinion was not endorsed by her contemporaries or by posterity. They got married in Boston on February 5, 1852. Her farewell American concert took place at Castle Garden on May 25, 1852, and *Dwight's Journal of Music* gave her a fond adieu: "Think of *seven thousand* faces, lit with sad enthusiasm. . . ." The reviewer said that Jenny Lind "has established a sort of moral and ideal empire in the hearts of this whole people." She and her husband were back in London in June. And yes, when Lind got settled in, she set up scholarships for Swedish musicians with part of her American earnings.

The Goldschmidts bought a house in London and lived a quiet life, though at one time there was a slight scandal. Some British papers wrote that Goldschmidt had gambled away his wife's fortune. Goldschmidt sued for libel and won. Jenny testified on his behalf, saying that since her marriage her fortune had doubled, thanks to her husband's wise counsel. Otherwise life was uneventful. They had three children. When Jenny resumed singing she and Otto worked together as a musical team. Goldschmidt accompanied her at the piano or was her conductor. Occasionally she would make trips to the Continent. On September 18, 1875,

Dwight's Journal of Music printed a letter from an American named Lyman Tremain, who was visiting Carlsbad. He had attended services at an English church there. The organist did not show up, and the rector asked the congregation if anybody could play the melodeon. A plain, quiet lady volunteered. She was Jenny Lind. "She played and sang. Her voice still exhibits much power, especially in the higher notes. . . . Can it be, I thought, that the woman before me, joining so devoutly in the religious services, is the same world-renowned Queen of Song, before whom the people of America formerly paid such wonderful homage? Is this the person to see and hear whom I had travelled one hundred and fifty miles with my wife and paid $20 for two tickets of admission . . . ?"

She specialized in oratorio singing, taught at the Royal College of Music, retired in 1883, and died on November 2, 1887. But even in her last days before the public, when she had lost a great deal of her voice, when the new vocal superstar Adelina Patti was conquering the world, Jenny Lind was still remembered by everybody as the world's greatest singer.

10 *Joseph Joachim*

THE INCORRUPTIBLE

EVERY age has opposing artistic currents, its yin and yang, and musical performers reflect it. For every romantic there is a classicist. Exaggeration is opposed to sobriety; mere entertainment to nobility of purpose; pure virtuosity to musical meaning. A certain type of performer *has* to exult in external display, letting the world know the unusual gifts bestowed upon him. Another type of performer *has* to subjugate his external skills to what he conceives as the Message, and he selflessly dedicates himself to an artistic ideal in the service of music. Generally it is the flashy extroverted performer of sensational skills who is the biggest box-office attraction; but it is the dedicated musician who achieves the respect of his colleagues and, in the long run, of the public. And once in a while a performer arrives who achieves the height of virtuosity and couples it with pure musicianship.

Joseph Joachim, the greatest classical violinist of the nineteenth century, was one of those men. He could have been a spectacular virtuoso like Paganini, Ernst, or Wieniawski. Instead, after he matured, he devoted his life to the cause of what he considered the best music. Until his time, every violinist who gave a concert played almost exclusively his own music. Joachim changed all that, even though he himself was a composer. He established the violin recital more or less as it is known today. He was the one who brought chamber music to the attention of European and British audiences. He was the one who consistently was heard in the solo sonatas of Bach, the quartets of Mozart and Beethoven, the sonatas and chamber music of Brahms. He was the stern, Jehovah-like corrective against rattle-brained exhibitionism. He was the one who changed the position of the violinist from entertainer to artist.

His age saw musical Europe split into two camps. Berlioz, Liszt, and Wagner, at mid-century, were the leaders of the avant-garde, spreading the gospel of the Music of the Future, using the publicity machine to disseminate their message, writing a new kind of music that attracted some and bothered most. Opposed to them were the upholders of tradition. Mendelssohn had been one; he died young in 1847. Robert Schumann, though an avant-gardist, also was one. The music of Liszt, Wagner, and Berlioz did not especially attract him, and his gods were Bach, Beethoven, and Schubert. The oncoming talent that interested him had to have roots in tradition; and around Schumann and his wife Clara an anti-Liszt, anti-Wagner group was assembled. In it was the young Brahms above all. And there was Joachim.

Joachim's talent was spotted early. In music there always has been a word-of-mouth transmission that apparently moves at the speed of light. All professionals everywhere seem to know who the major talents are from the very beginning. If a spectacular talent starts to create talk in Russia or Italy, or wherever, the entire music world seems to know about it in a matter of weeks. One musician tells another, who tells a third, who mentions it to a critic, who starts whipping up stories about a new genius. Then foreign papers pick up the stories. Or their own correspondents break the news of the appearance of a major talent. Joachim was brought to

American attention by Alexander Thayer, who wrote an excited report about him in *Dwight's Journal of Music.* It is a chain-letter effect, as true today as it was two hundred years ago.

In Joachim's case, Mendelssohn first heard the twelve-year-old violinist in Leipzig. Joseph Joachim had been born on June 28, 1831, in Hungary, studied in Budapest, started playing in public at eight, had gone to Vienna for further study, and then, in 1843, had enrolled in the Leipzig Conservatory headed by Mendelssohn. It took Mendelssohn only two or three hearings—professionals *know*—to appreciate the boy's magnitude of talent. Mendelssohn realized that there was nothing more that young Joachim could learn about the mechanics of his instrument, and saw to it that he instead concentrated on theory, counterpoint, and composition. Then Mendelssohn started bragging about this phenomenal talent. He told Clara. He told Moritz Hauptmann, the cantor of St. Peter's in Leipzig. He wrote a letter to his English friend, William Sterndale Bennett: "Of all the young talents that are now going into the world, I know none that is to be compared with this violinist. It is not only the excellence of his performances, but the absolute certainty of his becoming a leading artist." Bennett told Moscheles, who then told everybody what the great Felix thought of young Joachim. Thus Moscheles and the others were prepared when Joachim, who started to tour when he was thirteen, came to London. In those days Joachim was still a virtuoso violinist, and his repertory contained standard showpieces of the day, such as concertos by Mendelssohn's friend Ferdinand David and by Charles de Bériot. But already he had the Beethoven Violin Concerto under his fingers and was playing it in public. "Mendelssohn is right," Moscheles wrote. "Here we have talent of the true stamp."

Young Joachim seemed to have everything, and he startled his elders with his talent, his natural musicianship, and his sheer brilliance. At thirteen he was called upon at short notice to play Spohr's *Gesangsszene* Concerto, and he learned it virtually overnight, playing it from memory in a style, according to Moritz

Joseph Joachim, age twelve. The pencil drawing is by Frau Moritz Hauptmann. She was the wife of an important composer and teacher in Leipzig.

Hauptmann, "that would have charmed Spohr himself." Hauptmann knew whereof he spoke; he was a close friend of Spohr's.

Liszt, too, heard about the brilliant youngster, and in 1850 invited him to Weimar as concertmaster of the ducal orchestra. Joachim stayed there for two years, and like everybody else was captivated by the glittering Franz. Some of the letters Joachim wrote to him are positively fawning. Liszt also permitted Joachim to form a chamber-music group, and Joachim happily went through much of the literature. Liszt was generous to him and acted as his patron. But soon Joachim became disenchanted with what were to him meretricious aspects of Liszt and his circle. In 1852 he broke away and became violinist and musical director for George V in Hanover. Soon he would not even talk to Liszt. He heard Liszt conduct some of his own music in Hanover and wrote to Clara about his disillusionment: "A more vulgar misuse of sacred forms, a more repulsive coquetting with the noblest feelings for the sake of effect, had never been attempted. . . . I shall never want to meet Liszt again, because I should want to tell him that instead of taking him for a mighty errant spirit striving to return to God, I have suddenly realized that he is a cunning contriver of effects, who has miscalculated." Clara must have nodded her head approvingly. She *hated* Liszt and what he stood for. Joachim the next year finally wrote Liszt a letter saying that Liszt's music was "antagonistic" to him and that their aims were too different ever to work together again.

By that time Joachim was close to Brahms, who was two years his junior. To Brahms, Joachim was the musical hope of the age—the Galahad, the pure knight, lance at the ready to slay the dragons of mediocrity. Joachim was already famous as violinist, conductor, and composer, and Brahms was impressed no end. He wrote to Clara in 1856: "There is more in Joachim than all us young people put together," and he stood in complete awe of his friend. "I am always encouraged if my things come up to his standard," he said. For most of their lives Brahms, Clara, and Joachim had a close relationship. Brahms sent Joachim and Clara all of his music for comments and suggestions. Brahms and Joachim worked together on the Violin Concerto, Joachim helping Brahms with technical aspects of the solo part and writing the cadenza. Nearly all of the Brahms violin music received its world premiere at a Joachim concert. Clara and Joachim formed a sonata team and made music together for decades. Clara also was a surrogate mother who advised Joachim on any and all problems. She worried about his workload. She scolded him for his constant partygoing. A natural conservative in every respect, Clara fretted when she thought that her young friend was going to do something impulsive or rash. In 1860 Joachim told her that he was thinking of leaving Hanover. Clara was horrified. Why would he want to give up a position that paid so well? "Such a position, with 2,000 thalers [$1,600] for seven months!"

So Joachim stayed in Hanover until 1864, and when he left it was because of an unexpected series of happenings. Joachim had been born a Jew but had become baptized. Jews normally could not hold important court positions anywhere in Europe, so they became Christians to advance their careers. Nobody paid it any particular attention except anti-Semites. Joachim, like Mendelssohn (also baptized), never denied his ancestry. In Joachim's orchestra was a Jew named Grün, who had been denied promotion because of his race. Joachim wrote a strong letter in his behalf, pointing out that Herr Grün had been engaged with the express understanding that he succeed one Herr Kömpel:

> If Herr Grün, in spite of his excellent services and fidelity to duty, acknowledged by all his superiors, and after years of patient waiting, is not to be promoted after I have called attention to the matter, *because he is a Jew,* and if, for this reason, the promises made to me on behalf of a higher authority are not fulfilled, then according to my idea of honor and duty, I shall have no alternative but to justify myself by retiring from my appointment at the same time as Herr Grün. If I remained in my present position after the rejection of Herr Grün I should never be able to get over the purely personal feelings that because I had become a member of the Christian church I had gained worldly advantage and had

> obtained a privileged position in the Royal Hanoverian Orchestra, while others of my race were forced into humiliating situations.

A scandal followed, and Joachim was attacked in the newspapers. The king promoted Grün and, in a private audition, asked Joachim not to leave. But Joachim had been terribly disturbed about the anti-Semitic venom he had encountered for the first time in his life. He resigned. The following year George V smoothed things over and cajoled Joachim into returning. But he could never again be happy there and kept his eyes out for another position. In 1868 he jumped at the chance to become head of the Hochschule in Berlin at a starting salary of 2,000 thalers, the same sum he had been receiving in Hanover (of course his income was supplemented by his concert work), and he remained there for the rest of his long life. He thought that his salary of $1,600 was very high, and in 1869 wrote an exulting letter to his wife: "When we two are little old people we shall be able to live in peace and spend our capital on the children." Things are relative. In 1869 Mario was getting well over $1,600 *a performance*, and Patti was approaching $3,000. On the other hand, a workman in Germany would be fortunate to earn $350 a year.

In 1863 Joachim had married Amalie Weiss, a well-known contralto who had a touring life of her own. The union produced six children. One wonders, however, how happy the marriage was even from the beginning. His wife must have been a strong personality—singers are known to be temperamental—and she insisted on being the center of attention. She also had long periods of ill health. A hint is given in a letter from Clara to Brahms in 1879. Joachim visited Clara in Frankfurt, and she tells Brahms that "he was very charming, and as jolly as he always is when his wife is not with him." In 1881 relations between the couple took a nasty turn. Joachim accused his wife of having had an affair with the publisher Fritz Simrock and declared that their last child was illegitimate. The case went to court and Amalie was found innocent. Brahms had sided with her and written a letter in her behalf that was introduced as testimony. For several years Joachim and

Joachim, about thirty-five years old.

Brahms were not on speaking terms. Eventually their friendship was restored, but it never was as easygoing as it had been.

In Berlin Joachim supervised the administration of the Hochschule and taught. His life alternated between teaching and concert tours. In his forty years as a teacher he had some four hundred pupils, few of whom amounted to very much. From all accounts he was not a very good teacher. But as a performing violinist—that was another matter. His concerts with Clara in Germany and England were especially famous. Thayer was in Berlin in 1855 and wrote a report of one of their concerts. His account gives a wonderful idea of the free and easy recital mores of the day. Joachim and Clara played at the Singakademie, and a chorus participated in the program. When it was their turn to play, Clara and Joachim came forward from behind the choir "as calmly as in their own room." She went directly to the piano and played some solos. Joachim sat in an armchair on the stage and listened. When she finished she joined him in an adjoining armchair and they both listened to the chorus. Then the audience chatted for a few minutes, and so did she and Joachim. When quiet prevailed in the hall Joachim rose to play unaccompanied Bach while Clara listened from her chair. "There was no flourish about it, he laid his violin lovingly against his cheek, and his instrument sang old Bach's music so clearly, distinctively, powerfully, gently, and with such perfect ease, that one felt it was no difficult thing to do! You see in Joachim's entire personal appearance that he thinks of showing not what he can do; he loves Bach and enters into the very soul of his music, and that means his hearers shall also." After the Bach, Clara and Joachim joined forces in a Beethoven sonata.

He was always playing Beethoven. He forced Beethoven down people's throats. As early as 1859 he formed a string quartet and presented an evening of three of the late Beethoven quartets. Even Clara complained. Three of these difficult pieces, she told a friend, "were too much, all one after the other, and it was only his playing that made me endure it." Joachim was to be associated with his own string quartet for the rest of his life. The personnel might change, but the stout, bearded, dignified Joachim was always at the first stand, and serious musicians all over Europe slept better that night, knowing that Joachim was still around. He was their conscience, and a very stern Jehovah he could be. There was the time, at the turn of the century, when he was invited to meet the rising young French violinist Lucien Capet. At the soirée Capet was introduced as "the French Joachim." That did not get the evening off to a good start for the veteran. He glowered. In Joachim's honor, Capet played the Bach Chaconne. Joachim hated the performance and said (German musicians can be very arrogant, especially when confronted with French musicians), "Couldn't you play something typically French?" Instead, Capet played the Wilhelmj arrangement of Bach's Air for the G String. Joachim exploded. "How can you as a musician have the tastelessness to play such a shameless falsification of a work by Bach?" Capet broke into tears. The evening was not a success.

As an interpreter Joachim approached his music with a big sweep and a big sound. His interpretations were not pedantic. "The wonder of the age. . . . So bold. . . . So free!" marveled Amy Fay, the young American piano student. Without drawing attention to his own skills, he managed to make his audience enter his own world. He had solved all the technical problems of his instrument, took it for granted, and saw no reason for showing off. His fellow musicians, the critics, his audiences—everybody—recognized his total immersion in music rather than instrument. J. W. Davison, the testy critic of the London *Times,* hearing the young Joachim play the Beethoven Concerto, was struck with the combination of grandeur and chasteness, and he hailed Joachim's "unsurpassable" mastery of the instrument and "command of expression apparently inexhaustible." Chorley felt much the same way. *All* felt the same way. In Brussels a critic wrote: "If we are asked what are the qualities of the virtuoso which Herr Joachim represents, we answer without hesitation: *all.*" In 1879 the Berlin critic Otto Gumprecht wrote the standard Joachim review: "For the first time I have brought away with me from a performance an impresssion of absolute perfection. . . . After the concert it struck me that the greatest wonders of bravura had passed by unheeded.

. . . The virtuoso is merged completely in the artist." Hanslick, who had thought Vieuxtemps to be the greatest living violinist, changed his mind after hearing Joachim in 1861, paying him the usual tribute ("identified with the musical ideal") and adding that here was one violinist who did not scratch on the lower strings. This says something about the violin playing of the day.

Through his sixty-four years before the public, Joachim never received a bad review until he ran afoul of that idol-toppler, George Bernard Shaw, who blew hot and cold about him. Shaw, as always, was different. For all others to question the playing of the great, the sublime Joachim, the perfect musician, would be like taking issue with the Ten Commandments. It simply was not done. It was taken for granted everywhere that Joachim was the greatest violinist of his time. His time took in such major violinists as the Belgian Henri Vieuxtemps (1820–81), who carried on the Paganini tradition; the fiery Polish-born Henri Wieniawski, who died in 1880 at the age of forty-five; the poised August Wilhelmj (1845–1908), a German virtuoso who stopped playing when he was forty and devoted the rest of his life to teaching; and the eccentric Norwegian Ole Bull (1810–80). The later years of Joachim's life saw the emergence of Pablo de Sarasate and Eugène Ysaÿe. Joachim imperturbably went his own way, a mighty figure who dwarfed his competitors, and when he died in Berlin, on August 15, 1907, the last link to the great days of the nineteenth century went with him.

He played the violin with certain technical aspects that stemmed from Paganini. As described by Boris Schwarz in his *Great Masters of the Violin,* "Characteristic of Joachim's bow position was a very low upper right arm pressed against the body, which necessitated a highly angled wrist. He gripped the bow with his fingertips; the fingers were kept close together, the index finger touching the stick at the first joint (counted from the nail), while the little finger remained on the stick at all times. The change of bow at the frog was accomplished by a rotary wrist movement and stiff fingers." Joachim was a Stradivarius man. When he started playing he used a Guadagnini but, as soon as he

Joachim around the turn of the century. In 1905 the great veteran, who had been born in 1831, made a few phonograph records.

could afford it, purchased a Strad that he played until 1885, exchanging that instrument for another Strad. Carl Flesch, an important violinist and teacher, and a musician very much in the Joachim tradition, thoroughly described the Joachim approach in his memoirs. Flesch was thirteen when he first heard the fifty-seven-year-old Joachim. "The nobility of his cantilena . . . has remained an unforgettable experience for me." To Flesch, Joachim's playing represented spirit over technique, and a large-scale reformation of program-making. "We owe it above all to him that the virtuoso for virtuosity's sake came to be relegated to an inferior position, that the music itself was promoted to the first place." It might be, Flesch wrote, that Ferdinand Laub (a Czech violinist active in Russia) was as good a technician, that Wilhelmj was a greater virtuoso and had more beauty of sound, and that Sarasate purely as a violinist was the better instrumentalist. But nobody had Joachim's "unique spiritual and musical superiority."

Around 1905 the aged Joachim was lured into the recording studios and cut five sides: the Adagio from Bach's unaccompanied G minor Sonata, the Bourrée from Bach's Partita No. 1, the Hungarian Dance in G minor and Hungarian Dance in D minor by Brahms, and his own Romance in C. He was about seventy-five at the time, and naturally his bowing and intonation are not always reliable. But through the dated sound come authentic sweep and grandeur. The Joachim recordings are like the recordings that Patti made around the same time, when she was approaching her middle sixties. The listener has to extrapolate backwards, making allowances for age, deficiencies in recording technique, and a musical philosophy alien to today's, including a characteristic nineteenth-century portamento. With all that, the Joachim recordings stand up remarkably well. The playing is strong and confident, and obviously a great master is at work. Sarasate's own recordings made at about the same time are exciting and brilliant, but the Joachim playing on these records has its own brilliance—and something more: a bigness, a *conception,* a combination of violinistic strength and musical intelligence. One suddenly understands what the nineteenth century was talking about.

11 *Anton Rubinstein*

RUSSIAN ELEMENTAL

WITH Liszt out of action after his retirement as a touring concert pianist, with Thalberg no longer taken very seriously, the midpoint of the nineteenth century saw a vacancy for the title of the World's Greatest Pianist. It was promptly filled by the leonine Anton Rubinstein, who had no real competition. He was something elemental, a titanic figure who blasted the piano and snapped its strings, and yet who could be capable of the most intimate, sensuous playing. Karl Tausig would have been one of the immortals, but he died too young. Karl Filtsch, Chopin's genius of a pupil, would have made it (Liszt said of him that when Filtsch started playing in public he, Liszt, would shut up shop), but the poor boy died even younger. Adolf von Henselt had exiled himself to Russia and was a forgotten legend. The brilliantly talented American meteor, Louis Moreau Gottschalk, had returned to his country, to die in 1869 (in far-off Brazil) at the age of forty. Which left Hans von Bülow as Rubinstein's chief rival, followed by some ladies—notably Clara Schumann and Liszt's pupil Sophie Menter, yclept "the Valkyrie of the piano." Later in the century there would be Annette Essipov and Teresa Carreño. All of them were popular and had superb careers. But no woman seriously challenged the supremacy of the male giants.

Rubinstein did everything in a big way. He was a hard drinker, a profligate liver, a gambler, a womanizer, a man of emotions and high passions. He produced tremendous surges of sound that overwhelmed his listeners. He was known to ruin pianos at his recitals. Often he would have two instruments on stage. If he broke a string in one he would switch to the other, and at intermission a technician would repair the damage. He was the sloppiest of all the great pianists. He had an extraordinary technique, but other things were more important to him, and when he became excited he lost control. Nothing mattered but the Message, and the means were not important. As a result his concerts could be full of wrong notes, dropped notes, overpedalings, and outsized fortissimos. Bülow once ruefully and altogether accurately observed that "Rubinstein can make any quantity of errors during his performance, and nobody is disturbed by it; but if I make a single mistake it will be noticed immediately by everyone in the audience."

Naturally. Bülow was an intellectual, analytical pianist, considered "cold" by his audiences. That kind of pianist uses very little pedal, lets the fingers do the work, and as a result any mistakes spring into high relief. But who could care for a mistake or two while reveling in the Niagara of sound produced by "the Hercules of the piano"? As Hanslick pointed out, Hans von Bülow was a great pianist, but it was Rubinstein who had the immediacy and sensual energy that always attract a public more than intellectual integrity. "And that is why we listen to him with untroubled ears and uninhibited pleasure. He may excite anger now and then, but with the next movement all is forgiven. . . . His excesses derive from an irresistible primeval force rather than from mere vanity of virtuosity." George Bernard Shaw put it another way. Rubinstein, he said, specialized in "seizing his listeners by the ears with wings of golden fire." Whether or not wings can seize ears, Shaw had the right idea.

Rubinstein's style changed very little through the years. When Moscheles heard the thirteen-year-old boy he wrote that he had fingers "as light as feathers, and withal the strength of a man." As he grew older that strength intensified, and at some concerts Rubinstein actually gave his listeners headaches. Or so Amy Fay reports. In 1870, while in Tausig's Berlin class, Fay contrasted her teacher's perfection and precision with Rubinstein's "abandon." The first piece on Rubinstein's program was played so loudly it

> gave me such a violent headache that I couldn't hear the rest of the performance with any pleasure. He has a gigantic spirit in him, and is extremely poetic and original, but for an entire concert he is too much. Give me Rubinstein for a few pieces, but Tausig for a whole evening. Rubinstein doesn't care how many notes he misses providing he can bring out his conception and make it vivid enough. Tausig strikes *every* note with rigid exactness, and perhaps his very perfection makes him at times a little cold. Rubinstein played Schubert's *Erl König,* arranged by Liszt, *gloriously.* Where the child is so frightened, his hands flew all over the piano, and absolutely made it shriek with terror. It was enough to freeze you to hear it.

Rubinstein's colleagues, including many Liszt pupils, had a high opinion of him. Some pianists are prone to errors because they are not superior technicians. Rubinstein, who was a superior technician, made errors because he did not especially worry about the spit-and-polish aspects of piano playing, and also because he probably did not practice very much in his later days, relying on his fabulous memory. It had to be fabulous, considering the vast extent of his repertory. Only toward the end did he begin to have memory problems. When young he used to travel with a dummy keyboard on which to practice. Alice Diehl tells a pretty story about Rubinstein on a river steamer practicing on his keyboard. A passenger suggested he go on deck to admire the beautiful view. Rubinstein said, "This won't wait. The other will."

The young Anton Rubinstein. Those thick fingers produced a Niagara of sound.

Thus the professionals knew what he could do if he really put his mind to it, and they forgave him his lapses. Perhaps the American critic Henry Krehbiel had a point when he suggested that Rubinstein stirred up such tempestuous cyclones at the piano that he "scattered wide the wrecks of discriminating judgment." Bülow—somewhat unexpectedly, considering how different they were as musicians—called him the Michelangelo of pianists. Rachmaninoff called him "the most original and unparalleled pianist in the world." The venerable Wilhelm Ganz called him "the greatest pianist I have ever heard"—and Ganz had heard Liszt. Theodor Leschetizky, the famous pianist and teacher, was another who called Rubinstein the greatest pianist who had ever lived; there might be technical inadequacies, but never a letdown in tension or imagination.

Frederic Lamond, a Liszt pupil, claimed that Rubinstein towered above all pianists after Liszt and, for that matter, also "over those of succeeding generations." What especially struck Lamond was Rubinstein's enormous but never brittle sound. (Rubinstein once told Rachmaninoff how to get a singing tone: just press upon the keys until the blood oozes from the fingertips.) Like many others, Lamond marveled at Rubinstein's fat, thick, immense hands. His fingers were like "sausages," the hands were as soft as a woman's, but "with the strength of a lion's paw." And despite the tremendous personality that came through the man and his playing, he never tried to woo an audience. He was a careless and even sloppy dresser, and he never put on an act at the keyboard. He just came out and played, not using many gestures, seldom smiling. As described by Lamond, a Rubinstein concert must have had the kind of aura similar to the ones played several generations later by Vladimir Horowitz. "There was in the hall an air of suspense and tension such as I never experienced in any other audience in St. Petersburg. He appeared, and something in his looks, in his pale face, half Attila-like and half like Beethoven, with its mighty forehead and deep-set eyes, inspired awe."

There *was* a resemblance between Rubinstein and Beethoven, and some believed that the pianist was Beethoven's illegitimate son—a neat trick, considering that Beethoven died two years before Rubinstein was born. Rubinstein, one feels, played up the resemblance. But Lamond was right. Despite Rubinstein's unbounded virtuosity and ability to hypnotize an audience, he was not out to impress. He really got carried away with the music, did not know an audience existed, and certainly never played down to it. Rubinstein was one of the most uncalculating of artists, and he appears to have been completely single-minded in his dedication to the music under his fingers. After a tour with Ysaÿe in 1882 he wrote to the violinist telling him never to cater to an audience: "There is invariably a conflict between your conception of a work and that of your audience. Always keep before you one main objective, which must be to express the music according to your understanding and feelings, and not merely to give pleasure to those who listen."

Another Liszt pupil, Moriz Rosenthal, described the way Rubinstein took over music. Rosenthal said that Rubinstein was not merely the master of the music but rather its despot. At one of his concerts Rubinstein played a Handel suite, and Rosenthal reported Leschetizky as telling Rubinstein, "What a technique you must have to mess up the finale that way." Rubinstein was famous for his performance of the *Funeral March* in Chopin's B flat minor Sonata, and Rosenthal is one of the many who has left a description of Rubinstein's performance. It was at a concert attended by Liszt himself. The movement started with four crashing chords, then pianissimo constantly building to a tremendous fortissimo up to the trio; simple playing in the trio; then triple fortissimo at the resumption of the march with lessening dynamics down to a pianissimo ending. It made a grand effect, even if Chopin did not write it that way. Said Liszt, as quoted by Rosenthal, "Splendid, superb, quite good, hm, hm."

Rosenthal, himself as great a pianist as the period had to show, had a few interesting comments to make about Rubinstein's playing (he claimed to have heard the Russian pianist in some thirty concerts). "The greatness of his playing depended, in large measure, on his choice of program." Some pieces of his repertory he had mastered to perfection; in others he was uneasy. If there were a large number of "dangerous" pieces on his program, the result could be a bad evening. He always had an enormous tone, "about three times as large as that of Hans von Bülow." It was an orchestral approach to the piano, even if he could achieve intimate results in some music. Rosenthal considered his Chopin "too inflated in line" and technically sloppy. Yet, "I shall never forget his A flat major Polonaise, which he played with an unprecedentedly heroic power of expression."

On the other hand, there were pianists who despised Rubinstein's playing. Clara Schumann was one. She could not gear her tidy mind to such convulsive, manic wildness, to what she considered a sheer lack of discipline and musical proportion. By her lights she was right. An Anton Rubinstein playing today in a major competition would never be allowed to progress beyond the semifinals. Clara and the other academics on the jury would see to that. As late as 1893 she was writing to Brahms expressing her complete bewilderment about the Rubinstein craze.

Just as there was a standard review for a Joachim concert, so there was for a Rubinstein one. In Joachim's case the reviewers automatically mentioned the violinist's dedication to music, his high ideals and nobility of conception. In Rubinstein's case, virtually every review dwelt on his power and frequently slipshod technique. Here is the *Musical World* of London in 1881: "Surely the passionate Rubinstein is a phenomenon—a volcanic eruption attended by fire, noises and smoke. The thing is heroic in character and proportions. We may not recognize here a pianist in the act of performing pianoforte music, but we are in the presence of an amazing display of musical impulse and inspiration which fascinate even those who do not approve." Then Rubinstein could turn around and play simply, accurately, and elegantly, suddenly becoming "a flower-decked lion trained to walk in a festival procession." All of which meant that Rubinstein was one of those pianists "who evade criticism by the very splendor of their faults not less than by the glory of their excellences."

Some early reports had it that Rubinstein was one of Liszt's

Anton Rubinstein (right) and his brother Nicholas. Anton founded the St. Petersburg Conservatory in 1862, and Nicholas the Moscow Conservatory in 1866. Nicholas was reputed to be in his brother's class as a pianist, but he did not give many concerts.

pupils. He never was. His first contact with Liszt took place in Vienna, in 1846. As Rubinstein tells the story in his autobiography, he had great hopes about the generous Liszt and got an introduction to him. But Liszt received him in "a cold and distant manner" and uttered some banalities to the effect that a man had to make his own way in the world. It was uncharacteristic behavior, assuming that Rubinstein's account is true. A year and a half of poverty ensued. Later Liszt visited Rubinstein and they became friends.

Rubinstein was born on November 28, 1829, and his only teacher was Alexander Villoing, in Moscow. A prodigy, he made his debut at the age of nine, and at eleven started his European tours, accompanied by his mother. He was on the road until he was thirteen. In Berlin from 1843 to 1846, he studied composition then went back to Russia, where he became the protégé of the Grand Duchess Elena Pavlovna. He resumed touring in 1854. Back again in Russia, he married Vera Chekuanov in 1856, and they had three children. He was one of the founders of the Russian Musical Society in 1859 and conducted many of its concerts. In 1862 he founded the St. Petersburg Conservatory and was its director until 1867. Then came another triumphal tour of Europe and, in 1872–73, of the United States.

The Steinway piano firm brought him to America; it also engaged the great violinist Henry Wieniawski to share his programs. Rubinstein was to get $40,000 for 215 performances. He ended up playing 216 concerts in 245 days and returned home with $46,000. The tour started pleasantly enough, with the New York Philharmonic serenading him on his arrival. And certainly the reviews for his first concert on September 15, 1872, at Steinway Hall, could not have made him unhappy. *The New York Times* set the tone: "More remarkable piano playing cannot be imagined . . . inexhaustible variety . . . power and delicacy . . . exceeding science and taste. . . ." Wieniawski also got a rave review. In addition, two singers appeared on the program. No wonder the *Times* man complained that the concert was too long.

From there on it was all downhill. The tour was too long, too arduous, too much to handle. Sometimes they had to give two or three concerts in as many cities on the same day. Wieniawski after a while started to sulk, feeling that he was playing an inferior role. Which he was—he was getting half of what Rubinstein had been offered. The two musicians soon got on each other's nerves and weeks would pass without their speaking to each other. Rubinstein later wrote, in his autobiography, that he began to despise himself and his art. "So profound was my dissatisfaction, that when several years later I was asked to repeat my American tour, with half a million [francs, or $100,000] guaranteed to me, I refused point-blank." Rubinstein and Wieniawski gave their farewell concert in America on May 24, 1873, at Steinway Hall. Rubinstein played only his own music, including an arrangement he made of *Yankee Doodle,* an arrangement "prepared with all the canons of art, and (as to selection, at least, we opine) in opposition to all the canons of taste." So said the *Times* critic.

During all those years Rubinstein had been composing, and his conservative music (a combination of Chopin, Schumann, and Mendelssohn) turned out to be very popular. The *Ocean* Symphony, especially, was one of the most successful symphonic pieces in the last half of the century. His D minor Piano Concerto also was a repertory item and remained so for many years. In 1887 he resumed the directorship of the St. Petersburg Conservatory and died in that city on November 20, 1894, a tired man, blind in one eye and losing sight in the other, but still busy and still the elemental force he always had been.

It was a measure of his magnetism that he, a Jew (although he had converted), was able to be on such good terms with the Russian nobility. He was an internationalist with strong German leanings, and his remark about the way others considered him has often been quoted: "To the Jews I am a Christian, to the Christians a Jew, to the Russians a German, to the Germans a Russian, to the classicists a Wagnerite, to the Wagnerites a reactionary. . . . I am neither flesh nor fowl—an unfinished person." The major Russian composers—the famous Five (Balakirev, Mussorgsky, Borodin, Rimsky-Korsakov, and Cui)—hated him for what he

Rubinstein toured the United States in 1872–73, sharing the program with the violinist Henri Wieniawski.

represented. They were trying to create a national school of composition, while Rubinstein and his brother were preaching German academism. The brother, Nicholas, was a fine pianist who founded and headed the Moscow Conservatory in 1866. Anton Rubinstein made no secret about his conservatism. In his autobiography, published five years before his death, he insisted that "Composition has come to an end. Its parting knell was rung when the last incomparable notes of Chopin died away. All that enchanted us, all that we loved, respected, worshipped and admired, has ended with Chopin." Chopin died in 1849.

Not much of Rubinstein's music is heard today. His D minor Concerto is occasionally trotted out as a curiosity. It is a period piece but does have its virtues, and it can be tremendously exciting in the proper hands (listen to the Josef Hofmann recording). In Russia his opera *The Demon* is staged once in a while. Some of his piano pieces linger on. The rest of his large output has been forgotten.

It is as a pianist that Rubinstein is remembered, and there he made a mighty impact. Everything about him was authentically big. His programs were gargantuan. They could contain twenty pieces and run well over three hours. He often played a seven-concert historical series, a representative program of which would consist of Beethoven's *Moonlight,* D minor, *Waldstein, Appassionata,* E minor, A major (Op. 101), E major (Op. 109), and C minor (Op. 111) sonatas. Each concert also contained encores. Toward the end of his life he gave a two-year series of lectures for the students at the St. Petersburg Conservatory, and Rachmaninoff stated that during those thirty-six lectures he played 857 pieces, a staggering number. At his first lecture he played the complete Book I of Bach's *Well-Tempered Clavier.*

He was the first pianist to make a great fortune in his concerts, and his fees were sensationally high. His American tour had made a good deal of money for him—not equivalent to what the vocal superstars were getting, but enough (in his own words) to lay the foundations for his prosperity. Besides, he had an ample pension from the Czar. Toward the end of his life he was making really big money, more than any pianist before him. In 1881 he went home with $100,000 after a two-month tour of England. In London he was charging a $5 top, which old Ganz called "unheard-of," and he received $30,000 for his historical series in St. James's Hall. (Rubinstein was not the first to give a historical series. Max Paur, a fine German pianist, had given a survey of the repertory, in six concerts, a few years before Rubinstein's first one.)

As a teacher Rubinstein put his imprint on Russian piano playing for generations to come. He did not produce as many individual giants as did Liszt or Leschetizky. What he did do was establish a philosophy of piano playing and interpretation that was carried on for generations in St. Petersburg and Moscow, and then through all Russia. Broadly speaking, it was an emotional school of piano playing backed by thorough training. Russian pianists coming out of that school could differ as widely as, say, Emil Gilels and Sviatoslav Richter, but they all had certain things in common: a Romantic sonority, the ability to project a musical line, and a certain freedom in expression.

By far Rubinstein's greatest pupil was Josef Hofmann. The sixteen-year-old Polish pianist went to Rubinstein in Dresden and worked with him intensively for two years starting in 1892. Rubinstein would tower over him, never touching the piano himself, and allowed his pupil a great deal of leeway. But he never allowed Hofmann to bring to him any composition more than once, saying that he might forget in the next lesson what he had told Hofmann in the previous one and thus "only confuse my mind." His attitude toward technique was completely dismissive. Hofmann asked him for the fingering of a complex passage. Rubinstein did not want to be bothered with such things. "Play it with your nose, but make it sound well." No wonder Hofmann wrote that Rubinstein "was not a pedagogue in the usual meaning of the word." He would not let Hofmann get away with anything, and insisted that the exact letter of the text be followed. Hofmann found this strange considering the liberties that Rubinstein took when he played the same works. Hofmann got up the nerve to ask him about this seeming paradox. Said Rubinstein, "When you are as old as I am now you may do as I do"—adding, grimly, *"if you can."*

12 *Adelina Patti*

THE QUEEN OF SONG

JUST as Anton Rubinstein filled a vacuum to become the World's Greatest Pianist, so Adelina Patti filled a vacuum after her sensational London debut in 1861. The great bel canto singers had either died or retired. Angiolina Bosio could have given Patti a good run for her money, but that amazingly gifted soprano died of pneumonia in St. Petersburg in 1859 at the age of twenty-eight, already recognized as the greatest singer of her time. The big-voiced Sophie Cruvelli had retired in 1856 after a career that lasted only eleven years, during which time she gave the impression that she was much more interested in her amours than in her art. She was always in the papers, especially when the son of the Viceroy of Egypt drowned in the Nile and it was discovered that he had left Cruvelli a large legacy. That was, the papers said, straight-faced, because she had taught him French while he was in Paris. She finally did capture a baron. Then Patti came along and for the next forty years and more was the Queen of Song.

Scanning the millions and millions of words written about Patti is a stunning experience. Could any artist have been *that* good? Were there *no* dissenting voices until toward the end of her career? Everybody seemed to fall sway to her voice and personal charm. Even her colleagues, never a particularly charitable lot, bowed in homage. Clara Louise Kellogg, Blanche Marchesi, Nellie Melba, Marietta Alboni, Jenny Lind, Lilli Lehmann, Albert Niemann, Emma Eames, Frances Alda—all said she was the greatest of all singers. There were no qualifications. The composers of the day were equally excited about her. Verdi, who had good reason to dislike and distrust the prima donna as a species, first heard Patti when she was eighteen and wrote that he was "struck dumb not only by her marvellous technique but by certain dramatic traits in which she revealed herself a great actress." Verdi heard her Gilda and was especially impressed by her work in the last scene, where she says she still loves the Duke: "I cannot express the sublime effect of those words as she sang them." Berlioz, Gounod, and all the other composers who heard her were even more outspoken in their praise. Said the venerable Auber: "I remember Catalani, Pasta, Malibran, Grisi and Sontag. But I never heard so perfect an artist as Patti. As for her voice, it is without a flaw."

And the critics! They could not find words, so they repeated the same ones endlessly. Even George Bernard Shaw, who came in late, after Patti had been before the public over thirty years, who poked fun at her musicianship, wrote glowingly about "that wonderful vocal instrument, with its great range, its birdlike agility and charm of execution, and its unique combination of the magic of a child's voice with the completeness of a woman's." Patti especially knew how to put over a ballad, and the amused Shaw reported that when the immensely rich soprano sang *O give me my lowly thatched cottage again* there wasn't a dry eye in the house. The veteran Hanslick in Vienna called her "a musical organization perfected beyond all others—I may, indeed, say a musical genius." Krehbiel in New York topped that by calling Patti "a musical miracle" and said she set the standards by which all others are judged.

Obviously, then, in her prime she must have been one of the

greatest of all lyric sopranos, most likely the greatest. Nobody could have so gone on, year after year, decade after decade, from triumph to triumph with no dissenting opinion about the sheer beauty of her singing, unless she really was that gifted. She was paid accordingly, and no musician ever was so lavishly rewarded. Patti drove a hard bargain and, to put it bluntly, was as money-mad as Catalani had been.

Even before her London debut she was being talked about as the greatest of all singers. That was in America, where she grew up. When we speak about Patti, we are speaking of a woman who was born in 1843, who was singing in public at the age of seven, who became the spoiled pet of two continents, who sang in public until 1906, who made a series of recordings at that time, and who occasionally appeared in public even after that. We are speaking of an authentic diva, one who traveled in a private railway car especially made for her, with a large entourage, some fifty trunks, a fortune in jewels, a traveling menagerie of cats, dogs, and birds, a personal chef, and cases of her favorite potables, mostly champagne and Château Lafite. Patti gave a new meaning to the term *prima donna assoluta*. The royalty of Europe had given her a jewel collection second to none in private hands, and she was not loath to show it off. For one of her New York *Traviata* performances in 1882, the audience was treated to a display of the Patti jewels; and don't think the newspapers did not make a prime story out of it. She wore diamonds and emeralds in the first act, turquoises and diamonds in the second,

> but in the third act she was all diamonds. Twin solitaires, the size of walnuts, shone from her ears; a diamond butterfly fluttered and flamed from her shoulder; nine different necklaces rainbowed around her neck and the front of her corsage; rings flashed from her fingers, and on her arm blazed bracelet after bracelet, culminating in one band of selected stones, each of which scintillated like a star.
>
> No wonder Nicolini [her husband] loves her.

Traviata was the opera in which she made her stage farewell at Covent Garden in 1903. For that occasion she summoned her jeweler from Paris to her castle in Wales and had him take some of her stones out of their mounts. She had them put on her Violetta gowns, and the costumes were taken to the theater under heavy guard. The stones for this occasion were valued at $1 million; there were 3,700 jewels, some on the back as well as on the front of the costumes. Guards were in the wings when she came on stage, in a blaze of jeweled light. After the performance the guards conveyed her costumes back to the castle, the jeweler restored the stones to their settings, and the costumes went back into one or two of the five hundred trunks of costumes that Mme. Patti had in an air-conditioned room.

The size of her fees was another subject that fascinated the public and was constantly discussed in the newspapers. In the 1880's she was receiving $5,000 a performance, plus a percentage of the gate. Sometimes she got more, as at the Cincinnati Festival of 1882, when her impresario, Colonel Mapleson, paid her $8,000 a performance and trumpeted to the press that this was "the largest amount this invaluable lady has ever received in the shape of a salary." The world was intrigued and enchanted. In 1883 a mathematician counted all the notes in Patti's role of Semiramide and calculated that she received 42⅝ cents per note. Another calculating genius, in Boston, figured out that in *Lucia* Patti got 42½ cents for every note she sang. In America the current joke was that the only singer richer than Patti was the Singer Sewing Machine Company. Her fees were even front-page news, as witness the following box accompanying the headline from a New York newspaper in 1903:

ADELINA PATTI
Will Make Here
$5,000 for Each Concert
50 per cent of receipts that exceed $7,500
$375,000 for the sixty concerts
$56 for each minute on the stage
$2.60 for each second of time

$3.47 for each velvet note
$2.50 every time she breathes

Her farewell tours were also admiringly discussed by the international press. Patti started making them as early as 1884. For the next twenty years every season was announced as a farewell. In 1886 the Brooklyn *Eagle* worked out that Patti had made her "last appearance" twenty-seven times; her "positively last appearance" nine times; that she "had permanently retired from the stage" seven times; had "retired to spend her days in her castle" three times; and now she wanted to make another American tour and retire again. Thus nobody believed the announcement in 1903 that this tour was Patti's "absolute farewell." The announcement included a note: "Madame Patti has never before in all her career announced officially, as in this instance, her farewell to the Public." But this time it really was her farewell to America.

The damndest things were written about her. It was reported that kings and princes had proposed marriage to her. It was reported that the preservation of her voice was due to the fact that every night she ate, before retiring, a sandwich with the tongues of twelve nightingales on it.

From the age of seven she was constantly in the news. Patti was born in Madrid on February 19, 1843, almost on the stage. Her mother went into labor pains during a performance of *Norma* and she was born the following day. Both of her parents were Italians and both were singers. The family was always on the move and came to New York in 1844 or 1845. Her father managed the Astor Place Opera House as well as singing there. Patti, four years old, was taken to the opera every night. Soon it was discovered that she had absolute pitch and a retentive memory. She grew up hearing music at the opera house and at home, where her six brothers and sisters (there were three boys and a girl from her mother's previous marriage) all were singers or studying to be singers. Carlotta, the best, was a well-known singer for about twenty years. Once in a while she sang in the same cast with Patti. Adelina's stepbrother Ettore became her teacher. Apparently there

The seven-year-old Adelina Patti. Already she was a veteran of the concert stage.

was not much he could teach her. Adelina sang as easily and naturally as she spoke.

At seven she was amazing everybody with her flawless singing of *Casta Diva*. The family began to exhibit her as a child prodigy. *Dwight's Journal of Music* has an entry about the eight-year-old Adelina, who appeared in a concert with Miss Petit, the nine-year-old pianist, and "Master Marsh, the infant drummer," four years old. She was taken in hand by Maurice Strakosch, who had married Adelina's sister Amalia. Strakosch was a good musician—tenor, pianist, conductor, impresario. He took Patti on tour in 1850 with the popular violinist Ole Bull; she sang standing on a table. Strakosch was her vocal coach, and she learned a great deal from him. From all accounts Adelina was a willful, spoiled child with a temper, and she had to have her own way. She toured with a troupe assembled by the pianist Louis Moreau Gottschalk in 1857, and in 1859 made her operatic debut in New York. *Lucia* was the opera; she was sixteen years old and already had sung fourteen operatic roles, including Leonora in *Trovatore* and Valentine in *Les Huguenots*. She seldom sang those roles in later life. She also gave a series of concerts that year in New York.

In America she was considered a native. *The New York Times* wrote an editorial claiming her for the United States. A subsequent editorial offered a retraction. Perhaps the young singer was not, after all, officially an American; the *Times* said that it had claimed Patti as such "from pure covetousness." In this 1859 editorial was a remark that has a peculiar familiarity: "The old, old libel, that no artist could succeed in New York without the prestige of a European reputation, has been exploded once more." It is indeed an old, old libel, and not supported by the facts.

America was conquered. Now was the time for Patti to conquer Europe. She signed a contract with Frederick Gye, the manager of the Royal Italian Opera at Covent Garden, for three trial performances without pay. If she was successful, she would be engaged at $750 a month for the first season and up to $2,000 for her fifth. Her debut, in *La Sonnambula,* took place on May 14, 1861. It was an unheralded debut. American reputations did not mean much to London critics, a proud and independent lot that included James Davison of the *Times,* Desmond Ryan of the *Morning Chronicle,* Henry Lincoln of the *Daily News,* Henry Fothergill Chorley of the *Athenaeum,* Sutherland Edwards of the *St. James Gazette,* and Henry Hersee of the *Globe*. They all were at Patti's first appearance and, to a man, were carried away. The *Musical World* marveled. "Never did singer make her debut in this country with so little known of her antecedents, and with so little stir about her beforehand," the critic wrote. "Her name had appeared only four days in advance of her debut, and without a single remark in the advertisements. . . . Never was a surprise greater, no result more triumphant." The *Chronicle* pronounced the debut the most impressive since Jenny Lind's first appearance and described the voice as "a pure soprano of wonderful extent in the upper registers, reaching with positive ease F in altissimo. It is clear, sonorous, bright, and firm as a rock." She also sang on pitch, the critic noted, using her voice "with the perfectness of a player on a tuned instrument, and has an incomparable shake." Some critics gently said that there was room for musical maturity. None had anything against the quality of the voice.

It also helped that the eighteen-year-old Patti was slim, beautiful, and charming. Most superstar sopranos of that day (as they are today) were well padded and lumbered rather than walked. Patti was young, radiant, confident, and at that time something new on the operatic scene. Every subsequent Patti performance was sold out, a phenomenon that held true for almost the rest of her long life. She was immediately assigned top singers for her casts. In one *Don Giovanni* performance the tenor was Tamberlik, the Don was Jean-Baptiste Faure, the Leporello was Carl Formes (one of the all-time great basses), and the great Grisi, who had virtually no voice left and was making her last operatic appearances, was Donna Anna. Patti sang Zerlina. In *Il Barbiere* she was paired with Mario, the Prince of Tenors. Patti sang twenty-five performances of six operas in her debut season. The only complaint about Patti's Rosina was that, in the exuberance of youth, she overornamented her arias.

That overornamentation was something Rossini himself put a stop to. We owe it to the Saint-Saëns memoirs for the story. Patti made a brilliant entry into Paris in 1862, became the talk of the town, and sang the Rosina aria, *Una voce poco fa,* at one of Rossini's soirées with the composer at the piano. She embellished the music beyond recognition. When she finished Rossini looked up and said, "Who wrote that aria you just sang?" It was a slap in the face. Rossini was still angry when Saint-Saëns saw him a few days later. "I am fully aware that arias should be embellished. That's what they are for. But not to leave a note of them even in recitatives! That is too much." Saint-Saëns says that Patti thought it over for a few days, decided it was best not to have Rossini as an enemy, and returned to him for advice. "It was well for her that she took it, for her talent, though brilliant and fascinating, was not yet fully formed." Two months later, at another soirée, Patti sang arias from *La Gazza Ladra* and *Semiramide,* and this time, according to Saint-Saëns, "she combined with her brilliancy the absolute correctness which she always showed afterwards." In the lesson scene of *Il Barbiere* Patti inserted *Home, Sweet Home,* and it became identified with her from that point.

The musical Grand Tour followed Paris. Patti sang all over Europe, creating a furor everywhere, receiving presents in the form of the grandest jewels from the grandest nobility. Adored, she moved as royalty among royalty as Malibran and Sontag had done. She eventually got to the point where she could even afford to snub emperors. Kaiser Wilhelm I sent her a message asking her to walk with him early to drink the waters. "Certainly not!" she answered. "I get up early for no King in Europe."

Year after year she went on, singing much the same way, her voice showing not the slightest hint of deterioration, her figure unchanged, a picture of eternal youth. That was because she took very good care of herself and of her voice. As a very precious property she was shielded from anything that might distress her. She was a wise vocalist, seldom learning a role that was too heavy for her voice; and if she once in a while appeared in an opera that asked too much of her resources, she sang it only a few times. Her

Patti around 1870, at the height of her fame. This photograph was taken during one of her appearances in St. Petersburg.

contracts specified that she did not have to attend rehearsals. She did relatively little vocalizing—only a few scales a day for about ten minutes or so. Patti knew that she had a priceless asset in her voice and religiously took care of it. Her schedule was Spartan, and as a result she kept singing long after most of her colleagues had lost their voices. Kellogg, who knew her very well, has left an account of her schedule: "Such a life! Everything divided off carefully according to regime: —so much to eat, so far to walk, so long to sleep, just such and such things to do and no others!" Her husband—in 1868 she married the Marquis de Caux, a French nobleman without much money—saw to it that the outside world never bothered Adelina. Adelina's father had opposed the marriage. In his opinion—and Strakosch's too—no prima donna should ever marry. He pointed out as examples the sad marriages of Malibran, Bosio, Frezzolini, Grisi, Lucca, Trebelli, Sasse, Heilbron, and the dancer Marie Taglioni. All became separated from their husbands, who were bounders and spent or gambled away the hard-earned money of their wives. One wonders how much Papa's thought was colored by the fact that now Adelina would have a husband to manage her affairs and dip into her fabulous earnings. Patti had business agents, secretaries, and legal counsel to take care of her business affairs, and Alfred de Rothschild himself watched over her investments, but Papa was worried. A husband by law had control over his wife's income.

As a matter of fact, Papa's gloomy prediction came true. Patti separated from Caux. In 1867 she met a tenor who sang under the name of Nicolini (his real name was Ernest Nicolas), and felt an attraction for him, even if he was a married man with five children. Ten years later, while both were appearing in the Italian company in St. Petersburg, they had an affair. Appropriately, she was singing Juliet to Nicolini's Romeo in the Gounod opera. The affair exploded in the international press when the marquis stormed into his wife's dressing room and started screaming at her, saying that he had given her a title and she had acted toward him like a whore. Caux had to be bought off. Herman Klein, Patti's biographer, says that Caux settled for $300,000. Patti and Nicolini were Catholics,

Patti with her father. He warned her about the perils of marriage.

so no ecclesiastical divorce could be arranged. They got married in 1886 in a Protestant church near Craig-y-Nos, the castle in Wales she had just purchased. Queen Victoria, who had been a close friend, refused to talk to her after that. Nicolini was not one of the great tenors, and at his death in 1898 the obituary notice of the New York *Herald* twisted the knife: "Patti's devotion to Nicolini even went so far as to include her admiration for his singing, which shows love is not only blind but sometimes deaf."

No real vocal rivals appeared. For a while Pauline Lucca attracted some attention. She was a fiery, temperamental woman who walked out of opera houses because of imagined slights. In London, when she sang Marguerite in *Faust*, she was attacked in the press for her "risqué" acting and broke her contract, saying she would never return to London, "that city of fog and decayed vegetables." (Some years later she did return.) Patti replaced her as Marguerite and it became one of her greatest roles.

Another competitor, and a really great singer, was the brilliant Etelka Gerster. During the years of Mapleson's American touring company they both were members and alternately sang the same roles. Gerster was a wild Hungarian with a phenomenal voice, and had not Patti been around she would have been acclaimed as the world's leading soprano. In her fifteen years before the public she conquered all audiences and was Patti's only real rival. The two ladies hated each other and were not on speaking terms. Gerster would go into rages when she saw the Mapleson three-sheets with Patti's name in larger letters than hers. (It was in Patti's contract that her name on posters be in letters one-third larger than anyone else's. Nicolini would be out there with a ruler, measuring.) Once Gerster tore a costume to pieces just before curtain time and the audience had to wait half an hour while a new one was hastily fitted. On another occasion she saw a playbill with Patti's name not only in larger letters, but also with a price scale that put the admission higher for Patti than for her—$7 against $5. Gerster, who was supposed to sing that night, got on a train in a fury and returned to New York without telling anybody. The opera had to be canceled. Mapleson told the press that Gerster's baby had been taken ill and that the frantic mother had rushed to its side. Patti, who was superstitious, believed that Gerster had the evil eye and took pains to avoid her. If anything went wrong, it was Gerster's fault because of the baleful aura. They were in the same company in San Francisco during the 1884 earthquake. As soon as the earth started trembling Patti knew the reason. "*Gerster!*" she exclaimed. Gerster could pay back tit for tat. Patti once got an impulsive kiss from Governor Crittenden of Missouri, and reporters asked Gerster what she thought about it. "I don't see anything in that to create so much fuss," Gerster said. No? Nothing wrong? "Certainly not. There's nothing wrong in a man kissing a woman old enough to be his mother." Gerster seems to have been not much of an actress and was not a pretty woman. Patti remained the favorite.

Other great singers during Patti's reign included the eccentric Croatian soprano Ilma di Murska, Christine Nilsson from Sweden, and the German-born Therese Tietjens. Of these three, Tietjens was probably the greatest vocalist. A large, stout woman, she had an enormous voice (Wagner wanted her for his first Isolde), an equally enormous repertory, and was tremendously admired by the public and professionals. She was versatile enough to sing all three female roles in *Don Giovanni,* and like so many of the early sopranos was as comfortable in Rossini bel canto as she was in the heavy roles of Meyerbeer and Verdi. She was known primarily as a dramatic singer. Di Murska was in every way a flamboyant type—she with her giant Newfoundland dog, with which she dined every day; with her monkey, parakeets, parrots, cats, and whatever other pets she picked up en route. She specialized in romantic and fantastic characters, such as the Queen of the Night and Lucia, and would embellish everything with a florid boldness that made her listeners catch their breath. She would insert trills, cadenzas, arpeggios, staccato passages, octave leaps, and anything else that occurred to her busy little mind at the moment. She must have driven conductors crazy. A top singer who appeared all over the world, she made and spent a fortune, and died in poverty. Nilsson was a universal favorite, both for her looks and for the sweetness

Some of the greatest singers in history were rivals of Patti. The sweet-voiced Christine Nilsson from Sweden (upper left) even upstaged Patti in Russia. She sang at the opening of the Metropolitan Opera in Faust *on October 22, 1883. The versatile German-born dramatic soprano Therese Tietjens (upper right) spent much of her career in England and sang everything from Rossini to Wagner. Etelka Gerster (above, left), the brilliant coloratura soprano from Hungary, was considered by many to be Patti's peer. Ilma di Murska (below), a Croatian soprano, was flamboyant, eccentric, and a willful virtuoso.*

of her voice. She sang Marguerite at the opening performance of the Metropolitan Opera in 1883. Nilsson was one of the few singers genuinely admired by Patti, who also had good words to say about Alboni and Jenny Lind. Nilsson was one of the few singers who ever upstaged Patti. That was in St. Petersburg, where the two appeared on the same program in 1873. Patti sang first, and her technique and beautiful sound brought down the house. Nilsson, no mean technician herself, did not even try to compete. Instead she sang a slow, lyric Russian folk song, in Russian, and the audience went wild.

Patti instead of Nilsson could have opened the new Metropolitan Opera. She was approached, but asked for too high a fee. Mapleson, terrified that his top attraction would be leaving him, raised her salary to $5,000 a performance, and the Metropolitan did not care to match that. Patti always insisted on being paid in dollars before the curtain went up: no dollars, no performance. In her 1888–89 season she received a percentage of the gate as well as her normal fee. In six months she made about $500,000. From that period comes one of the best-known stories of that irrepressible raconteur, Mapleson. Short on cash before a performance, he gave her secretary, Franchi, $4,000. Franchi said Patti would not sing and that the contract now was void. Then Franchi returned with a deal. Give him the $4,000. He would escort Mme. Patti to the theater, and she would put on her Violetta costume, except for her shoes. As soon as the last $1,000 came in, she would go on stage. A half hour before curtain time, $800 had come into the box office. The money was given to Patti. Now she was only $200 short. Franchi notified Mapleson that Patti had put one shoe on. As soon as he sent her the rest of the money she would put on the other one. Patti waited until she was completely paid and then, "her face radiant with benignant smiles, went to the stage." Mapleson was filled with rueful admiration. Patti, he wrote, "is beyond doubt the most successful singer who ever lived. Vocalists as gifted, as accomplished, might be named, but no one ever approached her in the art of obtaining from a manager the greatest possible sum he could by any possibility contrive to pay."

A somewhat similar story came out of Chicago. Patti was there in 1889 to help inaugurate the new opera house. At the opening ceremony she made a single appearance, singing *Home, Sweet Home* and, as an encore, the *Swiss Echo Song*. For this stint she was paid $4,000. She went on to sing during the Chicago opera season, at $3,500 a performance plus 50 percent of the receipts over $5,000. In his lively history of the Chicago Opera, Ronald L. Davis tells of the influenza epidemic that swept the city. Patti was one of the few singers untouched. The management visited her hotel room to ask if she would replace an indisposed soprano. Patti received them while warming her feet at a fire and eating marshmallows. The following dialogue ensued:

"You are well, are you not?"

"Perfectly."

"Then can you sing tonight?"

"For four thousand dollars."

The management bowed and left. Emma Albani stepped in, and not for $4,000.

In the 1890's the bloom started to go from Patti's voice, but she still maintained a heavy singing schedule, concentrating more on concerts than opera. She sang her last American operatic performance in 1892. Generally, at that time, all of her music was transposed down, as much as a third. After Nicolini's death she married Rolf Cederström, an impoverished Swedish nobleman who was reputedly her masseur, in 1899. She was fifty-six and he about thirty years younger. Patti was still the Queen of Song, though new singers started to threaten her supremacy. Of the new breed, she thought Marcella Sembrich and Nellie Melba were the best—and she was right.

After the 1890's she was more entertainer than artist, singing the same sentimental songs and ballads again and again in her concerts. Critics became restive, but Patti defended herself according to her lights: "Every day I get letters to sing this old song, that old song," she told an American interviewer. "I hear that some critics grumble because I sing the same old ballads over and over again. But that is what the public wants. They like the songs they

Ernest Nicolini, Patti's second husband, in 1877. That was the year of their romance in St. Petersburg.

know. If I were to refuse to sing *Home, Sweet Home,* they would think me no longer Patti, no matter how well I might sing in opera. There are plenty of women to sing Wagner and new operas for the critics. I prefer to please my public."

In 1903 Patti made her last American tour, and it was a tragedy. The voice was almost gone; and Patti, who all of her life sang to full houses, canceled many concerts when ticket sales were not up to expectations. Her manager had loudly announced that Patti was being paid "the largest honorarium ever accorded to any artist in the history of the world," but word got around about the state of Patti's voice, the reviews were bad, and the public seemed disinclined to contribute to Patti's old-age fund. She gave her last concert in London in 1906, but she could not keep away from the stage and appeared in a few charity performances until she was seventy-two years old. She died on September 27, 1919, and there was universal grief at her passing. Patti not only had been the greatest of all singers; she also had been the last exponent of the bel canto style as taught to her by Rossini himself.

Let some of her colleagues, great singers themselves, discuss her style. Lilli Lehmann, who was born only five years after Patti and outlived her by ten, was a soprano who not only was the greatest Wagnerian of her time but also a lyric who could do coloratura roles. The redoubtable Lilli knew whereof she spoke, and when she spoke of Patti it was only in superlatives. In her book *How to Sing,* she wrote that "in Adelina Patti, everything was united. . . . All was absolutely good, correct and flawless, the voice like a bell you seemed to hear long after its singing had ceased." Lehmann once asked Patti how she did it. *"Ah, je n'en sais rien."* Emma Eames, one of the all-time great sopranos, first heard Patti in Boston and was struck by the fact that although the Queen of Song had been before the public for many years, the voice was entirely unimpaired:

> Hers was the most perfect technique imaginable, with a scale, both chromatic and diatonic, of absolute accuracy and evenness, a tone of perfect purity and of the most melting quality, a trill

> impeccable in intonation, whether major or minor, and such as one hears only in nightingales, liquid, round and soft. Her crescendo was matchless and her vocal charm was infinite. I cannot imagine more beautiful sounds than issued from that exquisite throat, nor more faultless phrasing, nor more wonderful economy of breath.

The young Frances Alda, studying in Paris with Mathilde Marchesi, heard Patti and "went home in a daze, unable to sleep all that night." The next day Alda told Marchesi that there was no point in continuing to study. "I know I'll never sing like that." When Clara Louise Kellogg first heard Patti she had much the same feeling Alda was to have. But at least Kellogg comforted herself, calling Patti unique: "What a voice! I had never dreamed of anything like it. But, for that matter, neither had anybody else."

And let Patti herself speak. She wrote an article for an American magazine about singing, and it was full of good sense. Cultivate the middle register. Do not harm the voice by trying to add top or bottom notes. In other words, never strain the natural compass of the voice. "My golden rule in singing is to spare myself until the voice is needed, and then never to give it all out. Put it in the bank. I do not push my voice for the pleasure of the moment. If you are prodigal of your powers at such times, the next time you wish to be generous you cannot." Patti knew exactly what she could do. She might try out an opera, such as *Carmen,* but if it did not work, she promptly dropped it. Her repertory consisted of forty-two operas, many of which she sang only a few times.

In her great days her voice went securely to a high F and she had a technique that would effortlessly allow her to do anything required of it. But when she made her 1905 recordings, her voice was pretty much gone. Fred Gaisberg, the legendary artists and repertory director of the Gramophone and Typewriter Company (later known as His Master's Voice), had to bring the equipment, engineers, and accompanist (Landon Ronald) to Craig-y-Nos. For four days, between 11 A.M. and noon, there were recording sessions. The following year there was another series. In all, Patti

Patti in the arms of Mario during a Covent Garden performance, 1863. The Mephistopheles is the famous French baritone Jean-Baptiste Faure.

recorded seventeen pieces, some of them twice. Most of them were popular songs, including her signature pieces—*Home, Sweet Home* and *Comin' Thro' the Rye*—but there were also operatic arias, including *Casta Diva, Batti, batti,* the *Jewel Song, Connais-tu le pays,* and, above all, the *Ah, non credea* from *La Sonnambula.*

It must never be forgotten that these records represent the singing of a woman of sixty-two who had been before the public for fifty-five of those years. The intonation is poor, she runs out of breath, phrases are broken up. Yet through the wreck of a voice something sweet and appealing comes through. Call it charm, spirit, style—whatever it is, one can (as with the Joachim recordings) extrapolate backwards and see what it is that so captured five decades of audiences. There are also some invaluable illustrations of Romantic performance practice. In *Batti, batti* the concluding six-eight section may have been a little too hard for Patti at this stage of her life. But her fast tempo is entirely convincing, and it gives an idea of how singers approached the aria in the middle nineteenth century (and, one feels, probably in Mozart's day). There are significant variances from current accepted practice in many of the arias. These too give an idea of the practice of the day. And then there is the Bellini aria, the *Ah, no credea mirarti,* in which the veteran Patti sings with a haunting line and produces some of the most beautiful trills ever heard on records.

Gaisberg rushed the wax records back to London and had a set of test pressings made up. Those were rushed back to Wales. Patti listened to them and broke into tears. "Oh, my God!" she cried. "Now I understand why I am Patti. Ah, yes. What a voice! What an artist! Finally I understand everything!"

13 *Jean and Edouard de Reszke*

THE SINGING BROTHERS

JEAN AND EDOUARD DE RESZKE were singing brothers. Edouard was probably the finest bass after Lablache. Jean was the most stylish tenor of the century, a matinee idol, a superior musician, and an admired human being. Jean, the elder, was born in Warsaw on January 14, 1850. Edouard was born there on December 22, 1853. For most of their lives, the two brothers were inseparable, appearing together in many operas, sharing adjoining apartments, working out their repertory together. There also was a singing sister, Joséphine, born in Warsaw on June 4, 1855, a soprano who had a relatively short career. She sang with each brother separately, and in 1884 the three of them were cast together in Massenet's *Hérodiade* at the Paris Opéra. A fourth sibling, Victor, had a fine tenor voice. He refused to study, saying that there already were enough crazy ones in the family.

Both Jean and Edouard were considered the finest in their categories. Edouard, who made his debut in 1876, was a giant of a man with a voice to match. George Bernard Shaw called it "alarmingly powerful." Edouard exulted in his voice, pouring it out in prodigal manner in all roles from Italian bel canto to Hagen in *Götterdämmerung*. Jean, who started as a baritone, developed into an all-purpose tenor who could sing Romeo, Radames, Walther, or Siegfried with equal authority. He was a virile, good-looking man (Shaw, who followed his career from the beginning, remembered him as "slim, and the handsomest young man I ever saw on the stage"), a fine actor, and a singer of unusual nuance and subtlety. He was Mario's legitimate successor in the line that culminated in Enrico Caruso. In de Reszke's singing was Mario's suavity coupled to a heftier vocal quality and a breadth of repertory that Mario had never shown. He was a universal favorite, and not only with the public. Sopranos from Patti to Nordica and Melba were eager to sing with him. The usual rewards followed. The de Reszke brothers became famous and very rich. Both were married: Edouard to Hélène Schütz in 1885 and Jean to the Comtesse Marie de Goulaine. That was her title in her own right. She had been married to the Comte de Mailly-Nesle before falling in love with Jean, and a dispensation for the marriage to Jean had to be obtained from the Pope. The announcement was made in 1896, at which time Jean told the New York *World* that they had been engaged for seven years. They had a son, who was killed in action during World War I—destroyed by a mine a few hours after the Armistice.

Jean's life was more interesting than Edouard's, if only because of his shift from baritone to tenor. Many Wagnerian tenors originally started as baritones—Ramón Vinay and Lauritz Melchior, to mention but two. As a baritone Jean, who made his debut in 1874 using the name of Giovanni di Reschi, did not impress anybody very much. After two indifferent years before the public, he went to Italy to work with a teacher named Giovanni Sbriglia and emerged with a new voice. But de Reszke was a slow developer. He also had patience. In 1875, in Madrid, he made his first appearance as a tenor, and then retired for another three years of study. The breakthrough came in 1884, when he sang John the

Jean de Reszke as Roméo in the Gounod opera. It was his most famous role.

Baptist in *Hérodiade*. It was a triumph, and Jean de Reszke immediately was recognized as the premier French stylist before the public.

For the rest of his life his activities were concentrated in Paris, London (where he first sang in 1887), and New York (his Metropolitan Opera debut took place in 1891). Toward the end of his career he began to take on the heavy Wagnerian roles. First it was Walther in *Die Meistersinger,* sung in French. In 1895 he started to sing Wagner in German, and he was the greatest Lohengrin, Tristan, and Siegfried of his time. German tenors had a tendency then (and now, too) to bark the vocal lines. To everybody's amazement, de Reszke showed that the vocal lines could actually be sung. Herman Klein, the singing teacher and critic, went so far as to say that de Reszke brought to these heavy Wagnerian roles a bel canto approach.

Of course, like all other superstars, he also made appearances in many other houses, and for the largest fees of any singer except Patti. It is true that in his first London season he was paid only £100 a night. (Edouard, who went with him, signed for £320 a month.) A few years later he would not have walked across the street for that kind of money. At the Metropolitan Opera for eight performances a month he was paid $10,000 a month and 25 percent of the gross over $25,000. (He was the only singer in the history of the Metropolitan ever to share the gross.) In his 1901 Metropolitan season (his last) he received $2,500 a performance plus 5 percent of the gross over $5,500. Melba that season also got $2,500 a performance but did not share in the box office. Emma Calvé had to be satisfied with $1,500 a performance. Edouard, of course, never made that kind of money. In New York they called him "the singing cannon" and everybody was crazy about him. But he was only a basso and, as such, more disposable and hence less highly paid, than superstar tenors and sopranos. An interviewer once asked Jean de Reszke if he thought he was overpaid. He answered with his customary suavity and intelligence. On nights when he was in good voice, then yes, perhaps he was overpaid. "But when I am out of health, voice and spirits, and yet have to make a superhuman effort not to disappoint my manager and the public, no sum in the world is too great to compensate me for what I have to go through."

Jean took to New York and the country. His only dislike was ice water, which was constantly thrust upon him as a potable. Jean explained to a journalist that he never had heard of ice water until coming to America. "We use water on the other side to wash in but not to drink." But in any New York restaurant ice water was a concomitant of the meal. "I have been hounded almost to distraction by ice water . . . it has become a nightmare." In New York he was such a hero that he could get away with anything. Considering the universal acclaim paid to his "artistry," it is a little disconcerting to read about some of the musical luxuries he allowed himself. Radames was one of his big roles; but Jean de Reszke, like so many tenors, quailed when faced with the difficult *Celeste Aida* so early in the opera. His solution more often than not was simple. He did not sing it. He told Giovanni Martinelli that in nineteen performances of *Aida* at the Metropolitan Opera, he had sung *Celeste Aida* only four times. "It was too difficult an aria to sing before I was properly warmed up," he explained. No singer today, no matter how great a superstar, would be allowed to get away with that nonsense.

He had few eccentricities. Emma Eames, who frequently sang with him, suggests that he was something of a hypochondriac who always thought he was catching a cold. Before every performance he went to a physician to get his throat sprayed "and invariably smelled of iodoform and ether through the whole of an opera." Eames also would catch him studying his vocal organs in front of a mirror with a laryngoscope before a performance. But as tenors go, he was completely sane. He was a conscientious, hard worker, as was brother Edouard. Amherst Webber, a vocal coach, worked with the brothers while they were preparing their Wagnerian roles at the Metropolitan Opera. They would arrive at the house early and experiment with phrasings and dynamics, one up in the balcony, listening to the other from the stage, and they "would criticize each note separately until the ideal was attained."

Edouard de Reszke as Mephistopheles. He was a physical giant and the greatest basso of his day.

Edouard was all singer. If Shaw is to be believed, he was less interested in ultimate refinement, as Jean was, than in showing the full power of his glorious voice. As an actor he competently went through the motions, but Shaw often found his work amusing. Shaw has left an inimitable description of Edouard as Mephistopheles in *Faust:*

> We all like to see him enjoying himself; and he never enjoys himself more thoroughly than in that outrageous crimson and scarlet costume, with two huge cock's feathers twirling in the Covent Garden draughts (especial boreal this year), his face decorated with sardonic but anatomically impossible wrinkles, and a powerful limelight glowing on him through the reddest of red glasses. His firm conviction that he is curdling the blood of the audience with demonstrations of satanic malignity when he is in fact infecting them with his mountainous good humor; his faith in the diabolic mockery of a smile that would make the most timid child climb straight upon his knee and demand to be shewn how a watch opens when blown on; the exuberant agility with which he persuades himself that his two hundred and forty pounds of generously nourished flesh and blood are a mere vapor from the bottomless pit—all these sights are dear to the hearts of stall and gallery alike.
>
> And then his singing! Singing is not the word for it: he no longer sings: he bawls, revelling in the stunning sound with a prodigality that comes of knowing that he has so much voice to draw upon that no extravagance can exhaust it.

If Edouard—in *Faust,* anyway—just reared back and let loose, Jean was a much more thoughtful artist. Gounod and Massenet, in whose operas Jean so triumphed, were among his most fervent admirers. Perhaps Jean's most famous role was Romeo in Gounod's *Roméo et Juliette.* After hearing him as Romeo against the Juliet of Patti (the composer had conducted the performance), Gounod sent a note off to de Reszke: "Never have you carried to such a height that beauty of diction and gesture, that correctness and expressiveness of accent, that control of voice production—in a word, that perfectly balanced proportion which alone makes the great artist." From all accounts it was de Reszke who, in the opinion of professionals and connoisseurs, fully blended voice and art. Tamagno had a bigger voice and Mario may have had one of more natural beauty but, as Klein pointed out, never had there been such a voice in which was blended "exquisite smoothness and equality all through the scale matched by the same perfection of phrasing or such complete technical control."

All critics said much the same thing. W. J. Henderson, the renowned vocal expert of the New York *Sun,* wrote a long article on the occasion of Jean de Reszke's death (in Nice on April 3, 1935). Henderson described de Reszke's voice as powerful enough for the most heroic roles, yet capable of the most delicate lyric flights. "It was not one of the great voices of history, as Caruso's was." But his art was incomparable. Henderson, who had heard everybody since the 1880's, said of de Reszke that

> He was the greatest Romeo that ever walked the stage. He was the greatest Tristan since Niemann. . . . He was great as Faust, great as Siegfried. He was matchless as Lohengrin. He was the ideal Walther von Stolzing. He was the finest Chevalier de Grieux [in Massenet's *Manon*], the unparalleled Raoul in *Les Huguenots* and John of Leyden in *Le Prophète.* No one except Italo Campanini rivalled him as Don José and perhaps only Caruso as Radames. As Vasco da Gama [in Meyerbeer's *L'Africaine*] he had no rival. . . . Mr. de Reszke's vocal technique was the greatest I have ever known in a man, with the one exception of Plançon. But his art was something far beyond technique. His searching analysis of every phrase he had to sing was based first upon a demand for the utmost significance of the text. Having satisfied himself as to this, he proceeded to construct a vocal delivery which would combine precisely the right degree of volume, the most illuminating color and the vitalizing dynamic curve. I learned more about singing from Jean de Reszke than from any other artist.

But it was not only critics who considered Jean de Reszke

unique. Nellie Melba considered him a greater singer than Caruso. De Reszke's great contemporary Lilli Lehmann, the foremost Wagnerian soprano at the turn of the century—Lilli, with her 170 roles in 119 operas, Lilli who was born in 1848 and was still singing wonderfully when she made her recordings around 1905, Lilli who in her youth could and did sing a different opera every night in the week, Lilli who as a teacher produced such pupils as Geraldine Farrar and Olive Fremstad, Lilli the most imperious of all the prima donnas—Lilli pronounced Jean de Reszke as in a class by himself, "such as one has no opportunity to hear elsewhere. His full, soft, noble and not over-big voice, his admirable distribution of breathing, his pronunciation—which is alike perfect in three languages—all these elements are fountains of purest delight to the listener."

Jean de Reszke also was in the record studios much around the same time that Lilli Lehmann was. After his retirement he made at least two recordings. A mystery surrounds them. In 1903 Edouard had made three sides for the Columbia Grand Opera series in America, and those were properly issued. But Jean's records contain elements of a detective novel. In 1905 Fonotipia announced two 13¾-inch de Reszke discs—the *Salut tombeau* from *Roméo et Juliette* and the *O souverain* from Massenet's *Le Cid.* But neither record was issued. Legend has it that de Rezke approved the records, then heard them once again, decided they did not do him justice, and had all pressings destroyed. Legend also has it that a de Reszke record is owned by a French collector who has it in a vault, not to be released until fifty years after his death in deference to de Reszke's wishes. There is another mystery. The Gramophone Company in England listed de Reszke as one of its artists in its 1910 catalogue. But no de Reszke records ever were released.

The only recorded samples of de Reszke's voice are to be found on the Mapleson cylinders. From 1901 to 1903 Lionel Mapleson, the librarian of the Metropolitan Opera, set up an Edison machine in the catwalk and recorded, on wax cylinders, snippets of actual performances. These cylinders eventually were thrown into a trunk and forgotten. Discovered some thirty years later, they were in shocking shape. It was next to impossible to make out the faint sounds through the loud surface noise. A few of them were issued in the 1950's by William Seltsam on an LP disc with a big warning: THIS IS NOT A HIGH FIDELITY RECORDING. In 1983 the Rodgers and Hammerstein archives at the New York Public Library in Lincoln Center subjected the cylinders to modern audio techniques in an effort to make available more accurate transfers. The results were not notably successful; the originals had deteriorated too badly. But the cylinders give an idea of what went on at the Metropolitan at the turn of the century, and some fabulous singers can be heard—Nordica, Eames, Calvé, Emilio de Marchi, Scotti, Sembrich, Gadski, Schumann-Heink, Adams. And Jean de Reszke. Listening to the few dim measures of his singing in Siegfried's *Forging Song,* one can see why Klein wrote that the tenor brought a bel canto quality to his Wagner singing. The music is sung, not yelled; the phrasings have grace; the utterance sounds as though it comes from the vocal cords of a young man. A few other Mapleson excerpts indicate that Jean de Reszke was indeed the paragon he was held to be in his own age.

Edouard retired in 1903 and went back to the de Reszke estate in Poland—an estate that covered thousands and thousands of acres. All of New York's Central Park could have been tucked into one corner of it. Jean retired in 1902 and was a frequent visitor to the estate. The brothers were enthusiastic racehorse breeders. One of the happiest moments of their lives occurred when their horse Le Sorcier won the Russian Derby in Moscow on the very same day that another of their horses, Pickwick, took the International Stakes in Paris. Jean also purchased a luxurious house in the Rue de la Faisanderie, had a little theater built in it, and began a new career as a teacher. His most famous pupil was Maggie Teyte. As a teacher Jean was an exponent of the *coup de glotte,* a glottal stroke that, some singing teachers believe, ruined any number of de Reszke pupils.

Jean's parties were famous. He was the most lavish of hosts, with the most distinguished guest list. Asked who would be at one

The de Reszke brothers in their Metropolitan Opera years. They sang together in many productions all over the world.

of his dinners, Jean might say in an offhand manner, "Oh, the King of Portugal, the Duke of Connaught, the Grand Duke Vladimir of Russia, le Duc de Morny, *et ainsi de suite*." Jean may have been deprecating but everybody else was impressed. Leo Slezak, the great heroic tenor of a following generation, took a few lessons with de Reszke, admired his house with its small stage, and spoke admiringly of the musical entertainments he gave there—little concerts "that were among the most sensational social events of the day." As for the famous parties, "de Reszke lived like a prince and he was a true *grand seigneur* in every respect. His house was a meeting place for all the royalties, distinguished nobility, artistic celebrities and great men of Paris." His dinners "were of a brilliance and elegant charm ordinarily associated with the most exclusive courts of Europe. At a dinner party for twelve persons, there would be a servant in gold-laced scarlet livery, silk stockings, buckled shoes and powdered hair behind every guest. . . ." Mary Garden, frequently at his parties, noted one eccentricity. De Reszke would stroll about with his pet on his shoulders—a green parrot that would bite anybody who tried to touch it.

14 *Ignaz Paderewski*

THE AUREOLED POLE

FROM the Hungarian Liszt to the Russian Rubinstein, the mantle of the World's Greatest Pianist next draped itself over the shoulders of the Polish Ignaz Paderewski. Paderewski became the most popular and highest-paid pianist in history up to that time, and the mystery to his colleagues was how he did it. He was not a great technician or a great musician in their estimation. But not since Liszt had a pianist so captured the public imagination, and certainly no pianist except Liszt had so captivated the women. Of course Paderewski, like Liszt, was handsome and magnetic; and, like Liszt, he came from an exotic, romantic part of the world. He exuded mystery and, his admirers thought, genius. He was everybody's dream of what a pianist should look like, and he cultivated the image.

And then there was Paderewski's glorious aureole of hair, reddish-blond, thick, and lustrous, falling to his shoulders. Naturally the image of Samson was evoked. In 1893 Paderewski gave a New York concert that he had to play with a disabled middle finger, and the *Spirit of the Times* wrote that it made no difference. "His admirers would have admired him just as much had he played with his toes. Like Samson, he depends for his effects not on his fingers but upon his hair." His concerts were largely filled with languishing, love-struck females; it was like a scene from *Patience,* with the lovesick maidens languishing over this pianistic Bunthorne. A newspaper reporter in 1899 described a Paderewski concert: "There I was, simply girled in. A huge and dominant gynarchy seethed around me. There were girls in short waists of silk and of flannel; there were girls in loose corsets and tight corsets. There were large and bouncing girls, and short and stubby ones. There were girls in hats and girls in bonnets. There were girls who wore wedding rings and girls who didn't. There were girls. . . ." An article in the March 1892 issue of *Munsey's* described the chain-smoking, insomniacal, highly nervous Paderewski and his effect on women: "From his feminine admirers he finds it impossible to escape. Nine tenths of the audience at an afternoon recital will invariably be of the fair sex. Hundreds of them will swarm around him when the performance is ended." Sometimes he was in actual danger. At a 1902 Carnegie Hall recital he was mobbed by hysterical women, losing a watch and chain given to him by the czar and valued at $1,000.

How much of this was spontaneous and how much engineered is a moot question. At the beginning, the imaginative hand of skilled publicity agents was employed. After that, nature took its course and Paderewski became the most idolized musician before the public. Paderewski was invited to the United States in 1891 by the Steinway piano firm, which still had fond memories of the 1872–73 Rubinstein tour. The idea was to add luster to the Steinway instrument. Paderewski played in the new Music Hall, later to be called Carnegie Hall, and Hugo Görlitz, his secretary and later business manager, was the one who thought up the Paderewski Crush. Görlitz gave fifty tickets at each concert to students, instructing them to run to the stage and cheer Paderewski after each performance. Whether or not Paderewski knew what his agent was doing, he himself had a secure sense of publicity. Alexander Greiner of the Steinway firm, in an unpublished memoir, says that Paderewski was a positive genius in that respect. Once, at a recital in a northwest city, a cab picked up Paderewski at his private railway car. The driver detoured to show Paderewski the sights of the city, for which the pianist tipped him $200. Of course this made the newspapers, and Paderewski got thousands of dollars of publicity for his $200. Greiner did not admire Paderewski very much; he wrote that Paderewski was an egomaniac who insisted on homage from everybody; that he was rotten, spoiled, and had a bad temper; that he took things out on underlings who were in no position to fight back.

What Paderewski accomplished pianistically, he did by sheer determination. He was born in Kuryłówka on November 6, 1860. His father, of an old but impoverished family, was of the gentry and was an administrator of estates; his mother died when he was young, and he was educated by tutors. Perhaps he had a major talent as a child. He was attracted to the piano as a baby and had lessons from local teachers. None of them was properly qualified, and as a result Paderewski grew up with ingrained bad pianistic habits. He never really overcame them. At the age of twelve he entered the Warsaw Conservatory, a boy full of musical ideas but without the technique to put them into effect. Nor was the faculty of the conservatory of much help. Paderewski made a few concert tours of Poland before his graduation in 1878, but did not make any kind of impression. He also started composing.

Some bad years followed. Paderewski married, only to see his wife die in childbirth. His son was born a cripple. He went to Berlin in 1882 and, listening to the music around him, discovered how little he really knew. He continued to slave at the keyboard, determined to become a real pianist. Some help came from friends interested in the handsome young man, among them the famous actress Helena Modjeska. Finally he went to Vienna to study with the great pedagogue Theodor Leschetizky. When Leschetizky heard him play he threw up his hands, stating that it was too late, too late. "Your fingers lack discipline! You do not know how to work!" Leschetizky took him on as a beginner, putting him on

The young Ignaz Paderewski. He became the most celebrated of all pianists by sheer willpower.

Czerny exercises. Thus Paderewski, in effect, did not really start studying the piano until he was twenty-two.

Paderewski worked with Leschetizky off and on for two years, going to Paris in 1888. His debut at the Erard salon was a success, and he was engaged by the Lamoureux Orchestra, where he played the Saint-Saëns C minor Piano Concerto. Offers began to come in. Paderewski had arrived in Paris with only one program and he worked like a maniac for three weeks to prepare another. His career started to gather momentum. There was something about the dashing, romantic young Pole and his obvious dedication to the keyboard that captivated audiences. Returning to Paris in 1890, he became the lover of the Princess Rachel de Brancovan. (He already had a mistress in Poland—Helena Gorska.) Paderewski was talked about as the coming pianist.

But not until London in 1890 did he become anointed. He made his debut at St. James's Hall and the first of his four announced concerts was a flop. Critics called him a banger. George Bernard Shaw complained about his rubato, which "goes beyond all reasonable bounds." His second concert attracted more attention and there was wild enthusiasm when he played his third. Shaw began to revise his opinion. Now Paderewski was "a spirited young harmonious blacksmith." It did not take Shaw long to admire him tremendously, and he ended by calling him the greatest living pianist. Women went crazy. London was the pre-Raphaelite center, and Paderewski looked as though he had stepped out of a pre-Raphaelite painting. The famous painter Edward Burne-Jones told everybody that an archangel had come to earth. Soon Paderewski became the rage of London and the pet of society.

He did not forget his teacher and kept Leschetizky up to date. A letter to Leschetizky from London, dated May 21, 1890, gives an idea of Paderewski's schedule. He tells his "dear master and friend" that the day after his first London concert he had to return to Paris for a benefit concert, then make an appearance at a private soirée, then return to London for his third concert, then go back to Paris for the Saint-Saëns Festival. "But that's nothing to what I have already done in Paris—four concerts of my own, the fifth a

Paderewski around 1890, the year of his London debut.

benefit, four others for charity, two Lamoureux concerts, two at the Conservatoire, concerts in different halls—in all, twenty-one public concerts." Paderewski says he had a huge success and that his four big concerts "have brought in the bountiful sum of 12,500 francs."

Then Paderewski pays homage to Leschetizky, attributing all the success to his teacher: "My heart fills over with gratitude." He says that his health is "absolutely deplorable"; that he doesn't eat, doesn't sleep, is tired. "It often happened to me that I practiced ten hours on the day of a concert. One doesn't do these things with impunity, but I believe just the same that I have a strong motive." He mentions the pianists currently in London—Sophie Menter, Helen Hopekirk, Franz Rummel, Vasilly Sapellnikov, Teresa Carreño, Bernhard Stavenhagen, Arthur Friedheim—"in a word, everybody." He did not think much of the famous Carreño. She had great sonority "for a woman" and a good mechanism; but "taste, spirit, finesse are absolutely missing." He mentions his forthcoming concert with orchestra, which he says is going to cost him a great deal. "The orchestra alone costs $500, but one has to do things well if they are to bring good results."

His tours started. On his return to London in 1891 he was commanding huge fees. But big as those fees were, they were nothing compared to what he was to make in America. To promote the Steinway piano he was promised $30,000 for eighty concerts in 1891. The $375 per concert was more than Rubinstein had made, but the fee was not particularly brilliant. Because of a clause in his contract that called for extra payment over a certain amount, Paderewski went home with $95,000. In 1891 that was enough for a man to live lavishly for the rest of his life. But the supermoney was to come in succeeding American tours. The success of the first tour was such that on his return Paderewski was able to charge ticket prices twice above that of any other musician. His second tour netted him $160,000, his third $248,000, and the American proceeds mounted steadily year after year. The Chicago *News* in 1896 was insulted by Paderewski's earnings. He had departed from the city with a profit of $10,000. "This is quite a tidy sum," fulminated the paper, "for a man who might rise to the dizzy heights of a ten-dollar clerkship if he were not a pianist with an aureole of hair that the ladies find irresistible. His American tour is estimated at a grand aggregate of $200,000, a sum which it would take 400 laborers an entire year to earn." As a matter of fact, the tour netted $280,000 for Paderewski. Make it 560 laborers at $500 a year. At the end of World War I, when Paderewski made his first tour after serving as Premier of Poland, he made some $500,000. And that was only in America. As early as 1907 a magazine estimated his 1906 income to be in the vicinity of $1.5 million. It must be said of Paderewski that he spent money as fast as he earned it.

On November 17, 1891, Paderewski made his American debut. With an orchestra conducted by Walter Damrosch he played the Saint-Saëns Fourth Concerto. Then followed with a group of Chopin solos and Paderewski's own A minor Concerto. The reviews were ecstatic. Three successive orchestral concerts followed. Between the second and the third, Paderewski practiced seventeen hours a day. Six solo recitals followed. New York went wild. Then Paderewski went on tour. In 117 days he played 107 concerts. No wonder he was exhausted. There was a major scare in Rochester during the tour. Paderewski developed a major hand problem. As recounted by Paderewski in the Adam Zamoyski biography,

> As usual, I struck two or three opening chords—when suddenly, something broke in my arm! A terrific pain—an agony—followed. I had the feeling that I must run from the platform, that I would never be able to play again. Of course, I mastered the feeling in a second, because I realized that it would be disastrous for me to do such a thing. But in such dreadful moments one sees everything black. I thought it was the end of everything—that my career was over, because something very serious, I knew, had happened to my arm. It became suddenly very stiff and the pain was indescribable. But somehow I held myself together and began the playing of Beethoven's *Appassionata*. How I got through it I shall never be able to tell you.

The problem was diagnosed as torn and strained tendons. The fourth finger of the right hand was useless. Paderewski was told to take a complete rest. Instead he continued with the tour, refingering everything to avoid the damaged digit, getting local doctors en route to massage the arm and otherwise do what they could. He believed that this would be his last chance to make a large sum from concertizing, and was prepared to go through with the tour no matter what the eventual cost. On his return to Paris he was told that the muscles were irretrievably damaged. He tried everything, and finally found a masseur who restored strength to the arm. Paderewski never was completely cured. In later years he had to cancel concerts and cut tours short because of neuritis or rheumatism.

His ailment cannot have helped his technique, but the international public could not have cared less. He was the symbol of great piano playing. Obviously something must have come through that his records do not suggest. Paderewski started recording shortly before 1910 and continued making records until shortly before his death. His total was about a hundred discs and some fifty piano rolls. When he started recording he was around fifty, an age when most pianists are in their prime. The records are disconcerting. Whatever the nobility of conception, it is handicapped by clumsy playing. Nor is this attributable to the acoustic (pre-electric) recording process. As a matter of fact, modern audio equipment at its best, with light-tracking tone arms, sensitive cartridges, and a variety of response curves in the preamplification circuits, can bring out things on acoustic discs that the makers never realized was on them. It is possible to get a very good idea from records of what such early recording pianists as Pachmann, Hofmann, Godowsky, Pugno, and Grainger represented. And singers, who focused directly into a horn, can sound glorious. There is a certain amount of surface noise even on mint copies of old discs, and a great deal of noise on badly used ones. But modern equipment can filter out much of the noise without interfering with the "flat response" of the records. That is, old records should be played flat, with the same linear characteristics that were put into them. Any attempt to reduce the surface noise with the high-frequency controls leads to loss of overtone and brilliance. That is why so many LP transfers of old records are nowhere near as faithful as the noisy originals. The transfers may be quieter, but they sound dull by comparison. In any case, the human ear is a remarkably discriminating instrument, and a listener intensely interested in the information on the disc invariably finds that the surface noise, so annoying at first, soon tends to be ignored.

What the Paderewski recordings indicate is a triumph of sheer application over mechanical limitations. The real effort in his playing is strongly noticeable. But a magnificent sound is suggested. Paderewski must have been able to produce an unbelievably rich sonority. As an interpreter, he was much more free in his use of rubato and tempo changes than most of his contemporaries. This is not guesswork. The records of his contemporaries—Rachmaninoff, Hofmann, Lhévinne, Rosenthal, Gabrilowitsch, and even the eccentric Pachmann (born in 1848)—have none of the stylistic idiosyncrasies of Paderewski's. Their playing was aristocratic and rhythmically flowing, surprisingly simple, with a certain amount of classic restraint, and altogether different from what constitutes today's accepted ideas about Romantic playing.

Very little is known today about Romantic piano performance practice. Many musicians have the idea that nineteenth-century piano playing is next to rhythmic and textual anarchy. The reverse is true; it was a highly controlled art, and the so-called liberties consisted mostly of delicate ritards and accelerandos, with a knowledge of how to handle a bass line and bring out the inner voices so carefully indicated by the composer. Paderewski may have been the one who gave Romantic piano playing a bad name; he was so famous and popular that his approach was often automatically equated with Romantic performance practice. But none of the other great pianists of the day played like him. Perhaps he indulged in his exaggerations as a cover-up for his technical limitations. It is not that Paderewski was entirely a keyboard cripple; but he was simply not in the same technical league as many of his illustrious colleagues.

Anyway, Paderewski returned to America in 1892 to start a life that no other pianist ever has matched, and only Patti among the singers. He traveled in his own railway car. It had a bedroom, sitting room, dining room, and grand piano. He traveled with his secretary, valet, chef, piano tuner, tour manager, and two porters. After 1899 there might also have been his wife; he married Gorska that year and she accompanied him on many of his tours. There was not a newspaper in America that did not print detailed, lip-smacking reports about the luxury of Paderewski's private car. In the meantime Steinway was sending pianos all over the country so that an instrument would be at the concert halls waiting for the great man to arrive.

At the turn of the century he was getting $3,000 for a concert. Not even Jean de Reszke could match his total earnings. Singers normally do not appear more than three times a week. Paderewski could play every night if he so wished. Of course he always played to full houses. His very name entered the language. "Paddymania" was coined to describe the furor he and his concerts created. As with Patti and Lind, various objects were named after him. There was Paderewski soap, Paderewski shampoo, and so on. He purchased a large estate in Poland (which he sold in 1903) and a villa in Switzerland on five hundred acres. It was there, during his summer vacations, that he did most of his composing. He also had a ranch in California. Wherever he went, he entertained lavishly. After 1896 his playing was not confined to Europe and America. He made world tours, traveling with his usual entourage and a hundred or so pieces of luggage. He spent as much time as he could in his beloved Swiss villa, Riod-Bosson. It would have been nice to have been at Paderewski's birthday party there in 1913. Among the guests were Leopold Stokowski and his wife, Olga Samaroff (a wonderful pianist), Rudolf Ganz, Josef Hofmann, and Ernest Schelling. The *pièce de résistance* was the *Blue Danube* Waltz played in ragtime style by Paderewski, Hofmann, Schelling, Ganz, and Stokowski, all squeezed together for a ten-hand performance.

Paderewski composed prolifically. Much to his dismay, his Minuet in G became his most popular work; he disliked it as much as Rachmaninoff detested *his* C sharp minor Prelude. Little of Paderewski's music has remained in the repertory. His opera *Manru* received some performances in the early years of the century and then disappeared outside Poland. His big Symphony in B minor has vanished. Nobody plays his Piano Sonata in E flat minor. Another ambitious work, the *Polish* Fantasy for Piano and Orchestra, held on for a while. It too has gone, though it is an ingenious piece and pianistically very effective. His A minor Piano Concerto is representative of such late Romantic virtuoso concertos as the Grieg A minor, and there are some fine moments in it. But it is considered far too old-fashioned to interest today's young keyboard lions. After 1917, though he lived another twenty-four years, Paderewski appears to have stopped composing.

When World War I came Paderewski took an active part in the Polish Relief movement. In 1915 he came to the United States and remained there during most of the war, giving many of the proceeds from his concerts to Poland, raising other money for his homeland, and working with President Wilson on the Polish problem. The Zamoyski biography goes into great detail about Paderewski's war work and his contributions after 1918 as Premier of Poland—and also the mistakes he made. His wife, the bossy Helena, made plenty of enemies for him by interfering in affairs of state. In 1919 Paderewski resigned as Premier and in 1922 returned to the piano. In 1928 he began to take pupils. Most of them were Poles, the most famous of whom was Witold Malcuzynski. Helena died in 1934. Paderewski continued to play long after he should have retired. At the outbreak of World War II he did his best to help Poland again. By that time he was almost senile. He died in New York on June 29, 1941.

Aspects of his character were not universally admired. Some called him anti-Semitic. Newspapers in 1913 carried stories about Paderewski and the Jews, and some Jewish groups accused him of anti-Semitism because of his association with the notorious Polish anti-Semite Roman Dmowski. Threatening letters were sent to him. But the Boston *American* on January 25, 1914, quoted Pade-

Paderewski in 1923. He had resumed his concert career the previous year, after serving as the Premier of Poland.

rewski as saying that some of his best friends were Jews. It appears, however, that there was a strong racist streak in the man. Normally he avoided talking about anything but music in his newspaper interviews, but a reporter for the New York *Tribune* on November 22, 1918, spoke with him in Poland and came away with Paderewski's invective against emigration to the United States. "All this foreign blood," said Paderewski, "is not wanted there. I should even say there is too much of it already. . . . They [the Americans] are spoiling their pure, rich Anglo-Saxon strain with a new vintage that comes from the waste products of the old world." And several provisions of his will show a streak of Polish anti-Semitism. Especially suggestive is Article F in a copy of the will translated by the wife of Sigismond Stojowski (one of Paderewski's pupils): "40,000 rubles to start economic associations to open little stores in villages to help fight Jews who mostly run these stores and refuse to be assimilated."

The influence of Paderewski on piano playing soon waned. After 1970 or thereabouts there was a sudden interest in Romanticism, with the avant-garde starting to look back to Mahler and Beethoven, and with young musicians beginning to look into nineteenth-century performance practice as illustrated by recordings of pianists and other musicians born before 1900. Paderewski interests them very little. Their magic names are Rachmaninoff, Lhévinne, Friedman, Hofmann, Moiseiwitsch. But if Paderewski does not live on for them, he still lives on in the memory of every concertgoer and, indeed, of the nonmusical public. The name has not been forgotten. To the great mass, Paderewski still means The Piano—which also means that the man had a magnetism, a charisma, a magic, an overwhelming stage presence that still makes him an object of mystery and veneration.

15 *Pablo de Sarasate, Eugène Ysaÿe, Jan Kubelík, and Fritz Kreisler*

A QUARTET OF VIOLINISTS

JOSEPH JOACHIM went through his long life serenely indifferent to competition. What did other violinists mean to *him*? He was the one with a mission, his closest friends were Bach, Beethoven, and Brahms, and a musician on such intimate terms with deities would necessarily have his head in the clouds. Mere mortals did not concern him very much. But midcourse in his career arrived Pablo de Sarasate; and later there were Eugène Ysaÿe, Jan Kubelík, and Fritz Kreisler. Each member of that quartet made a notable impression on violin playing and on the public. In 1910 Herman Klein, a critic who was with the New York *Herald* from 1902 to 1909, went home to England and, the following year, wrote a book, *Unmusical New York*. In it he mentioned that in all the world only a dozen artists were capable of selling out Carnegie Hall. Three of the dozen were violinists—Ysaÿe, Kubelík, and Kreisler. (The others were the singers Marcella Sembrich, Ernestine Schumann-Heink, Lillian Nordica,

Emma Eames, Johanna Gadski, and David Bispham; and the pianists Paderewski, Moriz Rosenthal, and Fannie Bloomfield-Zeisler.)

Sarasate would have been on the list had he not died in 1908. He always played to full houses. Part of his success stemmed from his physical presence: he was short but handsome, aristocratic-looking, careful of his dress and grooming, well-spoken, and utterly elegant. Fritz Kreisler's wife had a crush on him: she said that Sarasate was the greatest *grand seigneur* in musical history; that he looked like a grand duke with his gray hair and mustache dyed black. Everything was perfectly calculated for greatest effect. "When he had placed his violin under his chin and everybody thought he was about to start," Harriet Kreisler said, "he would drop it again, clamp a monocle into his eye and survey his audience. He had a way of seeming to drop his fiddle that would take the audience's breath away. That is, he would let it slide down his slender figure, only to catch it by the scroll of the neck just in time. It was a regular showman's trick of his."

With the showmanship came a fluent technique and what must have been one of the sweetest, most sensuous sounds in violinistic history. It was not the big, cellolike sound that Mischa Elman later was to produce; it was too refined for that. Rather it was all grace and suppleness, radiant in its purity and honeyed in its production. Leopold Auer, who knew as much about violin sound as anybody, described it as "a tone of supreme singing quality which, however, was not very powerful." His records bear this out. He recorded eight pieces around 1905, and each demonstrates his fluent technique and sensuous tonal characteristics. The American critic Peter Davis, reviewing a Sarasate reissue in 1984, marveled at the violinist's "feline, silky grace and polished verve" in the *Ziguenerweisen* and some of the Spanish dances. Sarasate was not in any way an important composer, but his Spanish pieces and a few others have very much remained in the repertory. Among his recordings, incidentally, is the first movement of Bach's Partita in E. It is interesting as an indication of the way virtuoso violinists used to approach the work: as a showpiece, played at a breathtaking tempo. Then compare it with the selfless, broad approach of Joachim in his recordings of the G minor Sonata movements.

No, Sarasate never had the powerful musical mind of a Joachim, and even in his day nobody ever thought so. Sarasate represented the elegant side of sheer virtuosity; and what a virtuoso he must have been! George Henschel first heard him at the Cologne Festival of 1877, playing the Mendelssohn Concerto. It was a performance that "came to German ears like something of a revelation, creating a veritable furore, and indeed I doubt if in lusciousness of tone, crystalline clearness of execution, refinement and grace, that performance ever has or ever will be surpassed." George Bernard Shaw also heard Sarasate in the Mendelssohn and decided that the violinist did not have a great brain. All music seemed to mean the same to him. "He never interpreted anything," wrote Shaw. "He is always alert, swift, clear, refined, certain, scrupulously attentive and quite unaffected." The Mendelssohn must have been the perfect vehicle for Sarasate; it has the elegance that matched his kind of musical mind. The fine American violinist Albert Spalding once remarked that Sarasate "made trivial music sound important and deep music sound trivial." Flesch, sneeringly, wrote that "In intellectual respects Sarasate was in the lower income brackets." There probably was some truth in the assessment. But if he was not profound he was, as Henry E. Krehbiel wrote on the occasion of Sarasate's visit to the United States in the 1888–89 season, "a most lovable wizard." Hans von Bülow summed him up as well as anybody. He spoke about Sarasate's "seductive speaking on the violin," and said that it was silly to compare Sarasate and Joachim. "Joachim plays like a god—but Sarasate plays like an angel, or like an archangel."

Sarasate was born in Pamplona on March 11, 1844, and went through the usual prodigy process, playing at five and making his debut at eight. He attracted such attention in Spain that Queen Isabella sent him to the Paris Conservatoire in 1856. There he studied under the famous violinist-pedagogue Delphin Alard, winning every prize in sight. In 1859 he started concertizing, and

Pablo de Sarasate, painted as a young man by Felix Moscheles (the son of the great pianist Ignaz Moscheles), and in a photograph taken around 1900.

his tours took him all over the world. He was the highest-paid violinist before the public, getting as much as $1,000 for a concert. Joachim seldom reached that figure. It was a measure of Sarasate's popularity that so many composers rushed to write major works dedicated to him, hoping that the great Sarasate would make them known. Among the composers were Bruch, Saint-Saëns, Lalo, Wieniawski, Dvořák, and even Joachim himself. Some of these pieces first played by him, such as Lalo's *Symphonie espagnole* and the Bruch G minor Concerto, remained repertory items. Sarasate died in Biarritz on September 20, 1908. He never married. The story was that the woman he loved married somebody else. In Sarasate's last years he was something of an anachronism, and Ysaÿe was the violinist who captured the public and professional admiration.

At the height of his career Sarasate was, as Flesch said, a great name. And more: Sarasate, in the opinion of Flesch, had real contributions to make to the art of violin playing. The great German expert quoted Ysaÿe, who once told him Sarasate had taught all violinists "to play exactly." From Sarasate, Flesch said,

> dates the modern striving after technical precision and reliability, whereas before him a somewhat facile fluency and brilliance were considered the most important thing. . . . With the precise and effortless function of both of his arms, he represented a completely new type of violinist. The fingertips of his left hand were quite smooth and ungrooved; they hit the fingerboard in a normal fashion, without excessive raising or hammering. His vibrato was rather broader than had hitherto been customary. . . . Sarasate's effect on his audiences depended, in the first place, on the complete lack of friction in his tone production, a circumstance which today [1931], in the age of a Heifetz, would hardly impress us so strongly, but which then, when listeners were still used to "scraping fiddlers," was regarded as absolutely unique. . . . It goes without saying that the last movement of the Mendelssohn Concerto came from his bow in a multicolored pyrotechnic display. . . . As an interpreter of the Beethoven Violin Concerto, on the other hand, he was impossible.

Hidden from the public was Sarasate's love for chamber music. Whenever possible he would join a string quartet for a quiet evening, reveling especially in Beethoven. But, Flesch says, he approached the music timidly, with the "shy respect" that Romantic musicians then had for the classics. His chamber-music playing was "scrupulous and musical, but dry and lacking in imagination." Flesch blew hot and cold about Sarasate. The Lord giveth and the Lord taketh away. But in his memoirs Flesch presented a graceful and appreciative summing-up of Sarasate's contributions to the history of violin playing: "When all is said and done, however, he remains one of the greatest and most individual figures of the nineteenth century, the ideal embodiment of the salon virtuoso of the greatest style; the history of violin playing cannot be imagined without him."

Flesch's remark about Sarasate's vibrato is interesting. There is not much of a scholarly literature on violin vibrato, the "trembling" of the fingers on the string to add color and variety to the sound. In the classic period vibrato was used only for special effects. But even in the 1750's, there apparently were violinists who used a continuous vibrato. Leopold Mozart, Wolfgang's father, fulminated against them in his famous book on violin playing. It is hard to figure out how much vibrato was used in the nineteenth century by Paganini and his successors. Some experts flatly state that not until Sarasate and Ysaÿe did concert violinists use a continuous vibrato. But we simply do not know.

Ysaÿe vibrated continuously, as can be heard on his many records. The young Flesch and all of his generation were influenced by him; and when, many years later, Flesch wrote his memoirs, he flatly said that Ysaÿe was to them a "revelation" and "the most outstanding and individual violinist I have heard in all my life." And the young Kreisler said that Ysaÿe, and not Joachim, was his musical idol. The great French violinist Jacques Thibaud doffed his hat, saying, "It was thanks to him that in the art of violin playing the spirit of freedom was revived—not of anarchism, but of a freedom based on the deepest love for art in the broadest sense of the word."

The young Ysaÿe in 1893 drawing by W. Berteaux, and, about fifteen years later, the obese Ysaÿe as he remained to the end of his life.

There have been an Italian, a French, a German, a Russian, and a Belgian school of violin playing. Ovide Musin, a highly regarded Belgian violinist at the turn of the century, once wrote a capsule outline of the Belgian school. It was started by de Bériot, who taught Vieuxtemps, who taught Ysaÿe and Jenö Hubay. Another Belgian violinist-teacher, Lambert Massart, taught Wieniawski, Camilla Urso, and Kreisler. Still another, Hubert Léonard, was the teacher of Martin Marsick, César Thomson, Henri Marteau, and Musin. Marsick taught Jacques Thibaud and Carl Flesch. Thomson taught Adolf Betti and Alfred Pochon. Ysaÿe himself taught several talented young people who went on to distinguished careers as teachers—among them Lea Luboschutz, Louis Persinger, and Joseph Gingold.

Ysaÿe carried the Belgian school to its greatest height. Yet he had an unusually short career. He was born in Liège on July 16, 1858. At four he was studying with his father, and at the Liège Conservatory he worked with Rodolphe Massart, a then-famous violinist and one of the founders of the Belgian school of violin playing (and the nephew of the equally famous Lambert Massart at the Paris Conservatoire). From 1874 to 1879 Ysaÿe studied with Vieuxtemps and then started his concert career. After 1881 he spent much time in Paris, where he became friendly with French composers and specialized in their music. He was the first great exponent of the Franck Sonata, the Debussy Sonata, and the Chausson *Poème* (all dedicated to him). He also played many chamber-music recitals with Raoul Pugno, the finest French pianist of the time. Both were exceedingly heavy men, and it was said that the stage would buckle when the two behemoths walked upon it.

After 1910 Ysaÿe began to experience physical problems, including a tremor in his bow arm and a loss of response in his left hand. His playing deteriorated fast. Flesch always maintained that the basic trouble stemmed from Ysaÿe's faulty grip on the bow, which finally led to a complete loss of stability. When Ysaÿe's technique started to go, around 1912, he turned to conducting, and from 1918 to 1922 was the director of the Cincinnati Symphony

Orchestra. He had fled to the United States in 1915 after the German invasion of Belgium and spent the war there. His wife died in 1924 and he married Jeannette Dincin, an American pupil. He was seventy, she twenty-four. His recitals after 1922 were weak; he suffered from heart trouble and diabetes, and had to have a foot amputated. He died in Brussels on May 12, 1931.

But from about 1890 to 1910 he was, in the eyes of his colleagues, *the* violinist. To many he still is. Isaac Stern considers him the greatest violinist (Stern plays the Guarnerius that Ysaÿe owned). When Ysaÿe appeared, Joachim and Sarasate were the two most important violinists, and they were antipodal: Joachim was all music, Sarasate all technique. Along came Ysaÿe to make a fusion of the two styles. He had all of Sarasate's technique, and he had Joachim's quality of complete musical immersion. He was a Romantic, with a concentrated quality of expression, and he could take liberties with the music, but he had such inner strength and such conviction that he carried everybody along with him. Scholars call him the real founder of twentieth-century violin playing.

For a while Jan Kubelík gave Ysaÿe some strong competition. Up to the beginning of World War I, Kubelík was probably the most popular violinist on the circuit. Born on July 5, 1880, in Michle, near Prague, he was a prodigy who studied with Otakar Ševčík at the Prague Conservatory. In 1898 he started touring and was immediately hailed as a second Paganini. He had a brilliant technique that he was never bashful to display, and he would toss off the most incredibly difficult things with the ease of a shark engorging a minnow. He came by this technique through hard work; it is said of him that as a student he would practice twelve hours a day to the point where his fingers bled.

But although he had a career that lasted forty years, his staying power was not markedly pronounced. For about ten years he was at the top, and then there was a precipitate drop. There were musical reasons for this. Audiences, at first startled and enthusiastic over Kubelík's amazing feats, could hear them just so many times. Then boredom set in. There simply was not enough *music* to be heard. In addition there appeared to be physical problems.

Jan Kubelík, who briefly set the world on fire and then disappeared. Audiences grew bored with his technical stunts.

Flesch says that even before Kubelík was thirty "there were clear indications of a decline." His tone became dry, his technique began to break down, and his unpolished interpretations, which had been attributed to youth, "proved to be a lack of musical culture." Musicians wondered about so sudden a collapse. To Flesch the reasons were simple. Kubelík, a talent of the highest calibre, was driven by an intense urge to perfection. But his virtually unprecedented precision was coupled to "a defective practicing hygiene . . . resulting in an atrophy of elemental feeling"; and, in addition, "a disregard of purely musical thought in favor of a perfect but lifeless, soulless mechanization of the playing elements." It was a major tragedy, Flesch concluded, that Kubelík never succeeded in escaping from the blind alley in which he found himself.

With Ysaÿe and Kubelík on the decline, Fritz Kreisler from Vienna became acknowledged as the world's top violinist around the time of World War I, although some new Russians, especially Mischa Elman and Efrem Zimbalist, were coming up fast. When Jascha Heifetz entered the arena, he and Kreisler more or less shared the top honors, though with a difference. The inhumanly perfect Heifetz ruled by might of bow arm and fingers. But nobody ever *loved* the cool, remote, antisocial Jascha Heifetz. Fritz Kreisler was genuinely beloved by all. The man had no enemies. He was great in all departments—as violinist, as all-around musician, as composer, as human being. He was a generous man, a genuinely aristocratic democrat, a wonderful colleague, a gentleman of the world, a patrician admired by all.

He was, of course, a prodigy, but it took him some time to reach the top. He was born in Vienna on February 2, 1875, and at four was studying the violin with his father, who was a medical man and a great music lover. The Vienna Conservatory accepted Fritz when he was seven, and he won the gold medal at ten. At the conservatory his theory teacher was Anton Bruckner. Sent to the Paris Conservatoire, Fritz worked with Lambert Massart and left in 1887, sharing the first violin prize. He also became a splendid pianist. After leaving the conservatory at the age of twelve, Kreisler never had further musical instruction of any kind. At thirteen he made his first American tour, sharing the program with the pianist Moriz Rosenthal, a highly touted Liszt pupil. Kreisler's contract called for $50 a performance, with a guarantee of fifty performances. Rosenthal, who went on to a major career, attracted all of the attention. Kreisler was scarcely mentioned.

For the next ten years little was heard of the young violinist. He seemed content to live a carefree life in Vienna, desultorily attending medical school and completing his military service. He apparently never even practiced the violin; but, then again, he never practiced in later life either. It never seemed to be necessary. All he had to do was play a piece several times, and he had it for life. His dear friend Rachmaninoff once said, perhaps a bit sourly, that Kreisler gave so many concerts he did not have to practice. At his height Kreisler maintained an enormous schedule. One year he gave 260 concerts. In October 1912 he gave thirty-two concerts in thirty-one days in the United States. Kreisler defended his lack of practicing by saying that if one worked correctly in his youth, the fingers would always retain their suppleness. It worked for him at least. One time in Tokyo he was asked to play a large group of sonatas he had not touched for years. His accompanist, Michael Raucheisen, has written that all Kreisler needed was one rehearsal. Kreisler went on stage "and played the sonatas, which he had not had in his repertory for many years, by heart, without a single flaw in memory."

Fortunately for the cause of violin playing, Kreisler took up the fiddle again in 1896 and, with his Berlin appearance under the baton of Arthur Nikisch in 1899, became a strong force. Aside from the rave reviews, the usual word of mouth operated. Ysaÿe was in the audience and after the concert ran around telling every violinist he met about Kreisler; and they passed on Ysaÿe's praise. The easygoing Kreisler seemed to be in no rush to make a major career. He even thought about playing in an orchestra. He took everything that came his way, never argued about his fee, and lived the life of a gay bachelor.

Things changed after his marriage in 1902 to an American, Harriet Lies. She was not the most popular woman around, and most thought her a shrew. Certainly she always said exactly what was on her mind, sometimes to her husband's discomfiture. As late as 1944, when Kreisler was all but canonized, Harriet gave an interview to the New York *World-Telegram.* She said that Fritz wasn't the sweet man everybody thought he was. "He isn't at all, and not only that. He's around the house all the time. Most women's husbands go to the office from nine to five every day." She said that Fritz was lazy and had to be nagged into practicing. He would be a marvelous musician, she said, if only he practiced. But if there was general dislike of Harriet, it also was conceded by all—including her husband—that she brought him into line. She forced him to work. She saw to it that he did not work for nothing, and his fees became legendary. In 1900 Kreisler was earning close to $3,000 a year, and happy about it. With Harriet on the scene, his fees started to mount—$300 a concert, then $500, then $1,000. In the 1920's he was the most highly paid violinist of all, Heifetz included, and was receiving $3,000 a concert. In addition he was making a fortune from his recordings, of which he made hundreds. One of the earliest instrumentalists to record, Kreisler was represented on records as early as 1903. He lived to see electrical recordings, which were introduced in 1925, and for the new process he could be heard in his sonata and concerto repertory. His recording contract with Victor in 1925 guaranteed him $750,000 within a five-year period.

Thus Kreisler could afford to indulge himself in his hobbies. Where Sarasate collected snuffboxes and walking sticks, Kreisler went in for violins and rare books, building up a very valuable collection of instruments and incunabula. Normally he played a Guarnerius in his concerts, but would occasionally switch to other violins. He owned a Gagliano, a Stradivarius that he purchased for $4,000 and grew to dislike, the Hart Guarnerius, the Hill Guarnerius, the Greville Stradivarius, the Lord Amherst of Hackney Stradivarius, the Earl of Plymouth Stradivarius, a Bergonzi, and a dozen or so other fine instruments that he picked up and sold. Unlike most violinists, he switched around. He believed that the Stradivarius was fine for small hands, while the Guarnerius had a bigger sound. He might play the Gagliano or Stradivarius in small halls, but he invariably used his Guarnerius for big ones. Kreisler maintained that he had terrible hands for a violinist. He told an interviewer, on his eighty-fifth birthday, that the little finger of his left hand was so weak that he had to refinger everything. In 1946 he started to break up his collection. That year he sold the Plymouth Strad to the American violinist Dorothea Powers, and the Lord Amherst to Jacques Gordon, the leader of the Gordon Quartet. In 1952 he gave his Guarnerius to the Library of Congress. Previously, in 1949, he had donated his collection of books and incunabula to the Golden Rule Foundation and to Lenox Hill Hospital, each of which realized $100,000 from the sale.

Year in and year out, Kreisler seemed to get more and more polish into his playing. Audiences could not get enough of this dignified man and his relaxed stage manner. He never seemed to have stage fright, never seemed to be bothered by anything. His playing had extreme finish and elegance, beauty of sound, and a warm, natural, aristocratic approach that seemed to encompass all styles except the music of his own time. Kreisler was an outspoken conservative. He played the world premiere of the Elgar Concerto in 1910, but that was exceptional. Unlike Ysaÿe and Sarasate, he did not ally himself with composers or their schools. He scornfully dismissed "the modernists, the cubists, the vorticists, and other offshoots of the new movement," admitting that the new men spoke a language different from that he had learned.

When he was not engaged in solo work he was playing chamber music, which he loved. In the United States in his early years he appeared in trios along with Josef Hofmann and the cellist Jean Gérardy, and in later years could be heard with Harold Bauer and Pablo Casals. One would give a great deal to have been able to eavesdrop on Kreisler's summers in Paris before World War I. He, Ysaÿe, Thibaud, Casals, and Pugno would go through the chamber-music literature. Both Ysaÿe and Kreisler liked to play the viola. The group would meet for lunch at Thibaud's quarters, play, break for dinner, and resume playing until 4 A.M. All the players except Casals and Pugno would switch instruments. Other

Fritz Kreisler gave trio concerts in the United States with the pianist Josef Hofmann (left) and the cellist Jean Gérardy (center).

musicians would be present, participating, page-turning, or cheering the heroes on. The Romanian violinist-pianist-conductor-composer Georges Enesco was a frequent visitor.

Until the outbreak of World War I, Kreisler lived in Berlin. He was called into service by the Austrian army as a lieutenant, saw active duty, and was wounded in the leg. He wrote a short book about his experiences. Demobilized as a captain in August 1914, he went to the United States and spent the war years there. At first he was received as fervidly as he always had been. But soon anti-German sentiment made itself felt, Kreisler was attacked, and when America entered the war Kreisler was forced off the stage. The Daughters of the American Revolution put him on their blacklist, and he had to cancel many concerts. Kreisler put out a dignified position paper, but there was still a great deal of fuss, and Kreisler withdrew from the concert stage toward the end of 1917 "because of bitter attacks that have been made on me as an Austrian and because at the outbreak of the war I fought as an officer of the Austrian army at the Russian front." To amuse himself he wrote an operetta, *Apple Blossoms,* which ran for a year on Broadway after it opened in 1919. In a *New York Times* interview Kreisler was quoted as saying, "I'm crazy about light music. I adore waltzes and have always wanted to write them." He went on to say that he composed the operetta to take his mind off the war. "It was the one thing that saved me. In seeking to write songs which should amuse people and make them happy, if only for a moment, I found I could forget myself." It is not generally known that Victor Jacobi composed half of the music for *Apple Blossoms.* Kreisler was to compose another operetta, *Sissy, the Rose from Bavaria Land,* which had its premiere in Vienna in 1933.

His return to concertizing in 1919 was a triumph, even though the American Legion tried to keep him off the stage. Soon his international career was in full swing again. As early as 1933 he took a firm stand against the Nazi movement and refused to play in Germany. Germany retaliated by banning all sales of his music. Kreisler became a French citizen in 1939. He spent World War II in the United States, giving many benefit concerts for the war effort and raising much money, and became an American citizen in 1943. The following year, at the age of seventy, he made his first radio broadcast. Like Rachmaninoff, he had refused to go on the air. But unlike Rachmaninoff, he relented and was to make many broadcasts before his retirement in 1950. Perhaps the size of the fee was the deciding factor. Kreisler was to get $5,000 for each of his five Bell Telephone broadcasts. But in those years, alas, his playing had started to slip. His retirement was hastened by an accident in 1941. Crossing the street, he was hit by a panel truck and rushed to the hospital with a fractured skull and internal injuries. He was unconscious for several days, and when he recovered, it was found he had a rare form of amnesia, during which he spoke only Latin and Greek. There were anxious moments until the day came when he picked up his violin and found he could still play. But surely the accident set him severely back. That, plus deterioration of hearing and a sight impairment, led to a near-collapse of his playing. He should have stopped then, but he could not keep off the stage. His last Carnegie Hall concert, in 1947, was sad; the hall was only half-filled and the poor old man struggled in vain to recapture his old glories. After three more years Kreisler finally called it quits, playing on a Bell Telephone broadcast for the last time. He died in New York on January 29, 1962, a few days short of his eighty-seventh birthday. His wife died the following year, at the age of ninety-three.

In 1935 the great scandal over his "forgeries" erupted. Through the years Kreisler had been playing certain works by classic and baroque composers, and everybody loved them. Kreisler claimed that he had discovered the music "in an old convent in the south of France." In reality he himself was the composer. While Kreisler was on a South American tour in 1935, Olin Downes, the critic of *The New York Times,* broke the true story. Downes had been trying to find the original of one of the Kreisler adaptations—specifically, the Praeludium and Allegro by Pugnani. Not surprisingly, he couldn't. He got in touch with Kreisler, and the hoax was revealed to the world. It was a great story, and there were very red critical faces. Ernest Newman, the esteemed critic of

Kreisler and his wife, Harriet, in 1932.

the London Sunday *Times,* had a fit and made great noises about the ethics of the situation. Kreisler answered with a letter defending his position. Newman came back with a savage attack, accusing Kreisler of being, in effect, a liar: "*You* gave the public to understand that what you had done was to operate upon an *original manuscript* by some famous composer or other when as a matter of fact *there was no such manuscript*. . . ." Downes, who also had been taken in, was amused. *The New York Times* hastened to print a bylined piece by Kreisler on February 18, 1935. Kreisler said that he had not written the music to deceive the experts and the public. "I wrote the pieces in question when I was quite a young artist with no other object in mind than to enrich my concert programs. Tact and modesty kept me from repeating my name endlessly in these programs as a composer." As a matter of fact Kreisler as early as 1910 had suggested to his publisher that the pieces be printed in his own name. His publisher, Carl Fischer, would not do it. It was a matter of business, explained William Kritsch, a Fischer executive, in 1935. "Heifetz, Zimbalist, everybody—all of them played them," said Kritsch. "And all of them, Zimbalist, Heifetz and the rest, thought they were the works of Pugnani, Francoeur, Padre Martini, Stamitz, Vivaldi, Porpora, Couperin and Dittersdorf. And they wouldn't have played them so often if they knew they were Kreisler's." Today it is hard to see how anybody could have been deceived. But the period before World War II was not a strong musicological age, very little was known about baroque music, and the skillful Kreisler created works that had all the surface characteristics of the period.

As for Kreisler the "real" composer, he left a series of lovely salon pieces—*Schön Rosmarin, Caprice Viennois, Liebesfreud, Liebesleid,* and the like—that immediately entered the repertory. During the serious dodecaphonic and serial period after 1945 they were rather disdainfully ignored by the younger generation of violinists, but in recent years they have returned, and all violinists eagerly rush to make recordings of these bonbons. They are elegant, tuneful, and beautifully written. Kreisler himself recorded most of them, with his inimitable grace and charm.

Charm was indeed one of the basic qualities of his playing. Flesch has described the Kreisler technique, which was one followed by no other violinist. Even in the 1880's, Flesch says, Kreisler did not use a wrist vibrato but rather a finger vibrato in which the pitch oscillated hardly at all. If Ysaÿe had been the first to use a broader vibrato than customary, Kreisler was the first to use a continuous vibrato, which meant a correspondingly increased intensity of expression. His bowing was entirely his own, too. He did not use the entire bow, as all previous violinists had done; he used only the middle of the bow. Then there was the unique Kreisler sound—"unmistakable, incomparable and unequalled"; and the steady Kreisler rhythm; and the Viennese charm that permeated his performances, complete with a portamento (sliding from note to note) that violinists today would never think of using.

All surrendered to the Kreisler charm, even the severe German violinists, who were a bit uncomfortable in the presence of such tonal luxury and relaxed music-making. Flesch was one; he described Kreisler's long phrases as "an unrestrained orgy of sinfully seductive sounds, depravedly fascinating, whose sole driving force appeared to be a sensuality intensified to the point of frenzy." Listening to the Kreisler recordings, it is difficult to see where Kreisler was so sinful; but that was how he impressed some of his colleagues. As a good musician Kreisler, after all, did know something about musical architecture, and he was able to bring out the relationships within any work he played, even though the emphasis was on beauty of sound and the delicate rubatos that were so uniquely his own. He also could do certain things that no other violinists could begin to bring off. A few New York listeners with long memories may remember a Carnegie Hall performance of the Brahms Concerto with the Philadelphia Orchestra in the 1930's. Kreisler played the cadenza (his own, rather than Joachim's) and at the end, just before the entrance of the orchestra, he bowed in a manner that flooded the hall with glorious sound. It was a sound that did not appear to come from the stage, and listeners looked around to see where the other violinist was. The effect was sheer magic, one of the unforgettable musical experiences of a lifetime. But there were moments like that at every Kreisler appearance.

One of the prettiest stories in music has to do with a Kreisler-Rachmaninoff concert. The two great musicians adored each other and, when their schedules permitted, gave concerts for charity. (They recorded several pieces, too, including the Grieg C minor Sonata, the Beethoven *Kreutzer,* and the Schubert Duo.) The story goes that during one of these affairs Kreisler lost his place during the *Kreutzer.* He desperately started to improvise or, as violinists say, noodle. Rachmaninoff was so amused that he refused to help his friend. He anticipated every Kreisler noodle and went along with him. In desperation, Kreisler sidled up to Rachmaninoff while noodling.

"For God's sake, Sergei, where am I?" he whispered.

"In Carnegie Hall," Rachmaninoff whispered back.

When Kreisler was a very old man he was told this story by a young interviewer, who asked him if it were true. Kreisler howled with laughter. He said it was the funniest thing he had ever heard. But, he said, it was not true. First of all, he and Rachmaninoff always took over the Metropolitan Opera for their charity performances. And, second of all, "I *never* lost my place in the *Kreutzer,"* Kreisler said, drawing himself up.

16 *Nellie Melba*

THE SINGING MACHINE

MATHILDE MARCHESI, formerly a singer herself, hung out a shingle as a teacher, with stupendous results. Among her pupils were Ilma di Murska, Gabrielle Krauss, Emma Eames, Etelka Gerster, and Emma Nevada—great singers all. From the Marchesi studio also came Suzanne Adams and Emma Calvé, the latter considered the all-time great Carmen. Marchesi trained Rosa Papier, who went straight from Marchesi to the Vienna Opera as Amneris, and who soon ruined her voice by pushing it to heavy soprano roles. Marchesi trained the great Clementine Proska, a coloratura soprano who was content to remain in Dresden for thirty years and thus never became an international superstar. Another Marchesi pupil was the meteoric Sybil Sanderson, of the incredible high notes in full voice. Frances Alda, who so distinguished herself at the Metropolitan Opera, was still another Marchesi pupil.

But the greatest of them all was Nellie Melba, the exemplar of the Marchesi method. Marchesi regarded the singing voice as an instrument, to be produced from lowest to highest note without a break in register, with perfect freedom, and with little vibrato. All of the Marchesi pupils produced this kind of rather white-voiced sound, but Melba produced it better than anybody else. She was *the* soprano after Patti—the one considered, and rightly so, the most phenomenally flawless technician before the public. And Dame Nellie fully agreed. She had no illusions about herself. She told a reporter in 1919, "There is no Anno Domini in art. I have the voice of a genius. Then why should I not always sing beautifully as long as I take care of it and do not forget what I have been taught? Why should I not sing for a thousand years?" At the Metropolitan Opera she told the press, "I know I have the most beautiful voice in the world, and as long as I know that, I will continue to sing." From the beginning she had that kind of confidence in herself. As a still untried singer in London, before she went to Marchesi, she listened to such stars as Emma Albani and Christine Nilsson, and said she could sing better than the former and as well as the latter. The only singer who really impressed her was Patti. "I shall try to do as well as that," Melba said.

She became the archetype of the prima donna—rich, spoiled, outspoken, jealous of competition. She defended her territory and would not let anybody enter into it without a royal fight. Nobody could call her a good colleague, and she was full of naughty tricks. She attended a *Bohème* performance at Covent Garden in 1903 and, from her box, sang the high B at the end of Musetta's waltz. Fritzi Scheff was the Musetta. When the curtain fell Scheff, who had not been amused, went into hysterics and was unable to continue the performance. Melba was always feuding with singers. She never got along with John McCormack. She kept Titta Ruffo out of her *Rigoletto* cast, not liking the competition of his glorious baritone. Her excuse was that he was too young for the title role. The story goes that some years later Melba asked Ruffo to sing with her in *Hamlet*. "Tell Melba," Ruffo said, "that she is too old to sing with me." At least, that is how Ruffo tells the story. Melba kept Selma Kurz of the Vienna Opera, a potential rival, out of

Covent Garden. When Melba heard that the promising Frances Alda had been offered a Metropolitan Opera contract, she wired New York: "Either Alda or myself." Alda did get into the Metropolitan—in 1908—only after Melba deserted the house for the Hammerstein opera. Some years later Melba was asked what she thought of Alda. "In *my* day she might have been good enough for the chorus."

Melba was a holy terror. Her accompanist, Landon Ronald, said that one of Melba's marked characteristics was her bluntness. That was putting it mildly. In the 1890's Melba appeared with Mary Garden and others at a command performance in Windsor Castle. Garden was then a young, promising singer, a brainy and beautiful girl who was picked by Debussy as his Mélisande in 1902 and went on to a fabulous career. During dinner at the castle Melba turned to Lord Farquhar, the Court Chamberlain, and loudly said, "What a dreadful concert this would have been if I hadn't come." All eyes turned to Garden, who quietly said, "I love Melba's rudeness. It amuses me."

For a section of the world so remote, Australia has produced some remarkable artists, from Melba and the dramatic soprano Florence Austral to the pianists Percy Grainger and Ernest Hutcheson, the baritone John Brownlee and so to Joan Sutherland. Nellie Melba was born in Melbourne on May 19, 1861 (and returned to Australia to die there). Melba was her stage name. She was born Helen Porter Mitchell. Like Patti, she was a natural singer as a child. She started serious vocal studies with Pietro Cecchi, who had been an operatic tenor in Europe. He knew what kind of talent the girl had and predicted a great career for her. She also proved to be a fine musician, becoming proficient on the piano, organ, and violin. When she was twenty-one Nellie married a dashing man named Charles Armstrong, and the result was a clash of two egocentric, stubborn people. They had a boy. Deciding to be a singer Nellie went to Europe in 1886, stayed in London for a while, and then sang for Marchesi.

In Melba's autobiography she says that when Marchesi heard her voice she rushed to her husband saying she had found a star.

Nellie Melba, around the time of her Covent Garden success in 1889. She became the archetype of the prima donna in the post-Patti period.

Perhaps the story is even true. In the Marchesi studios Melba met the musical elite of Paris. Marchesi's reputation was such that managers and composers from all over came to hear her students; and when Marchesi told them that a singer was ready, that singer would be offered a contract. Most singers worked with Marchesi for several years. Melba was there less than a year before Marchesi arranged for her debut, in 1887 at the Théâtre Royale de la Monnaie in Brussels. Her debut role was Gilda. At that time she dropped her married name and called herself Melba. She and her husband were no longer living together; the marriage was over, though there was no divorce for thirteen years.

Melba was successful in Brussels, but much less so when she sang at Covent Garden the following season. Not until 1889 did she conquer London. That was in a performance of Gounod's *Roméo et Juliette* with Jean de Reszke as her lover. For the next forty years Nellie Melba was the reigning queen of Covent Garden—and any other opera house in which she sang. It was fitting that the Gounod opera be the work that made her famous. She loved the work, sang it throughout her career, and it also was the opera in which she heard two great singers who were to inspire her. After her Brussels debut Melba had heard de Reszke and Patti as Romeo and Juliet and was swept away, as all were. Patti had always been her goddess; she had "the most golden voice to which I had ever listened . . . I took my lesson from her, and she had much to teach." As for de Reszke, with whom she sang many times, "He was a god." At a *Lohengrin* performance in which Melba was his Elsa, she was so moved by his singing that she burst into tears during the last act.

Through the years there was very little deterioration in Melba's voice except toward the very end, and what Londoners heard in 1889 was pretty much what they heard for the next thirty-five years. She had a pure, clear, large-sized soprano that went from low B flat to F above high C. It was a cool voice, perfectly produced, seamless in its scale. Her chromatic runs, leaps, gruppetti, staccati, and arpeggios were models of precision. Her trill was fast, even, and always on pitch. George Bernard Shaw admired her accurate intonation: "You never realize how wide a gap there is between the ordinary singer who simply avoids the fault of singing obviously out of tune and the singer who sings really in tune, except when Melba is singing." What Melba had that none could duplicate was a kind of frozen perfection in which *every* vocal problem was nonexistent. The woman was a singing machine. Probably not even Patti had this kind of sheer mastery, though Patti's voice was a much warmer instrument. Melba once admitted that "my voice is like a glorified boy's voice." Connoisseurs and colleagues wondered how she did it. Even her teacher confessed to wonderment. Melba, wrote Marchesi, was without a rival on the lyric stage. "As a vocalist, she more resembles a bird than a human creature, and it is impossible to conceive anything more musical or more flexible than her marvellous voice, which is always as clear as a silver bell." Yet some found the voice curiously sexless and even boring. To Ernest Newman, Melba was "uninterestingly perfect and perfectly uninteresting." Modern criticism has a tendency to support Newman's view. Melba never really sang as though the music had much *meaning,* and while her phrasing and style always were correct, it was all curiously impersonal. Take her recording of *Depuis le jour* from Charpentier's *Louise.* It is sung in an absolutely even manner, all difficulties triumphantly resolved, but none of the music's rapture is suggested. The same is true of most of her other records. But nobody could deny the technical mastery that went into her singing, and that alone, on so exalted a level, can be its own esthetic reward.

Her rivals paid homage. Jean de Reszke wrote, in a letter to her, "Nature has given you a voice of gold, positively the most beautiful of our time." Said Calvé to Melba, *"Comme un ange vouz chantez avec votre voix divine."* Mary Garden was overwhelmed by her vocalism in *La Bohème:* "My God! How she sang it!" The high C at the end of the first act was "the strangest and weirdest thing I ever experienced in my life. The voice came floating over the auditorium of Covent Garden: it left Melba's body, it left everything, and came over like a star, and passed us in our box, and went out into the infinite. I have never heard anything like it in my life, not from any other singer, ever." Melba made everything sound *so* easy. W. J. Henderson, the famous New York critic, was stunned by Melba's ease. She never gave the impression that she was preparing to sing. "She opened her mouth and a tone was in existence. It began without any betrayal of breathing; it simply was there."

About her only limitation on the stage was acting. Melba was a woman of ample proportions who barely went through the motions of acting, if that. "I never saw such a fat Mimi in my life," said Mary Garden, adding that Melba looked no more like Mimi than the contralto Schumann-Heink did—and no singer had the girth of the fair Ernestine. (Schumann-Heink once came on stage during a rehearsal with the Detroit Symphony and, en route, knocked over a whole row of violin stands, and some violinists, too. Ossip Gabrilowitsch, the conductor, watched her admiringly and said, "Tina, why don't you walk sideways when you come from the wings?" Schumann-Heink looked at him in disbelief. "Ossip," she said, "you know that with me there is no sideways.")

Melba had about twenty-five roles, but concentrated on relatively few—Juliet, Lucia, Gilda, Violetta, Mimi, Marguerite, and Desdemona above all. Some of those were Emma Eames's roles. The two great sopranos bumped into each other when Melba went to the Metropolitan Opera in 1893. The two ladies hated each other. In Eames, Melba encountered a singer just as stubborn, just as temperamental, just as egoistic—and just as talented.

Emma Eames (1865–1952), an American, was a few years younger than Melba. She was a beauty who conquered as much by her looks as with her marvelous voice. She was a strong-minded young woman who resembled Melba in many respects: she said what was on her mind, she was abrasive, and she had no respect for her elders, including her teacher Marchesi. Eames made a brilliant debut at the Paris Opéra in 1889, opposite Jean de Reszke in Gounod's *Roméo et Juliette,* sang at Covent Garden in 1891, and seldom appeared in Europe after that. Had she Melba's drive and money-lust, she could probably have made just as brilliant a career, but she was content to stay mostly in New York, singing at the

Emma Eames, Melba's great rival and a more versatile singer.

Metropolitan Opera from 1891 to 1909. She was a typical Marchesi product, with a big, cool, silvery voice and an easy singing method. Her repertory was bigger than Melba's, encompassing Tosca, Santuzza, Sieglinde, and Donna Anna (Melba never sang Mozart), as well as Melba roles. Like Melba she was an inferior actress (at the Metropolitan she was called "the operatic iceberg"), reserving her temperament for matters outside the stage. Only once was she known to lose emotional control. In 1905, during a *Lohengrin* performance, she slapped her Ortrud, Kathie Sanger-Bettaque, in the face while both were standing in the wings. They had had an argument over who would go on stage first in the second-act sequence. "You shall apologize for this, on your knees!" shrieked Sanger-Bettaque. Eames later apologized. The press heard about it and descended upon both singers in their respective hotels. Sanger-Bettaque was asked how she felt about the situation. Oh, she said, Mme. Eames's conduct was disgraceful. "But I was so glad to see some vestige of emotion from her."

Eames, then the queen of the Metropolitan, did not welcome Melba to New York. In Europe, Eames had become convinced that Melba was trying to ruin her. She admitted that Melba had a "divinely beautiful" voice, but she let it be known that Melba was treacherous and had worked behind her back to keep her, Eames, off the stage; that Melba had put all kinds of obstacles in her way, had told lies about her, had tried to alienate her friends. Perhaps Eames was correct. Melba never was hospitable to potential rivals. Melba played it cool on her arrival in New York. Asked about the feud, she cooed, "I do not know Madame Eames." New York had a hotter climate with the two ladies in residence; and also just about the best opera the city ever had. In those days the Metropolitan Opera could stage a *Huguenots* with Melba, Jean and Edouard de Reszke, Nordica, Plançon, Victor Maurel, and Sofia Scalchi—a dream cast. Or a *Faust* with Eames, the de Reszke brothers, and the great baritone Jean Lassalle—another dream cast.

Melba tangled with Lillian Nordica as well as with Eames, and Nordica was not a woman to be trifled with. She was a big woman, abundantly endowed in every respect, with a trumpet of a voice and yet a flexibility that allowed her to sing coloratura roles. She was born Lillian Norton in Maine, was an outspoken suffragist, often quarrelsome, thrice married. Husband No. 1 was Frederick Gower, who went up in a balloon and was never seen again. Husband No. 2 was Zoltan Döme, a second-rate singer whose real name was Solomon Teitlbaum. Husband No. 3 was a banker named George Washington Young, who immediately lost his fortune on Wall Street. Her death was as tumultuous as her life. In 1914, returning from an Australian tour, her vessel was shipwrecked off Java and she died in Batavia (now Jakarta) of complications resulting from overexposure.

It was in 1896 that Nordica took on Melba. That year Melba made the one vocal mistake of her life. She decided to sing the *Siegfried* Brünnhilde. After all, Brünnhilde appears only in the last scene of the opera. What Melba wanted Melba got, and her contract for the season specified exclusive rights to the role. Jean de Reszke was one of her supporters, and he too threw a great deal of weight around. Nordica was furious, called in the press, raised a fuss, and left the Metropolitan amid clouds of newsprint and recriminations. Melba sang the role—once. It was too heavy for her, and halfway through she lost her voice. "I have been a fool. I will never do it again," she said in her dressing room. She had almost ruined her perfect organ and had to take several months off before it recovered from the strain. Fortunately there were no permanent ill results.

Melba left the Metropolitan Opera in 1906 to join Oscar Hammerstein's Manhattan Opera. She left because Hammerstein, who had put together a company to challenge the Metropolitan, offered her $4,000 a performance and the option of naming her own roles. She sang there in Hammerstein's first season and again in 1908–09. For her first Hammerstein season, Melba took a leaf out of Patti's book, singing Violetta with gowns encrusted with her own jewelry. Hammerstein called the police and then thoughtfully called the press. He demanded that the police put a twenty-four-hour surveillance on the costumes, and he told the press that

Lillian Nordica.
In 1896 Melba elbowed her aside at the Metropolitan to sing the Siegfried *Brünnhilde. It was a total disaster for Melba.*

Luisa Tetrazzini, the brilliant coloratura soprano who, for a few years after 1907, was Melba's chief rival.

the jewels were worth $500,000. Melba was insulted. Her valuation, she indignantly told reporters, was $2.5 million.

Her last Metropolitan Opera appearances were during the 1910–11 season. Thereafter her headquarters was Covent Garden, where she beat down all competition, though there were those who said her encounter with Luisa Tetrazzini was a draw. Tetrazzini (1871–1940) made her Covent Garden debut while Melba was touring Australia in 1907, and many believed that Melba would not have let the Italian coloratura soprano anywhere near the house had she been around. The short, fat Tetrazzini was nobody's dream of romantic love, but she had one of the most brilliant upper registers in operatic history, and she took London by storm. By the time Melba returned from her tour, Tetrazzini was such a favorite that Melba could not dislodge her. The two rivals did not like each other, and Tetrazzini could be as bitchy as Melba. When she heard Melba vocalizing in a room at the Savoy, she asked the manager, "Have you *many* cats in your lovely hotel?" The real victor in the battle was Covent Garden, which sold out every performance whenever either singer was announced. Poor Tetrazzini lost her voice early; she had only about seven good years left after her sensational Covent Garden debut, though she sang until 1934. Melba lasted to 1926, and those were years of concentrated work and touring all over the world.

Until the 1920's, when her voice finally started to go, Melba was the queen of sopranos. Her work was officially recognized when she was named a Dame of the British Empire in 1918. She lived like a queen and probably earned more money than most of them. Once she established herself, Melba demanded the highest fees of any singer, Caruso included. It was not the money; it was the principle. Thus Caruso had to receive less than Melba did—she to get $2,000 a performance, and he $1,995. Similarly, when she started making records, they had to be sold at a higher price than those of anybody else—a guinea each, rather than £1. For she was Melba. She found concert work lucrative, and at one concert in Sydney she made $13,300, a world's record at the time. At her height she was making $225,000 a year, to which could be added another $100,000 from her records (which she started making in 1904, ending with over a hundred). It is estimated that she earned $2 million from her records alone. Alfred de Rothschild was her financial adviser, and the income from her investments matched what she made through her voice. She did not throw money around, but she spent a great deal—on herself. When she traveled she had to have her favorite edibles, such as plover's eggs *en croûte* with fresh caviar, and her entourage saw to it that she was fed according to her desires. She purchased a London house in Great Cumberland Place and remodeled it in the style of Versailles. All female singers have pets, and one of Melba's was a parrot that she taught to fall into a faint at the mention of Emma Calvé's name. Or, at least, so the papers said. She moved in the highest of society, and was a snob who relished everything about it. In her autobiography she lamented the disappearance of the great days of London wealth and splendor, when they really gave parties. "Who today, for example," she wrote, "would give a dinner party in which there was a pearl in each soup plate? And yet that is the way Hector Baltazzi celebrated his winning of the Derby." She had affairs off and on, the most publicized one being with the Duke of Orleans. At her divorce from Armstrong in 1900 she almost immediately announced her engagement to the Australian playwright Haddon Chambers. Nothing came of it. There also was a persistent rumor linking her name to—of all people—the grave, bearded Joseph Joachim. Another musician who may have figured in her love life, if there is any foundation to the gossip, was Timothee Mamowski, a violinist with whom she toured.

On June 8, 1926, Melba made her farewell to Covent Garden, singing the Balcony Scene from *Roméo et Juliette,* the Prayer Scene from *Otello,* and the last two acts of *La Bohème.* She had been before the public for thirty-nine years and, at sixty-five, did not have much voice left. Then came a series of farewell recitals. Melba could not keep away from the stage. She returned to Australia and even there appeared in several operatic performances. She died in Sydney on February 23, 1931. At the end she suffered, and her face and body were disfigured. The proud Melba would not have liked that. One likes to remember her as she was at her height, around the turn of the century, when she was the toast of the world, when she became immortalized through a dessert (*pêche Melba*), when she was singing in Covent Garden, the Metropolitan, and the Chicago Opera. That great chronicler of society, Lucius Beebe, described her procession into the Twentieth Century Limited en route to Chicago. "Melba," he wrote, "acted the part of the star performer both on stage and off and travelled in a cloud of hothouse flowers, couriers, personal attendants and the gastronomic prejudices of the well placed and determined of the world. . . . Before she boarded the train, her personal staff remade her bed and toilet appointments with the diva's own specially scented bed linen and towels, and the adjacent drawing room which she used as a sitting room was decorated with Melba's own sofa pillows, silver candlesticks and a few gold framed and autographed likenesses of crowned heads for company to Chicago where she was to sing *La Bohème*. It was all approximately as Bohemian as life in Buckingham Palace."

17 *Enrico Caruso*

THE TENOR OF TENORS

PERHAPS the Golden Age really was the period of Patti and Melba, the de Reszke brothers, Eames and Sembrich, Plançon and Maurel, Tamagno, Nilsson, and the other great figures. Perhaps. And perhaps an even better case for a Golden Age can be advanced for the decade between 1915 and 1925. Those ten years brought together a concentration of great singers unique in operatic annals. There were dozens of them, and any single one would have been a star in any opera house today. Consider: Frances Alda, Pasquale Amato, Michael Bohnen, Celestina Boninsegna, Lucrezia Bori, Karin Branzell, Sophie Braslau, Enrico Caruso, Feodor Chaliapin, Toti Dal Monte, Giuseppe De Luca, Emmy Destinn, Florence Easton, Geraldine Farrar, Miguel Fleta, Johanna Gadski, Amelita Galli-Curci, Beniamino Gigli, Alma Gluck, Frieda Hempel, Louise Homer, Maria Ivogün, Hermann Jadlowker, Maria Jeritza, Barbara Kemp, Alexander Kipnis, Giacomo Lauri-Volpi, Lotte Lehmann, Frida Leider, Vanni Marcoux, José Mardones, Giovanni Martinelli, Edith Mason, Margarete Matzenauer, Richard Mayr, John McCormack, Lauritz Melchior, Francesco Merli, Lucien Muratore, Claudia Muzio, Sigrid Onegin, Aureliano Pertile, Alfred Piccaver, Ezio Pinza, Rosa Ponselle, Rosa Raisa, Marie Rappold, Maurice Renaud, Elisabeth Rethberg, Léon Rothier, Titta Ruffo, Tito Schipa, Friedrich Schorr, Elisabeth Schumann, Ernestine Schumann-Heink, Antonio Scotti, Margarethe Siems, Leo Slezak, Riccardo Stracciari, Conchita Supervia, Richard Tauber, Marian Telva, Maggie Teyte, Eva Turner, and perhaps a dozen others one could name.

Of all these names, the one that still rings forth as loudly as ever, and evokes the most magical response and instant recognition, is that of Enrico Caruso, most likely the single most famous singer who ever lived. He earned it, with his glorious voice, but there was something in addition that has kept him alive. This jolly, fat, peasantlike Neapolitan, so unlike his immediate, elegant predecessor Jean de Reszke, had something that transcended his singing and made him a universal favorite. He communicated something—enjoyment of life? good nature? love? the common touch? child of nature? innocence?—with which Everyman seemed to identify. There were elements of tragedy, too, felt by all when Caruso died at the early age of forty-eight. It somehow was not *fair* that such a voice, in a body so resonating with a love for life, was permanently stilled.

And so Caruso has never been forgotten. It is not only the memory of his singing that keeps him alive. Movies are made about him. His recordings continue to be released, in "improved" techniques that are not so much of an improvement. His name remains synonymous with the art of singing. In *The Record of Singing,* Michael Scott makes a good point. "Traditionally," he writes, "it had been the prima donna who enjoyed universal fame; brilliant voices, by their very nature, are more affecting. Since the eighteenth century and the disappearance of the castrati, no male singer had ever challenged their supremacy: Rubini, Mario and Jean de Reszke were greatly admired, but their reputations had not extended far outside the opera house or beyond the society that patronized it."

Caruso changed that. His recordings helped immeasurably. All over the world people could read about Caruso's triumphs. Now they could actually hear what he sounded like, and in living rooms everywhere were Caruso recordings. He first recorded in 1902, but it was not until his great American successes in the 1903–04 season, followed by his first batch of American recordings, that he became the first recording superstar. The phonograph was then a new invention, and Caruso was the first great singer to ride to glory on the new medium. Something in the timbre of his voice, in its resonance and overtones, made him and the phonograph the happiest of marriages. For some reason his voice sounded fuller and firmer on discs than that of any other singer. His records sold in the millions.

There was, of course, the voice—the richest, most colorful, most idiosyncratic tenor voice in history. It took a little time developing. Caruso was born in Naples on February 27, 1873, the first of his parents' eighteen children to live beyond infancy (Enrico was followed by a brother and a sister). His first teacher was Guglielmo Vergine, and he made his debut in Caserta, in a forgotten opera by Morelli, in 1895. At that time he was a slim young man frightened of high notes. Yet something in his singing seemed to attract audiences. Tetrazzini heard him about that time, "before his voice was yet rounded and the different registers smoothed out. I recall the difficulty he had even with such ordinary notes as G or A." But several years later, in 1899, she sang with him in St. Petersburg and was amazed at the progress he had made. "I can hear that velvet voice now, and the *impertinenza* with which he lavishly poured out those rich, round notes. It was the open *voce Napolitana,* yet it had the soft caress of the *voce de la campagna Toscana.* There never was a doubt in my mind. I placed him then and there as an extraordinary and unique tenor. From top to bottom his register was without defect."

For a while Caruso sang in small Italian houses, happy to

work for a ten-week season, for which he got paid $140. In Livorno he sang with a soprano named Ada Giachetti, and a liaison ensued. It lasted until 1908, and two children resulted. Caruso began to make a name for himself, and his fees started to go up. Genoa paid him $1,000 for a three-month season in 1897. In Milan, at the Teatro dal Verme in 1898, he sang in the world premiere of Giordano's *Fedora.* In the same year, in St. Petersburg, he joined a company that exposed him to world-class singing for the first time. In addition to Tetrazzini, there were Sigrid Arnoldson, the bass Vittorio Arimondi, and the baritone Mattia Battistini, known as *La gloria d'Italia.* Battistini had one of the wonder voices. The following year saw Caruso in South America at $2,400 a month. In 1900 he made his La Scala debut, in *Bohème* with Toscanini conducting, and in 1901 toured South America with Toscanini and a Scala group. Now, making $7,000 a month, he started to indulge himself, put on weight and became a chain-smoker. A temporary setback in his career occurred in 1901, when he sang in Naples, his hometown. He had a poor reception and vowed never to sing there again. He kept his vow. His Covent Garden debut was made in 1902, in *Bohème,* with Melba as Mimi. The irrepressible young Caruso, already a prankster on stage, pressed a hot sausage into the diva's *gelida manina* during his famous first-act aria. Melba yelped with shock. Caruso whispered to her, "English lady, you like sausage?" How Caruso did not get fired by the furious Melba is a mystery. Or perhaps she ended up amused with the double entendre? For his debut Caruso got a prophetic notice from Percy Betts of the *Daily News.* Betts hailed him as "that heaven-sent rarity, a pure tenor voice of the old Italian type, a voice . . . which will undoubtedly make him a power in the operatic world." Covent Garden became Caruso's second home; he was to return there many times before the theater was closed during World War I.

But it was the Metropolitan Opera that was his base, and he arrived there for the 1903–04 season. Caruso had signed a contract with Maurice Grau, the general manager, for $1,000 a performance. Grau was looking for a successor to Jean de

Reszke. Before the season started Grau resigned, to be replaced by Heinrich Conried, a man of the theater who did not know much about music. Who was this Enrico Caruso? He asked the Italian consul to name the greatest Italian tenor. "Caruso!" He asked his bootblack the same question. "Caruso!" He asked the president of his bank. "Caruso!" Conried felt happier about the situation.

The debut, on the opening night of the season, November 23, 1903, was not a pronounced success. Caruso sang the Duke in *Rigoletto*. Sembrich and Scotti were the other principals. The reviews were cautious. One reviewer, however, had no doubts at all. Herman Klein, who admired Caruso's voice more than his acting, wrote about "the rare sostenuto; the even scale climbing to easy, vibrant head notes; the perfect diminuendo to a soft mezza voce." Klein was especially struck by "the extraordinary rich, dark tone—the *voix sombre,* as Manuel García called it—which pervaded the organ throughout its full two octaves from the low to the high C." After a few performances the beauty of Caruso's voice became apparent, and every performance was a sellout. Conried's bootblack stood vindicated.

For some years Caruso established a routine that would take him to European opera houses during spring and summer, and then back to New York for the Metropolitan season. His fees kept going up, and eventually he was getting $2,500 a performance at the Metropolitan Opera. He could have had more. Otto Kahn, who financed the opera house, was willing to give Caruso a blank check. But Caruso, who took large fees as a matter of course, was never money-mad. He was perfectly satisfied with $2,500. For his concerts he could get a great deal more; and there was an enormous income from his recordings. Caruso was a very rich man, so rich that he could loftily ignore the Chicago Opera, which tried to lure him from the Metropolitan in 1918 with an offer of $5,000 a performance.

He was always in the news. America took to him and the press followed him everywhere. Once in a while the news was not to his liking. There was the Monkey House episode in 1906. Ca-

The young Enrico Caruso in his early years at the Metropolitan Opera. He made his debut there on November 23, 1903, the opening night of the season.

ruso, in the Central Park Zoo, gave a woman the supreme Italian accolade. He pinched her derriere. She called the cops, who seized Caruso and put him in a cell. The newspapers had a field day. At the court hearing the plaintiff, Hannah Graham, did not appear. Caruso was found guilty and fined $10. He was paralyzed with fright at his next performance. Would New York boo him off the stage? He got an ovation. All was forgiven.

Then there was the Trentini episode. Emma Trentini came to New York in 1906 as a member of Hammerstein's Manhattan Opera. She was a tiny woman, effervescent, temperamental, and a good singer. Critics were amazed at the range and volume of voice produced from so diminutive a body. In 1910 she left opera for operetta, taking the lead in Victor Herbert's *Naughty Marietta.* The response was ecstatic. A star was born. Then, in 1911, American newspapers erupted in headlines. CARUSO AND TRENTINI TO WED NEXT SUMMER. When asked if it were true Trentini confirmed it, saying she had been engaged to Caruso for a year and a half. The Chicago *Examiner* of September 23, 1911, carried a long interview with Trentini under a New York dateline. Some of it is worth quoting:

> "Boys will be boys. Monsieur Caruso has had what you call his flirts. Now he will settle down. Besides, who flirts if Trentini marries him?"
>
> For sixteen months Caruso has been wooing Madame Trentini with bonbons and kisses. Every Wednesday and Saturday night he called, and now she is to be his wife. Trentini, the tiniest prima donna on the stage, in truth a doll and a very "naughty Marietta," told all about it today.
>
> "We love—ah, how we have loved—for over a year. Long time ago—sixteen, eighteen months—we say to each other we marry. And this summer, near Rimini, we do what you call our courting. Wednesdays and Saturday evenings, moonlight by the seashore, ah. Sometimes I sing to him, very low, very sweet. Caruso, never. He fears the salt air on his throat."
>
> "Do you think that you can hold Monsieur Caruso's love after you have married him?" the reporter ventured to ask.

Emma Trentini, with whom Caruso was supposed to have had an affair. The American papers breathlessly followed their verbal exchanges for several months.

> "Me, Trentini, hold this Monsieur Caruso's love?" almost shrieked the little prima donna. "But it is Monsieur Caruso who must hold my love. Mine, you see. Trentini can get many other husbands. But where can Caruso get him another Trentini?"

Caruso could not be reached for comment. He was somewhere in Italy. In the meantime the uninhibited Trentini told the world that she wanted to adopt Caruso's illegitimate children. "I shall be a real mother," she said. Shortly after this interview Trentini went on tour with *Naughty Marietta*. All over America lady reporters pursued her. "Madame Trentini wants to reform Caruso" was the refrain of the sob sisters. Finally the great day came when Caruso returned to New York. Reporters rushed to the dock on November 8 to ask him about his beloved one. They were greeted with a "Pah! I don't get married." The reporters were thunderstruck. But Trentini? they asked. Caruso looked calmly at them. "Trentini?" he repeated, tapping his forehead reflectively. "What Trentini? Who is Trentini? How do you spell her name? What does she do?"

Delighted reporters in Chicago confronted Trentini with Caruso's statement.

"Caruso, he lie!" she was reported saying. "Caruso, he like publicity. I don't care. I just as happy as before. Happier, maybe." This was reported back to Caruso, who rather ungallantly said that Trentini reminded him of a peanut, or maybe a cake of soap. Trentini was not amused. "What does he know about soap?" she told a *New York Times* correspondent. The affair degenerated into a mudslinging match, with remarks about "Ze fat Italiano," soap, and peanuts. Eventually it petered out, but it was a great story while it lasted.

Caruso had enough woman on his hands with his great leading soprano, Geraldine Farrar. She was a fireball who burst over America in 1906. An American, a radiant beauty, she had come out of Melrose, Massachusetts, to study in Europe with Lilli Lehmann and make a tremendous debut at the Berlin Opera in 1901. There also were rumors of her liaison with the Crown

Caruso drew thousands of fast caricatures. The drawings have a good deal of life. Here he is before a recording horn and at a rehearsal with Geraldine Farrar.

Prince and, later, with certain musicians. (When she finally married, it was to the American film star Lou Tellegen, and it was not a happy marriage.) Caruso ceded the opening night of 1906–07 to her; it was the only opening he missed in his years at the Metropolitan Opera. She was not the greatest vocalist of her time, but her flaming personality and temperament, coupled to her looks and acting ability, made her second only to Caruso in the popularity sweepstakes, and they became the supreme couple in the Metropolitan's history. Farrar had sung with Caruso before coming to the Metropolitan, in Monte Carlo, and she almost missed her cue because she was so enthralled by Caruso's voice, with its "unique, velvety quality." Not that they sang together at the Metropolitan very often. Giulio Gatti-Casazza, who became general manager of the house in 1908, saw no reason why he should waste his resources. He did not have many singers who could sell out the house, and so he seldom put Caruso and Farrar in the same cast. Each alone could be depended upon for a sellout.

Farrar was always in the news. There were constant interviews, written mostly by women, about her gowns, her way of exercising, her diets, her cooking, even sometimes her singing. When there was no Farrar news, she managed to make it. In 1915 a news story led off with "Three days have gone by without any Farrar news." Few singers better knew and understood the value of publicity and how to manage the media. Farrar left the Metropolitan shortly after Caruso's death. Her voice was beginning to go, and she was faced with the competition of the new Viennese bombshell, Maria Jeritza. And anyway she always had said she would quit when she reached the age of forty. So Farrar retired while she was still on top. Her last performance in 1922 created a near-riot; her "Gerryflappers" took over the house and all streets leading into it.

Rosa Ponselle entered Caruso's life toward the end of his career, and hers was a remarkable story. Like Farrar she was American. Unlike Farrar, she had had no operatic experience before going to the Metropolitan Opera. Indeed, she had been to the opera only three times in her life. Her family name was Ponzillo.

Rosa was born on January 22, 1897, studied with local teachers in her hometown of Meriden, Connecticut, and then started a vaudeville act with her elder sister Carmela, a fine contralto who eventually had an operatic career of her own. In 1918 Caruso was looking for a dramatic soprano for a revival of Verdi's *La Forza del Destino.* Word spread about this phenomenal girl singing at the Palace Theatre (the Metropolitan Opera of vaudeville houses). Rosa was auditioned three times and given a contract by Gatti-Casazza. She had to learn *Forza* immediately, followed by Rezia in Weber's *Oberon* and Santuzza in *Cavalleria Rusticana.* Nino Romano was engaged to coach her in those roles.

Thus it was as an unknown that the twenty-one-year-old Rosa Ponselle made her debut opposite Caruso in 1918. The critics went wild. "A Caruso in petticoats," exulted James Huneker. It was indeed a remarkable voice that Rosa displayed: big, rich, seamless up to a high C and down probably to a baritonal low D, handled in a musically tasteful manner. It was a voice that struck awe in everybody, and most likely Ponselle was—vocally, anyway—the greatest dramatic soprano of all time. The veteran conductor Tullio Serafin, who had heard everybody, always claimed that he had known but three vocal miracles in his long life—Caruso, Ponselle, and Ruffo.

Ponselle always said that there never was a voice like Caruso's, and in her memoirs she tried to explain why:

> What made the Caruso voice unique were its timbre, or sound quality, and its range. It combined the ease of a lyric tenor and the power of a dramatic baritone. (In fact he could have passed for a baritone anytime and no one would have been the wiser.) He could so darken his voice that once he even went so far as to record, privately, the bass aria from the last act of *Bohème.* Because of his unique voice, he could sing a pleading, lyrical aria like *Una furtiva lagrima* from *L'Elisir d'amore,* then toss off the *La donna è mobile* from *Rigoletto,* and yet have the sheer power needed for such dramatic roles as Samson or as Eléazar in *La Juive.* Except possibly for certain of the early bel canto and Mozartean roles, to

which the color of his voice, as I heard it, would have been unsuited, Caruso could have sung nearly everything.

The story behind the bass aria mentioned by Ponselle stems from a *Bohème* performance on December 23, 1913. Andrés de Segurola, the Colline, ran completely out of voice in the fourth act, so Caruso sang the *Vecchia zimarra* aria for him. The audience did not realize what had happened. Caruso's private recording has been transferred to LP, and several versions are available, including a pressing in RCA's complete Caruso series.

A detailed analysis of Caruso's technique can be found in the biography written by Pierre Key and Bruno Zirato. Key, a well-known vocal specialist, believed that Caruso was in most respects self-taught—that the singer had worked out a way to relax the throat and tongue muscles. Caruso used a minimum amount of breath, distributed with the utmost conservation. Almost never did he force. "He sang beautifully because he sang naturally; and one of the secrets, if there be any in singing technique, was the purity of his vowels, and his clear attack of consonants." No apparent physical effort was involved, no more than in talking. "He was able to reinforce the resonance of each tone through 'letting it filter' to the places where it could radiate to all the spaces which yield resonance. . . . If there were any real secret to the Caruso method, it would seem to lie, to a considerable extent, in the fact that he 'talked' his tones."

Not a learned musician, Caruso always sang with unfailing good taste. Even his sobs were relatively restrained. He was not a fast study, but he had a total of about sixty operas in his repertory, a very respectable number. At the Metropolitan he was heard in thirty-seven roles. He also was an influence on the next generation of tenors, who tried to belt out the music *à la* Caruso. And some, like Gigli, abused the Caruso sob. So Caruso's influence was not altogether beneficial. The trouble was that nobody could begin to do what he had done.

Caruso lived almost exclusively for his singing. He had a few hobbies, among them stamp and coin collecting. His ten-second

Caruso's two greatest leading ladies were Geraldine Farrar (top) and Rosa Ponselle. The glamorous Farrar made her Metropolitan Opera debut in 1906. She and Caruso were the most popular team in the history of the house. Ponselle, arguably the greatest dramatic soprano of the century, sang with him only in his last three years.

and very skillful, amusing caricatures have real quality, and have been collected in a book. He liked to eat, as his figure showed, and he was a chain-smoker to the end of his days. Completely sedentary, he played golf—once. He tried tennis—once. He liked women; those he did try more than once. He never took care of himself. His life was at the opera, and he would get to his dressing room two hours before a performance. At those moments he was irritable and nervous. Warming-up consisted of a few scales and simple exercises. He would pull at his tongue; he thought that made it supple. Then he would use an inhalant, insert a pinch of Swedish snuff to clear the nostrils, gargle with lukewarm salt water, and take a sip of diluted Scotch. Then he would light a cigarette. His valet would help him into his costume. The curtain would not go up until Caruso was ready. Ludivico Viviani, the assistant stage manager, would be constantly peering into Caruso's room to see if he was ready. Finally, "May we begin, Mr. Caruso?"

His voice started to thicken as he grew older. It still had the unmistakable Caruso timbre, but a darker, even more baritonal quality was apparent. Top notes became more of an effort. When young, Caruso had a high C and even a D flat, as shown in his recording of the *Cuius animam* from the Rossini *Stabat Mater*. Later he had high C's transposed down. Still no tenor could come near him. James Huneker wrote that he had heard tenors from Brignoli to Gayarré, from Campanini to Tamagno, Masini and Nicolini, "yet no one possessed a tithe of the vocal richness of Camerado Enrico. Some have outpointed him in finesse, Bonci; Tamagno could have outroared him; Jean de Reszke had more personal charm and artistic subtlety; nevertheless, Caruso has a marvellous natural voice, paved with lyric magic. It is positively torrential in its outpouring, and with the years it grows as mellow as a French horn."

Everybody adored him. Caruso was a good colleague, never had bad words to say about anybody, and was always eager to help a friend—which meant everybody. The stagehands especially loved him; he was a generous tipper. And he came backstage at

Christmas to dispense cheer. Frank Garlichs, the treasurer of the Metropolitan, once described Caruso playing Santa Claus. He would fill a big plate with gold pieces and walk around passing them out to everybody. He also gave presents of watches, scarf pins, and pens. He was always ready to write out a $500 check for needy musicians. Italian compatriots with their hands out invariably found Caruso a soft touch.

Good soldier that he was, Caruso was a regular on the annual Metropolitan Opera tours (many top singers hate the tour and avoid it when they can). He was with the company during the San Francisco earthquake of 1906 and was seen wandering the streets, wearing a fur coat over his pajamas and clutching a signed portrait of President Roosevelt. "'Ell of a place," Caruso said. "I never come back here." He sang in the world premiere of Puccini's *La Fanciulla del West* in 1910; it was one of the great evenings in the house, with the composer present and enthusiasm running high. Emmy Destinn, a wonderful singer, was the Minnie, and Pasquale Amato sang Jack Rance. Year after year Caruso was the mainstay of the Metropolitan Opera. He even learned to act in a dependable manner. He married an American woman, Dorothy Park Benjamin, in 1918. He made two films. The first, *My Cousin,* was a flop. The second, *The Great Romance,* was withdrawn.

Then came the dreadful night of December 11, 1920, at a performance of *L'Elisir d'Amore* at the Brooklyn Academy, where the Metropolitan Opera used to give regular performances. During the first act Caruso had a hemorrhage on stage. Fresh handkerchiefs were passed to him from the wings. Caruso wanted to continue the performance, but the management called a halt. William J. Guard, the press representative of the Metropolitan, told the audience what had happened, to their gasps of horror. The curtain went down and stayed down, and for the first time in the history of the Metropolitan Opera a performance failed to be completed. Caruso's personal physician misdiagnosed the case; he said it was nothing but a small ruptured blood vessel in the tongue. His doctor permitted him to sing in *Forza del Destino* on December 13 and in *Samson et Dalila* on the 16th, not realizing how desperately ill the man was. Then Caruso developed pains in the side. Again a misdiagnosis. Just neuralgia, the doctor said. On December 24, 1920, Caruso sang in *La Juive*. It was his 607th and last appearance at the Metropolitan. The next day he was in dreadful pain, specialists were called in, and the diagnosis was pleurisy and pneumonia. Several operations were necessary. Caruso went to Italy to recuperate and died in Naples on August 2, 1921.

His friends and colleagues found the world a darker place. Caruso was genuinely loved. Frances Alda spoke for everybody when she said that "something warm and vibrant happened to the house when he was on stage. . . . The great tenor was the finest artist, the truest friend and the kindest person I ever knew in the theatre."

18 *A Digression on Tenors*

FROM the very beginning, tenors have attracted bemused attention from their colleagues, opera managers, the public, critics, feature writers, and other such caterpillars of the community. There always seems to be something *different* about them, and it was not for nothing that the admirable soprano Frances Alda, no mean temperament herself, went so far as to separate tenors from the human race, creating for them a separate phylum, or branch, of the animal kingdom. *Men, Women and Tenors* she called her book. Giulio Gatti-Casazza, a man of infinite size, dignity, and experience, would shrug his shoulders whenever anything went wrong during his many years as general manager of the Metropolitan Opera. "The head of a tenor," he would say. That explained any stupidity.

Sopranos too had their little eccentricities, but in the days before women's lib those were explained away simply because they were *women,* and it was taken for granted that women were not rational creatures. God had ordained it so. But tenors were, after all, men, and thus it was harder to understand the wonderful, amazing way they went through life. The great tenors were overpaid, oversexed, vain, and spoiled. They offered a new and exalted meaning to the word *egoistic;* were insatiable in their demands for praise; were susceptible to the most egregious flattery; and made crazy demands, expecting society to bend to their wishes. Often they acted like spoiled children, and managers thought they *were* children. Colonel James Mapleson, who knew as much about them as anybody, wrote in his memoirs about a tenor named Antonio Giuglini, who was one of his crosses in the 1860's. "Giuglini," Mapleson said, "was in many ways a child. So, indeed, are most members of the artistic tribe, and it is only by treating them and humoring them as children that one can get them to work at all." Also, Mapleson darkly added, "with their childishness a great deal of cunning is also mixed up." He knew. Sopranos he somehow could cope with. He merely acceded to their demands and all was well. Tenors scared him and reduced him to despair. He never knew what they were going to do next; they always had nasty little tricks up their sleeves. Read about his adventures with Volponi, Mongini, Masini, Ravelli, Bertini, Fancelli, Campanini, and a few others who caused him grave anguish. The above-mentioned Giuglini, who had a beautiful voice and was considered by many the successor of Rubini, liked to fly kites on busy London streets. His other hobby was making fireworks. The poor fellow died mad in 1865 at the age of thirty-eight.

In the 1850's Max Maretzek, who produced and conducted opera in the United States, had tenors to deal with, and in his *Crotchets and Quavers* he described the species as he saw it, centering on one Signor Lorenzo Salvi, who

> believed himself in the Operatic world, a fixed star of the first magnitude, around whose twinkling lustre . . . all and the other planets had slowly and respectfully to revolve. He supposed himself to be the brilliant Sun from whom the nobodies who were his satellites had to obtain the whole of their light and warmth.
>
> If, perchance, he descended from the height of self-

> appreciation upon which he dwelt, and for a moment admitted himself to be an ordinary mortal like you or myself . . . it was only that he might indulge in playing the role of a despotic sovereign. Then, I felt, that he believed himself to be the Louis Quatorze of the lyric drama, and, at times, was under the impression that I should hear him exclaim, *"L'Opéra, c'est moi."*

Signor Salvi's attitude toward the sopranos in his operas was symbolically related to cannibalism. At least, according to Maretzek, sopranos were there for Salvi to pluck, squeeze, "and be sucked like a ripe and golden orange." When the juice had satisfied him, it was to be thrown away and kicked into the street. The public, however, was a necessary evil. "He regarded them somewhat as a band of savages, whom he, however, like a second Orpheus, could appease with the wondrous melody of his voice." Salvi was with Maretzek's companies for some years; he apparently was a brilliant-sounding tenor and an audience favorite. But in 1853 he ruined Maretzek's benefit. Salvi suddenly decided, on the afternoon of the concert, that he wanted his fee in advance. Max, the last one to submit to blackmail, closed down Niblo's Garden instead. *The New York Times* did some digging and learned that Salvi was in debt and being dunned. Among the debts was $253 to the druggist Dubuic for eighty gallons of cod liver oil. Tenors are eccentric folk, but it was the feeling that eighty gallons of cod liver oil was a bit unusual. What on earth did Salvi do? Bathe in it? (It later was found that he had purchased it for delivery to Italy.) The *Times* pointed out that in the previous twenty months Maretzek had paid Salvi "upwards of thirty thousand dollars." Was Salvi worth it? The *Times* said no. "Signor Salvi cannot be ranked with the first tenors of the present day except by a traditional and extremely unsatisfactory fiction. He is passé and tolerated simply because he is the best we have among us."

At about the same time Berlioz, in 1852, devoted a chapter in his *Evenings with the Orchestra* to the tenor as a species: "His salary is 100,000 francs, with a month's leave annually. . . . Art is for him nothing but a gold coin and laurel wreaths, and the most likely means to obtain both quickly are the only ones he cares to use. He has noticed that certain melodic formulas, certain vocalizations, certain ornaments, certain fortissimi, certain concluding platitudes or vulgar rhythms have the property of immediately drawing applause of a sort. This seems to him reason enough to rely on those devices."

Berlioz goes on to describe in detail the musical sins of great tenors. But to the tenor or his public, Berlioz writes, it makes no difference. "The tenor lords it over everyone and tramples on everything. He struts around the theater with the air of a conqueror; his crest gaily glints about his proud head; he is a king, hero, demigod, god." After all, the prima donna gets only a mere pittance of 40,000 francs. A few decades later, George Bernard Shaw was observing much the same thing. "Good tenors are so scarce that the world has always condoned any degree of imbecility for the sake of an *ut de poitrine*"—that is, a stentorian high C.

The famous American soprano Clara Louise Kellogg encountered many tenors during her long career, and she mentions one of them, not giving his name, whose hands always were so dirty that her Violetta gown became greasier and greasier. She finally asked him to wash his hands before a performance. Back came the cheery reply: "All right! Tell her to send me some soap!" Mme. Kellogg did for the rest of the season, figuring it was cheaper than buying new clothes. She wrote in her autobiography that most tenors are enormously pleased with themselves, have their eccentricities, and the best a soprano could hope for was that the eccentricities were innocuous. "I used to find it in my heart, for instance, to wish that they did not have such queer theories as to what sort of food was good for the voice. Many of them affected garlic. Stigelli usually exhaled an aroma of lager beer; while the good Mazzoleni invariably ate from one to two pounds of cheese the day he was to sing." Mazzoleni ate cheese while the curtain was going up. In *Faust* he would munch cheese during the basso's arias in the first act, and he continued to eat cheese during the intermissions. His body and breath reeked of cheese, to the dismay of his sopranos. Then there was Pasquale Brignoli, a popular tenor on the American circuit in the post–Civil War period. Brignoli had one major peculiarity: he did not like to be touched. "Imagine," says Kellogg, "playing love scenes with a tenor who did not like to be touched." She brooded about him and his colleagues. "Tenors are queer creatures," she concluded.

Later in the century there was the great Francesco Tamagno, the tenor with the trumpet of a voice who created Otello for Verdi. He probably was the loudest tenor who ever lived. He also was one of the best paid until his retirement in 1903, and at one point the Monte Carlo Opera was paying him $5,000 a performance. He died a multimillionaire. But the thing about Tamagno is that he was born a peasant, died a peasant, and has come down as the stingiest singer who ever lived. He was never known to pick up a check. At restaurants he would wrap up any uneaten food—and not only his own—stash it in a pocket, and eat it the next day. He once had an engagement in South America at $2,250 a performance. His contract called for first-class passage from Genoa to Buenos Aires. Tamagno traveled steerage and pocketed the difference. He owned an estate and would run all over the grounds picking up and saving empty bottles, which he would then sell. Blanche Marchesi, in her memoirs, says that Tamagno would avoid buying even the smallest bit of ribbon or thread for his costumes. Instead he would go to the women in the company and wheedle everything he needed. "For the part of Raoul in *The Huguenots* a tiny little ostrich feather was necessary for his velvet hat. He passed his whole day in the second-hand shops to find a cheap ostrich feather, and in the evening came to Madame Campanini, asking her if she would lend him one, as they were too expensive to buy, though at that time they could be purchased with a few shillings."

Even the great Enrico Caruso, normally a well-adjusted man, was not immune to tenorism. Child of nature that he was, he was easily amused, and nothing amused him more than pranks and practical jokes on stage. He would pour flour in Colline's stovepipe hat in *La Bohème* and wait breathlessly until the basso put it on. Then he would become dissolved in laughter. Or he might put water in the hat. It is a well-known scientific fact that bassos never put water into tenors' hats. Nobody does things to tenors; tenors do things to other people. Singers on the stage learned to be very wary of Caruso and moved with great caution.

Tenors have been described as usually short, stout men (except when they are Wagnerian tenors, in which case they tend to be large, stout men) made up predominantly of lungs, rope-sized vocal cords, large frontal sinuses, thick necks, thick heads, tantrums, and *amour propre*. Some physiologists have advanced the theory that where their brains should be are, instead, acoustic cavities that enable them to throw tones higher, harder, and faster than members of the human race can. Whether or not this is true, it *is* true that tenors are a race apart, a race that seems to operate reflexively rather than through due processes of thought.

The species came into full flower in Rome on the afternoon of January 21, 1958. For the several hundred years since the invention of opera everything had been leading toward this dress rehearsal of Verdi's *Don Carlo*. Franco Corelli was the tenor (one exception to the rule that tenors are short and stout, he was a handsome six-footer, built along the lines of an Olympic swimmer). During the rehearsal Corelli got the idea that Boris Christoff, the bass, was trying to upstage him. Words passed. Suddenly Corelli drew his sword and went for Christoff with the single-minded intention of laying his liver bare for all the world to see. Christoff had to draw *his* sword in self-protection, and the Rome Opera was filled with the clink-clank of thrust and parry until stagehands pulled Corelli and Christoff apart. It was the greatest duel scene since Errol Flynn faced Basil Rathbone in *The Adventures of Robin Hood*. Christoff suffered a wounded finger. He stalked from the house, understandably discouraged, and never returned for this particular cast in this particular opera. The management did not ask him to return. Bassos are much easier to replace than top tenors.

Not much later Corelli was singing in Naples. A heckler in a box said something that displeased the great man. Corelli stopped singing—this was *not* during a rehearsal—rushed offstage, broke down the door of the box with his shoulder, and was preparing to assassinate the miserable wretch when the stage managers caught up with him. Corelli's boiling point strongly resembled atomic fission, and he exploded with much the same result.

Richard Tucker, who in his day was one of the stalwart tenors of the Metropolitan Opera and indeed had a wonderful voice, never came to a boil. He merely made the management boil. In 1960 the Metropolitan, in the final week of the season, gave a performance of Flotow's *Martha* in a brand-new English translation. Tucker was, of course, the Lionel. Things went swimmingly until about 10:20 P.M., when Tucker advanced to the footlights and broke into *M'apparì* instead of the expected English version, *One Lonely Night*. Nino Verchi, the conductor, and the others in the cast were caught completely by surprise. So was Rudolf Bing, the general manager, who immediately delivered himself of some tart comments about tenors, artistic responsibility, and teamwork. The only one who was not surprised was Tucker's press agent. She was in the office of *The New York Times* at 10:30 P.M. with the stop-press item.

Tenors have always been adding to the gaiety of the nations. On November 10, 1953, David Poleri was singing Don José in Chicago opposite the Carmen of Gloria Lane. Poleri, who had a short career, was talented, moody, temperamental, and unpredictable. During the performance this and that kept going through his mind, and everything collided in the last act. Glaring at the conductor and at Lane, he loudly said, "Finish it yourself" and walked out, leaving Carmen with no Don José to stab her. Lane watched Poleri's departure with what must have been a certain amount of surprise. Having nothing better to do, as she later told reporters, "I just dropped dead."

Even those dignified battleships known as Wagnerian tenors are not immune to the disease that eventually afflicts all high-voiced singers. The great and stately Lauritz Melchior drove the Metropolitan Opera stage managers crazy toward the end of his career. Melchior could well have been the greatest Wagnerian tenor who ever lived, but at that time he had sung one too many performances, was bored, did what he wanted, and knew he was irreplaceable. He generally would have a card game going with the stagehands, and sometimes he would arrive on stage just in time for his cue. Or at other times he just about wouldn't. His sopranos were afraid that when he had nothing to do on stage he would fall asleep. He once did, during the last act of *Tristan und Isolde,* and Kirsten Flagstad had to poke him to stop his snores during her *Liebestod.*

Melchior's behavior in *Parsifal* was uniquely his own. In his latter days he refused to follow the stage directions, which call for Parsifal to stand voiceless, motionless, and rapt during the entire Grail scene. This is about a half hour of standing voiceless, motionless, and rapt, and Melchior did not like it. He would sidle to the wings, imperceptibly, without appearing to move: quite a trick. It was a living demonstration of the quantum theory, in which particles go from one place to another without passing through intermediate territory. Melchior seemed immobile, all 285 pounds of him. He was a very big particle. But suddenly he would be a yard to the right. Then another yard. Soon he would be in the wings, presumably picking up his card game.

The theory has been advanced that no high-voiced singer has been normal since the castrato Caffarelli. Around 1725 Caffarelli was studying with Porpora in Naples. Porpora, so the famous story goes, kept the male soprano for six years on the study of a single page of exercises and then sent him forth into the world. "Go, my son. You are the greatest singer in Europe." But, say the experts, such a course of training over so long a period would be enough to make anybody insane or, at the very least, eccentric. Working on a single sheet of exercises for six years would be shattering to the psyche. Perhaps, say the experts, talking learnedly of genes, DNA, and the collective subconscious, the Caffarelli Effect has been transmitted to tenors through the ages. Certain it is that they all are highly emotional, to the point where they can do grievous harm to themselves. Did not the great Nourrit in 1839 hurl himself from a window to his death because he was depressed about the success of his rival Duprez?

Of all tenors the Italian tenor—that is, the tenor who specializes in Italian opera—seems to have the slenderest grip on reality. He seems to live in a world consisting only of high C's (which he always has at the beginning until he has to transpose down), rivalries with sopranos, jockeying for curtain calls, and strange offstage behavior; and he swims in the operatic ocean with the grave behavior of Leviathan among the lesser fishes of the sea.

But why should such things be with tenors? And why, specifically, Italian tenors for the most part? Why not pianists, violinists, and conductors, who also have their own considerable share of ego? There is a combination of reasons. A pianist or violinist starts around the age of six or before (if he starts later, the chances are against his making the big time) and, in the process of mastering his art, generally gets a complete musical education. But male singers have to wait until adolescence before their voices settle. Some great male singers did not discover they had a voice until their middle twenties or even later. A few, such as Ezio Pinza, who was one of the great bass singers of the century, could not even read music.

As a result their musical education is far from complete. They do not have the mental, physical, and musical discipline imposed by years of study from childhood on. They know little of the literature outside the operatic literature. And—the fact must be faced—what Italian tenors *do* study is a long way from Beethoven's Op. 131 or Bach's *Kunst der Fuge,* or *Tristan und Isolde*. The roles of Alfredo, Manrico, or Radames do not impose an intolerable intellectual strain. As a result Italian tenors are apt to be naïve, musically speaking. (There are always exceptions, of course.) They live in what is musically a very restricted world.

If they are very good, they enter a world in which there is mad competition for top tenors. At any age there are only a few. Pianists, violinists, and conductors—and very good ones, too—go a-begging. Not a very good tenor. In the 1980's world of many opera houses, incredibly fast transportation, and abnormally high fees, he can sing seven nights a week if he chooses. He will be fought over, even if his ideas of acting are rudimentary. That superb vocal stylist Carlo Bergonzi was a case in point: his singing had grace, style, and flexibility, and he made a brilliant career even though he could be singing of love, hate, war, revenge, or murder with never a change of expression on his face; and physically he looked like a pear that needed a shave. *Prima la voce,* it is said. First the voice; and if a tenor has a really great voice he learns early that he does not need anything else.

So he goes his own way, as observers since the days of the castrati have chronicled. He gets away with things for which any other singer would immediately be fired. He resents the conductor telling him what to do, he resists coaching, and he relies on his lung power and high notes to carry him through. Until recent times, when conductors and stage directors started to usurp the holy place held only by top singers, tenors did not even bother much about things like refined phrasing, musical meaning, and the relation of an aria to the action as a whole. One of the curiosities of recordings is the sob that the tenor Hipolito Lazaro creates at the climax of his disc of *E lucevan le stelle* from *Tosca.* It is a positive Vesuvius of sobs. It gets under way slowly, with gurgles and chokes, then erupts with a grinding, creaking, and ultimately explosive sound that suggests a particularly orotund belch from a volcano letting loose.

All this applies only to the big-voiced tenor, who always has gotten away with anything because of the glory of his natural vocal endowments and the brilliance of his top. Smaller-voiced singers necessarily have had to compensate with finesse, musicianship, and beauty of phrase. Tito Schipa was a tenor of that school, whereas in the following generation a tenor like Mario Del Monaco never saw any particular reason why he should not bawl his way through any kind of music. The Del Monaco kind of tenor gets along fine without any real degree of musicianship (although Caruso, for one, was instinctively a tasteful musician, on the whole). A lieder singer cannot, and a Wagnerian tenor cannot, but an Italian tenor can and only too often does. In addition he is exposed to a psychological element that few men are big enough to resist. A tenor is accustomed to the center of the stage. In most operas he is the hero and, with the soprano, has the lion's share of the evening. So incessant is the spotlight on him that eventually he may end up living in a world of his own. Luigi Ravelli, a top tenor in 1881, was signed for a new opera by Colonel Mapleson. When Ravelli learned that it was the *baritone* who put the tenor to death, he refused to go on. Colonel Mapleson could not budge him. Ravelli wanted to know why the habitual impersonator of heroes should fall beneath the sword of one who was accustomed to play only a villain's part. Ravelli "cried, screamed, uttered oaths and at one time threatened to kill with his dagger not only his natural enemy, the baritone, but everyone around him." He had made up his mind. "I will kill them all!" he shrieked. Finally he consented to sing, but only on condition that he receive the equivalent of a state funeral on stage.

Thus the tenor gets used to being a hero on stage and receiving adulation during and after the performance. It is not surprising that he has a tendency to carry this over into his private life. And it is a fact that many tenors have had abnormal living patterns. They get mixed up in paternity suits and other scandals. In Gatti-Casazza's reign the outraged wife of a tenor demanded that he, Gatti, stop her husband from sleeping with the ballet girls (and also with the ballet boys, for that matter). Gatti looked at her sorrowfully. "What can I do, madame? It is the custom of the opera."

In the 1750's Gluck started his operatic reform to curb the excesses of singers. But there never really was a "reform," and when great voices appeared they continued to do just what they wanted to do. In the 1960's there was talk about "ensemble opera," in which great voices would be subordinate to the vision of the *Gesamtkunstwerk,* the total work of art. But that noble conception held true only when there were no great voices in the cast. Certainly the public resisted it. The public wanted its heroes and heroines of the lyric stage to sound forth in all their uninhibited glory. It is said by cynics that "ensemble opera" is merely a euphemism for cheap opera, in which less than great singers, paid less than top fees, are seen in less than great performances. Ensemble opera may provide expert staging, better acting than that offered by most superstars, a more searching look into the musical values. But what it does not offer is, *au fond,* the basic reason for opera, which is glorious singing. Fortunately for the cause of art, there have been singers with glorious voices who also were abundantly endowed musicians, who could shape a quiet phrase with melting beauty. In them, opera has been fructified throughout the ages. But when a choice has to be made between an inferior voice with a superior musical mind, and a superior voice with an inferior musical mind, the history of opera amply demonstrates that it is the latter who wins out.

19 *Josef Hofmann*

THE POLISH KEYBOARD MASTER

WHEN Josef Hofmann, not yet twelve years old, made his American debut, he already was a veteran of the concert stage. He was born in Cracow, Poland, on January 20, 1876, and had studied with his father from the age of three. Both parents were musicians. Casimir was director of the Cracow Opera and his wife was a soprano in the company. They soon found out that Josef and the piano were made for each other; the child's progress was miraculous. So they put him on exhibition, and Josef was touring Europe as a prodigy at seven. He was a good-looking child, but so short that his feet could not reach the piano pedals, and a contraption (metal stilts attached to his shoes) had to be rigged so that he could operate them. When he made his London debut in 1887, playing the Beethoven C major Concerto at a Philharmonic concert, the critics went wild and weekly recitals plus a tour of the provinces followed. The *Musical Times* reported that young Josef drew larger numbers of people to his concerts "than any other living pianist, Rubinstein not excepted."

But that was nothing compared to the furor Josef created in New York. There was a great deal of advance buildup about the prodigy, and his father, Casimir, rented the Metropolitan Opera for Josef's debut on November 29, 1887 (Carnegie Hall had not yet been built). But before the concert Casimir put Josef on exhibition before an audience of professionals and newspapermen at Wallack's Theatre. Several musicians tested the boy. Among them was Rudolph Aronson, a composer, who played for the child sixteen bars of a waltz he had just composed. "While I played," Aronson recalled some years later in *Musical America,* "young Hofmann listened attentively, then seating himself at the piano he played my waltz correctly, modulated from one key to another, interpolated other melodies, and after five minutes of this extemporising, reverted to my waltz in the original key and note for note."

The debut program consisted of the Berlioz *Roman Carnival* Overture, Beethoven's Piano Concerto in C, the Saint-Saëns *Phaeton,* a set of Rameau variations played by Josef, Mendelssohn's *Midsummer Night's Dream* Overture, Josef's own Berceuse and Waltz, Chopin's E flat Nocturne (Op. 9, No. 2) and E minor Waltz, and the Weber-Liszt *Polacca* for piano and orchestra. Adolf Neuendorff was the conductor.

There was not a dissenting critical voice about the amazing gifts of the youngster. The *New York Times* critic said that the boy was already in the front rank of pianists. "Perhaps the one thing which struck the educated hearer most forcibly was the fact that the boy did not play like a boy. It was not necessary to think 'That is extremely good work from a child,' because it would have been extremely good work from a man." Henry E. Krehbiel of the *Tribune* called him "the wonderful boy . . . gifted in music far beyond any child presented to the public in recent years." Krehbiel invoked the ghost of Mozart and said that Hofmann was a "phenomenal" technician, mature far beyond his years. He ended, "The taste of the lad is exquisite, his command of tone-color amazing, his reposefulness of delivery would reflect credit on any older artist, his sense of symmetry is most delightful, and his digital ability as great as that which the majority of pianoforte players attain after practicing as many years as this little lad has lived." All the New York papers had similar evaluations. Thus all New York fought for a chance to hear the genius and see if he was indeed as good as everybody said.

A series of concerts followed that would have taxed the resources of a mature pianist. Within a two-month period Josef played the Beethoven C minor Concerto, Mendelssohn's *Capriccio brillant* and G minor Piano Concerto, the Weber *Konzertstück,* many solos, and even some improvisations on themes suggested from the audience. He played at the Metropolitan Opera on November 29 (his debut), December 1, 3, 6, 8, 13, 15, 22, 27, and 31, on January 3, 18, 21, and 25, and on February 8, 15, and 18, sharing most programs with a pianist and singer. Sometimes Josef played two-piano pieces with his father. Interspersed with the Metropolitan Opera programs were appearances in Boston, Brooklyn, Philadelphia, and Baltimore. The press became worried about this crazy schedule for so young a boy, and there also were accusations of exploitation by a greedy father. The Society for the Prevention of Cruelty to Children stepped in, forbidding any more performances, and the February 18 concert at the Metropolitan Opera was the last. In later years Hofmann said that the marathon had not taxed him; that he liked to play the piano and would have been just as happy had he been allowed to continue. As things worked out, the philanthropist Alfred Corning Clark, a New York banker, offered Casimir $50,000 to remove his son from the stage, with a further stipulation, accepted by Casimir, that Josef was not to play in public until he was eighteen.

After it was all over, Krehbiel in a retrospective article wrote that "the interest in the lad Josef Hofmann early got beyond the phase which is defensible on art-grounds, and degenerated into a craze so silly and irrational that a sordid father and grasping managers did not hesitate to encourage it with mountebank tricks." And the boy was being exploited only for money, Krehbiel said,

The eleven-year-old Josef Hofmann on the occasion of his American debut at the Metropolitan Opera on November 29, 1887. To a man, the New York music critics were overwhelmed.

for in Germany, Austria, and France Josef could not command more than $150 a concert. But in the United States the boy's unquestioned talent, the enthusiastic reviews, "and a flood of gratuitous advertising" transformed Josef into "one of the biggest money-makers in the musical profession. To the cupidity aroused by this discovery the lad was sacrificed."

Exploited, yes. Sacrificed, no. Hofmann grew up to become one of the greatest of all pianists. Casimir took Josef back to Europe, where he worked with Moritz Moszkowski and finished with Anton Rubinstein in Dresden. Rubinstein had heard Josef as a child of eight and had been so impressed that he said he was a boy such as the world of music had never produced. Twice a week for two years Josef worked with the Russian grandmaster, and on March 14, 1894—shortly before Rubinstein's death—Hofmann made his public reentry, starting the life of a touring pianist and making Berlin his headquarters. He returned to the United States in 1898, where after a few years he was received as the giant he was. In Russia he enjoyed unprecedented popularity to the point where in 1911 the czar gave him the keys to the Russian railroads, allowing him to travel anywhere as the personal guest of the ruler. In 1912, in St. Petersburg, the demand was such that Hofmann gave twenty-one consecutive concerts, not once repeating a piece. Altogether he played 255 different works.

At that time Paderewski was the king of pianists—to the public, anyway. Hofmann, though he made a fine career at first, was no threat to the Polish charismaticist. But Hofmann's colleagues knew him for what he was. Before Rachmaninoff started his career around 1920, there were three pianists above all who instilled awe among the professionals. One was Leopold Godowsky, an amazing technician and a superior musical intellect. Godowsky, however, seemed to tighten up in public; it was in his studio that he did things that made other pianists go out talking to themselves. Then there was Ferruccio Busoni, another remarkable pianist who devoted himself to Bach, Beethoven, and Liszt (and, toward the end of his life, the Mozart piano concertos). Busoni from all accounts could be eccentric in his interpretations, but he had the

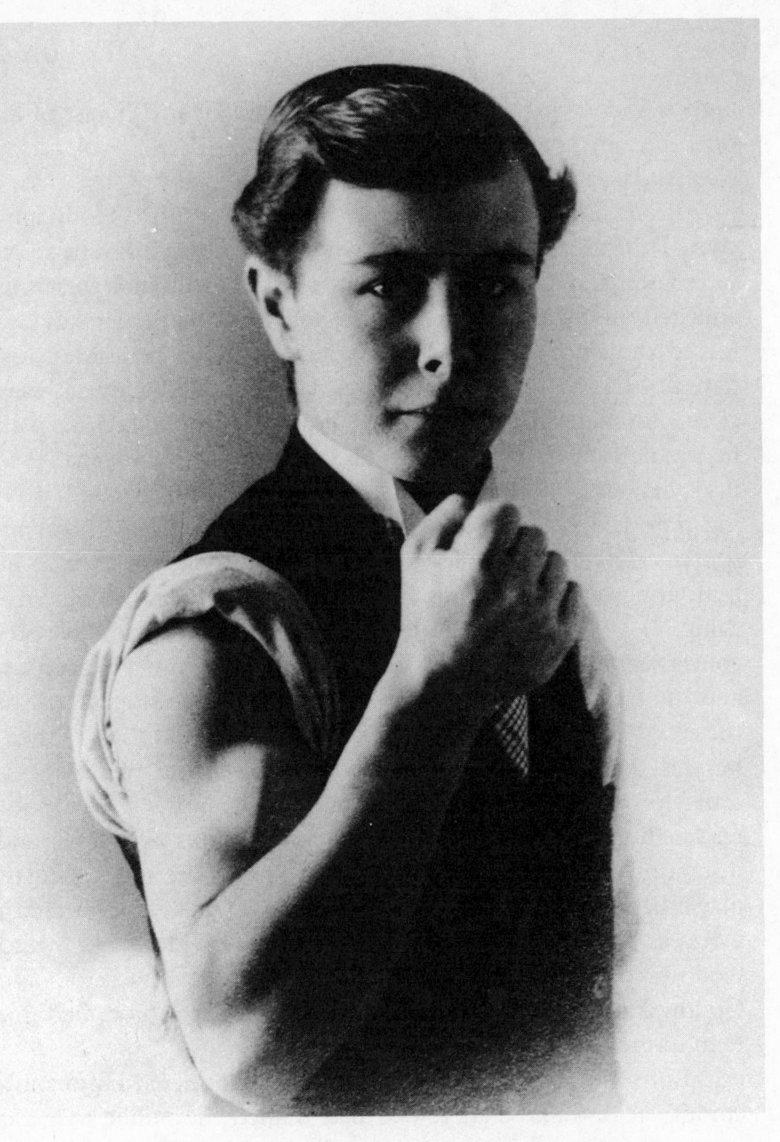

The short, compact Hofmann in 1905, proud of his musculature. Many considered him the most perfect pianist of his time.

biggest vision and the most individual ideas of any pianist of his time. He must have been a colossal figure.

And then there was Hofmann.

Professionals respond to craft, and no pianist had Hofmann's craft. Difficulties ceased to exist when he was playing. His scales were faster and clearer than anybody else's, his trills more perfectly adjusted, his octaves light and elegant, his tone perpetually unforced and singing, never losing control even in the loudest fortissimi. His rhythm never faltered. His ideas about music were clear and uncomplicated. For a Romantic pianist, which he was, he was unusually strict. Later in his life there was to be a change in his style, but from the 1890's to the early 1930's Hofmann's playing represented elegance, exquisite finish, and the height of resource. He was the coolest of the Romantic pianists, just as he himself never appeared flustered or, indeed, bothered about anything. If he is to be believed, he never went through the preconcert agonies of most performers; he said he was never nervous, and the only thing that concerned him was "adjusting myself to the acoustics of a hall." His colleagues could find no flaw; to them he was the perfect pianist. The one weak aspect of his musicianship was his sight-reading. Hofmann always was a poor reader. But he compensated for that lack with his perfect ear and instant memory. He could hear a piece a few times and be able to play it back perfectly—and that included so insanely complicated a work as Godowsky's *Fledermaus* paraphrase. Hofmann heard Godowsky play it a few times, and then played it back for him. Godowsky, who was composing the piece at that time, had not even written it out completely.

But some experts chafed at what they considered Hofmann's emotional restraint. Paderewski had trained the public to great surges of tone and heart-on-sleeve drama. Hofmann hated overemotionalism. He once told an interviewer: "Perfect sincerity plus perfect simplicity equals perfect achievement." He was a nonsentimentalist, and in his book *Piano Playing, with Piano Questions Answered,* he cast scorn on musicians who perform with excessive feeling. Too many young pianists anxious to impress public and critics, he wrote, are tempted

> to resort to esthetic violence in order to make sure of "good notices"; to use power where it is not called for; to make "feeling" ooze from every pore; to double, treble the tempo or vacillate it out of all rhythm; to violate the boundaries of both the composition and the instrument—and all this for no other purpose than to show as quickly as possible that the various qualities are "all there." These conditions produce what may be called the pianistic nouveau-riche or parvenu, who practices the vices of the dilettante without, however, the mitigating excuse of ignorance or a lack of training.

But that did not mean Hofmann's interpretations were cut and dried. The reverse is true; he was a spontaneous pianist and seldom twice played a piece the same way. Always there was a feeling of improvisation, and often one felt that he was trying out new ideas as they occurred to him during public concerts. He admitted as much. W. J. Henderson, the critic of the New York *Sun,* wrote in 1913, in an otherwise flattering review, that Hofmann's playing was extremely controlled. Hofmann wrote a letter to Henderson, saying that Rubinstein had never played a piece precisely as he had played it before,

> and that I cannot do it either. . . . I think that the model made at home can and ought to establish the *general lines* and that the performance in public may differ in so far as it admits certain improvisatory elements. This results in a much higher function of artistry because it is—with certain limits—free, *in statu nascendi,* spontaneous, and—if you will—personal! That this freedom presupposes the artist's mind and taste to be so well trained as to warrant him to rely on his inspiration, is a matter of course; and that however quickly, with flashlight speed, the plan must be made; a plan there *must* be.
>
> No compliment, therefore, pleased me more than to read that

> I am not an "impulsive" player, that I prepare every nuance and detail at home—for it *proves* that I can place some reliance into the promptings that come to me on the stage; sufficient, at any rate, to make even a profound connoisseur think that everything was planned at home.

Hofmann believed in the subconscious. "In every art form," he wrote not long before his death in 1957, "expressive greatness is not achieved consciously. If it is planned, the listener always becomes aware of the artist's intent and falls out of the mood. Naturally one must study the work to fall into its spirit, but from that point on the performance must be intuitive—otherwise it is worthless."

Hofmann's early recordings support his words. He had a peculiar recording career. It is believed that in 1887, Thomas A. Edison, who had invented the phonograph only ten years previously, took the prodigy to his laboratory, where Josef made a few cylinders. (Edison, who had a hearing impairment, knew nothing about music; his tastes were abysmal. But like everybody else he was intrigued by the young pianist and wanted to see how he would sound on the Edison machine.) Those cylinders have long disappeared. In 1890 Hofmann, who had been sent a machine by Edison, made some cylinders in Berlin. The young man, who had a scientific bent (in later life he had his own laboratory and workshop, built a steam automobile, and held patents on automobile shock absorbers and piano actions), tinkered with the machine and made some improvements on it. Unfortunately the 1890 cylinders were destroyed during the bombing of Hofmann's home during World War I. His first commercial records were issued in 1904 by the Gramophone and Typewriter Company (known to collectors as G&T) in Berlin, and five records were released. For Columbia, in America, he recorded fifteen discs between 1912 and 1923; and, for Brunswick, eight between 1924 and 1926. All of those recordings were acoustic. The electrical recordings that came in after 1925 did not interest him. He said that they could not do justice to his kind of playing, and he never again made a commercial recording. He did make some test pressings for Victor and HMV in the 1930's but never allowed them to be released, although he was altogether satisfied with the HMV results. After his death, however, those were transferred to LP discs. His golden jubilee concert at the Metropolitan Opera in 1937 was privately recorded by Victor, and that too has been released; it contains the Rubinstein D minor Concerto, Hofmann's own *Chromaticon* for piano and orchestra, and a large group of solo pieces. He gave a concert at Casimir Hall in the Curtis Institute of Music, and the acetates of that performance have been saved and issued in a two-disc album.

Fortunately for posterity, Hofmann made many appearances on the radio. In the middle 1930's many record collectors and music lovers got their own recording equipment and started to take music off the air on acetate discs. Thus some Hofmann performances have been saved, among them Rubinstein concertos, the two by Chopin, the Beethoven G major, and excerpts from several others (Hofmann's concerto repertory was very small, purposely so). A few of these radio performances should never have been released; they show the great Hofmann in his decline. By that time he was an old, bitter man with an alcoholic problem. But all of the important items were made available by the International Piano Library, later called the International Piano Archives. The archives, founded by Gregor Benko, currently are at the University of Maryland.

Hofmann never recorded large-scale works on his commercial records. His first efforts were in the days of single-sided records, which meant that no piece could last longer than five minutes. Around 1910 some genius figured out that *both* sides of a record could be used, and Hofmann took advantage of it a few times, playing such relatively long works as the second Liszt Rhapsody and the Chopin B minor Scherzo (both cut) on both sides of a single disc. In the early 1920's and the last days of the acoustic process, large-scale works began to be recorded—complete symphonies, operas, and the like—but Hofmann never got around to recording an entire sonata or anything really major. He also made many piano rolls, signing a fifteen-year contract with Aeolian Duo-Art to record a hundred pieces for $100,000. In the 1960's many Hofmann rolls appeared on LP records, often with their provenance so carefully concealed that buyers thought they were hearing Hofmann flat-disc recordings. These LP transfers of piano rolls are a disgrace and should be avoided. They give no idea of Hofmann's playing, even though he himself endorsed them.

The early Hofmann flat-disc recordings accurately represent his art, faded in sound though they may be. He plays everything with an inhuman perfection and an aristocratic musical approach. Young pianists today, who mistakenly think that technique has improved, cannot believe their ears on encountering early Hofmann. Somehow he makes every other pianist sound *thick*. There is a peculiarly alive quality to the playing, with the rhythmic bounce unique to Hofmann. Yet there also is a strong classic side, in that it is objective, unfussy, and almost always textually literal. His Romanticism, as with other top pianists of the day, can be seen in his delicate adjustments in tempo, and in his ability to marshal bass lines and inner voices. And, above all, there is the unique, soaring, beautiful Hofmann sound, as revealed in his 1935 HMV tests and remembered by all who heard him play.

Later in life he did not seem to concentrate as much on sheer accuracy. His approach was broader, and a few missed notes did not bother him. The late Hofmann can be sampled in the International Piano Library recordings of the two Chopin concertos, both off the air with the New York Philharmonic conducted by John Barbirolli. The slow movement of the Chopin F minor gives an idea of what Romantic rhetoric at its best was all about: the pacings sounding inevitable, the melodic lines shaped by a master, the recitative sections all but talking, the technique all-encompassing.

In the 1920's Hofmann became, with Rachmaninoff, one of the two leading pianists before the public. But he was not a happy man. His personal life was in a mess, for one. He was a womanizer, and his marriage was breaking up. In 1905 he had married Marie Eustis, eleven years older than he, of a distinguished family, and a divorcée with a child. Hofmann left her in 1927 to marry one of his pupils, who was thirty years younger than he. After a while she became very stout and reclusive. Hofmann started drinking heavily, and eventually became an alcoholic. He played during those years, sometimes with distressing results.

In the 1920's the Curtis Institute kept him busy. Back in his prodigy days he had met Edward and Mary Bok, who ran the Curtis Publishing Company (the *Ladies' Home Journal* and *Saturday Evening Post* were the flagships of that fleet). They remained friends, and he stayed with them whenever he was in Philadelphia. The Boks founded the Curtis Institute of Music in 1924, appointing Hofmann the head of the piano department. He had never taught and was attracted by the idea of working with top students admitted only on a full scholarship basis. The initial faculty was glittering. Among the piano teachers was Isabella Vengerova, who taught some outstanding American pianists. The head of the voice faculty was Marcella Sembrich. Leopold Stokowski was in charge of conductors and Carl Flesch was the head of the violin department. Hofmann became director in 1927, and promptly hired such musicians as Leopold Auer, Efrem Zimbalist (who later became director of the Curtis Institute), Fritz Reiner, and Arthur Rodzinski. The salaries paid the faculty were stupendous for those days. Hofmann's was $72,500. Later, during the Depression, he took a cut to $42,500. He became very active in Curtis affairs, but in 1933 resumed his European tours. In 1938 the Curtis board had to effect economies, and faculty salaries were heavily cut. Hofmann protested, offering to waive his own salary if that would help. He resigned over the issue and moved from Philadelphia to Los Angeles. As a teacher he never produced many artists who became stars. Of his many pupils, the only famous one currently (1984) in action is Shura Cherkassky.

Like his friend Kreisler, he composed graceful salon pieces for the piano and, like Kreisler, hid his identity. Where Kreisler "discovered" music by composers of the past, Hofmann "discovered" music by one Michel Dvorsky. The only difference was that when Kreisler's hoax was unveiled, there was a major scandal. When

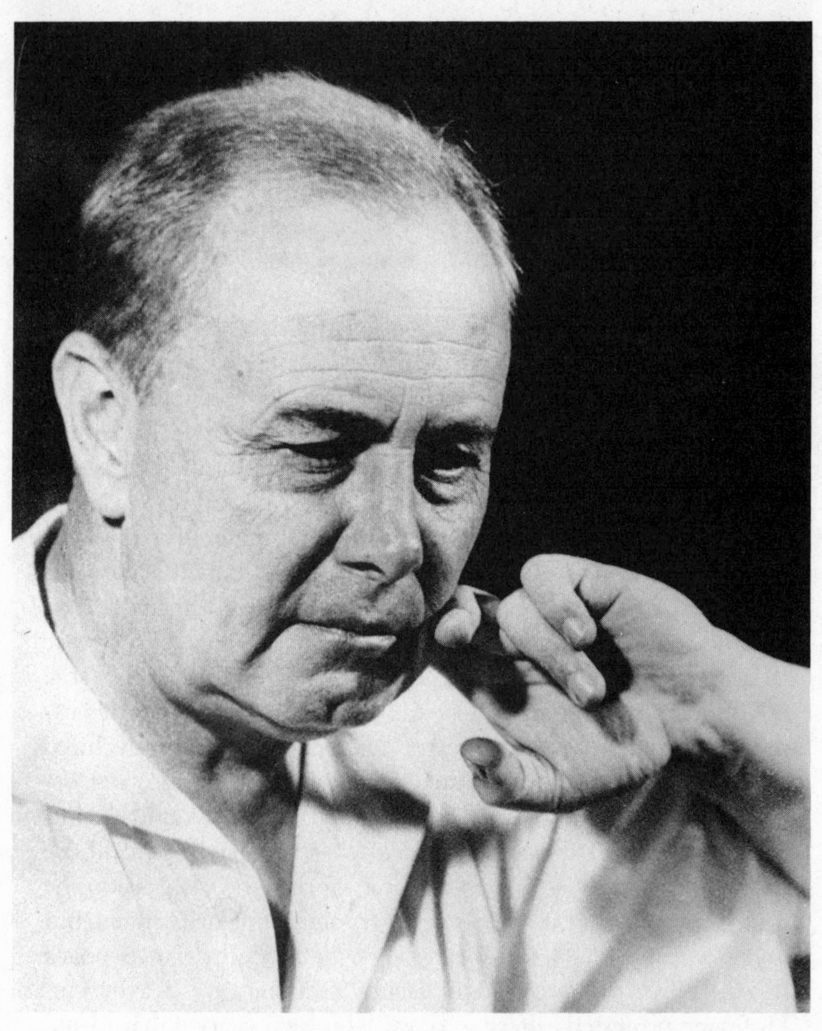

Hofmann toward the end of his career. He had a small hand that could barely stretch a tenth.

Hofmann 'fessed up, nobody cared one way or the other. By that time, in any case, everybody in music knew who Michel Dvorsky really was.

After his last concert in 1946, Hofmann retired to Los Angeles. He also had a house in Long Beach, at which he spent much time. His Los Angeles house did not even have a piano in it; he had got rid of the two instruments specially built for him by Steinway. Many pianists believe that because of his small hands Hofmann's custom-made pianos had considerably smaller keys than regulation instruments. But that was not the case; each key was shaved down a bit, and the net result was something like a tiny fraction of an inch to the octave.

Little was heard of Hofmann in his retirement. The younger pianists were much more interested in Rachmaninoff and in Rachmaninoff's successor, Vladimir Horowitz. Every pianist in the 1940's and 50's was trying to be Vladimir Horowitz. But the reissue of the solo part of Hofmann's Golden Jubilee concert by Columbia in 1957 (and, several years later, of the entire concert by IPA) sparked a revival of interest in the contributions of one of the greatest pianists of history. With the Romantic revival of the 1970's and the return to the repertory of music hitherto sneered at, young pianists began to regard Hofmann and some of his great contemporaries—especially Josef Lhévinne, Ignaz Friedman, Benno Moiseiwitsch, and Leopold Godowsky—with more than cursory interest. The old masters did, after all, have secrets that disappeared with them. Could those secrets, their manner of playing, the musical philosophy that enveloped all of them, their way of producing sound, the conventions that all of them obeyed—could these secrets be rediscovered? Possibly. But the particular combination of perfection, aristocracy, masculinity, energy, and poetry that typified Josef Hofmann in his great days went to his grave with him.

20 *Sergei Rachmaninoff*

THE RUSSIAN MASTER

SERGEI RACHMANINOFF came to the piano early and he came to the piano late. He came to the piano early because he followed the usual prodigy path—born with a perfect ear, starting at the age of four, impressing everybody with his talent, winning prizes. But as a young man he became more interested in conducting and, especially, composing than he was in piano playing. Not until the Russian Revolution, when he fled the country, did he decide to make his living with his fingers. He was about forty-five years old, and had to learn an entire repertory. In effect, he was coming to the piano late, starting from scratch, although he was not entirely unknown. Was he not, after all, the composer of that universal favorite, *the* Prelude in C sharp minor?

He and Josef Hofmann, the two pianists who bestrode their times, were the closest of friends. Henry Pleasants, as a young music critic in Philadelphia, once asked Rachmaninoff who, in his estimation, were the greatest living pianists. Rachmaninoff thought a bit. "Well," he said, "there's Hofmann . . ." and he thought a little bit more, "and there's me"; and he then closed his mouth and would not say another word. The two pianists were polar opposites. Hofmann was short, Rachmaninoff tall. Hofmann was voluble and affable, Rachmaninoff dour and laconic. Hofmann was a colorist at the keyboard; Rachmaninoff projected strength, structure, and form. Hofmann's playing sounded spontaneous, while Rachmaninoff's gave the feeling that everything had been planned in advance.

Both pianists had all the gifts, including the infallible musical memory that all top performers have to possess. But judged even on the highest plane Rachmaninoff's gifts were something special. Born in Semyonovo on April 1, 1873, he was taken to St. Petersburg as a boy of ten. His father had dissipated the family fortune, and he was immediately enrolled as a scholarship student at the Conservatory. Two years later he entered the Moscow Conservatory and also the classes of Nikolai Zverev.

Zverev was an unusual man. He was a piano teacher who took only young boys into his house—they had to live with him—and superintended their entire cultural as well as musical development. He charged a great deal for pupils who could afford it and nothing at all for pupils who couldn't. Demanding and irascible, he ran a tight ship, expecting immediate obedience from his young charges. The boys had to get up at six, practice, play four hands, study scores, and whatever else Zverev demanded. They had to read the classics of Russian and European literature, learn table manners, go to the opera and to the theater, learn the difference between a claret and Beaujolais, learn how to hold one's liquor. When Zverev considered them ready, there were visits to nightclubs and, maybe, brothels. Nobody knew if Zverev could even play the piano; he never played anything at any time. But he must have done something right; through his hands passed Lhévinne, Scriabin, Konstantin Igumnov, and many others who achieved fame as recitalists and teachers. Zverev also was a great party-giver whose affairs would attract notables of Russian society and all of the important Russian musicians. Zverev's pupils often played at

Sergei Rachmaninoff (right) and his good friend Josef Hofmann. The two great pianists met in Russia early in the century, when this picture was taken, and remained close all their lives.

these events, and it was there that Rachmaninoff met the Rubinstein brothers and Tchaikovsky. Tchaikovsky was impressed and predicted a great future for the boy. Rachmaninoff worshiped Tchaikovsky, who became the greatest influence on his musical development. One other thing: Zverev's pupils had to act like young gentlemen at these affairs, and woe betide anyone who committed a gaffe or had a lapse in etiquette.

Rachmaninoff left Zverev after about three years. He probably was the most talented pupil Zverev ever had, but he was more interested in composition than playing the piano, and they broke up over the issue. Returning to the Conservatory, Rachmaninoff studied piano with his cousin Alexander Siloti, the Liszt pupil, and won the gold medal not as a pianist but as a composer. His award-winning composition was an opera, *Aleko*.

Thus it was as a composer that Rachmaninoff first made his mark, though in Moscow he also was recognized as a fabulous pianist and as a formidable all-around musician. His mind was a magnet to which musical particles were attracted and, once secured, clung for life. Rachmaninoff, like Liszt, could do things that scared musicians. He also was something of an object of mystery to his fellow students. One of them, Mikhail Bukinik, has left a description of the sixteen-year-old Sergei—bass voice, heavy smoker, stony but expressive face, a listener rather than a talker. "Though we know he is our age," Bukinik said, "he seems an adult to us." Many years later one of his classmates, Alexander Goldenweiser, wrote his recollections of Rachmaninoff. Both were Siloti pupils. Once Siloti, at his Wednesday class, gave Rachmaninoff the long Brahms-Handel Variations to study. Three days later Rachmaninoff came to the Saturday class with the piece memorized. On another occasion Goldenweiser and a friend, Ivan Alchevsky, visited Rachmaninoff:

> Rachmaninoff was interested in knowing what we were composing. I had nothing of interest with me, but Alchevsky had the first part of a symphony that he had just finished sketching. He showed it to Rachmaninoff, who played it through and praised it

> highly. After this, quite a long time passed—not less than a year or a year and a half. Then at one of my musical evenings Rachmaninoff saw Alchevsky, recalled the symphony and asked how it had worked out. Alchevsky, who always abandoned his undertakings midway, told him that he hadn't finished it and that there was only the first part, which he had already seen. Rachmaninoff said, "That's a great pity, for I liked it very much." He sat down at the piano and played from memory almost all the exposition of this quite complicated work.

Another classmate, B. L. Yavorsky, recounts a similar story. In the early 1890's, he says, the composer Sergei Taneiev held a musical evening and Alexander Glazunov was present. Glazunov was asked to play something of his own and obliged with a movement of a symphony that he had just finished and had not shown to anybody, not even to his mentor, Rimsky-Korsakov.

> When Glazunov sat down at the piano [Yavorsky continues], Taneiev got up and left the room to close all doors so that there would be no interruption. He locked the doors, returned and invited Glazunov to begin. Glazunov played the first movement, after which there were discussion and conversation. Some time passed. Suddenly Taneiev said, "Oh! I locked all the doors. No one can get in. Maybe someone has come." He left the room and shortly returned with Rachmaninoff, whom he introduced as his pupil, saying that he was very talented and had also just written a symphony. Rachmaninoff sat down and played the first movement of—Glazunov's symphony. Glazunov, amazed, asked, "*Where* did you get to know this? I haven't shown or played it to anyone." Taneiev said, "He was sitting in my bedroom. I had locked him in."

Musicians found out that whatever composition was mentioned—orchestral, piano, opera, anything—Rachmaninoff, if he had at any time heard it, could go to the piano and play it as if it were a work he had thoroughly studied. "Such phenomenal power," Goldenweiser said, "I have never met with in anybody else." Naturally, Rachmaninoff was one of the great sight-readers in history, and when he read through a work for the first time it was generally a finished performance. Only once was he known to admit difficulties. When he read through Scriabin's murderously complicated Etude in C sharp minor (Op. 42, No. 5) he told his classmate Leo Conus (both were in Anton Arensky's composition class), "Difficult Etude! I spent a whole hour on it."

For the next decade Rachmaninoff composed diligently, conducted at the Private Opera (a company set up by the wealthy industrialist Savva Mamontov), and there met the new star bass, Feodor Chaliapin. A lifelong friendship resulted. After the failure of his First Symphony he went into a depression and temporarily ceased to compose. César Cui's review would have sent any young composer into a decline. "If there's a Conservatory in Hell, and one of its gifted pupils should be given the assignment of writing a programmatic symphony [Rachmaninoff's work was named *The Bells*] on the Seven Plagues of Egypt, and if he should write a symphony resembling Mr. Rachmaninoff's symphony—this assignment would have been carried out brilliantly and he would enchant all the inmates of Hell, so devilish are the discords he dished out to us." Rachmaninoff did give concerts, however, playing his own music. He started to travel, and made his London debut in 1899. Everybody wanted to hear him play *the* Prelude, which Siloti had introduced to England a few years previously. The public doted on it, and so did publishers. Everybody made money from the piece except him. He had sold it outright to a publisher for $40. Had Rachmaninoff held a copyright on the Prelude in C sharp minor, he would have been a very rich man on the proceeds from that work alone. He ruefully mentioned this more than once later in his life.

It took Rachmaninoff three years to work himself out of his depression. A medical man, Dr. Nikolai Dahl, cured his problem with a combination of hypnosis and autosuggestion. The immediate result was his ever-popular Second Piano Concerto. In 1902 Rachmaninoff married his first cousin, Natalie Satin. Then followed a conducting engagement at the Bolshoi Opera and a stream of compositions, including the Second Symphony in E minor and the Piano Concerto No. 3. Rachmaninoff played the world premiere of the concerto on his first American tour in 1909, with the New York Symphony, Walter Damrosch conducting. Neither the conductor nor the orchestra made him very happy, but about two months later Rachmaninoff played the concerto with the Philharmonic under Gustav Mahler, and was ecstatic about the experience, saying that Mahler was the only conductor who could be classed with Arthur Nikisch. This D minor Concerto, his greatest, was dedicated to Josef Hofmann, who never played it, saying it was not for him. The stretches would have been uncomfortable for Hofmann's small hand.

From 1911 to 1914 Rachmaninoff conducted the Moscow Philharmonic. World War I arrived. Rachmaninoff remained in Russia. He gave several concerts of Scriabin's music after the composer's death in 1915, and did not make everybody happy. Many felt that Rachmaninoff's playing was too severe, too lacking in improvisatory feeling for the mystical Scriabin, whose own playing had a shimmering quality. At that time Serge Prokofiev was the *enfant terrible* of Russian music; he had recently graduated from the St. Petersburg Conservatory and was a brilliant pianist himself. He heard one of Rachmaninoff's Scriabin concerts. Scriabin's own playing had been all allure and suggestion, recollected Prokofiev, "but with Rachmaninoff all its notes stood firmly and clearly on the ground." Prokofiev went backstage after the concert and told Rachmaninoff that he had played very well. Rachmaninoff was furious. "And you probably thought I'd play badly?" he icily asked. The two men were not on speaking terms until many years had passed. During the war Rachmaninoff toured Russia with an orchestra conducted by Serge Koussevitzky. He also accompanied the soprano Nina Koschetz in some of her recitals, and there were those who said that their relationship was more than one of mere friendship.

In 1918 Rachmaninoff left Russia for good, with wife and two daughters, and settled first in Stockholm and then in Copenhagen. He received offers from American orchestras: both the

Boston Symphony and the Cincinnati Symphony invited him. But Rachmaninoff felt unprepared; his symphonic repertory was too small. So to the piano he went. Up to that point his public appearances as a pianist had been almost exclusively devoted to his own music. Now he had to memorize a repertory ranging from Beethoven onward. Like all Romantic musicians, Rachmaninoff did not spend much time on Mozart, Haydn, or Bach. He probably never had more than three or four Bach or Mozart piano pieces in his repertory. Of Handel, the *Harmonious Blacksmith* was the only work he played. He did not play many piano concertos. In his first years in America he offered the two Liszt concertos and the Tchaikovsky B flat minor. Then he played only his own concertos. Not until the last years of his life did he play anything else. One concerto was, unexpectedly, the Beethoven Piano Concerto No. 1, which entered his repertory in 1940. He also put into his repertory, in his last six seasons, the Schumann A minor and the Liszt *Totentanz.*

Almost immediately Rachmaninoff secured for himself a place among the piano immortals. It was not only his remarkable playing that attracted audiences. He also had a reverse kind of charisma. Audiences were awed when this grave, stately, tall (he was six feet three), unsmiling man, with his slightly Mongoloid features and close-cropped head of hair (unlike the wild foliage that topped the heads of so many musicians of the day) walked quietly to the piano. There was no show when Rachmaninoff played. Gestures were down to a minimum: the body was immobile; everything was done with forearm and fingers.

From those fingers came an unforced, bronzelike sonority and a feeling of infallibility. He was one of the most accurate of all pianists. Correct notes seemed built into his very constitution; a wrong note at a Rachmaninoff recital never seemed to occur. Rhythmically he was representative of the best in Romantic performers. His was a rhythm that never lost the basic metrical pulse and was always clearly defined, and yet was constantly being varied. The young Vladimir Horowitz may have got this kind of rhythmic snap from Rachmaninoff. All of his playing had extreme

Rachmaninoff in 1933. Unlike Hofmann, he had huge, beautifully shaped hands.

musical elegance, the melodic lines shaped with ineffable authority. It possessed a manly, aristocratic kind of poetry hard to describe; without ever becoming sentimental, Rachmaninoff managed to wring dry the emotional essence of the music. He did it by a kind of subtly nuanced phrasing within his strong, clear, unfussy projection of the lines. Unlike most pianists, he had a very large hand that easily disposed of the most complicated chordal configurations; and his left-hand technique was unusually powerful. His playing was marked by *definition;* where other pianists became blurry through abuse of the pedal, or deficiencies of finger, Rachmaninoff's textures were crystalline, and only Hofmann had his kind of clarity. It took some years for this kind of playing to become the model for the new generation of pianists. Rachmaninoff's brilliance, of course, was immediately recognized. Most critics hailed him as the greatest of living pianists, and he attracted huge audiences right off. At every concert he had to play *the* Prelude, which he grew to hate. But he knew what was expected of him, and he grimly faced the inevitable. "Don't worry," he would tell his manager. "I know my duty. I shall play it." His initial appearances put him into the top echelon of pianists. But some of the older critics, among whom was the esteemed James Huneker, were thrown off by Rachmaninoff's kind of austerity. They were used to Paderewski, or the thunderous Rosenthal and the other representatives of High Romanticism. Rachmaninoff, like Hofmann, was too cool for them at the beginning.

After his arrival in the United States, and his subsequent success, the pattern of Rachmaninoff's life was set. He would concertize in America or abroad and take the summer off in Switzerland to compose. In private life he was a warm friend and far from the majestic figure he was on stage. But when he was composing, he was unapproachable. His sister-in-law, Sophie Satin, has described his schedule. He rose at eight, had breakfast, read the newspapers, and practiced for two hours—scales and other finger exercises. At 2 P.M. he dictated letters and worked with his secretary. After lunch he took a short rest and practiced for another two hours. The rest of the day was reserved for himself and his family.

"But this schedule changed completely when Rachmaninoff was composing. Then he practiced no more than an hour and a half and kept away from everybody. During those periods we saw him only at meals, but even then, sitting with us at the table, he seemed to be absent. He was obviously not listening to the conversation and ate the food put before him almost automatically. After dinner he would rapidly disappear again. We all knew that one should never ask him what he was composing or how his work was progressing. He was then another man, and the mood of Rachmaninoff the composer was quite different from Rachmaninoff the pianist and man." He was *very* Russian. He never mastered English. In his twenty-five years in America, he seems to have read only one book in English—*Main Street* by Sinclair Lewis. He read much Shakespeare—in Russian translation. His friends for the most part were Russians. He gave very few interviews and was not in the least interested in publicity. He became an American citizen only a few months before his death.

In his professional life he was austere, seldom relaxing, a man of habit who operated by the clock and expected all others to do likewise. Schedules had to be maintained; what else were schedules for? He once arrived at the Academy of Music for an 11 A.M. rehearsal. Stokowski was working on a Tchaikovsky symphony. The hour of eleven came and went. Rachmaninoff waited about three minutes, walked to the piano, sat down, and hit a few thunderous chords. "The piano is here," he told Stokowski, "I am here, and it is eleven o'clock. Let us rehearse."

Such was the demand for him that he could have made any number of concert appearances. But he considered himself primarily a composer, and he turned down many dates. By the middle 1930's he had cut down his schedule to forty or forty-five appearances a season. Yet toward the end of the decade he was back to sixty or so, and he could have doubled that number had he wished. He and Hofmann were the two highest-paid pianists of their time. In the depths of the Great Depression, when the head of a family blessed himself if he was earning $3,000 a year, when a five-course meal at an elegant restaurant cost $1.25, Rachmaninoff was making about $135,000.

He never made a radio appearance. His official reason was that radio was "not perfect enough to do justice to good music." Also, "It makes listening to music too comfortable. . . . To appreciate good music, one must be mentally alert and emotionally receptive. You can't be that when you are sitting at home with your feet on a chair." Even more important: "An artist's performance depends so much on his audience that I cannot imagine even playing without one." Often he was asked to make radio appearances, and offered fabulous fees, but to the end of his life he refused. His contracts with the New York Philharmonic specified that he would not play the Sunday matinee performances, which were broadcast. Rachmaninoff felt that he could not be at his best without an audience to stimulate him. The year before his death he told his friend Alfred Swan that he was "like an old grisette. She is skinny and worn, but the urge to walk the streets is so strong that in spite of her years she goes out every night. And so it is with me. I am old and wrinkled, and still I have to play. Oh, no, I could not play any less. I want to play all I can." He needed his public, and he played as long as he could before cancer immobilized him, which was about a month before his death. He played his last concert in Knoxville on February 17, 1943; he was ill at the time and canceled the rest of his tour. On March 28, 1943, he died in Beverly Hills.

At least Rachmaninoff made records, many of them, including such large-scale works as the Schumann *Carnaval* and Chopin B flat minor Sonata. One wonders how he reconciled his views about the necessity of an audience with the lonely task of making records. First he recorded for Edison in 1919, making a few discs. Then in 1924 he moved to Victor. Toward the end of his life he proposed putting a series of his recital programs on records and was turned down. The loss is posterity's. In the 1970's Victor released five albums containing everything Rachmaninoff had ever recorded, including the Edison discs and a few that he never

Rachmaninoff a few years before his death in 1943. His expression was one of habitual severity. Seldom did anybody see him smile in public.

passed for release. He had some reservations about recordings, and said to a friend:

> I get very nervous when I am making records, and all of whom I have asked say they get nervous too. When the test records are made, I know that I can hear them played back to me, and then everything is all right. But when the stage is set for the final recording, and I realize that this will remain for good, I get nervous and my hands get tense. I am very pleased with the Schumann *Carnaval.* It has come out very well. Today I recorded the B flat minor Sonata by Chopin, and I do not know yet how it has come out. I shall hear the test records tomorrow. If it is not good, I can always have the records destroyed and play it over again. You know how severely I judge myself and my compositions. But I want to tell you that I have found some old records of mine. They are very well played, without a hitch. There is some Johann Strauss, Gluck, I think. They are very good.

The Gluck to which Rachmaninoff referred was the Sgambati arrangement of the *Mélodie* from *Orpheus,* recorded in 1925; and the Strauss was the Tausig arrangement of *Man lebt nur einmal,* recorded in 1927. In the history of Strauss waltz arrangements for piano on recordings—and the discography, played by very great artists, is very large—only Josef Lhévinne's coruscating performance of the Strauss-Schulz-Evler *Blue Danube* Waltz stands up to Rachmaninoff's of the Tausig arrangement. Rachmaninoff is in such incredible command of the notes in this fairly difficult piece. It must be remembered that until magnetic tape started to be used in the late 1940's there was no way to correct a recording. If the performer did not like what came out, he had to record the entire side over again. Since no such electronic hokery-pokery as splicings could be done, the old 78 r.p.m. discs are more honest than modern ones and they give a truer idea of what the artist really represented. In Rachmaninoff's Strauss-Tausig recording, he takes a pleasant enough but minor piece and makes something perfect out of it—perfect technically, perfect musically. On the published recording, incidentally, Rachmaninoff played Side 1 in a single "take." That is, Rachmaninoff sat down, played it once, listened to a test, and said it was fine. No splicings, no engineers riding gain—nothing but pure, unadulterated Rachmaninoff at his spectacular best. Side 2 is the third take. When he died he left a quantity of unapproved recordings in the Victor "icebox," among them Liszt's *Spanish Rhapsody.* Copies have never been located. It has been said that Victor, to help the war effort, donated all of its metal masters to be melted down, and among them was the *Spanish Rhapsody.*

Nobody grieved more about Rachmaninoff's passing than Josef Hofmann, who wrote a eulogy in 1945: "Rachmaninoff was made of steel and gold; steel in his arms, gold in his heart. I can never think of his majestic being without tears in my eyes, for I not only admired him as a supreme artist, but I also loved him as a man."

21 *John McCormack*

IRISH GOLD

ALTHOUGH Caruso was the greatest operatic tenor of his time, the greatest male voice on the recital circuit belonged to John McCormack. McCormack, however, had his fling at opera, and no more beautiful stylist existed, a fact that Caruso recognized. The two men were close friends and admired each other. McCormack first heard Caruso in 1904 and was overwhelmed. "My jaw dropped," he told *Musical America*. "Such smoothness and purity of tone, and such quality, it was like a stream of liquid gold." One of the nicest stories about singers concerns an accidental meeting of Caruso and McCormack on the street.

"Well, Rico, how's the world's greatest tenor today?" asked McCormack.

"John," said Caruso, "I didn't know you have turned into a baritone."

McCormack achieved a good measure of fame as an opera singer. He never had the power of a Caruso, and never sought it.

It was not that his singing lacked strength; but he knew exactly what his voice could do, and he remained a lyric tenor all his life, pouring forth long, liquid phrases that seemed to go on without end. The violinist Jan Kubelík said that McCormack must have had a Stradivarius in his throat. McCormack's advice to singers, in a letter to the New York *World* on April 14, 1918, stressed above all the necessity of resisting any temptation to force. "A great many singers—and some good singers, too—have an idea that the public wants bigness of voice. That is a mistaken notion. The public wants nothing of the sort; it not only never has, but it never will. The history of the world's greatest singers brings not one supreme artist who was not essentially lyric. . . . What the public enjoys most of all is the smooth, pure and beautiful tone in the singing voice."

McCormack could have added that it is not necessary to have a big voice to fill big areas. Good technicians never have to force. A well-placed voice—and no voice ever was more well-placed than McCormack's—can fill any house, with the most delicate pianissimo penetrating to the farthest corners. At the old Metropolitan Opera, that enormous cavern with about 3,700 seats, small-voiced singers like Lucrezia Bori and Bidú Sayão had no trouble; they had secure techniques, well-placed voices, and could face an audience without feeling the necessity to force.

Nor did McCormack have any vocal problems in any house. But he never was very happy on the operatic stage. If nothing else, he was the world's worst actor. He admitted that he acted like a stick, and he could go into a kind of trance on stage, wondering what to do with his hands, his feet, his body. Frances Alda was once his Mimi during a Metropolitan Opera *Bohème*. When she made her entrance McCormack was standing between her and the chair on which she was to sink. "You're in the way, John," she whispered. He did not move. "Get out of the way!" Alda says that McCormack became panic-stricken and froze up. "What'll I do?" he whispered. "Move, you fool!" McCormack made the sign of the cross and got out of her way.

Yet this inhibited figure on stage was the most genial, relaxed,

John McCormack, the most popular of all song recitalists. All professionals paid homage to the unparalleled sweetness and smoothness of his voice and the utter security of his technique. In the photograph above, he is seen with Fritz Kreisler.

and communicative of all recital singers. There he was at home. After 1910 he was a recital phenomenon, and his only real competitor was Ernestine Schumann-Heink. That stout, homely lady with the incredible contralto voice was at that time already America's earth mother, and she kept on going until she became America's grandmother. She liked to eat. Caruso once saw her in a restaurant attacking a steak as big as a manhole cover. "Are you having that alone, Tina?" he asked, preparing to join her. "Ach, no," said Schumann-Heink. "Mit potato, und wegetable, und. . . ." Blessed with an enormous voice and a perfect technique, she was indestructible. Hers was a career of almost unprecedented length; she was born in 1861, made her debut in 1878, and fifty-four years later, in 1932, made her Metropolitan Opera farewell. During World War I she had sons fighting in the German army and sons in the American army. She would tell this sad story while raising money for the American war effort, and there was not a dry eye in the house. One of the first radio stars, she sang *Stille Nacht* every Christmas for millions of radio listeners and became an American institution.

She and McCormack became the first concert superstars in history. There were great recitalists before them, but none ever so captured the public imagination, with a consequent earning power that exceeded even the fortunes made by the operatic superstars. Opera houses at any time pay top fees only to a handful of singers, and those fees are much lower than what top recitalists can get. Where Caruso at his peak would be getting $2,500 a performance, McCormack as a recitalist was making much more—and he could sing in bigger houses seven days a week if he felt so inclined. McCormack, with his concerts and income from records, sometimes earned $1 million a year. Financially he left Caruso and Schumann-Heink far behind. *The New York Times* of March 7, 1918, had a story saying that McCormack paid a bigger income tax than Caruso—$75,000 as against Caruso's $59,000. *Musical America* reported in March 1916 that McCormack's income from royalties on the sales of records alone "equalled the combined salaries of the President of the United States, the governors of New

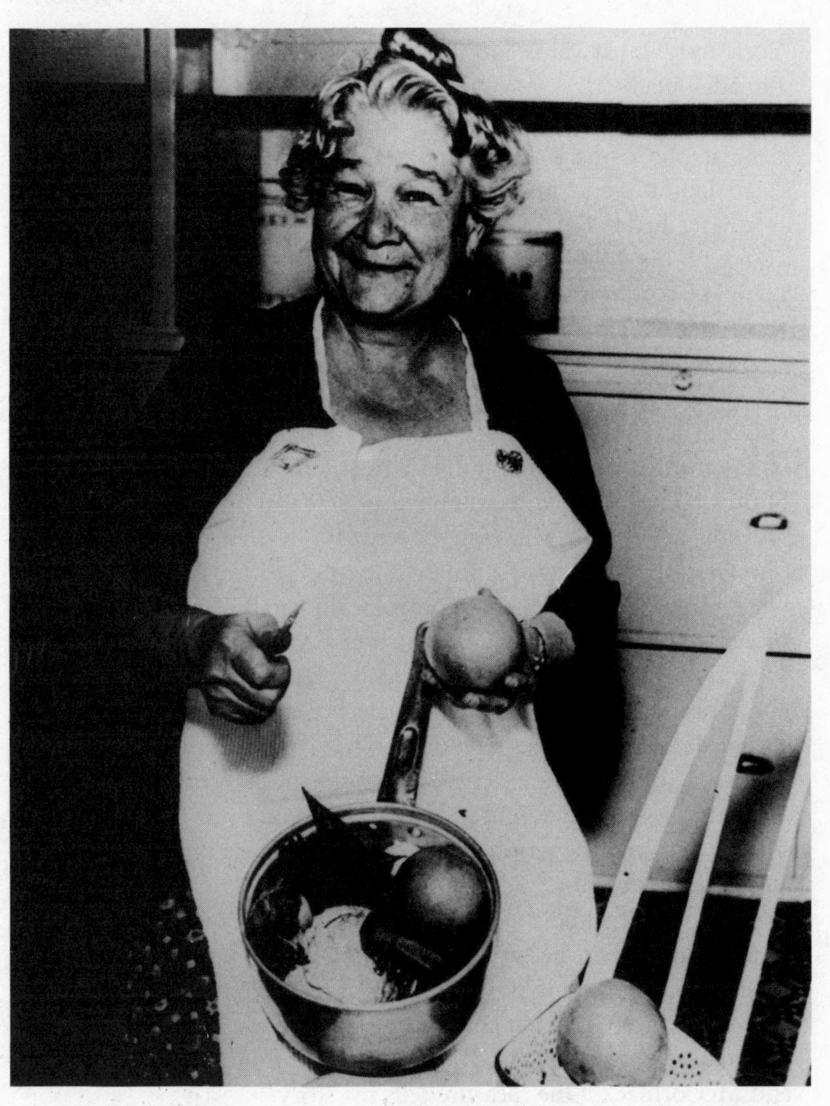

Ernestine Schumann-Heink, the contralto who was one of McCormack's few rivals as a recitalist. She had a phenomenal voice, and her career was phenomenally long.

York and Pennsylvania and the mayors of New York, Boston and Philadelphia."

What drove international audiences to a frenzy was the sweetness of McCormack's voice, its secure technique, his incredibly clear diction—and his repertory, with its mix of popular songs from the lieder repertory, a few operatic arias thrown in, and above all his Irish songs and ballads. All of these he sang with complete commitment and purity of style; and after 1920 he even took a look at songs by Hugo Wolf, Schumann, Grieg, and Brahms. It was inevitable that some serious critics and music lovers refused to take him seriously. To them he was a mere entertainer. They were wrong. A unique voice like McCormack's, used so tastefully, is in itself an esthetic treat; and McCormack applied himself to his music with complete artistry. All musicians could—and still can, on the McCormack records—learn a great deal from him about how to shape a phrase, how to breathe, how to inflect, what a legato line and breath control really can be, how to imbue a piece with infinite charm without ever becoming sentimental or too obvious. McCormack, incidentally, had a few words to say about his diction. He told an interviewer for the Duluth *Herald* in 1916, "It is because I have studied so hard that I have good enunciation. I do not sing exactly as I would speak. I exaggerate the consonants somewhat, and sometimes even add very slight vowel sounds between the words to make it clear where one word ends and the other begins."

He was Irish all the way through: he was born and died in Ireland, and when he sang his Italian and German music a pronounced brogue came through the perfect diction. That too was part of the McCormack charm. Of all the thousands of singers who made records, two are always instantly recognizable—Caruso and McCormack. One measure tells the story.

McCormack was born in Athlone on June 14, 1884. He sang in school, he sang in a Dublin cathedral, and at nineteen—the youngest tenor competing—won first prize in the National Music Festival. Another prizewinner was a soprano named Lily Foley, who became his wife a short time later. (They had two children,

Cyril and Gwendolyn.) He gave concerts and, in 1904, made his first recordings—all of Irish ballads. McCormack knew he had a voice, but he was almost self-taught and needed help. He therefore went to Italy in 1905 and worked with Vincenzo Sabatini, who extended his range to a top C (though McCormack never was to be a high-note singer). Sabatini told him that God had placed his voice, and that it would be best to leave it alone. On January 13, 1906, McCormack made his operatic debut with a provincial company in Italy. Back in London he gave more concerts and, in 1907, was engaged by Covent Garden. He was twenty-three and hopeless on stage, but the sheer beauty of his voice and the elegance of his style in such roles as Turiddu, Don Ottavio, and Rodolfo attracted admiring attention. Later he was to make a record of Don Ottavio's *Il mio tesoro* that has remained the exemplar of Mozart singing.

McCormack sang at Covent Garden every season until it was closed during the war. In all, he had fifteen roles. Among his operas were *Lucia, Rigoletto, Madama Butterfly, Roméo et Juliette, Tosca, Mefistofele, La Sonnambula,* and *Lakmé*. In those he appeared with such all-time great sopranos as Melba, Tetrazzini, Destinn, and Muzio. New York, in the person of Oscar Hammerstein, beckoned, and in 1909 McCormack made his Manhattan Opera debut in *La Traviata* with Tetrazzini. She had requested him, and he also was her tenor in *La Fille du Régiment* and *Lakmé*. When the Metropolitan Opera bought Hammerstein out in 1910, McCormack was taken over by the Met and made his debut there in *La Traviata* opposite Melba. He left the Metropolitan in 1911 and did not return until 1918, when he sang a few performances there. America adopted him as her own—which he indeed was, having applied for citizenship in 1914 and receiving his papers in 1919. By that time his concert career was in full swing, and he was recognized as the most potent box-office draw in the musical world. His operatic life was about over, and he left that world for good with a season at Monte Carlo in 1923.

In recitals he could be himself without having to worry about characterization, costumes, movement, and the other thousand

and one things faced by singers on the operatic stage. A naturally pleasant, outgoing, gregarious man, he made audiences feel at home. In 1909 he gave his first American concert, taking over the Metropolitan Opera, and he followed it with another the next month. So immediate was his success that little time was left for opera. During the 1914–18 period, for example, he appeared in opera only nine times, but he sang 400 concerts. Soon even the Metropolitan Opera was too small for the McCormack craze, so his manager, Charles Wagner, took over the Hippodrome, which seated about 7,000. Wherever he went, McCormack broke all box-office records. In Boston he sold out Symphony Hall four times in one week. *Every* concert he ever sang until he lost his voice was an immediate sellout, with extra seats placed on the stage and hundreds turned away. He was getting $4,500 a concert—more than Kreisler, more than Paderewski, more than anybody except Caruso. But Caruso did not like concerts very much and gave relatively few. In New York McCormack filled Carnegie Hall ten times in a single season, never once repeating a song. No wonder the Buffalo *Evening News* called him "The Modern Pied Piper of Hamelin." Like all musicians, he did his bit for the American war effort, and in 1917 raised $500,000 for the Red Cross and Liberty Loan Drive. He was not popular in England and Ireland, though. When word got out that McCormack had applied for American citizenship he was condemned and accused of being a slacker. It took some years before his compatriots were able to forget. Indeed, he had to cancel an Australian tour in 1920 because of demonstrations against him.

His audiences came to hear him sing *Mother Machree, Macushla, I Hear You Calling Me,* and other such favorites. As the Newark *Star Eagle* pointed out in 1917, "Mr. McCormack's appearances would not be real without them." *Musical America* knew the reasons for McCormack's success (not that it took an overwhelming intellect to figure it out), and explained them in 1916: "He gives the music-hungry world the music that it can understand, and with it he gives himself, a compelling, democratic, I'm-one-of-you personality." In addition there was "the most wonderfully sympathetic, God-given, natural tenor voice that ever rolled out of the throat of a human being." McCormack had a few words to say about his choice of music in 1916: "This talk about educating the public as to what kind of music it should or should not like annoys me. There is no use trying to force any particular kind of music down the throats of the public. Give them the kind of music they like."

McCormack, as an international idol, was constantly in the news and in the rotogravure sections. Often he was photographed on the golf course, and it is clear that he had a terrible swing. As a millionaire many times over, McCormack could afford to indulge himself. He became exceedingly stout from rich food and champagne. He maintained houses in Ireland, California, London, Connecticut, and New York. He drove, or was driven, only in Rolls-Royce automobiles. He became a collector. Although not a violinist, he owned a Stradivarius and a Guarnerius. In his art collection hung paintings by Gainsborough, Raeburn, Van Dyck, Hassam, Rembrandt, Hals, Whistler, Teniers, and Corot. He maintained a stable of racehorses in Ireland, and his only regret was that none of his mounts ever won the Derby. He was a pioneer in radio concerts, appearing on WEAF in New York in 1925 with Lucrezia Bori, with whom he had made so many records (is there anything lovelier than their *Parigi, o cara* from *Traviata?*). In 1928 he was made a papal count, and he rushed to get a coat of arms: three harps upon a shield, the crest topped by a black cat. The motto was *Felis Demulta Mitis*—"a stroked cat is gentle." In 1929 he made a talking film, *Song O' My Heart,* with a young actress, Maureen O'Sullivan, and received $500,000 for the eight weeks it took to make it.

His legacy on records is considerable. The ballads he recorded in 1904 were released on about twenty cylinders and eighteen discs. In 1906 he recorded for Odeon in London. In 1909 Victor bought out his Odeon contract, and McCormack stayed with that company for as long as he continued to record, which was almost to the day he died. His voice started to go in 1932, but he kept on singing all over the world until 1937, and he called it quits with a

Richard Tauber, whose career in Germany and Austria ran parallel to McCormack's in the United States and England. He too was a supreme vocalist and stylist.

London recital in 1938. During World War II he toured the British Isles with other singers for the Red Cross. He also did some BBC broadcasting and even made a few records. On September 16, 1945, he died in Booterstown, near Dublin.

There was one tenor whose career ran somewhat parallel to McCormack's, and that was Richard Tauber. Like McCormack, Tauber, who was born in Austria on May 16, 1891, first made his mark in opera. But where McCormack went into the Irish ballad business, Tauber switched to Viennese operetta, becoming a world-famous exponent of Lehár's music. He also was a noted recitalist. Vocally he was something like a combination of Caruso and McCormack. He had a bit of Caruso's heft of voice and a good deal of McCormack's artistry. Many connoisseurs consider him perhaps the most versatile tenor of the century, and his recordings support that high estimate. But McCormack was a purer singer who almost never went in for the musically cheap falsetto effects that Tauber so often used. On the other hand, Tauber's concerts contained more musical substance than McCormack's. He may not have been a better vocal technician than McCormack —who was?—but there was nothing wrong with his way of singing; he had a more extensive repertory and was a better all-around musician. He died in London in 1948.

Tauber sang until the year before his death from cancer. McCormack had almost twenty years of vocal inactivity after he retired. In *The Great Singers* Henry Pleasants concludes his study of McCormack with a sad little vignette: "Toward the end of his life, when nothing but the records was left, he would play them again and again, exclaiming happily, and a bit wistfully—possibly a bit incredulously: 'I was a damned good singer, wasn't I?'"

22 *Feodor Chaliapin*

BASS FROM MOTHER RUSSIA

ABOUT fifty years after Luigi Lablache, another bass arrived who was the talk of the world. Feodor Chaliapin, the handsome giant with a lust for life, the incomparable Boris Godunov, the greatest of singing actors, the spoiled child who always had to have his way, became a superstar in an age that included Caruso, Melba, Paderewski, and McCormack. There were great bassos before or contemporaneous with him. Carl Formes, Edouard de Reszke, and Pol Plançon, to name but three, were universally admired and had wonderful careers. Alexander Kipnis, also Russian, was Chaliapin's successor and had a beautiful voice and superior all-around musicianship. But they were not superstars in the sense that Chaliapin was. It was Chaliapin who got the top fees, who was always in the news, who was bigger than life, who created the kind of excitement normally reserved for superstar sopranos and tenors. Indeed, Chaliapin eclipsed Caruso in popularity, if a *Musical America* story of 1914 is accurate. Chaliapin sang in Sir Thomas Beecham's Russian season that year, and a correspondent reported that prices had been raised for all Chaliapin performances, and that for the first time in many years a bass singer was the number-one attraction of the world, drawing more of an audience than even Caruso, who was singing at Covent Garden. "Caruso's existence is forgotten by his former fashionable admirers," wrote the *Musical America* reporter, "to whom Chaliapin's rugged, masterful, virile personality makes an irresistible appeal."

The man was a giant in every way. It was generally agreed that he was six feet four inches tall, though some newspapers insisted on six feet six. He was a stupendous eater and drinker—drinker especially. On his first trip to the United States, in 1907, he was interviewed by Carl van Vechten. Chaliapin rattled off a speech that contained all the English he knew: "I spik English. How do you do? *et puis* good-bye, *et puis* I drrrink, you drrink, he drrrinks, *et puis* I love you." Soon van Vechten discovered it was not an accident that Chaliapin had selected "to drink" as the first verb he learned to conjugate. Nobody could keep up with him in the potables department. He was also a great lover who had plenty of affairs and two wives. From the first, an Italian dancer named Julia Fornaghi, he had eight children. From the second, a Russian woman named Maria Petzhold, he had four children. He had not lived with his first wife for many years, and when his divorce was granted in 1927 he immediately married Petzhold. Chaliapin defended his immense fees on the grounds of his large family. With two wives, twelve children, and numerous needy relatives, he claimed he had to get $3,000 to $5,000 a performance because he had twenty-six mouths to feed.

He had immense physical strength. Rosa Ponselle, no sylph, was once running to get into a moving train when Chaliapin leaned out and lifted her off the ground like a baby. She admitted to weighing 160 pounds, which means that she probably carried ten or more pounds than that. Chaliapin was proud of his strength. There once was a report in the papers that he had had his nose broken by a tenor. Chaliapin's pride was hurt. He sent cables to all papers that had run the story saying that it was not true; but that if it *had* been true, the news would have been accompanied by the announcement of the tenor's funeral. He was not averse to drawing attention to himself. His sartorial combinations were resplendent. In cold weather he usually wore an immense raccoon coat, gloves of English wool, a black-and-white checked suit, a shirt with brown stripes, and a checked cap. After a tour of South America he returned to Paris with two monkeys, a cockatoo and other brilliantly colored birds, and two alligators, all of which he installed in his hotel room. No matter where he went, he had to be the center of attraction, and that held true on the operatic stage. Ponselle was not happy about it. "If a colleague gave him an inch he would steal an entire scene. He was so artful about it that one wouldn't realize what was going on until it was too late." But Ponselle paid him due homage, saying that he was "unrivalled as a singing actor in his age or any subsequent one." Geraldine Farrar said that though Chaliapin had a voice like "melodious thunder," he could drive stage directors and other singers crazy; he seldom did what had been agreed upon at rehearsals and would do things on the spur of the moment. Farrar, who sang with him in Monte Carlo, echoed Ponselle in saying that "Chaliapin was a wonderful opera partner, but one had to be watchful for sudden departures from the rehearsed plan, and touches of originality favorable only for the aggrandizement of Chaliapin."

Chaliapin had temperament, charisma, and one of the most sonorous of all bass voices, and he brought new standards of acting to the operatic stage. His impact was tremendous, and he so changed the idea of what music drama means that his conceptions remain in force today. Michael Scott, in *The Record of Singing,* ranks Chaliapin with Caruso and Maria Callas as "one of the three greatest singers and most potent and influential artists of the twentieth century." As a young man Chaliapin challenged the established notions of operatic acting, finally had his own way, and became by far the most electric figure on the stage—and not only the operatic stage, as his two films, *Ivan the Terrible* (1915) and *Don Quichotte* (1933), demonstrate. He tried to get into the mind and conformation of any character he represented. Great singers

Feodor Chaliapin (right) and his friend Maxim Gorky, around 1905. Chaliapin was the first operatic bass superstar since Luigi Lablache, and he also was equally popular on the concert stage.

up to then were primarily interested in themselves and how *they* looked on stage. A Patti, a Melba, would have Parisian couturiers design their gowns, so that Aida would expire in an elegant Worth costume that had nothing to do with the opera or with what the other singers were wearing. Chaliapin demanded historical accuracy. He also probed into the meaning of the words he was singing, weighting each one with emotional significance. When he appeared on stage, all other singers were dwarfed, and not only because of his gigantic stature. It was also because he lived his part.

Chaliapin was born in Kazan on February 13, 1873 (the same year as Caruso), had only four years of school, knocked around quite a bit, lived in poverty, and was almost entirely self-taught as a singer. Not until 1892 did he work with a teacher, and that was only for a year. In 1894 he became a member of the Imperial Opera in St. Petersburg. He made his debut as Russlan in Glinka's *Russlan and Ludmilla* and did not attract much attention. He was promptly put into smaller roles, and had plenty of time to sit out front and study the productions. He did not like what he saw. "I realized that sham predominated," Chaliapin wrote in his memoirs. "The settings were lavish to a degree . . . and yet, curious to relate, all this splendor seemed to be only a cloak for naked poverty." The singers moved majestically through the operas but "the whole effect was as lifeless and mechanical as a marionette show."

Soon Chaliapin enjoyed a success, as the Miller in Dargomyzhsky's *Russalka,* and was promoted to leading roles. He wanted nothing to do with the bel canto style of singing, which he considered boring. "I thought of singers I knew, with magnificent voices, so perfectly trained that at any moment they could sing piano or forte, but who nearly all sang notes to which the words were of secondary importance." These smooth singers sang about love or hate the same way. So Chaliapin decided to "learn the true art of acting in the school of Russian dramatic actors." Every free night found him at the theater, studying the declamation of the cast and making friends with the actors. He was striving for the ultimate union of word and music, wondering if opera and drama could not combine, "and would there not be a great gain, a great stride forward, by a new road?"

In 1896 he joined Mamontov's Private Opera in Moscow and had a chance to put his theories into effect. He made his debut as Mephistopheles in *Faust* and had a great success. He also learned a great deal about musicianship from his close friend Sergei Rachmaninoff, who was one of Mamontov's conductors. Rachmaninoff taught him how to analyze a score and insisted that he memorize not only his role but the roles of every singer in the cast. With Rachmaninoff, Chaliapin studied the role of Boris Godunov, with which he was forever identified. When, after two years, Chaliapin returned to the Imperial Opera, he had the clout to make demands in matters of costuming and acting. And when he went to the Bolshoi in 1899 (he remained a member of the company until 1914) he dominated the house. He was huge, he was a world-class wencher, he was arrogant, disputatious, a troublemaker. He was not very popular. He was constantly interfering, telling singers how to act, conductors how to conduct; getting into fights with stagehands; and constantly being in the newspapers, which delighted in reporting "Chaliapin scandals." Sometimes his behavior could be downright unprofessional. He would sulk and refuse to go on stage. Or he might go back to his dressing room during a performance, get into street clothes, and leave the theater. Some called him a brawler, and Rachmaninoff agreed. "Feodor *is* a brawler. They are all scared of his very spirit. He shouts suddenly or even hits someone! And Feodor's fist is powerful. . . . He can take care of himself. And how else should one behave? Backstage at our own theatre it's just like a saloon. They shout, they drink, they swear in the foulest language." The companies in which Chaliapin sang put up with his antics because he had a phenomenal voice, was a brilliant actor, and, above all, was a crowd pleaser. Chaliapin sold tickets. He had everything worked out, including his bows, and he once took Rachmaninoff aside and explained to him that an artist should greet an audience with a happy smile. Rachmaninoff, who never smiled in public, took the remarks under advisement. He said wryly, "Though Feodor was a bass, he bowed like a tenor."

Around the turn of the century Chaliapin started to appear outside Russia. In 1901 he sang in Boito's *Mefistofele* at La Scala under Toscanini and was not impressed. He admired Toscanini the musician but had only contempt for Toscanini the director and the stock gestures he insisted upon. "He would wind up one of my legs around the other corkscrew fashion, or make me fold my arms *à la* Napoleon. In fact, what I was being instructed in was the technique of provincial tragedians." Chaliapin had wanted to play Mefistofele semi-nude. Toscanini would have none of it. But when Diaghilev in 1908 presented his first seasons of Russian opera and ballet in Paris, Chaliapin was part of the entourage and was given his head; and he conquered the city with his Boris.

Not until Chaliapin appeared at the Metropolitan Opera in 1907 did he present a nearly naked Devil in the Boito opera. Much ahead of his time, he had a disastrous New York season. He sang Basilio in *Il Barbiere di Siviglia* as well as Mefistofele, and the critics hated both impersonations. Here was a seedy Basilio, a vulgar, unctuous, greasy-looking priest who picked his nose, wiped it on his cassock, and kept spitting all over the stage. This was realism with a vengeance, and Chaliapin was taken apart. Among other criticisms, he was accused of debasing religion. He defended himself. Basilio, he said in an interview, "is a Spanish priest. It is a type I know well. He is not the modern American priest, clean and well-groomed; he is dirty and unkempt, he is a beast, and that is what I make him, a comic beast." Heinrich Conried, the manager of the Metropolitan Opera, was not displeased at the poor reception Chaliapin received. The singer had demanded, and was receiving, $1,600 a performance. Normally only top sopranos got that kind of money. Conried frankly thought that Chaliapin was not worth it. Some of his colleagues also were not displeased that the Russian giant had come a cropper. Geraldine Farrar was amused. She later recollected that Chaliapin, after being spanked by the critics, "dissolved in a huge Russian pout all winter."

In Russia, Chaliapin was a hero. Not only his voice and inter-

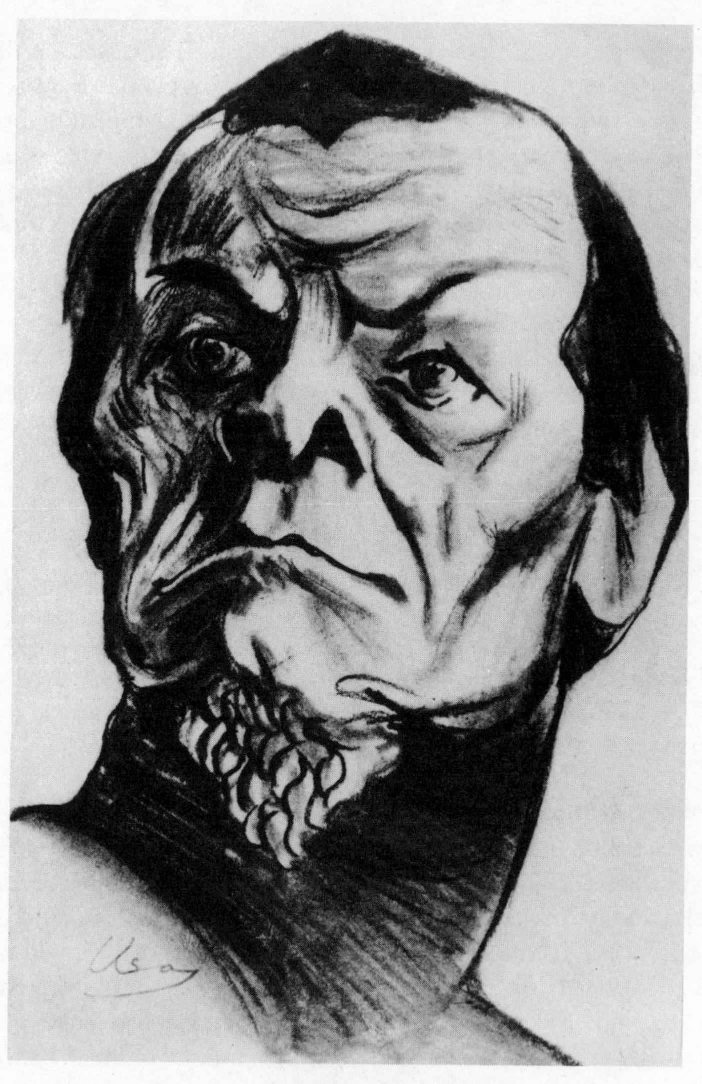

A pencil drawing by the Russian caricaturist Usa Gombarg of Chaliapin in one of his most famous roles—Mefistofele, in the Boito opera.

national accomplishments made him popular. It also was felt that Chaliapin represented the spirit of the Russian people, as Maxim Gorky wrote in a letter to a friend in 1911. Chaliapin and Gorky were close friends. They were born in the same city, where Chaliapin had been apprenticed to a cobbler and Gorky to a baker. For many years they were in close contact. Chaliapin, wrote Gorky, was

> a symbolic figure, yes, and an astonishingly integral image of democratic Russia. This huge personality embodies in himself all the best and talented that is in our people, and it does not exclude the bad or the weaknesses that lie in us all. He reminds us all how powerful, beautiful and talented is the Russian people. He is flesh of its flesh, a man torn through the thorns and great hustle of life, yes, and he proudly takes his place among the best of the world, for he sings to us all about Russia, to reveal that she, in her inmost depths, is big and talented and enchanting. . . . And that is what Chaliapin is always singing about; it is what he lives for; and we in turn should bow to him in gratitude, in friendship. . . . Chaliapin will always remain what he is, blindingly bright, a joyous cry around the world. Here is Russia, and this is what her people are like.

When the war came Chaliapin returned to Russia. He got into a bit of trouble before the Revolution. As a friend of the revolutionist Gorky, he was on the police blacklist. Vladimir Telyakovsky, the administrative director in the Moscow office of the Imperial Theatres, wrote in his diary that the czar himself demanded that Chaliapin be chased out of the theaters. After the Revolution Chaliapin sang for the workers and, at first, supported the new cause. In 1918 he was appointed director of the Marinsky Theatre in Petrograd. He left in 1921 to sing at the Metropolitan Opera, promising to return in three years. He also left his wife and children. Chaliapin never returned to Russia. Some of his children made it to the West. The Russians did not take his defection lightly. In 1927 the Russian government was unhappy about Chaliapin's contributions toward the support of Russian refugees in Paris (many of them the hated White Russians). His title of People's Artist was taken from him and his country home confiscated. Later, in 1932, Chaliapin was invited back. He refused. "I do not object to the Soviet ideas, nor do I object to the Soviet leaders," he said. "But in my work and in my way of doing things, I refuse to be prevented from acting as I wish. I am a man who must be free." By this time his friendship with Gorky had cooled. Gorky, living in Italy, accused Chaliapin of lying about what he had been able to take out of Russia, and called him a coward. This was in 1930, after Chaliapin had sued the Soviet government for 2 million francs for unauthorized publication of his autobiography (which had been written by Gorky). Chaliapin lost the suit.

In 1921 New York was finally ready for him. He sang Boris, and it was a revelation. Even so experienced a critic as Lawrence Gilman was swept off his feet, writing, "There is little to say about Chaliapin's Boris except that it is in all probability the greatest performance the lyric stage has ever known." Deems Taylor in the New York *World* called Chaliapin "the most stupendous stage personality in the world. . . . The thing he inspired is belief, instant, absolute, unquestioning." Chaliapin received an unprecedented fee of $3,000 a performance and was worth every cent of it. After the first Boris every Chaliapin appearance called forth a full house, with thousands turned away. Gatti-Casazza promptly raised the admission prices to a $10 top. At these performances of *Boris Godunov,* Chaliapin sang in Russian and the rest of the cast in Italian. In addition to the Mussorgsky opera, he was heard in *Mefistofele,* as Leporello in *Don Giovanni,* in the title role of Massenet's *Don Quichotte,* and as Don Basilio in *Il Barbiere.* He had a critical triumph in everything but the Rossini; his Basilio was still too rank for the gentlemen of the press. Chaliapin *had* to show the New York critics they were wrong. So a few years later, in 1927, he put together a company for *Il Barbiere* and gave several performances at Mecca Temple in New York. Most critics still didn't like it. Boris was one thing, Basilio another. W. J. Henderson of the *Sun* called it "low comedy." Olin Downes in the *Times* complained that

Chaliapin, in what after all is a minor role, hogged the show and turned comedy into burlesque.

In the operatic world Chaliapin was still a holy terror, getting into fights with conductors and his colleagues. He was singing in Vienna in 1927 when he got into a dispute with the conductor Karl Alwin, a very experienced man. Chaliapin complained about Alwin's slow tempos in *Boris* and *Faust*. During a performance of *Faust* he tried to conduct the orchestra while singing. Alwin was, not unexpectedly, furious and withdrew from all Chaliapin appearances. The audience sided with the conductor, holding Chaliapin's tantrum to be bad form. It is said that Chaliapin often started fights to take the public's attention from the fact that he was not in very good voice that particular evening.

As a recitalist Chaliapin again was different from all others. He never announced a program in advance. Instead there was a booklet on sale in the lobby, in which seventy-four songs and their texts were listed by number. No. 1 was *The Minstrel,* described as a "dramatic ballad," and No. 74 was Varlaam's *Kazan* aria from *Boris.* In between were songs by Grieg, Brahms, Schubert, and Schumann, and a few operatic arias, such as Leporello's *Madamina* from *Don Giovanni.* Mostly, though, the songs were Russian. At every concert Chaliapin could be counted upon to sing *The Song of the Flea, The Two Grenadiers,* and *The Song of the Volga Boatman.* He would select a piece from a pile of music on the piano and announce the number to the audience. For concerts his fee could ascend to $6,500. But that was no guarantee that he actually would sing. Chaliapin's waywardness was legendary. He constantly was canceling concerts, and that could be one reason Sol Hurok, his American manager in the 1920's, lost his hair. Chaliapin delighted in keeping everybody on tenterhooks the day of a recital. He would call in the morning and say that his throat felt like raw beef. At 3 P.M. he was still sick and at 5 he was still sick. At that hour he would issue instructions to be called at 7:30. At 7:30 he would say that maybe he would be able to sing if it were announced from the stage that Chaliapin was appearing even

Chaliapin in the 1930's. He was a giant in every way—physically, in his appetite, in his capacity for alcohol, and in his lust for life.

though he suffered from a cold. Though Chaliapin was one of the most popular recitalists before the public, he was more entertainer than artist, and most musicians did not take him seriously as a song interpreter. Gerald Moore, who was his accompanist for a while, wrote that Chaliapin was primarily an opera singer, far too egocentric for lieder. Moore never knew what was going to happen with the unpredictable bass. But one thing he did know: egocentric or not, musicianly or not, Chaliapin was always exciting.

He sang at the Metropolitan until 1929, and was giving concerts and making records almost to the day of his death in Paris on April 12, 1938. His artistic legacy is well represented on records. Chaliapin was one of the earliest of the great recording artists; he was in the studios as early as 1901, and he made some six hundred discs. Fortunately some excerpts from *Boris Godunov* are among them; and they give a good idea of the shattering effect his performance must have had on stage. To hear this Boris, in its majesty and fear, is almost to see Chaliapin, so vivid is the interpretation, so awesome the projection, so faithful to what Mussorgsky was trying to convey. An indescribable force comes through these old discs—and it is not only Chaliapin. Gorky was right—the spirit of Russia was embodied in the man.

23 *Arturo Toscanini*

THE MAESTRO

IT is hard to believe that Arturo Toscanini, whose name and memory are still so much with us, was born as long ago as 1867. Virtually the entire history of modern conducting was encapsulated in the man. During his long life many of the great conductors of history were in action. At his birth, Liszt and Wagner were still occasionally on the podium. As a young man he was contemporaneous with Hans Richter, Hans von Bülow, Arthur Nikisch, Anton Seidl, Felix Weingartner, Richard Strauss, and Gustav Mahler. In later life he had such eminent colleagues as Otto Klemperer, Erich Kleiber, Bruno Walter, Leopold Stokowski, Willem Mengelberg, Thomas Beecham, Serge Koussevitzky, Wilhelm Furtwängler, Pierre Monteux, Fritz Reiner, and George Szell—giants all.

But of this distinguished galaxy, to the public there was only one conductor, and his name was Arturo Toscanini. Nobody in the music world was prepared to dispute Toscanini's title as the

World's Greatest Conductor until the latter years of his life. Toscanini lived to see himself an anachronism, attacked by a new generation for his "rigidity," his objectivity, and, above all, his supposed lack of musical culture. Today the pendulum has swung toward Furtwängler. In the 1930's Furtwängler was considered much too romantic and self-indulgent. But with a more responsive attitude toward Romanticism on the part of the tastemakers in the 1970's, Furtwängler was reassessed and found to be more sensitive and musicianly than Toscanini. Thus the merry-go-round continues, each age applying its own esthetic to measure the esthetic of a previous age; each age drawing universal truths from its own experience and thinking it and it alone knows what the final answer is.

In Toscanini's case the attacks on him have a special kind of irony. The man many today accuse of being next to a musical illiterate conducted the Italian premieres of *Götterdämmerung, Siegfried, Eugene Onegin, Euryanthe,* and *Pelléas et Mélisande.* He conducted the world premiers of *Pagliacci, La Bohème, La Fanciulla del West, Madame Sans-Gêne* (by Giordano), *Nerone* (by Boito), and *Turandot.* In his repertory were 117 operas by 53 composers. His symphonic repertory consisted of over 480 works by 175 composers. It could well be the largest repertory of any conductor in history. All of these works he conducted from memory.

And it was Toscanini who revolutionized orchestral playing, bringing to the orchestra a previously unimagined kind of unified ensemble, accuracy of intonation, power, and rhythmic steadiness. He did for the orchestra what Heifetz was to do for the violin, setting a technical standard that became the goal of all who followed. As an interpreter, he above all others established the preeminence of the printed note as the guide, trying to do away with the excrescences of tradition. He was one of the first literalists, and his philosophy guided two generations of conductors. Although he never taught, he nevertheless founded a school that continues to thrive, and his influence is still strongly felt. It is manifested in the work of so many talented conductors who have all of his basic

Arturo Toscanini around 1900, when he was artistic director of La Scala.

approach and virtually nothing of his ability to kindle an orchestra and the audience. For Toscanini the literalist—the musician who looked only to the printed note as the guide, the great objectivist who was believed to keep himself out of the music—conducted with tremendous personality. He had an aura that only a few musicians in history have ever achieved; there was something about his passion, his total commitment and eternal search for perfection, that communicated itself to an extraordinary degree.

Thus his place as one of the supreme musical performers in any field is secure. Even his detractors admit that he was incomparable as a conductor of Italian opera. All one has to do is listen to his recording of Verdi's *Falstaff* to realize what a supreme and aristocratic musical mind can do to make an orchestra "talk." In the Falstaff monologue that ends the first scene, Toscanini has the orchestra doing things—and such perfectly controlled things!—that make all successive conductors sound pale. In areas outside Italian opera, his interpretations have been criticized. Toscanini's technique is not in question; all admit he was a complete master of his medium. But there are those who feel that in the classics, the German classics especially, he never achieved the identification that he displayed in Italian opera. This may be true—by the standards of the 1980's. It was not true for previous generations, which believed that Toscanini's Beethoven, Brahms, and Wagner had a concentrated strength and intensity that left all competition behind. And his Mozart or Haydn? Well, what conductor born in the nineteenth century, the revered Bruno Walter and Thomas Beecham included, conducted pre-Beethoven music according to today's dictates?

The early history of conducting has never been fully explored. Conducting as we understand it today is a relatively recent phenomenon. Until the turn of the nineteenth century, orchestras had divided leadership, with the duties shared by the "leader" (concertmaster) and clavier player. Generally the composer was the one officiating at the keyboard instrument. In the first decade of the century, certain musicians faced the orchestra and conducted it without help, though divided leadership was still common until the 1840's. The first who made a habit of using a baton was Ludwig Spohr. Prior to him, conductors used a violin bow or a rolled-up sheet of paper. The first conductors who worked in much the same manner as today's were almost always composers—Spohr, Weber, Mendelssohn, Spontini. François Habeneck in Paris, who did such pioneer work in introducing the Beethoven symphonies, was an exception to the rule of composer-conductors. Berlioz, Liszt, and Wagner, three more composers, took up the baton mostly to introduce their own music and, in Liszt's case, music of the then avant-garde. From the Wagner camp came many of the great conductors of the time, all originally disciples of *Der Meister* who went on to command orchestras of their own. These included Hans von Bülow, Hans Richter, Felix Mottl, Hermann Levi, Anton Seidl, and Arthur Nikisch.

The Wagner school of conducting took its cue from Wagner himself, who wrote several treatises on conducting and interpretation. It was a school that represented fluctuation of tempo, that depended on the inspiration of the moment to achieve its effects, that was highly personal. Opposed to the Wagner school was the stricter style that descended from Mendelssohn and Berlioz to Felix Weingartner, Toscanini, and his followers. This school discounted "inspiration" in favor of an accurate, polished presentation of the notes. That accomplished, the interpretation would take care of itself.

Arthur Nikisch (1855–1922) was one of the Wagnerians, but nowhere near as mannered as, say, Bülow was. He was the first of the modern conducting stars. He was not a composer and after his affair with the Wagner opera did not ally himself with any particular school. He was a professional conductor, nothing more, and he conducted what came his way. Born in Hungary, he grew up to be a magnetic, dapper little man with piercing eyes and an all-encompassing knowledge of his trade. No intellectual, he did not read much; he was interested only in cards, women, company, and his music. Orchestra players adored him. He never was a browbeater, he never lost his temper, he was on good terms with everybody—and yet he always got exactly what he wanted. He

Arthur Nikisch, the brilliant Hungarian conductor, who was a legend in his day. It is hard to locate a single critical or disparaging remark about his work; he received universal accolades from his peers and the public.

could lift blasé players right out of their seats. A musician in the London Symphony Orchestra wrote an article about Nikisch for the *Musical Times* in 1905. He said that he and the other members of the orchestra were overworked, tired, and sullen. At that point Nikisch entered for a rehearsal of the Tchaikovsky Fifth Symphony:

> Before we had been playing for five minutes we were deeply interested and, later, when we came to the big fortissimos, we not only played like fiends but we quite forgot we were tired. For my part, I simply boiled over with enthusiasm. I could have jumped up and shouted—as a matter of fact, when we reached the end of the first movement, we all did rise from our seats and actually shouted because we could not help it. . . . He simply *looked* at us, scarcely moving his baton, and we played as those possessed; we made terrific crescendi, sudden commas before some great chord, though we had never done this before.

Composers as well as orchestra players adored him. "He does not conduct, but rather imparts a kind of hidden magic," Tchaikovsky said of him. Tchaikovsky was impressed by the fact that Nikisch was no showman, never drew attention to himself, did not appear to exert himself, "and yet one has the feeling that the whole orchestra is completely subject to his will." And Brahms was simply overwhelmed when he heard Nikisch conduct his Second Symphony and bring out things that Brahms never knew were implicit in the score. "Is that possible? Did I ever write that?" he marveled. Brahms later told Nikisch, "You have changed everything. But you are right—it *must* be like that."

As orchestra players and composers admired Nikisch, so did his fellow conductors. They recognized a master when they met one. Nikisch was especially famous among his colleagues for being able to get more results after one rehearsal than they could get in a week. He had a positive genius for immediately centering on the salient points of a work and clarifying them; and doing it with a minimum of effort. Weingartner, no slouch himself, described

Nikisch at work in the last pages of *Tristan und Isolde*. He said that the orchestra was transformed, and he couldn't understand how Nikisch could get such beauty of sound and depth of feeling with a single rehearsal: "The mighty crescendos were absolutely uncanny. Where other conductors flail away with both arms, Nikisch just slowly raised his left hand until the orchestra roared around him like the sea." Even Toscanini, who was contemptuous of most conductors, had words of praise. When Nikisch conducted the Orchestra of La Scala he complimented Toscanini on its fine quality. Said Toscanini, "My dear, I know this orchestra very well. I am the conductor of this orchestra. It is a bad orchestra. You are a good conductor."

Nikisch must have been remarkable. All professionals were united in his praise, without a single dissenting opinion one can find. The severe Carl Flesch found Nikisch a revelation when he first heard him. "For the first time," Flesch wrote, "I saw a musician who, impressionistically, described in the air not simply the bare musical structure, but above all the dynamic and agogical nuances as well as the indefinable mysterious feeling that lies *between* the notes; his beat was utterly personal and original." With Nikisch, Flesch believed, a new era in conducting started.

Nikisch was all over the place. He did the Wagner operas all over Europe with Angelo Neumann's touring company. He made his debut in Leipzig in 1878 and stayed there for eleven years. He was associated with opera houses and orchestras in Vienna, Budapest, Hamburg, London, and Berlin. From 1889 to 1893 he was the conductor of the Boston Symphony. And he guest-conducted everywhere. He left some recordings, among them the first complete symphony ever put on discs—the Beethoven Fifth, naturally, released in 1913. His records do not do him justice, for not until electrical recordings in 1925 could the sound of an orchestra begin to be captured on records. Conductors before then had to use a greatly curtailed orchestra, and it is doubtful if Nikisch had more than twenty-five players for the Fifth. But through the Nikisch interpretations come temperament, high Romanticism, and a wonderful feeling of spontaneity.

If Nikisch was the first star conductor, Toscanini was the first superstar, with all the perquisites of superstardom—international fame, billions of words in all the media, his name a household word, tremendous fees, unbounded ego, the standard to which all others had to aspire. He was born in Parma on March 25, 1867, of poor parents. As always with superstars-to-be, his talent was noticed when he was a child. Toscanini never was a child prodigy, but he had a natural aptitude for music and a simply extraordinary memory. He could hear a piece once and never forget it. At nine he was in the Parma Conservatory, studying cello, piano, and composition. After his graduation in 1885 he started to play the cello in orchestras. The story of his conducting debut is well known. Toscanini was the principal cellist and chorusmaster in an opera company that was touring South America in 1886. The conductor was one Leopoldo Miguez, who seems to have been incompetent. Tensions arose in the company, and in Rio de Janeiro on June 30, 1886, Toscanini took over the podium for an *Aida,* which he conducted from memory. He then conducted ten other operas, all from memory. He was nineteen.

Back in Italy he resumed his career as a cellist, and was in the Scala orchestra for the world premiere of Verdi's *Otello* in 1887. He also managed to get some engagements as a conductor with minor companies, achieving a reputation as a severe drillmaster and as a young man with a foul temper. Even then he would go into insensate rages when he felt the players were not giving their best. He began to be well known and was given major assignments, such as the world premieres of Catalani's *Loreley* and *La Wally,* Leoncavallo's *Pagliacci,* and Franchetti's *Cristoforo Colombo,* all in 1892. His first big engagement came in Turin in 1895, and he opened with a real splash: the Italian premiere of *Götterdämmerung,* followed in 1896 with the world premiere of Puccini's *La Bohème.* Puccini was deliriously happy with the new conductor, who turned out to be everything a composer could have desired—musicianly, strong, rhythmically perfect, possessed of an ability to make the orchestra sing as beautifully as the soloists. It was in 1896, too, that Toscanini, in Turin, made his debut as a symphonic conductor, with a program very much of the kind he was to be conducting fifty years later. It consisted of the big Schubert C major Symphony, Tchaikovsky's *Nutcracker* Suite, the Brahms *Tragic* Overture, and the *Entrance of the Gods into Valhalla* from Wagner's *Rheingold*. That year he conducted forty-four symphonic concerts at the Turin Exhibition.

La Scala called, with all kinds of inducements. Under the terms of the proposed contract, Toscanini was to work under Giulio Gatti-Casazza, the general manager. But Toscanini was to be the artistic director, with full authority over choice of repertory, singers, the orchestra and its rehearsal schedule, and the selection of stage directors. His salary was to be $2,400 for five months. Toscanini, now a married man (to Carla De Martini, in 1896), accepted and went to Milan in 1898, opening his season with *Die Meistersinger*.

At La Scala, Toscanini did what Mahler was doing as manager of the opera in Vienna. La Scala was Toscanini's house to rule artistically as he wished, and he overhauled everything that had to do with the final product. He aimed for a standard to which no previous Italian conductor had aspired, and which no opera conductor anywhere except Mahler could begin to match. He said he wanted to rid opera of its silly "traditions" and get back to what the composer had written. Naturally he met opposition. There was a grand row with Giulio Ricordi in 1902. Ricordi, who published Verdi and Puccini, among others, complained that Toscanini was too rigid in his musical approach, and refused La Scala permission to stage *Il Trovatore*. Toscanini was adamant, and finally Ricordi gave in. Meanwhile the parade of Italian premieres conducted by Toscanini continued: *Siegfried* in 1899; *Eugene Onegin* in 1900; *Euryanthe, La Damnation de Faust* by Berlioz, and *Parsifal* in 1902; *Salome* in 1906; *Pelléas et Mélisande* in 1908. And then there were world premieres—Mascagni's *Iris* in 1898 and Franchetti's *Germania* in 1902.

Among Toscanini's innovations, one that was considered especially high-handed was his prohibition of encores. Italian audiences are volatile. When they like a singer's performance of an aria they want it to be repeated; and there is nothing more a singer loves than to clutch the audience to the bosom and deliver a repeat to great applause. Things came to a head in 1903. At a *Ballo in Maschera* performance the public screamed for the tenor Giovanni Zenatello to repeat an aria, and would not let the performance continue until he did so. Toscanini walked out of the opera house, letting an assistant continue, and told La Scala he was through. Was it purely a matter of artistic standards? Or was it childish petulance at not having his own way? Whatever the reason, Toscanini stayed away for several years, conducting in Buenos Aires and in various Italian houses and touring Italy with the Turin Orchestra (with which he conducted the Italian premieres of works by Richard Strauss and Debussy). When he returned to La Scala in 1906, it was on his own terms—no encores.

In any case, he did not stay long at La Scala. In 1908 he went to the Metropolitan Opera with Gatti-Casazza, at $5,000 a month. Immediately there was a problem. Mahler, who had left the Vienna Opera in 1907, was in New York for his second season at the Metropolitan Opera. In 1907 Mahler had conducted *Tristan* there and considered it "his" opera. But Toscanini wanted to do it on his arrival in 1908. Mahler protested; and Toscanini, who had high regard for Mahler as a conductor (but not as a composer), ceded *Tristan* to him. It was Mahler's opera until he left the Metropolitan in 1909 and took over the New York Philharmonic. Toscanini opened his New York season on November 16, 1908, with *Aida* and an all-star cast—Caruso, Destinn, Homer, and Scotti.

At the Metropolitan his repertory was wide-ranging, including German, French, and Italian opera. Russian opera, too; he conducted *Boris Godunov* in 1913. He ran into the temperaments of sopranos accustomed to having their own way. One of them was Farrar, and there were some merry spats between them before they became lovers. Emma Eames, who sang at the Metropolitan from 1891 to 1909, was convinced that neither Gatti nor Toscanini cared anything about singing. The great Emma, after all, did not care to be taught phrasing and musicianship by Toscanini.

They clashed, and Toscanini had nothing but contempt for her. The feeling was reciprocated. As late as 1940 in a newspaper interview, Eames, who never forgave or forgot, called Gatti the "vandal" of opera managers because he came to the Metropolitan as "the dry nurse" of Toscanini. Nor did the Metropolitan Opera orchestra take kindly to Toscanini's flares of temperament and constant screams of outrage. On January 29, 1912, the musicians sent a letter to the Metropolitan management:

> The common courtesy practiced in all public and private institutions by superiors to their subordinates has been grossly violated in the Metropolitan Opera House by the behavior of Mr. Toscanini publicly using insulting language toward the orchestra and otherwise reflecting on the efficiency of individual players as well as whole sections of the orchestra thereby creating a nervous tension unbearable in the course of time. The orchestra therefore demands an apology from Mr. Toscanini and unless such is forthcoming at once will refuse to play under him any more.

It is not known if Toscanini apologized. If the orchestra was unhappy, so was Toscanini, and tensions were building up to his unexpected departure in 1915. Frances Alda, the great soprano who was also Gatti's wife, said in her memoirs that Toscanini left because the Metropolitan Opera could not maintain the artistic standards he demanded. This may be true. Harvey Sachs, in his biography of Toscanini, quotes a letter in which Toscanini told a friend, "I have given up my position at that theater because my aspirations and artistic ideals were unable to find the fulfillment I had dreamt of reaching when I entered it in 1908. Routine is the ideal and basis of that theater." Cynics had another story; the gossip was that he was fleeing from Farrar, who was insisting that he leave his wife and family to marry her. Gatti indirectly referred to that when he told the board of the Metropolitan Opera that Toscanini was leaving because of "special motives, which have nothing to do with art." The Metropolitan made every effort to keep Toscanini, promising him anything he wanted. All over the world, after all, Toscanini was known as the greatest of opera conductors. But Toscanini had made up his mind, and when he left, it was never to return.

During the war Toscanini was in Italy and rather quiescent. He did a little opera conducting and worked for the war effort. After the war he had a brief flirtation with Mussolini. When he returned to La Scala in 1920 it was as supreme commander. Pending the opening of the opera house he toured the United States in 1920 with the Scala orchestra and made a few records for Victor. On December 21, 1921, La Scala reopened with a Toscanini-led performance of Verdi's *Falstaff*. In 1924 he conducted the world premiere of Boito's *Nerone*. Boito, who had died in 1918, was Toscanini's (and Verdi's) old friend. Two years later came another posthumous premiere—of Puccini's *Turandot*. Also in 1926 Toscanini conducted the New York Philharmonic-Symphony (as it was then named) for the first time. In 1928 he was named the Philharmonic's associate conductor, sharing the duties with Willem Mengelberg. The Dutch conductor was a master who had made the Amsterdam Concertgebouw one of the great orchestras of the world and who specialized in the big pieces of the repertory—the symphonic poems of Strauss and the symphonies of Mahler, of which he was an early exponent. But he did not have much of a chance against the electric, dynamic Toscanini, and was completely eclipsed.

Whatever friendly associations Toscanini may have had with Mussolini and his fascists vanished in 1926. Mussolini had ordered Toscanini to conduct the fascist anthem, *Giovinezza*. Toscanini refused. He had been initially attracted to the new movement in the hope that Mussolini could rejuvenate Italy. Soon he saw where the dictator was heading and disassociated himself. Toscanini appears to have been a genuine libertarian who opposed social injustice in any form and who gave his services and moral support to causes about which he had strong convictions. In 1930, for instance, at the request of the violinist Bronisław Huberman, he conducted the first performances of the new Palestine Symphony Orchestra (and, in 1936, the inaugural concerts of the

Toscanini with Vladimir Horowitz (center) and Bruno Walter, around 1935. Walter was one of the few conductors for whom Toscanini had any respect.

Israel Philharmonic). He spent more and more time away from La Scala, and in 1929 left for good, signing a contract with the New York Philharmonic that called for ten weeks of concerts at $110,000. But before leaving he took La Scala on tour. In Vienna the young Herbert von Karajan heard Toscanini's *Lucia* and later said, "From the first bar it was as if I had been struck by a blow. I was completely disconcerted by the perfection that had been achieved." In Berlin, where Toscanini conducted six operas, the city went wild. One critic, in a burst of enthusiasm, echoed the prevalent feeling:

> This past week, all of Germany seemed like one single megaphone that echoed one single name: Toscanini. In Berlin, the excitement came to such a fever pitch that it actually made us fear for German art, for the prestige of a German musical culture. We ask ourselves whether a Blech, a Kleiber or a Klemperer would have aroused similar delirious enthusiasm in Italy had he gone there at the head of the Berlin Opera.—No!—Because these three conductors put together could not make one Toscanini.

When Toscanini toured Europe in 1930 with the New York Philharmonic he evoked similar remarks about his interpretations of the symphonic literature. But he had not dropped opera. He conducted *Tristan und Isolde* and *Tannhäuser* at the 1930 Bayreuth Festival, and added *Parsifal* the following year. He was the first non-German conductor ever invited there. The old guard, headed by Karl Muck, was furious and did its best to keep Toscanini off the sacred premises. What was an *Italian* doing there? Muck, in protest, even refused to conduct at Bayreuth in 1931 when he learned that Toscanini had been invited back.

There was an international incident in 1931. Toscanini was in Italy for a concert in Bologna. He refused to conduct *Giovinezza* and was roughed up by young fascists. After that he no longer conducted in fascist Italy. In 1933 he also left Bayreuth for good, telling the Wagner family that Bayreuth was no longer a temple but rather just another theater. Toscanini also protested the ban on Jewish musicians at Bayreuth. In 1938 after the Anschluss he severed associations with the Salzburg Festival, proclaiming that he would not associate himself with Furtwängler and other conductors who were Nazis. To show where he stood, in 1938 he conducted in Lucerne with an orchestra composed entirely of refugees from Nazi Germany.

At the end of the 1935–36 season he left the New York Philharmonic. He was sixty-nine, he no longer was associated with any musical organization, and it was assumed that he had retired. Possibly Toscanini himself thought so. But he could not resist the offer made by the National Broadcasting Corporation through Samuel Chotzinoff, a close friend and the music critic of the New York *Post*. The proposition was that a radio symphony orchestra containing America's best players be formed, to be trained by Artur Rodzinski. Toscanini was to conduct ten concerts at $4,000 each. Toscanini found himself lured back to the podium and on Christmas Eve 1937 he directed the NBC Symphony in its first nationwide broadcast. He remained with the orchestra until 1954, touring with it and also taking a little time off for Philharmonic and other guest appearances. In 1946 he conducted the first concert in the rebuilt La Scala, which had been destroyed during the war. Toscanini was, of course, a legend, and no concert hall or opera house was big enough to contain the hordes who wanted to hear him. When he conducted the London Philharmonia in 1952, 6,000 seats were available, but 60,000 clamored to get in.

His last concert took place on April 4, 1954, and it was a sad ending to a glorious career. It was a Wagner program with the NBC Symphony. In the *Bacchanale* from *Tannhäuser* Toscanini's beat faltered and he dropped his arms. In the control room was Toscanini's protégé, Guido Cantelli, and Cantelli panicked. He told the engineers to cut off the program; and for a few moments the strains of the Brahms First Symphony filled the airways. In the meantime Frank Miller, the orchestra's first cellist, cued the players, Toscanini picked up the thread of the music, and the program went back on the air. Toscanini, in some kind of mental confusion or despair, walked off the podium while the orchestra was finishing the last piece on the program, the *Meistersinger* Prelude. He sent a letter of resignation to NBC and this time, at the age of eighty-seven, really retired. He died three years later on January 16, 1957. The following month the body was flown to Milan, where Toscanini was buried.

Almost every young conductor in the 1930's and thereafter tried to imitate Toscanini, and that included conducting without the score. Toscanini *had* to conduct without a score because his eyesight was so bad. But soon memorization became the fashion. Hans Knappertsbusch, a great German conductor, was once asked why he always used a score, whereas Toscanini. . . . "Because I can read music," growled Knappertsbusch. One thing the young conductors did not do was duplicate Toscanini's legendary rages. Toscanini could go completely out of control—screaming, yelling, ranting, calling the offenders all kinds of unmentionable names. His behavior is still of intense interest to psychiatrists. At a meeting of the Psychoanalytic Association of New York on May 24, 1982, Dr. Martin H. Blum read a paper entitled "Toscanini's Relation to His Orchestra." Dr. Blum discussed Toscanini's isolated childhood, his break from parents he did not like, and his adulthood as a man who callously degraded or ignored his wife and children. Toscanini tolerated no opposition to his will from them or his musicians, and "actually seemed to lack human decency." How, then, could he inspire such exalted performances? Because, concluded Dr. Blum, his talent and strength were so exceptional that he was able to destabilize his musicians' own self-representation, leading them into "trance-like peak experiences of pre-verbal fusion with the personified ego-ideal in the form of Toscanini." As for Toscanini himself, music enabled him to unite with his own parental object (the composer) and in this way undo the pain and rage of his childhood deprivation. But Dr. Alan J. Eisnitz saw it somewhat differently. The orchestra, he said, became to Toscanini an external source of self-esteem, a special phallus with which he could unite genetically the maternal breast-phallus through which he could regain the sense of completeness lost in childhood.

Toscanini in action with the NBC Symphony. No conductor had his kind of precision and unfaltering rhythm.

Through the years Toscanini put much of his repertory on records, thus presenting future generations with an idea of what he represented—but only an idea. Many of the records were made in the infamous Studio 8H of Radio City in New York, with its dry acoustics, and the majority of Toscanini's discs consequently suffer badly from lack of color and overtone. Nevertheless his basic characteristics come through—the whiplash attacks and releases, the intensity, the clarity of the orchestral balances, the surges of power, the singing line—and, sometimes, the fast tempos. But Toscanini's tempos often sounded faster than they actually were. Musicians know—or should know—that a fast passage played cleanly and accurately sounds faster than the same passage taken at a breakneck speed but executed in a sloppy manner. As Alan Shulman, a cellist in the NBC Symphony, once pointed out, "We played Strauss with conductors whose way of achieving excitement was to take it at a virtually unplayable speed, in which we didn't play half the notes. Toscanini took it a third slower, in tempos in which we could play all the notes, and it sounded twice as fast."

Toscanini was no intellectual. He relied on his technique, his musical instinct, and the printed note. As regards the printed note, he was not the absolute and uncompromising purist he was commonly held to be, and he would make slight changes in the orchestration of masterpieces when he felt it was in the composer's interest to do so. He had sublime belief in his approach, and there was only one way of interpreting a piece of music—*his* way. Charles O'Connell, who worked with him on many of his recordings, said that Toscanini's three main characteristics were "energy, determination and drive." But O'Connell had reservations. "I think that somewhat less of each would have made a greater artist and a nobler man." There was no room in Toscanini's world, says O'Connell, "for gentleness, for tolerance, patience, humility, humanity or love." Toscanini was not interested in a union of wills, only in the imposition of his own will.

He lived and died a complete egomaniac, spoiled and petted, surrounded by frightened people and sycophants who never dared

Toscanini rehearsing. His rehearsals were always charged with intensity. His musicians never knew when he would lose his temper and explode.

disagree with him, much less dispute him. All top musicians have big egos, but Toscanini's was unique in its inability to see things in any way but his own. Yet, curiously, he actually seems to have been humble in the presence of the great creative musical minds of history. With all his heart and soul, with all of his ability, he strove always to create *the* perfect performance as he visualized it, and there was something Beethovenian about his rages when imperfect musicians came between him and his vision. He was a monomaniac. He lacked the urbanity of a Beecham, or the philosophy of a Walter, or the flashy coloristic ability of a Stokowski. But he did have a total conception that broke entirely away from German sentimentalism, focusing squarely on the notes and their realization in order to create a unified structure of sound. This he did better than anybody before or after, and he was defiant in his belief that nothing mattered but the symbols that composers scribbled on paper to express their vision. "The tradition," Toscanini once said, "is to be found only in one place—in the music!" Mengelberg once gave Toscanini advice on how to conduct Beethoven's *Coriolanus* Overture. He told Toscanini that he had received the true interpretation from a conductor who had got it straight from Beethoven. "Bah!" said Toscanini when telling this story. "I told him I got it straight from Beethoven himself, from the score."

24 *Jascha Heifetz*

UNRUFFLED PERFECTION

THE career of Jascha Heifetz paralleled that of Arturo Toscanini in some interesting ways. Both brought new standards to their art, and their successors had to try to match the technical perfection that both achieved. Both dominated their respective fields. Both lived to see themselves called musical anachronisms by such idol-breakers as Virgil Thomson, who questioned Toscanini's intellect and who disposed of Heifetz by calling him merely a great player of encores. The younger generation sneered at his repertory and his habit of playing fluffy or crowd-pleasing transcriptions.

But to the public Heifetz always was *the* violinist, just as Toscanini was *the* conductor. And, as a matter of fact, Heifetz always remained *the* violinist to his colleagues. They all stood in awe of him, for his craft if for nothing else. Nobody had his kind of easy execution, arched tone, accuracy of intonation, and ability to get an infinite variety of nuance in one bow. Isaac Stern, for one, has said that Heifetz "represents a standard of polished execution unrivalled in my memory by any violinist either by book or personal knowledge." It was that way from the beginning. When Kreisler heard the eleven-year-old Heifetz in Berlin, with the Berlin Philharmonic under Nikisch, he said, "I'm told that I don't play the Mendelssohn Violin Concerto exactly badly. And yet when I heard Jascha Heifetz play it the first time he came to Berlin, I don't think it has ever been played before and probably never again will be played so well." Heifetz had that effect on his colleagues. His playing was so effortless and natural, so untainted with any appearance of physical effort, that they were in despair. Perhaps Fritz Kreisler had more charm. Perhaps Josef Szigeti was his intellectual superior. Perhaps Mischa Elman made more luscious sounds. Perhaps Bronisław Huberman was more representative of the German school. It made no difference. It was Heifetz who remained the criterion.

He would come out on stage, poker-faced as always. He trailed power and dignity, and that feeling of authority so peculiarly his own. For the audience it was a shivery experience. Heifetz was unique and everybody knew it. From his childhood he was unique, and his teacher, Leopold Auer, would throw up his hands when discussing him. Talents on the order of a young Heifetz or, at the piano, a young Hofmann, cannot be rationally explained. The violinist Benno Rabinof delighted in telling a story about Heifetz's Berlin debut. It seems that a few days after the concert the critic and musicologist Arthur Abell invited the young Russian, all of eleven years old, to his house for a dinner party in his honor. Abell rounded up every important violinist in town. After dinner the boy wanted to make music and decided to play the Mendelssohn. To his embarrassment he discovered that he had forgotten to bring the music for his accompanist, whereupon a distinguished-looking gentleman with a monocle stood up. "May I have the honor of accompanying you?" The gentleman was Kreisler, almost as good a pianist as he was a violinist. After Heifetz had finished the concerto, with Kreisler of course playing the piano part from memory, Kreisler got up and looked at the guests—among them Huberman, Carl Flesch, Juan Manén, Willy

Hess, and Jan Kubelík—and said, "Well, gentlemen, we can now all break our violins across our knees."

Born at the turn of the century, Heifetz inevitably reflected the nineteenth-century kind of playing. His instrumental and intellectual approach were geared to Romanticism. Like nearly all musicians of his generation his concentration was on music from Beethoven onward, though he played a great deal of Bach and Mozart. His performances of those earlier classics disturbed the generation after World War II. Heifetz, they believed, was always identified more with the *instrument* than with the *music*. His way of playing the Bach Chaconne or a Mozart concerto represented the bad old ways of doing things, they said—surface gloss, no real identification with the style, elegance without substance. Szigeti or Adolf Busch were much more to their taste.

The new criticism condemned Heifetz for the very traits that were considered so marvelous when he first appeared. He had interpretive mannerisms common to most violinists at the turn of the century—certain expressive devices involving slides, emphases, accentuations, and highlightings with crescendos and decrescendos on individual notes, which today are considered old-fashioned, not to say vulgar.

Yet, it was conceded, of all the Romantic violinists Heifetz was always the coolest, the most restrained, the most patrician. His vibrato never wandered into adjacent regions and he never slobbered over the music, as did some of the Romantic violinists. If anything, the one criticism heard about Heifetz until the younger generation of musicians arrived was that his interpretations were "cold." It also is very possible that this "coldness" was read into his playing because of his unemotional platform behavior. Heifetz never smiled, never changed facial expression, never teetered, never waved his bow arm, never became physically involved with the music. That gave the impression of aloofness, where really it was part of his discipline. The fact is that Heifetz never really was a cold violinist. He was reserved, which is a different thing entirely. Perhaps the inhibitions he displayed, his reluctance ever to put on a display of feeling in public, carried over into his

Jascha Heifetz at seven years of age. He had just started making concert appearances.

performances. But when the musical challenge was there in a work with which he had emotional affinity, he could be the complete musician. Certainly when he spun out the melody of the slow movement of the Brahms Concerto he managed to create something in which descriptions like "cool" or "aloof" were completely beside the point. There he played with ultimate authority, and it was enough that this kind of flawless projection existed. Nobody else ever had it in such measure.

His style changed very little. A methodical man, he could be counted upon to do much the same thing year in and year out. "Now, take Heifetz," Sir Thomas Beecham once told Irving Kolodin. "You may like what he does or you may not like what he does. But when he agrees to something in a rehearsal, what he plays is *exactly* what he has agreed to do beforehand. That includes standing precisely at the distance from the microphone where we had set the balance—rather than edging closer to it as some I could name."

The best analysis of Heifetz's playing comes from the Carl Flesch memoirs, published in 1958. Flesch, an important violinist and teacher, wrote from the lofty viewpoint of one who had heard everything, met everybody, knew everything in the literature, and had for all his life pondered the secrets of the violin. In his book he paid due homage to Heifetz the technician, who "represents a culmination of the contemporary development of our art. . . . His tone is of a noble substance and is of a magical beauty, and there is not the smallest flaw in his technical equipment." What puzzled Flesch was why so many musicians were unaware of Heifetz's high artistic achievements "whereas as a violinist he delights all the world." Flesch blames this, paradoxically, on Heifetz's talent. Since he was "well-nigh perfect at the age of twelve" he never had to struggle. Everything came too easily. Thus, thought Flesch,

> he was soon led towards neglecting, to some extent, his personality; his unparalleled routine seemed to suffice. He got used to playing often with his hands alone and allowing his mind

> a Sleeping Beauty's rest. When, however, it was roused by the Prince of Inspiration, a work of art of the very first rank came into being, such as his interpretation of the Sibelius Concerto. . . . When, on the other hand, he played without inner participation, then a marble statue, perfect but mercilessly cold, was the result. The absolute infallibility of his technical apparatus is his worst enemy because it promotes a certain emotional inertia. . . . People [i.e., musicians] would forgive Heifetz his technical infallibility only if he made them forget it by putting his entire personality behind it. He is a living example of the relativity of a virtue which, when it overshadows something more essential, may come to be felt as a defect.

Heifetz added fuel to his colleagues' nagging doubts about his innate musicianship by putting a great deal of second-class music on his programs, often his own arrangements of various popular pieces; he published over a hundred of them. Why, it was wondered, should such a flawless instrumentalist have sullied his image by playing so many trite and even trashy salon pieces? One answer is that Heifetz did so because it was part of his background and the period from which he arose. Nobody objected, for instance, when Kreisler played fluff, and the reference here is not to Kreisler's own charming vignettes. Kreisler sometimes played and recorded some real trash, and nobody thought the worse of him for it. All performers seventy years ago constantly were heard in certain repertory pieces today regarded with disfavor. Even the greatest of singers would entertain their audiences with pieces like *Ma Curly Headed Baby* or the latest Carrie Jacobs Bond opus. They could no more be blamed for this than kittens can be blamed for being cuddly. The entertainment function of a great artist bulked much larger in years past than it does in today's serious age. That helps explain Heifetz and his approach. It may be regrettable—indeed, it *is* regrettable—that he never outgrew it. But at least in many of the great works of the violin repertory he achieved a quality as close to perfection as any violinist has done, as Flesch was the first to admit.

Heifetz was a product of the Russian school. Born in Vilna on February 2, 1901, he was taking lessons with his father at the age of three, after which he worked with Elias Malkin. At six he had mastered the Mendelssohn Concerto and other major works. At seven he was playing in public. At nine he was accepted by Leopold Auer at the St. Petersburg Conservatory. "I have been teaching for forty-five years," said Auer, "but this is the first time in that period I have heard a violinist of such remarkable qualities." Among those qualities was an ear of such discrimination that it could tell the difference between a 440-A and a 441-A. At ten Jascha made his debut and started concertizing in Russia, and at eleven was playing the Mendelssohn and Tchaikovsky concertos in Europe. Word about the prodigy began to appear in American newspapers and music magazines. A correspondent for *Musical Courier* started preparing America for what to expect. "If I had not heard with my own ears. . . ." In a later report he said that the eleven-year-old boy was "already beyond the pale of criticism . . . a great artist in every respect." One of the pieces Jascha played was that touchstone, the Bach Chaconne. When he played in Dresden in 1913 the correspondent wrote that he "combines the demeanor and air of an elderly gentleman in his quaint gravity and dignity." The Heifetz man was already in the Jascha child.

To come to the United States while Russia was at war, the Heifetz family had to travel from Vilna across Siberia to Japan and then take a steamship to San Francisco. Heifetz, sixteen years old, made his American debut on October 27, 1917, in Carnegie Hall. His program consisted of the Vitali Chaconne, the Wieniawski D minor Violin Concerto, the Twenty-fourth Caprice by Paganini, and a group of light, short pieces. The next day he was famous all over America. Seldom has a debut created such excitement. Every violinist and musician who could get to the concert was there, and one of the most famous of all musical stories emerged. Mischa Elman listened, mopping his head. "It's hot in here," he said to his friend, the great pianist Leopold Godowsky. "Not for pianists," Godowsky answered. The critics went wild. Sigmund Spaeth in the *Evening Mail* wrote a representative review:

Heifetz in 1918, the year after his Carnegie Hall debut. He immediately was accepted as the supreme violin virtuoso before the public.

> When Jascha Heifetz is called the perfect instrumentalist, the words are used advisedly, and by no means in the first flush of hysterical enthusiasm. It has always seemed to this writer that it ought to be possible to play the violin with every note clear and in tune, with a correct rhythm in fast as well as slow passages, and with a pure, musical tone, neither scratchy nor shaky, neither lifeless nor maudlin. Until last Saturday afternoon he had never heard any one actually do it. Then a tall Russian being with a mop of curly hair walked out on the stage of Carnegie Hall and made the ideal a reality. . . .

A few days later, Heifetz gave a second Carnegie Hall concert and then made his orchestral debut, playing the Bruch D minor Concerto (not the more popular G minor) with the New York Symphony under Walter Damrosch. The enthusiasm grew even more intense, and the media swung into action. "If press superlatives mean anything," reported the *Musical Courier,* "there has not been within the memory of living critics a musical success so immediate, so sweeping." Inevitably Heifetz was compared to other violinists, and the *Courier* interviewed a musician who had accompanied Vieuxtemps and Wieniawski. "Heifetz," said the veteran, "equals them in the elegance, grace and resourcefulness of his bowing, the polish of his style and the distinction and yet breadth of his conceptions." The *Courier* thought Heifetz closest to Emile Sauret and Sarasate, but better than either:

> His fingers are infallible and his bow arm is a doer of almost incredible deeds. Such up and down bow staccatos, spiccatos, harmonics, octaves, sixths, tenths, chords and trills, performed with such impeccability and so little outward effort, have not been heard here since the days when that human violinola, Jan Kubelík, was at his best.

Almost immediately Heifetz started his American tours. Phrases flew from critical pens. The Boston *Globe* called him "an inscrutable master of magic" (not a bad description), a violinist who played "without outward sign either of pleasure or of annoyance at applause." He was hailed as music incarnate, a demigod, a giant of the bow, the musical wonder of the age. The experienced James Huneker waited a year before making a full assessment. In 1918 he wrote in *The New York Times:*

> Much has been said of Heifetz and his musical gifts compared with those of great violinists of the time—Ysaÿe, Kreisler, Elman, Zimbalist, Kubelík and Maud Powell. He has the integrity and purpose of Ysaÿe, although he has only one-third his age; and the upward flights of Kreisler, although his tone is not so sensuously sweet and juicy as that of the Austrian. As for the others mentioned, he has all their best assets—and many more. Indeed, his God-given gifts are so amazing that a magic pen would be needed adequately to describe them. As the years add their depth of feeling and imprint, his listeners will realize that they are hearing the master of the times.

From that point the pattern of Heifetz's life for about the next forty years was established. He was constantly on tour, all over the world, and when he was not on tour he was making records or playing in radio broadcasts. Of course he received top fees. Two years after his debut he was getting $2,250 for a concert and was the highest-paid violinist in history (Kreisler was getting $2,000 at that time). His recordings sold more than those of any other violinist, Kreisler included. Even after Heifetz stopped making records he got an annual retainer of $100,000 from Victor. Heifetz was set in his ways from the beginning. Through the years his programs remained largely the same—meaty things for three-fourths of the recital, then always a concluding group of lollipops. He was one of the last to adhere to the outmoded practice of playing concertos with piano accompaniment at his recitals, generally with the orchestral introduction cut. He played a 1741 Guarnerius and a 1731 Stradivarius (the Guarnerius had once belonged to Ferdinand David, who had helped Mendelssohn with the Violin Concerto and who then played its premiere on that very instrument). He did not care for contemporary music, and when he commissioned new concertos, as he did once in a while, they were from conservative composers—Walton, Gruenberg, Castelnuovo-Tedesco, Korngold. In 1925 he became an American citizen and in 1928 he married the film star Florence Vidor, from whom he was divorced in 1946. They had two children. In 1947 Heifetz married Frances Spiegelberg. They were divorced in 1963.

Unlike so many musicians before the public, Heifetz never had the need to keep performing all of the time. He took a sabbatical for twenty months starting in 1947. At that time he figured out that he had played 100,000 hours and traveled two million miles. In 1956 he took a two-year leave. Normally, enthusiastic audiences act like an aphrodisiac on the egos of top musicians. Heifetz gave the feeling that he could get along very well without the public adulation, and perhaps he really could.

Heifetz had never been associated with chamber music, and thus it caused some surprise when in the late 1930's a series of trio recordings came out featuring Heifetz, Arthur Rubinstein, and Emanuel Feuermann. Feuermann was a brilliant cellist who died young. Gregor Piatigorsky took his place in the trio. In 1959 Heifetz started to give master classes at the University of Southern California in Los Angeles, and Piatigorsky also became associated with the music department there. So did the eminent violist William Primrose. One offshoot was a series of chamber-music concerts in Los Angeles with Piatigorsky, Primrose, and others in 1961, followed in 1964 by the Heifetz-Piatigorsky concerts in Carnegie Hall. By this time Heifetz was doing less and less solo work. Arthritis in his right shoulder was beginning to set in, and playing was painful. His last actual concert took place in Los Angeles in 1972, though he played two years later for a French documentary. As a teacher Heifetz produced two violinists who have had respectable careers—Erick Friedman and Eugene Fodor.

In the latter years of his life Heifetz disappeared completely from the public eye. His was apparently not the happiest of lives. Perhaps he was paying the price for his prodigy childhood. Musical prodigies, after all, do not grow up and develop the way normal children do. They are born with a spectacular order of talent that has to be nourished, and virtually as babies, from the age of four or five (or, in Heifetz's case, three), are subject to a ferocious discipline of practice and study for years to come, well into early adulthood. Everything else, very often including a general education, is neglected. Most great performers manage to pick up at least a superficial gloss along the way, and a few develop into well-read, cultured people. But it is surprising how many musical prodigies grow up with emotional and sexual problems and a lack of real contact with the world. They know their art supremely well but outside music tend to be innocents.

Heifetz guarded his private life exceedingly well, and little is known about him as a person. He managed to keep to himself whatever emotional problems he may have had. But often his behavior could be eccentric. Always precise and punctual in his habits, Heifetz developed a mania for exactness and promptness as he grew older. One had to be on time, and there was a joke to the effect that Heifetz himself had to make an appointment to see Heifetz. He gave a party once for his students. They assembled outside the electric gate of his home. It opened at 4 P.M. and promptly closed. Those who arrived at 4:01 never did get in. Raymond Kendall, the head of the music department at the university at which Heifetz taught, believed that the man was "tortured by a thousand demons." Perfection exacts a toll. Perfect technicians have to live up to their reputation, and where other musicians can get along on style, artists of the Heifetz class are expected always to be transcendental. No drop from the pluperfect standard is allowed. The violinist Daniil Karpolowsky has theorized about the difference between Heifetz and Kreisler. The latter would come out with the attitude that he was going to play for 2,000 friends. Heifetz "always came out like a killer. He believed that out of the 2,000 people in the hall, 1,999 had come to hear him play a wrong note."

After he stopped playing Heifetz became a recluse, shunning publicity, refusing to give interviews. It was said of him that he did not have a face; it was a mask and nobody could get behind it.

The Heifetz everybody remembers—handsome, impeccably groomed, imperturbable, never smiling, accomplishing technical miracles with never a suggestion of effort.

He was even remote from his children. In one of his rare interviews, given to Howard Taubman of *The New York Times* in 1968, he explained why he had not appeared in a New York solo recital for thirteen years: "I've had my share of touring. I have no further interest in that kind of career. And I can't say I admire the pace at which today's musicians travel. They move too fast; they play too often; they don't pause to reflect." Somebody once asked him why he had not written his autobiography, or why no biography of him had been written. "Here is my biography," answered Heifetz. "I played the violin at three and gave my first concert at seven. I have been playing ever since." At his eightieth birthday he disappeared from his Beverly Hills home; he did not want any celebrations or parties. A persistent newspaperman tracked him down, got him on the telephone, and demanded an interview. Heifetz refused. "I have nothing to say."

"But, Mr. Heifetz," pleaded the interviewer, "the history of twentieth-century violin playing is your history."

"I have nothing to say," repeated Heifetz, and he hung up.

25 *Kirsten Flagstad and Lauritz Melchior*

THE TWO WAGNERIANS

WHEN the Norwegian soprano Kirsten Flagstad made her Metropolitan Opera debut as Sieglinde on February 2, 1935, listeners of the Saturday afternoon nationwide radio broadcast did not anticipate anything out of the ordinary. Geraldine Farrar, an intermission commentator, had listened to the first act from a booth. When she went on the air she threw away her script. "Ladies and gentlemen," she said, "you have just been in the presence of the most exciting thing in the theatre—the birth of a new star." And she went on to describe what she had heard. Some years later, Farrar said in an interview that "I had never thought to hear from human lips, since the passing of Lilli Lehmann, such a performance."

Nobody had expected the glory that poured forth from that throat. Flagstad was thirty-nine years old and had been active as a singer for about twenty of them, making no particular impression. She was at the Metropolitan as, almost, a measure of desperation. Frida Leider, who had sung the big Wagnerian soprano roles for two seasons, had elected not to return. Anny Konetzni had been tried and found wanting. Gertrude Kappel was past her best days. So the Metropolitan Opera turned its attention to Flagstad. She was not an inexperienced artist. She had sung all kinds of roles in her career, including musical comedy. In 1933 she had been given small parts at Bayreuth, and in 1934 was promoted to Sieglinde and Gutrune. Nobody paid much attention. Flagstad did not care too much. Married to a wealthy Norwegian industrialist, she had seriously been considering retirement. Gatti-Casazza and Artur Bodanzky, the chief conductor of the German wing at the Metropolitan, auditioned Flagstad in St. Moritz in 1934 and signed her to a contract. Apparently they were not very impressed, but they needed a Wagnerian soprano. Not until the dress rehearsal of *Die Walküre* did Bodanzky realize the calibre of singer with whom he had been dealing. He gave his baton to an assistant and rushed to the office of Gatti's assistant, Edward Ziegler, dragging him back to the auditorium. A messenger also was sent posthaste to summon Gatti himself downstairs. When the reviews appeared over the next few days, and again after Flagstad's Isolde on February 6, the surprised critics were flopping around like fish at low tide, gasping and evoking the magic names of Olive Fremstad and Lillian Nordica. Lawrence Gilman in the *Herald Tribune* was especially ecstatic, and he, whose memory extended back to the Golden Age, put Flagstad in a class entirely by herself. "A transcendently beautiful and moving impersonation," he wrote of her Isolde. "An embodiment so sensitively musical, so fine-grained in its imaginative and intellectual texture, so lofty in its pathos and simplicity, of so memorable a loveliness, that experienced operagoers sought among their memories of legendary days to find its like. They did not find it."

There are those who believe that Flagstad was the savior of the Metropolitan Opera. When she arrived in the dark depths of the Great Depression, the company was in poor financial condition. The Flagstad furor brought money into the house; she commanded a full audience every time she appeared. She also did not cost much; as an unknown singer she had signed on for much less

Kirsten Flagstad, who came to the Metropolitan Opera in 1935 and immediately made vocal history.

than superstar rates. With Flagstad heading the Wagnerian casts, singing in a company that boasted such great Wagnerians as Lauritz Melchior, Friedrich Schorr, Lotte Lehmann, Helen Traubel, Maria Olszewska, Kerstin Thorborg, Elisabeth Rethberg ("Never in my life have I heard such a beautiful voice as Elisabeth Rethberg's," Flagstad said after hearing her Sieglinde), Ludwig Hofmann, Alexander Kipnis, Emanuel List, and Karin Branzell, it was recognized that a very great age of Wagnerian singing was at hand. Audiences rushed to take advantage of it.

How could so phenomenal a voice as Flagstad's have remained unknown for so long? There are occasional cases of late development, and Flagstad's is the *locus classicus*. Wagnerian singers often take a long time developing. George Bernard Shaw used to argue that Wagner was more grateful to sing than Verdi, pointing out that whereas Verdi was mostly interested in the upper fifth of the singers' voices, Wagner spread the work over the entire compass. This is as it might be; but Wagner also used a much larger orchestra than any opera composer up to his time, and a singer has to have a heroic voice to ride over the volumes of tone that the Wagnerian orchestra produces. Great Wagnerian singers always have been a rare commodity. In 1985, for instance, Birgit Nilsson had all but retired from the stage, after her glorious career, and there was not a single soprano in all the world to replace her. Thus the line descending from Lilli Lehmann to Nordica, Fremstad, Leider, Flagstad, and Nilsson had come to a halt—a temporary halt, one hoped.

It takes years to develop the volume, strength, and underpinning needed to deal with Wagnerian roles. Flagstad did not achieve that ability until the middle 1930's. Neither opera managers nor music critics are deaf, and it is inconceivable that the voice Flagstad displayed on her debut would have been ignored had she reached that kind of level before coming to New York. It could well be that not until she was almost forty did everything come together for her. It also must be remembered that for most of her life she had been, in effect, isolated, singing in provincial Scandinavian centers. At that, Oscar Thompson, the music critic of the New York *Sun,* had heard her in Stockholm in the early 1930's and wrote an article trumpeting her praises. He was one of the few Americans who had heard her.

For her Siegmunds, Siegfrieds, Lohengrins, and Tristans, Flagstad had a singer with a voice to match hers. Lauritz Melchior —the Great Dane, as he was called—was a big, stout, jolly man with a golden voice that seemed to have unlimited power. When he sang there always was a feeling of something left in reserve. He could fill the opera house with a clarion trumpet blast, and yet give the impression that he could have doubled the volume had he so wished. Most likely he was the greatest Wagnerian tenor who ever lived. Jean de Reszke may have been a greater vocal stylist and more convincing actor, but he came to the big Wagner roles very late in his career and at his best never had the incredible endowments of Melchior—that poised projection, that beautiful and unforced sound, and the sheer size of the organ.

Most of Melchior's career was spent at the Metropolitan Opera, where he sang only the major Wagnerian tenor roles—Walther in *Die Meistersinger* excepted. He did, however, also make appearances in Covent Garden, San Francisco, Paris, and Buenos Aires. There were those who called him lazy. He could have sung Otello, Radames, and some of the Strauss roles. But he was content with what he was doing and, toward the end, a bit sloppy about it. Yet even at the end his was a voice of unparalleled glory, and he and Flagstad proved to be the most impressive stage partners since the great days of Caruso and Farrar. They stimulated one another, and possibly never in the history of opera have two great voices of such amplitude and generosity worked together to such brilliant and musical effect. In recent years, critics have been sniping at Melchior's musicianship, accusing him of taking liberties and of being rhythmically inaccurate. Would that today we had a Melchior, even with his alleged liberties and inaccurate rhythms! His species died when he left the stage in 1950.

Probably the trouble with Melchior was that he had no competition. Singers—and not only singers—work better when they have the competition of hungry colleagues snapping at their heels.

Lauritz Melchior, the greatest Wagnerian tenor of his time and, very likely, of all time.

Franz Völker and Max Lorenz were admirable singers and artists, but they were not real competition; neither had the clarion sound of a Melchior. Thus he became careless and indifferent, ending up doing things by rote. A pity. He had *the* unique tenor voice after Caruso.

Melchior was born in Copenhagen on March 20, 1890. Trained in his native city, he made his debut there in 1913 as Silvio in *Pagliacci*. At that time he was a baritone (many Wagnerian tenors, including Jean de Reszke, started as baritones). Five years later, Melchior started singing Wagnerian roles, and in 1924 appeared in Covent Garden as Siegmund. He also sang in Bayreuth in 1924 and went to the Metropolitan in 1926, remaining there until 1950. Toward the end of his career he was a constant source of trouble. He would not only skip dress rehearsals but would in addition even duck orchestra rehearsals. He was a law unto himself, and he worked on the assumption that since he knew the music so well, why waste time on rehearsing it? Max Rudolf, one of the Metropolitan's conductors and musical advisers, wryly said that Melchior was dependable; he could always be counted upon to make the same mistakes. There probably was a sigh of relief when Rudolf Bing, in his first year as general manager, did not renew Melchior's contract. But the Great Dane's career was not finished when he left the Metropolitan. He made some films, including one—*Two Sisters from Boston*—in which he sang a duet with the great comic Jimmy Durante. He also made radio appearances, did a vaudeville turn at the Palace in New York, and appeared in a Jones Beach extravaganza, *Arabian Nights*—at $5,000 a week. When he played the Palace he uttered the usual nonsense about "bringing music to the people" that artists inevitably make when they soil themselves artistically. Melchior was one of the highest-paid singers of his day. At the Metropolitan he was getting $1,000 a performance—small beer today but then the top fee paid by the house. For a concert he could command up to $5,600, and he sang many concerts; for radio appearances his fee was $3,000, and for a film, $100,000. In 1949 he was making an estimated $600,000 a year. To celebrate his seventieth birthday in

1960 he sang Siegmund with the Danish Radio Orchestra. He died on March 18, 1973, in Beverly Hills.

In many respects he was a clown, and he could have had a great career as a film comic. There were no inhibitions about Lauritz Melchior. He was a big eater, a big drinker, a gregarious man, a mighty hunter who owned an enormous 3,000-acre tract in Germany where he shot wild boar and other game, and who decorated his apartment with the stuffed fruits of his African safaris. Thrice he took a wife, and his second marriage, to Maria Hacker, called "Kleinchen" by everybody, was a success. She was a film star, called the Mary Pickford of Germany; she was lovely and petite—all the more petite when she went arm in arm with the elephantine Lauritz. She also had brains inside that pretty head, could read and understand the small print in all contracts, and took care of the family finances. "I make the noise," Melchior said, "and she makes the business." Managers were very wary when Kleinchen approached, and girded themselves for a real fight. She died in 1963. Melchior then married his secretary. That relationship was very short-lived.

When he discussed singing with a knowledgeable interviewer Melchior, of course, had something to contribute. He once described the Heldentenor—heroic tenor—as a singer with a voice "a little darker-colored than the ordinary Italian lyric tenor. A baritonal quality points the way to the dramatic or heroic Wagner tenor, the so-called *Schwerheld* [heavy hero]—Siegfried, Tristan and Tannhäuser. The higher *Held* is Lohengrin and Walther. . . . The heroic tenor must learn to conserve his energy, because it's such a long stretch. It's like a horserace: if you try to lead the field the whole time, you'll never make the finish." One of the basic requirements, he said, was "a natural lower register to build high notes. You can't put a skyscraper on sand." He gave an interesting explanation of why he never sang Walther, and warned Heldentenors to keep away from that role. It belongs, he said, to a *jugendlicher Held* (a young Heldentenor with a lighter voice). "The music [of *Die Meistersinger*] lies more in the top of the voice. The heldentenor goes from low to high, then downhill, then up

Melchior and his wife, Kleinchen. "I make the noise," he said, "and she makes the business."

again. He has a baritone quality down, a shining high on top. In *Meistersinger* there are no real mountains and valleys, so a heldentenor gets tired. When we walk on the same high level every time we lose strength." Melchior spent a summer studying the role and decided it was not for him. "Before I got to the *Prize Song* I had no strength left."

It is interesting to note that Eva in *Die Meistersinger* was one major Wagnerian role that Kirsten Flagstad never sang after her early days in Scandinavia.

Flagstad was born in Hamar on July 12, 1895. Her father was a conductor, her mother a singer and coach. At the age of ten Kirsten had memorized the role of Elsa in *Lohengrin,* and a few years later had Aida by heart. Of course she never really sang them at that age. At eighteen she made her debut in Oslo, in d'Albert's *Tiefland,* and for the next eighteen years was heard only in Scandinavia, singing everything from revues and musical comedy to dramatic operas. She married Sigurd Hall in 1919, had a baby, and left the stage for several years. Flagstad's mother talked her into resuming her career, and when she returned to the stage she discovered that her voice was about twice the size it had previously been. Now the biggest roles of the repertory were within her capability. At the Gothenburg Opera in Sweden she sang Eva in *Die Meistersinger,* Nedda, Minnie in *La Fanciulla del West,* Agathe in *Der Freischütz,* Amelia in *Un Ballo in Maschera,* and even Marguerite in *Faust.* One wonders what such a mighty vocal organ as Flagstad's would have sounded like in the Gounod opera. And did she have the trills for the *Jewel Song*?

She separated from Hall and in 1930 married a wealthy Norwegian industrialist, Henry Johansen. Again she retired from the stage. But when the director of the National Theater in Oslo asked her to sing Isolde, she—prodded by her husband—decided to learn the role, and she sang it there in 1932, in Swedish. Then came the Bayreuth summers and the spectacular Metropolitan Opera debut. In her first season in New York she sang, in addition to Sieglinde and Isolde, Brünnhilde and Kundry (she had never sung in *Parsifal* and had to learn her role in about three weeks), and also

Leonore in *Fidelio,* making twenty-three appearances in all. Suddenly the provincial, virtually unknown Kirsten Flagstad became internationally famous.

In her first season she received $550 a week. That went up to $750 a performance the following season. After that she received the Metropolitan's top price—$1,000. The Depression had cut salaries severely, even for superstars; but it should be remembered that Flagstad was earning, for one performance, more than most American families were earning in a year. It was in her contract that no singer be paid more than she. Whatever she made at the opera, she made much more through her concerts and recordings. She developed all of the stigmata of superstardom. Although she was a quiet and even shy woman who did not entertain much or play the society game, she could be very demanding and stubborn in her professional relationships. She would fight with Melchior over curtain calls, would sulk or storm when reviews did not pay utter homage, could be rude and biting. Indeed, she and Melchior had a feud for a few years; they had to sing together, but they were not on speaking terms.

A large-sized but not stout woman in her early years at the Metropolitan Opera, Flagstad conquered with her voice and instinctive musicianship rather than with temperament. She never was much of an actress; but at least she had the good sense not to make a fool of herself by indulging in excessive gesture or movement. Thus many called her a "cool" singer, which in a way she was. For the most part she stood solidly and stolidly where she was planted, throwing her head back and emitting cascades of glorious sound. It was an enormous sound. Flagstad had one of the biggest voices of the century, and it never sounded pushed or tired. She always sang out in full voice, even at rehearsals. She also was a workhorse, and once at the Metropolitan, in an emergency, she sang three Wagnerian roles three nights in a row. "I knew I could do it without harm to my instrument," she said. But her singing was not just pure sound. Phrases were shaped in an authoritative manner, and there was meaning to the vocal utterance. Flagstad, after all, had had about two decades of intensive operatic

Flagstad and her accompanist, Edwin McArthur. She moved heaven and earth to get him into the Metropolitan Opera as a Wagnerian conductor.

work before her fame. She well knew the relationship between word and note.

But she certainly was no intellectual. Edwin McArthur, her accompanist and conductor, has said that her understanding was acute but intuitive. "When a profoundly analytic article about her portrayal of this or that character appeared, she seldom had any idea of what the author was talking about." She and McArthur enjoyed an unusually close relationship, and she fought hard to get him into the Metropolitan Opera. When Bodanzky died in 1939 she immediately shot off a telegram to Edward Johnson, the general manager:

> Am distressed with sad news of Bodanzky's passing. The Metropolitan will not be the same without him, but life goes on and we must all keep up with the musical tradition so firmly established by him. I know that Melchior will join me in requesting that you give Edwin McArthur the opportunity to conduct our Tristan performances which he did so brilliantly in California and in which opera we both feel so perfectly at ease with him in the pit. I know that our dear departed friend himself would have approved such a choice if he could have heard him and I would feel privileged to have been instrumental in thus establishing a gifted young American musician.

Johnson would have none of it, and in that he was seconded by the musical community, who knew that McArthur was a competent accompanist and musician, but lacking in pit experience. The Metropolitan hedged. Flagstad vigorously pursued her goal. "I have done the Metropolitan so many favors and this is the first time that I have ever asked a favor of the Metropolitan and if you wanted to you could of course grant it," she wrote to Johnson. Eventually Johnson gave in and granted McArthur a few performances. In his biography of Flagstad, McArthur indicates that he was made uncomfortable by Flagstad's endeavors in his behalf. McArthur frankly admits that he could never have filled Bodanzky's shoes. He adds that neither could he have filled Erich

Leinsdorf's. Leinsdorf was the young conductor who inherited the Bodanzky operas.

In 1941 Flagstad canceled all engagements to return to her husband in Norway. Apparently she sang only four times in Europe during the war—in Zürich and in Sweden. Unfortunately her husband became a member of the Norwegian Quisling party, and musical circles and the press were ready to believe the worst about her. It was rumored that she sang in Germany and was on the best of terms with the Nazi leaders. Some ugly stories circulated about Flagstad's alleged Nazi connections. Her husband died in 1946 while awaiting trial as a war criminal. During the years Flagstad was away from the Metropolitan Opera, Helen Traubel took over her roles and handled them in a noble manner.

When Flagstad returned to America in 1947 there were demonstrations against her—pickets, stink bombs at her concerts, audience uprisings within the halls. Passions ran high. The pros and cons of her case were argued by newspaper editorialists and columnists. She professed to be nonpolitical, and perhaps she was. Only an innocent could have answered in so naïve a way some of the questions thrown at her. A *New York Times* reporter asked her if she had ever met Hitler. "Yes, and he had such wonderful blue eyes," she said. Apparently that was all she knew or cared to know about Hitler. She was not asked back to the Metropolitan Opera, and gave only concerts. Not until the 1950–51 season did she return. It was Rudolf Bing's first season as general manager, and the previous year he had started negotiations with her. The announcement of her return was a front-page story in the *Times*. There still was a great deal of unrest, but Bing held firm. "I would feel myself a coward," he said, "if I had let my personal feelings influence the artistic position of the Metropolitan." Flagstad was still the greatest Wagnerian soprano, and Bing said that the house needed her. On January 22, 1951, she sang Isolde there. For the first time in many years she sang the opera without Melchior; her Tristan was Ramón Vinay. She also sang in *Fidelio* that season under the direction of Bruno Walter. But Flagstad was not to remain at the Metropolitan Opera for a long time. Her career was drawing to a close. Her last Metropolitan appearances were in Gluck's *Alceste* in 1952, and her last appearances on the stage were at the tiny Mermaid Theatre in London, when in 1953 she sang Dido in the Purcell opera. For a few years after that she was the director of the newly formed Norwegian State Opera. She died in Oslo on December 7, 1962.

Like all superstars, she set standards. It is possible that she was the greatest of all Wagnerian sopranos. Judging from records, Nordica may have had a bigger and more flexible voice (though Nordica never was very successful in her recordings, and this opinion is merely a guess), but it could depart from the pitch and was not as easily produced as Flagstad's voice. Experts also say that Fremstad's recordings do not do her justice. In any case, Fremstad was a pushed-up mezzo who paid the ultimate price, and her high notes were never as secure as Flagstad's. In Flagstad's own day there was the admirable Frida Leider, a better actress and musician with a beautiful voice. Many consider her the greatest of all Isoldes; and it certainly was a more feminine and sensitive realization than Flagstad's. Yet Leider never had the monumental quality of voice that Flagstad could summon forth. And Leider never created the excitement, the public frenzy, that Flagstad somehow did. Nor did Helen Traubel with her rich, warm, powerful voice. Flagstad's great successor, Birgit Nilsson, had the power, range, and brains to establish herself as one of the all-time great Wagnerian sopranos, but that "white" voice of hers could never compete with Flagstad's in terms of color. If (to paraphrase Orwell) all great singers are unique, some are more unique than others; and the fact is that Flagstad was *the* unique Wagnerian soprano of her time. With Melchior she left an unmatched standard that still rings in the memory of all who heard them.

26 *Arthur Rubinstein*

JOIE DE VIVRE

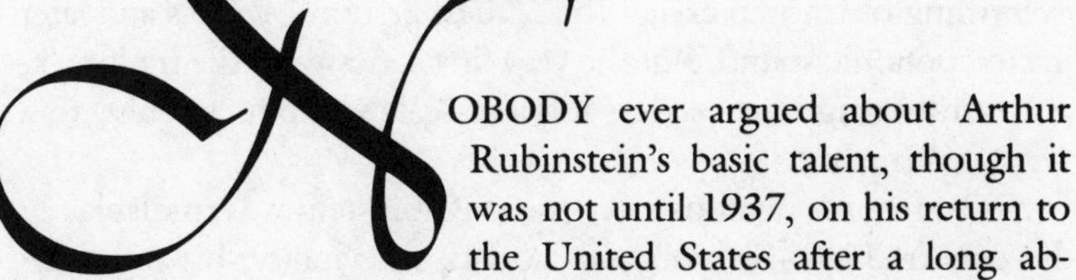

OBODY ever argued about Arthur Rubinstein's basic talent, though it was not until 1937, on his return to the United States after a long absence, that he was taken to the collective American bosom. But many music lovers had known in advance what to expect. Rubinstein had been preceded by his records. His career was not made by recordings, but they certainly helped. In America during the middle 1930's, Rubinstein was the first pianistic hero of the electrical era of recording—more than Alfred Cortot, more than Vladimir Horowitz (who at that time did not have many records), more than Artur Schnabel.

In those days if you went to a symphony concert at which the Tchaikovsky B flat minor Concerto was being played, you could count on many in the audience starting to rise at a certain point in the first movement and then settling back with silly grins. They were getting up to turn over the first disc of the Rubinstein recording. Those were, of course, 78 r.p.m. discs, and they did not contain much more than four and a half minutes of music. Electrical recording was then in its infancy, having been introduced only a short time previously, in 1925. Up to then single discs rather than albums were the norm. Now music lovers could and did revel in complete symphonies, operas, string quartets, and sonatas; and getting up every four minutes or so to change a record was a very small price to pay for the new world that had opened up. (Serious collectors refused to have anything to do with record changers, which in the early days were a threat to the health and longevity of the disc.) Electrical recording, too, marked a tremendous difference in fidelity; they were so much more faithful, colorful, and brilliant than the old acoustic records.

That was where Arthur Rubinstein entered. From him came the beginnings of the first complete Chopin series in history—the two concertos, the complete scherzos, nocturnes, mazurkas, and polonaises. Eventually he was to record and re-record substantially everything of Chopin except the études, first on LP discs and later in stereophonic sound. But the very first series were the trailbreakers, introducing music lovers to large-scale Chopin, and also to a very great pianist.

The records demonstrated what Rubinstein was to display in the concert hall—his gorgeous sound, his vitality, his big technique, his unflagging rhythm, his feeling for a sinuous shape to a phrase, the drama he could infuse into the interpretations, the sheer joy that comes through the playing. His playing changed somewhat through the years, but never did it lose the *joie de vivre* that set him off from all other pianists. He represented highly charged but disciplined emotionalism in music, the opposite pole from what he called the "intellectual" approach of Artur Schnabel, whose Beethoven playing he did not like.

His ideas about music were at once Romantic and modern. He was, after all, born in 1887, which meant that he was trained and grew up with the Romantic sound in his ears. To the Romantics, sound was an esthetic in itself, whether it came from the piano, violin, or voice. An artist had to produce a beautiful sound, and he or she then had to have the technique to put the sound to expressive use. Rubinstein had that sound; it was rich, varied, subtle, or powerful, as the need might have been, and never did it sound forced or ugly. That he had in common with all of the Romantics.

But his playing differed in many respects from nineteenth-century Romanticism. Metrically it was more regular, with a minimum of the fluctuation of tempo that was characteristic of some of the old pianists. There never was any tampering with the text or an empty display of virtuosity for virtuosity's sake. As such he was more modern than most nineteenth-century pianists. But to suggest, as so many have done, that he brought a completely new light to Chopin, is to misunderstand his contribution. In 1983, a year after his death, a series of his pre–World War II Chopin recordings were released, and in each liner note the annotator automatically went into the received opinion about the way Rubinstein "revolutionized" Chopin playing. The inference was that only Rubinstein understood the true way of playing Chopin.

This is nonsense. Were the annotators trying to tell us that the great pianists of Rubinstein's generation—pianists like Hofmann, Rachmaninoff, Ignaz Friedman, Josef Lhévinne, Benno Moiseiwitsch, Guiomar Noväes, Leopold Godowsky—had no idea of how to play Chopin? As a matter of fact, they could demonstrate an order of Chopin playing that has left everything far behind. One example: listen to the Friedman performance of the E flat Nocturne (Op. 55, No. 2). In its color, chord weightings, polyphony, control, and command of a singing line, it leaves even Rubinstein far behind. Or listen to the tensile strength and classic, nonsentimental playing of Hofmann in the familiar F sharp Nocturne. Or listen to the majesty, sweep, and refinement of Lhévinne in the A flat Polonaise. (All of these performances are available on LP transfers.) These pianists were completely different and each had his own individuality, but they all had certain things in common—sound as an esthetic ideal, the organization of basses and inner voices that gave a pronounced polyphonic structure and a much richer harmonic texture to the music, and the way they were able to float a melodic line.

Rubinstein had some of these traits, but his more modern outlook made him avoid the bass-inner voice delineations that were so much a part of Romantic playing. In his autobiography Rubinstein has some points to make about Chopin playing, but he goes about proving them in a peculiar manner. He says that in the 1920's his Chopin "found some detractors, who found it brilliant but a little dry. Paderewski's exaggerated sentimentalism and Alfred Cortot's too delicate conception were still considered the true way to play the Polish master, and Cortot's treatment of Chopin as the weak, tubercular artist was still in public favor. My own conception of Chopin was always based on the conviction that he was a powerful, masculine creator, completely independent of his physical condition. . . ." But few connoisseurs took Paderewski seriously in the 1920's; nor, *pace* Rubinstein, would many agree that Cortot was all that effeminate. Certainly Cortot's recordings of such pieces as the F major Ballade, the Fantasy, and the Preludes are valuable documents that are the work of a strong pianist with a fascinating mind. Rubinstein was not being very fair to Cortot. And Rubinstein does not mention the great Liszt and Leschetizky pupils who thrilled the world with their Chopin.

At least one can agree with Rubinstein's estimate of himself as a direct player. There never was a trace of affectation in his performances. Everything was clear, unneurotic, healthy, spirited, infused with a manly kind of poetry. And he had the technique to put his ideas into effect, even if he could have momentary memory lapses or had to scramble through a difficult section. Most of this stemmed from his distaste for practicing. A natural pianist, he seldom worked more than two or three hours a day, if that, and the day before a concert all he did was read through some of the more difficult sections. He was once asked what kind of exercises he used to keep his fingers in trim. Simple, he said. Take the Second Etude of Chopin—the one with the fast right-hand chromatic scales—and play the passages with the left hand. He went to the piano and zipped it off.

He was born in Lodz on January 28, 1887, and was a prodigy almost on the Hofmann order. At the age of three he was taken to

Berlin to play for Joseph Joachim, who encouraged further music studies. Arthur made his debut at seven and returned to Berlin in 1897, where Joachim supervised his education. Heinrich Barth was Rubinstein's piano teacher. At thirteen he was judged ready for his official debut, and he played Mozart's A major Concerto (K. 488) with Joachim on the podium. Soon he had an adult repertory and started concertizing. He also discovered girls, fancy clothes, good food, cigars, wines, and cognac. Young Arthur became one of Berlin's men-about-town.

He took a few lessons from Paderewski and was not impressed by the man as either pianist or teacher. Paderewski, Rubinstein wrote in his memoirs, was handicapped by technical defects "especially in the articulation of his fingers, which resulted in an unbalanced sense of rhythm." For a while, Rubinstein lived a hand-to-mouth existence, which apparently did not bother him very much. He was having too good a time. He nevertheless managed to learn an immense repertory, much of which he admitted he did not play particularly well. In 1906 he made his first American tour; his debut took place with the Philadelphia Orchestra under Fritz Scheel, and he played his particular warhorse, the Saint-Saëns G minor Concerto. He had a good but not overwhelming success and was characterized as a talented pianist who still had a good deal to learn. "I must admit," he wrote in his autobiography, "this was also my opinion." Returning to Europe, he made Paris his headquarters, supporting himself by everything that came his way—accompanying singers, giving concerts, playing Strauss's *Salome* as a piano solo at parties (at least he got free meals that way). *Salome,* of course, was the naughty, deliciously risqué musical scandal of the day. There was one bad period for Rubinstein, however. For a while he was so distressed that he thought of suicide. Or so he says in his memoirs.

In 1910 he competed for the Rubinstein prize in St. Petersburg and ended up sharing first place with Alfred Hoehn, a pianist never heard of again. Some playing in Russia followed, including appearances with Koussevitzky, who (with his wife's money) had purchased an orchestra to learn how to conduct. Whatever money

The teenage Arthur Rubinstein, drawn by Joseph Muller. Brilliantly talented, he was already very much the bon vivant *and eternal bohemian.*

Rubinstein made he immediately spent. He was always broke, almost always happy. World War I found Rubinstein in Paris, penniless as usual, giving piano lessons. In 1916 and 1917 he played in Spain and fell in love with the country. One result was the inclusion in his programs of music by Granados and Albéniz. For many years Rubinstein was known as an exponent of Spanish piano music. Then he went to Buenos Aires, where he became the rage. For the first time in his life he started making real money. By this time his repertory was expanded with the then new music of Debussy, Prokofiev, Ravel, and his compatriot Karol Szymanowski.

Rubinstein became a busy touring pianist, darting from Paris to London to Spain to South America to the United States. In the middle 1920's he played in New York under the management of Sol Hurok, and it was an association that was to bear fruit the following decade. After the middle 1920's, Rubinstein avoided America for a long time. He started to make recordings for HMV in London in 1926 (up to then he had made only piano rolls). Those first recordings are very interesting. Rubinstein always claimed that he had been a sloppy pianist before his marriage; that it was his marriage that determined him to settle down and really work at the piano. But those early recordings tell a different story. Among them are such pieces as the Albéniz *Navarra* and *Evocación* and the Liszt Tenth Rhapsody, played with a glorious technique, controlled abandon, excitement, and a wonderfully aristocratic sense of phrase. It is doubtful if he could ever play them as well later in life.

In 1932 the gay bachelor got married. His wife, Aniela, was the daughter of the Polish conductor Emil Mlynarski. She had previously been married, to a pianist named Mieczyslaw Munz. Rubinstein resumed touring, but after 1932 refused to play in Germany. He never had been an orthodox Jew, but he foresaw the rise of the Nazi movement, with all of its implications. Nor did he ever return to Germany. In later life he said that there were only two countries in which he would not play—Tibet, because it was too high, and Germany, because it was too low.

He heard the young Vladimir Horowitz and was both exhilarated and depressed. Exhilarated because of the way Horowitz played. Depressed because he was so good. "There was more than sheer brilliance and technique; there was an easy elegance—the magic something which defies description." Rubinstein went backstage to pay his respects and found Horowitz unhappy; he said that he had played a wrong note in Chopin's Polonaise-Fantasy. "I would gladly give ten years of my life," Rubinstein wrote, "to be able to claim only one wrong note after a concert." The two pianists did not hit it off very well, and for the rest of their lives had an uneasy on and off friendship. Basically, one feels, they really detested one another. They became the two top pianists of their time and found it difficult to share the throne. Rubinstein felt, in their years in Paris, that while they were friends,

> I began to feel a subtle difference between us. His friendship for me was that of a king for his subject, which means he *befriended* me and, in a way, used me. It caused me to begin to feel a deep artistic depression. Deep within myself, I felt I was the better musician. My conception of the sense of music was more mature, but at the same time I was conscious of my terrible defects—of my negligence for detail, my treatment of some concerts as a pleasant pastime, all due to that devilish facility for grasping and learning the pieces and then playing them lightheartedly in public; with all the conviction of my musical superiority, I had to concede that Volodya was by far the better pianist.

Rubinstein, incidentally, felt much the same way about Jascha Heifetz who, with Horowitz, "treated me as an inferior in our profession from the heights of their American-dollar superiority. As a matter of fact, I never envied either of them their great success and I took it for granted that Heifetz was the greatest violinist of his time, who never touched my heart with his playing, and Horowitz the greatest pianist, but not a great musician. On such premises our trio got along together quite well."

These remarks reveal a good deal about Rubinstein. To the

world he was the eternally civilized, debonair bon vivant. But he did have another side to his character. He needed and demanded respect, and his ego was no whit smaller than the ego of any other superstar. If he never surrounded himself with the flatterers and sycophants that were in the Horowitz or Toscanini circle, he nevertheless made sure that the wishes of Arthur Rubinstein were to be respected.

Sol Hurok signed Rubinstein for an American tour in 1937. The contract was sealed only with a handshake. For his return, Rubinstein played the Brahms B flat Concerto (for the Thursday and Friday concerts), and the Tchaikovsky B flat minor (on the Sunday broadcast) with the New York Philharmonic conducted by John Barbirolli, a musician he greatly admired (and, indeed, Barbirolli was one of the best accompanists in the business). He followed the orchestral appearances with a solo recital. From that moment he was America's most beloved pianist.

The time was right for him. Hofmann and Rachmaninoff, the two big keyboard lions, were nearing the end of their careers. Horowitz was their heir-apparent, but the field was big enough for two, and Rubinstein moved in. Horowitz scared audiences; he seemed Olympian and he hurled his pianistic thunderbolts in so highly charged an atmosphere that everybody felt nervous. Audiences were always more relaxed at a Rubinstein recital; there were none of the tensions that the Horowitz recitals evoked. Rubinstein clearly loved playing the piano and making music, loved the reception he got from his audiences, had just the right amount of—can one say?—ham in him to keep his listeners perpetually enthralled. His was one of the great entrances. "Without trying," a *Times* critic wrote, "he lets the audience immediately feel that it is facing a Presence. Look, my lord, it comes. Polite, agreeable, not gushing, he accepts the homage due him. He seats himself, and his nose points toward the stratosphere like the prow of a jet going upstairs. The audience waits, breathlessly. Rubinstein is in no hurry. He must compose himself; he must think of the opening piece; he must wait for the last cough to dissipate before he puts

Rubinstein in the late 1930's, at the beginning of his great American successes. He had an immense hand, capable of spanning C to G.

his hands on the keyboard. Suddenly the auditorium is filled with golden sound. A typical Rubinstein concert is under way."

It is interesting that in his two books of memoirs, Rubinstein has very little to say about Hofmann and Rachmaninoff, the two pianistic giants of his time. Hofmann he seems to have flatly disliked; he thought him cynical and without any real love for music. When he speaks of Rachmaninoff, it generally is in disparaging terms. There is one amusing anecdote in the Rubinstein memoirs about Rachmaninoff, who invited the Rubinsteins for dinner because the Stravinskys were coming. Everybody knew that the two Russians had no use for each other and, as Rubinstein wrote, "The two men had spoken with such disgust of each other's works that it was inconceivable to imagine them dining together." At dinner the conversation was hesitant and stilted. Suddenly the conversation became dangerous. Rachmaninoff taunted Stravinsky with the fact that his two most popular works, *Firebird* and *Petruchka,* had never given him a cent of royalties. Stravinsky flushed and became angry. "What about your C sharp Prelude and all those concertos of yours, all published in Russia, eh? You had to play concerts to make a living, uh?" Rubinstein thought a nasty scene would develop:

> But, lo and behold, quite the contrary happened. Both great masters began to count out the sums they could have earned and became so involved in this important matter that when we got up they retired to a small table and continued happily daydreaming of the immense fortunes they might have earned. When we were leaving, they exchanged a hearty handshake at the door and promised each other to find more sums to think of.

There is a Stravinsky postscript. "When, on my advice," Rubinstein wrote, "he discovered the easy way of making money by appearing in public, whether as pianist or conductor without any real talent for either, but relying entirely on his great name as a composer, he never stopped making concert tours and amassed a considerable fortune." Perhaps Rubinstein was repaying a debt.

Stravinsky had arranged for him as a piano solo the formidably difficult *Three Scenes from Petruchka,* with which Rubinstein had made such a brilliant effect when he put it into his repertory. It has remained one of the favorite virtuoso pieces of all pianists.

Unlike Horowitz, Rubinstein took on an enormous concert schedule. He also, of course, made many appearances with orchestra, playing with conductors who were not very good accompanists, such as Koussevitzky, and others who were, such as Ormandy and Toscanini. Rubinstein played only once with Toscanini. Their piece was the Beethoven C minor Concerto, and at the first run-through Rubinstein was appalled. Can *this* be the great Toscanini? he asked himself. They were not together, their ideas differed, and Rubinstein knew he was faced with a catastrophe. After the initial run-through Toscanini asked Rubinstein if that was the way he was going to play the work. Rubinstein said yes. Very well, said Toscanini, and faced his orchestra. *"Ancora!"* Then, says Rubinstein, a miracle happened. Toscanini had been listening while Rubinstein was playing, and the second time around everything was perfect. Toscanini had memorized all of Rubinstein's tempos, expressive devices, rubatos, and dynamics. It was as though they had been playing together all their lives.

Naturally, Rubinstein received top fees. Through the years he also put his entire repertory on records, and many of those records were best-sellers. Those included many pieces of chamber music, which he played with his typical bounce and élan, yet with due respect for the nature of the medium. World War II sent him from Paris to a permanent American home and citizenship. In 1955 he gave a Carnegie Hall concerto series, playing seventeen works for piano and orchestra in five concerts. He was to top that in 1960, when he gave a series of ten Carnegie Hall recitals, all for charity. Some believed that it was Rubinstein's answer to Sviatoslav Richter's series of six recitals in his first New York season.

Rubinstein seemed indestructible. He never seemed to show his age until toward the very end, and he was before the public until the age of ninety. It was around that time that he left his wife

Rubinstein in his seventies. He was before the public until he was ninety, and he still had five more years to live.

and had an affair with Annabelle Whitestone, his secretary. Rubinstein had always prided himself on his machismo. In the last years of his life he became blind. But if he did not play anymore, he was still a presence. Among other things, he interested himself in the Arthur Rubinstein International Piano Competition in Tel Aviv. The first winner, in 1974, was Emanuel Ax, who went on to a fine career. Rubinstein, who never had taught, was a jury member who did what jury members should not, and that is get involved with the contestants. He would have meetings with them, listen to them play, offer advice and suggestions. It also is said that he did not like it very much when other jury members had the temerity to differ with his evaluations. But he was an inspiration to the young pianists who came to Israel for the competition. They all had grown up with the Rubinstein legend and had been weaned on his recordings.

He died in Geneva on December 29, 1982, at the age of ninety-five. It had been a wonderful life, a fact that he freely admitted. He said that he had enjoyed every minute of it, and that the only price he had to pay was stage fright before a performance. He had met everybody, done whatever he had wanted to do all his life, had achieved supremacy in his field, and had had fewer frustrations than almost any of his colleagues. He had no musical worlds left to conquer. Perhaps the only regret he had leaving this life was for the great wines in his cellar that he had not yet drunk and the great cigars he had not smoked.

27 *Vladimir Horowitz*

ELECTRICAL ENERGY

IF Arthur Rubinstein was the most beloved pianist of his time, Vladimir Horowitz was the most legendary. He was a mysterious figure, living a very private life, seldom mixing with society the way Rubinstein did. He took long sabbaticals from the concert stage, fighting his real or imaginary ailments. The man had problems. He did not especially like playing with orchestras, and of all the great pianists he had the smallest concerto repertory, being identified primarily with the Rachmaninoff Third, the Brahms B flat, the Tchaikovsky, and the Beethoven *Emperor*. Toward the end of his career he whittled them down to one concerto, the Rachmaninoff, and then to none at all. He played relatively few concerts in the latter part of his career, but the ones he gave were more royal processions than concerts. Not since the great days of Paderewski had a musician traveled in this kind of style, with his wife, her companion, a television director, his tuner, a Steinway representative, a valet, a record producer, his physician, his manager, and, often, his chef. Horowitz was royalty and expected his retainers to keep him happy. When he gave a concert in Florida, for instance, the sponsors had to fly from New York, at no little expense, his daily portions of Dover sole for his finicky stomach.

To the public his recitals were the highlight of the season. In his latter years he would play only at 4 P.M. on Sundays. He was Vladimir Horowitz, and he got what he wanted. Every Horowitz recital was sold out, with seats overflowing on the stage. The audience would be assembled well ahead of time, waiting quietly, as though in church. A Horowitz audience was like no other. There was an air of expectation in the hall as everybody awaited the wonders to come. People spoke in hushed whispers. Horowitz never was in a rush to come out. Often he would make his audience wait for twenty minutes or so. When he did come out, it was in morning clothes. Horowitz was the last to wear the cutaway and striped trousers. He would bow politely and address himself to the keyboard. He played with few physical mannerisms. But those connoisseurs who followed him—and those who watched the close-ups in his television broadcasts—often wondered how he did it. He had a peculiar way of playing. The little fingers of his hands would be curled, awaiting the proper moment, when they would strike like a mamba. His hands had a peculiar turnout, at an angle from the wrists. Liszt had recommended that, but Horowitz had never studied with a Liszt pupil. For the most part, Horowitz kept his fingers close to the keys, often in a flat rather than the normal curved position, raising his hands only in moments of emotional excitement.

From this rather immobile pianist came a sonority probably not heard since the days of Anton Rubinstein. Horowitz produced a simply enormous sound, helped by pianos tuned a bit high. Sometimes the instruments were under such tension that critics complained about Horowitz's "metallic" sound. He orchestrated at the piano. One could hear horns, cellos, bassoons, flutes, and the panoply of the full orchestra. He was not primarily a banger or a loud pianist. But when he unleashed his full power he had a kind of demonic energy that was equivalent to mighty surges of electricity. Coupled to this was a technique that, it was generally agreed, was the most infallible and awesome of his time.

No wonder that in the period from about 1940 to 1960 all young pianists wanted to be Vladimir Horowitz. He was their guru. What he played they played. If Horowitz brought back Schumann's *Kreisleriana,* it automatically followed that all young pianists would be playing it two years later. If Horowitz played the Haydn E flat Sonata, it was sure to be on programs all over the world in a short time. The youngsters strove for the unique kind of finger independence that Horowitz had, for the clarity of his playing, for his crisp pedaling and easy resolution of all technical difficulties.

What they did not have was his style—a style centered in several aspects of nineteenth-century Romanticism. Musicians today are literalists who have been trained to believe in the urtext—the one printed edition supposedly faithful to the composer's intention, purged of all Romantic editing and other excrescences. So they grimly pursue the goal of "faithfulness to the composer's intentions," not realizing that there is no such thing, as composers were always the first to admit. Most composers were performers themselves, and they realized that the performance of music lay as much between the notes as in the notes themselves. Today performance tends to be more a blueprint than a work of art.

But as a Romantic, Horowitz always realized that it was a performer's actual *duty* to take the notes—the blueprint—and attempt a synthesis that mingled the mind of the composer with the mind of the interpreter. If once in a while he strongly felt that it involved touching up the notes, then Horowitz had no hesitation to do so, though he was very careful in whatever modifications he made in Beethoven and Chopin. In virtuoso music he had no hesitation in carrying the composer's point one step further, adding octaves or other reinforcements. In one notable case he all but rewrote Mussorgsky's *Pictures at an Exhibition*. Pianists of the previous generation did this constantly—some with taste, some with vulgarity. But few today except Horowitz would dare to alter the printed note. Even such exponents of nineteenth-century Romanticism as Jorge Bolet and Shura Cherkassky do not tamper with the text. The younger ones could not, even if they wanted to. Their training forbids it: tampering with the notes would be equivalent to murder.

Horowitz was admired by the professionals much the same way that Heifetz was admired, and for many years he was critically untouchable. Both Heifetz and Horowitz represented the ultimate in craft, and the older generation of critics fell all over themselves to pay homage. But with the new generation of critics after World War II it was a different story. The older generation, brought up in a period when emotion and what the baroque theorists had called the *Affekt* governed musical thinking, responded to the Horowitz style. The younger generation, though, found it mannered and impossibly fussy, full of effects that tortured the line out of all recognition—and it is true that from the 1970's, this became a characteristic of his playing. To the New Criticism this was Romanticism at its worst. Horowitz no longer was an untouchable.

The trouble was that not many new critics had heard the Horowitz of yore, except on recordings. Through the years there have been two Horowitzes. The first Horowitz, from the time of his appearance in the West to his twelve-year retirement starting in 1953, was on the whole a responsible pianist who represented the Anton Rubinstein tradition, though with much more technical accuracy. He was something of a stylistic maverick, and his interpretations had little to do with what such Romantic pianists as Hofmann, Lhévinne, Godowsky, and Moiseiwitsch represented. Compared to Horowitz, they were models of rectitude, much more restrained in their use of expressive devices. Horowitz was closest to Rachmaninoff, also an Anton Rubinstein offshoot, but here too there were significant differences. Rachmaninoff, much more aristocratic in his interpretations, never took the rhythmic liberties that Horowitz did. And Rachmaninoff was a healthier pianist. There was a tense, neurotic quality to the brilliant playing of Vladimir Horowitz, manifested in sudden, outsized explosions that may have been thrilling but that also were unsettling. But it nevertheless was clear that Horowitz was the spiritual godchild of Rachmaninoff. He had taken over the patented left-hand thrusts of Rachmaninoff, the technical infallibility, and the bigness of conception. He had mastered the authentic Rachmaninoff sound.

The first Horowitz was a much more direct player than the second. After 1965, when he returned to the stage, mannerisms started creeping into his playing, though the performances still had many moments of glory. Around 1970 the second Horowitz came into full flower, and his playing then was often a travesty of what it had been. The idiosyncrasies of his approach, which had added such spice in the old days, now took over completely. Horowitz had created his own monster. A comparison of his three recordings of the Rachmaninoff Third Concerto is instructive. Horowitz first recorded the work around 1928, with Albert Coates. This is a strong, unaffected, brilliant performance, very much in Rachmaninoff's own manner. It pursues a straight line from beginning to end, with confidence and strength. About thirty years later Horowitz made a recording with Fritz Reiner, and mannerisms enter—a teasing of the melodic lines, much more variation in tempo, and a slower feeling. Finally, in 1978, his recording with Eugene Ormandy was altogether a mannered, self-indulgent performance, overladen with sentimental lingerings and a lack of the grand design that Horowitz had displayed in his first recording and, to a large extent, in his second.

So Horowitz changed, and not for the better. The first Horowitz was indeed a spectacular pianist, well deserving of the idolatry lavished on him; and his early recordings bear this out. The Rachmaninoff Third, the Liszt Sonata, the single discs of the Liszt-Paganini E flat Etude, and the Fourth Scherzo by Chopin—all these are the work of a thoroughbred. It was not only technique. There were pianists around who could match him finger for finger, but none conveyed his special kind of demonic drive and sonorous thunderings. And his daring, too. Horowitz took perilous chances, and audiences would gasp at his tightrope-walking. Could he finish a passage at the wild tempo at which it had begun? Can octaves possibly be played that fast? How on earth could he manage to delineate so clearly the crazy fingerwork and the combinations of themes in his arrangement of *The Stars and Stripes Forever*? Yes, a Horowitz recital always had its circus elements.

At the same time he would take care to put much quiet music on his programs, determined to show that he was more than a technician. Schumann's *Kinderscenen* and *Arabesque,* Scarlatti sonatas and occasionally one by Mozart, Chopin mazurkas, or some Debussy would always be popping up in his programs. He had a lovely way with these, playing the music with a singing tone and all kinds of subtle finger and pedal colorations. Some had the feeling that Horowitz, he of the breathtaking fingerwork and colossal sonorities, was at his best in miniature works. He may have had trouble pulling together a Beethoven sonata, but he played short pieces with ravishing sound, delicacy, and finish. That finish did not come by accident. Horowitz was a monomaniac who spent hours and hours a day refining his craft, working on his programs, endlessly trying out different chord weights and dynamics, constantly searching for his kind of pianistic and musical ideal. If not all musicians regarded him as a tremendous intellect, they all bowed to his supreme craft.

Horowitz put together his programs with great care. He created programs that he thought would interest "the public" and looked with scorn on programs that contained only three Beethoven or Schubert sonatas. Consciously or unconsciously, he was more entertainer than educator. He was very concerned with his public; he wanted to play a mixture of music that was of high quality and, just as important, pianistically effective. Almost always he picked as a major work something that he had not previously played in America or that he had not touched for many years. For his 1982 tour, for instance, he selected the Schumann *Carnaval,* which—to everybody's surprise—he had never previously put on his programs. In other years he had played late Scriabin sonatas, such relatively unknown Liszt as the Nineteenth Rhapsody and B minor Ballade, and a handful of Clementi sonatas. In that he was different from most pianists of his generation. Rudolf Serkin, to cite one case, kept refining his repertory down to the point where, year after year, he would be repeating much the same late Beethoven or Schubert sonatas.

When Horowitz prepared to give a concert, the day of the performance resembled some sort of purification rite. At least, such is suggested by an interesting page in the Glenn Plaskin biography. In the morning, Horowitz would begin to wash, shave, and dress. "The public," he said, "pays money and they want to hear and see something esthetic. I'm the boss of the situation. I have to look like that. I want to have a completely clean body and hands, perfume, too. I think about small details. To put on the socks so they don't press me. To see the shoes are closed. The fly is closed. Then, at the moment I feel that cutaway—the moment I am in uniform—it is like a race horse before the races. I start to perspire. I already feel some electricity. At this moment, I am already an artist. . . ." All this amounts to the ablution before a service, the ridding of defilement when a holy act is to be performed. It is a gesture rooted deep in the Old Testament and, indeed, in the subconscious of all mankind—a sort of baptism, the washing for forgiveness, the plea for renewal, for a new life and religious commitment. Substitute *vestments* for *clothes, holy oil* for *perfume,* and what emerges is a priest about to perform his office and face his God. In passing, it might be noted that very few of the younger generation of male musicians have this commitment. Far from cleansing themselves before a concert, they often appear dressed in clothes in which they apparently have slept for several months; they look unshaved and unshorn; their platform manner is not only deplorable but also actually insulting, showing nothing but contempt for an audience that expects an artist to look and act like an artist.

Horowitz was one of the few major pianists who did not set the world afire as a prodigy. He was born in Kiev on October 1, 1904. His mother was a pianist and an uncle a professional musician. Horowitz's sister, Genya, also was a talented pianist. Naturally, Vladimir's abilities were spotted early. He seemed to be able to read any music at sight, and his memory was infallible. When he was eight years old he heard Josef Hofmann in a pair of recitals and was inspired to work much more seriously than he hitherto had done. He had several teachers, but his first important one was Sergei Tarnowsky at the Kiev Conservatory, with whom he worked between the ages of twelve and sixteen. Tarnowsky was very permissive, letting the talented Volodya study the repertory that appealed to him. Then Horowitz went on to Felix Blumenfeld, an exponent of the Rubinstein school. Blumenfeld concentrated on tone and the production of a singing line. Nineteenth-century teachers from Chopin on were very interested in singers, and were constantly urging their students to try to duplicate on the piano the flowing lines of a Jenny Lind, a Patti, a Nilsson. Horowitz grew up loving the singing voice. One of his favorites was the Italian baritone Mattia Battistini, who had a wonderfully flexible bel canto voice. As a teenager Horowitz could go to the piano and play many operas in their entirety. (Modern piano teachers seem to have forgotten how much piano music of the nineteenth century was inspired by the art of great singers. It could be a valuable clue to their students about the interpretation of a Chopin nocturne or a Mozart slow movement. Mozart's piano concertos are saturated in the opera.)

Horowitz was the outstanding pupil in his classes, and he knew it. He could be difficult and arrogant. After the Russian Revolution, Horowitz's family, formerly well off, was reduced to poverty. In 1920 Horowitz graduated from the conservatory and made his debut the following year in Kharkov. His gifts were immediately noticed, and he became one of the most talked-about pianists in Russia. Often he gave concerts with Nathan Milstein; they had met while Horowitz was at the conservatory, found that they thought about music the same way, and became lifelong friends. In 1925 Horowitz left Russia for good, first settling in Berlin, which at that time was a major center of European culture. Even Paris took notice. A city in which were working such outstanding persons as Klemperer, Kleiber, Walter, Furtwängler, Mann, Albert Einstein, Brecht, Weill, Kandinsky, Schoenberg, Berg, Webern, Hindemith, the painters of Die blaue Reiter group, Reinhardt—this was a city of ideas and accomplishment. Artur

Vladimir Horowitz in Russia around 1920, photographed à la *Chopin. His profile did have a slight resemblance to Chopin's.*

Schnabel and Walter Gieseking were the big pianists there, and Horowitz respected both of them. He made his Berlin debut on January 2, 1926, and was received as just another good pianist. What created a furor was an unscheduled appearance with the Hamburg Philharmonic. A last-minute substitute for an indisposed pianist, Horowitz was told to report to the concert hall and play the Tchaikovsky B flat minor. It was too late for any rehearsal. Eugen Pabst was the conductor, and he and Horowitz discussed tempos at the intermission of the concert. Pabst told him just to watch his baton, and nothing wrong would happen. As Plaskin tells the story in his biography of Horowitz,

> After the Concerto's short orchestral introduction, Horowitz's first crashing chords sent Pabst spinning around, staring in amazement at the slim, pale young man at the keyboard. A few more measures and Pabst abandoned the podium altogether, incredulously watching Horowitz's hands. Until the end of the first cadenza, Pabst's face was reportedly a study in disbelief, as his hands beat mechanically, following Horowitz's tempi. The flood of sound continued and by the end of the work orchestra and conductor were euphoric and overwhelmed, the audience was beside itself, and the piano "lay on the platform like a slain dragon" while a perspiring Horowitz stood nearby with a modest smile on his face. The entire house had risen two measures before the end with a thunderous roar of applause. Bravos resounded, programs waved. Pabst rushed over to Horowitz, grabbed him by the shoulders, and hugged him repeatedly. One critic declared that "not since Hamburg discovered Caruso has there been anything like it."

Word spread all over, and Horowitz was in great demand. He had a grand success in Paris, then in Rome, then all over Europe. He came to the United States in 1928, making his debut with the Tchaikovsky at a New York Philharmonic concert directed by Sir Thomas Beecham. It also was Beecham's American debut, and he was much more interested in himself than in his soloist. Horowitz has entertained dinner parties with accounts of his first American performance, and is most amusing on the subject. He says that Beecham gave him only an hour of rehearsal. (Here Horowitz is taking an anecdotist's liberty. They had several rehearsals.) What is more, Beecham decided to conduct the concerto from memory and, in Horowitz's estimation, did not know the score *that* well. At the rehearsals Horowitz found the tempos impossibly slow. "But who was I, a scared little Jewish boy from Kiev, unknown, to argue with the great Beecham?" In the opening number of the concert, an overture, Beecham's suspenders broke and he had to conduct while holding up his trousers with one hand. That did not put him in a good mood. When the concerto started, the tempos were even slower than they had been at rehearsal. Horowitz felt the audience slipping away from him. At the beginning of the last movement he felt that he had nothing to lose. His American career already lay in ruins. So he took off on his own, with a wild burst, making the startled Beecham follow him as best he could. Horowitz says that they finished "almost" together. The critics loved this show of spunk, and Horowitz got rave reviews.

But, says Horowitz, he felt that Beecham was a bad colleague, could not forgive his behavior to a nervous debutante, and resolved never to play under his baton again. About five years later Horowitz was in London to play the Tchaikovsky and discovered that Beecham was his conductor. Should he play? Should he become "ill" and cancel? Horowitz decided that he would play and went to the hall. Beecham saw him enter, stopped what he was doing, grinned, and loudly said, "Librarian! Bring the score!" So Horowitz also grinned and they made up.

Aside from his crashing successes in his first American tours, the big thing in Horowitz's life was his meeting with Rachmaninoff. They became close friends, and Horowitz worked with the composer on the Third Piano Concerto, with Rachmaninoff playing the orchestral reduction on a second piano. Now Horowitz started the life of a busy touring and recording artist. His fees went up and up, soon to achieve epical heights. In the last years of his career he was one of the two most highly paid classical musicians before the public (Luciano Pavarotti was the other). Horowitz was receiving 80 percent of the gross of all concerts, and often there were such spin-offs as television and recordings made from live concerts. His profits could run into the hundreds of thousands and even millions. Horowitz was not bad as a spender, too. He was a natty dresser, loved luxury and loved being pampered, started collecting art (top specimens of Picasso, Degas, Rouault, Renoir, Modigliani, and others) and buying expensive cars.

He played the Beethoven *Emperor* in 1933 with Toscanini and the New York Philharmonic and, also that year, married Toscanini's daughter, Wanda. They had a daughter, Sonia. In his biography Plaskin goes into great detail about Horowitz's relationship with the Toscanini family. It is his belief that Toscanini browbeat Horowitz and made him feel insecure. In 1936 Horowitz stopped playing for two years; it was the first of his three retirements. Many of Horowitz's associates call him a hypochondriac, and perhaps he is, but apparently in 1933 he suffered from hypertension, stomach trouble including colitis, and phlebitis. Plaskin also suggests that Horowitz was trying to escape the terrible, lowering shadow of Toscanini. On his return to the platform Horowitz continued to be the top box-office draw of pianists. He spent World War II in the United States and became a citizen in 1942. After the war he started playing in Europe again.

His second retirement was a long one, from 1953 to 1965. Again many believe that it resulted from a combination of real and imaginary ailments. For a time he did not even go near the piano. When he resumed playing, he began to concentrate on Clementi and the later music of Scriabin. He spent most of the time in his New York town house. He made a few records (soon leaving Victor to go to Columbia) and took a few pupils. Horowitz never had taught anybody until Byron Janis in 1944. But between 1953 and 1965 there was a small procession—Gary Graffman, Coleman Blumenfield, Ronald Turini, Alexander Fiorillo, and Ivan Davis. Of these, Janis and Graffman had fine careers; the others never went very far, though Davis became respected as an exponent of nineteenth-century Romanticism. During all this time Horowitz showed no interest in returning to the stage, and there was a general belief that he would never play in public again.

But return he did, in Carnegie Hall on May 9, 1965. There was incredible excitement when the announcement was made, and an equally incredible press buildup. When tickets went on sale about two weeks before the concert they vanished within a few hours. Panting Horowitz admirers had started queuing up at the box office two days before, and when the box office opened there were an estimated 1,500 people four abreast in a line that extended far down Fifty-seventh Street. Every musician and celebrity who was in town and could get a ticket was there. On the program were the Bach-Busoni Toccata in C, the Schumann Fantasy, the Ninth Sonata by Scriabin, and a Chopin group topped with the G minor Ballade. Horowitz was nervous, and there were some wrong notes in the Bach. But it was grand and spacious, as was the Schumann. The Scriabin was amazing. It is a difficult work, but Horowitz was able to clarify the writing, achieve an extraordinary range of colors, and evoke the spooky and magical atmosphere of the strange piece. He played three encores but the audience refused to go home. When he left the hall he was almost mobbed at the Fifty-sixth Street doors. Horowitz had come back; and he was correct when he referred to his return as a "resurrection." Because of the special circumstances, in addition to the proof that Horowitz had lost few if any of his powers, it was one of the most exciting, dramatic concerts of the twentieth century.

Although he resumed his career, he gave fewer and fewer recitals. At the fees he charged he did not have to give very many. He stopped playing entirely between October 1969 and May 1974. When he started again it was with several out-of-town concerts followed by an appearance at the new Metropolitan Opera in Lincoln Center (it had opened in 1966). The recital brought in slightly over $100,000, of which Horowitz got half. (The concert had been advertised as a benefit for the Metropolitan Opera, but Horowitz also benefited.) In 1978 he gave a golden jubilee concert at Carnegie Hall. Four years later he played in London; it had been thirty-one years since he had last played there. Again there

Horowitz at the height of his fame. No pianist of his time had such an electrical impact upon audiences.

was great excitement, with a worldwide television broadcast. His 1983 tour, during which he gave some concerts in America and then a pair in Japan, was a tragedy. For the first time, Horowitz seemed unable to do what he wanted to do. He had memory lapses and actual incoherencies wherever he played. The feeling in musical circles was that the veteran this time would really quit for good. But in April 1985, he filmed a concert in his home, to be shown in Carnegie Hall and elsewhere in the world in lieu of a concert. At that time Horowitz told the press that he wanted to give "real" concerts again.

Horowitz will, of course, live permanently in the annals of pianism. He was the most electrifying pianist then in action, and all of his concerts were events charged with thousands of musical volts. There could be a lovely quality of artistry at his concerts, but that was not what his public came to hear. His public wanted the thunder and lightning, and that is what in the end made Horowitz the highest-paid musician of his era. He realized the fact and was torn in half about it. He resented it that the public regarded him as a musical trapeze artist. Yet at the same time he catered to it. He never fully resolved the problem, which could account for the neurotic quality of his playing and his frequent retirements. Nevertheless, Horowitz at his best was a fascinating, fearsome pianist and musician, full of interesting ideas, capable of flights of poetry and fancy; a virtuoso whose stupendous feats created a standard that many of the newer pianists tried (unsuccessfully) to duplicate; a musician who was regarded in pianistic circles the way Heifetz was among violinists; one of the supreme Liszt and Scriabin players in history; the very last symbol of a certain aspect of unbridled Romanticism. Heifetz, at least, had a true successor in the brilliant Itzhak Perlman. When Vladimir Horowitz stopped playing, there was nobody to succeed him.

28 *Maria Callas*

THE WILL TO SUCCEED

IN a way, Maria Callas was like a female Paderewski. Like him, she had a great career in which brains and determination triumphed over a deficiency of natural ability. Just as Paderewski had nowhere near the technical equipment of many of his contemporaries, so there were singers in the Callas period who were much better vocalists—Renata Tebaldi and Joan Sutherland, to mention but two. And just as Paderewski had that indefinable *something* to make him the World's Greatest Pianist in the eyes of the public, so Callas was the World's Greatest Singer.

After the period following World War II, Maria Callas emerged as the singing superstar. She was *La Divina,* the most exciting vocalist before the public, the one who sold out every house, the one who was always in the news because of her singing, her tantrums, the scandals swirling around her, and her extramusical activities involving Greek billionaires and the Beautiful People. She gave a new meaning to the word *ego.* Hard, tough, frequently unethical, she was monumentally self-centered, and the world had to revolve around her. She needed constant praise, and she had to be in the newspapers at all times. Almost everything she did was thoroughly calculated. In New York, after a Metropolitan Opera performance, John Coveney of Angel Records put together a big party to which celebrities in every walk of life had been invited. They waited for her, but she never showed up. She had been discussing the party with a friend and wondered how much attention it would get in the papers. It would be good for a paragraph or two, she was told. "Then what if I do not go at all?" Oh. That, she was told, would be in all the papers. "So I won't go," said Callas.

In every respect it was a peculiar career. It was very short, for one thing. She scored her first success in 1947 and was at her peak in the 1950–60 period (though she started having problems as early as 1954). Thus she had only about thirteen good years before the public. And even at its best, her instrument was one that normally would never make a great career for a singer. It did not have an equalized scale, and one could hear three distinct registers when she sang. As an exponent of bel canto roles she was called upon to sing high notes, but nobody, including herself, ever knew what was going to come out above a high B. She had all kinds of technical inadequacies, including unreliability of pitch, a beat, and a tremolo. She was not a very good colleague and had all kinds of feuds with other singers. She was supposed to be a great actress, but many critics poked fun at what they called her three gestures and her overcalculated way of making a dramatic point.

Yet this woman thrilled audiences to a degree unmatched since the days of Caruso and Chaliapin. If *they* were great singers—and nobody will dispute the point—then what did Callas, with her assortment of inadequacies, have that put her on their level as a superstar?

Brains. Musicianship. Magnetism. Presence. Intensity. The ability to work hard. Ambition. Ruthlessness. Mystery. Her autocratic behavior, which so delighted the public; here was a singer who went through life the way the public expected a diva to live. An acting ability which, if not supreme, enabled her to get into a role in a much more believable way than did her competitors. A voice that, if not especially beautiful in itself, had great expressive and communicative power. An unerring instinct for publicity, which continually built up her glamour and her mystique.

Singers of the past, such as Geraldine Farrar and Mary Garden, were also constantly in the news and knew how to manipulate the press. But there was something different about Callas. Garden and Farrar were all-woman. In Callas there was something demonic rather than feminine. Singers of the past and present have worked according to the conventions. Callas observed no conventions. She made her own rules; she was *different:* the Bobby Fischer of singing, so to speak. And so the world breathlessly followed her musical and personal adventures, and would throng the opera houses to see her in the flesh.

Did she do these attention-getting things on purpose? Everybody in the musical community had theories. A popular one was that, deep down, Callas was insecure, with a massive inferiority complex. Therefore she compensated heavily on the opposite side. Arianna Stassinopoulos suggests as much in her biography of Callas. Walter Legge, the recording executive who was associated with Callas for many years, the husband of Elisabeth Schwarzkopf, and a great connoisseur of singing, says it outright. Callas, he wrote, had "a superhuman inferiority complex." That was why she drove herself, and it helped explain her "monumental egocentricity and insatiable appetite for celebrity." That was why, in the early 1950's, she slimmed down from over 200 pounds to 140. As a student in the Athens Conservatory she was a driven girl—stout, a compulsive eater, dressed in shabby clothes, an obsessive worker without friends. This carried over into the days when she was famous. She could never forget the unhappiness of her youth.

All are agreed that she was a loner, with many acquaintances but few friends. She always felt herself to be in a jungle, and nobody but she herself could take care of her. In her own words, "I hate to be pitied and I never pitied anyone. . . . One thing I learned—don't ask anybody for favors. You won't get anything, anyway. . . . When I am old, nobody is going to worry about

The young Maria Callas (above) before she took off weight. It is a sharp contrast to the Callas (below) remembered by most opera-goers.

me. . . . I understand hate. I respect revenge. You have to defend yourself. You have to be strong, very, very strong. That's what makes you have fights." Once she made up her mind she was inflexible. "They say I am stubborn. No, I am not stubborn. I am right." With this kind of working philosophy, it is no wonder that her whole life seemed to be a perpetual struggle, with Callas pitted against opera managers, her colleagues, the press, the world. Legge, who worked with her on many of her recordings, called her vengeful, malicious, vindictive, ungrateful. She was icier than the ice Princess in *Turandot* and could dismiss people, even her own mother, with awesome detachment. "Don't come to me with your troubles," she wrote to her mother. "I have to work for my money and you are young enough to work too. If you can't make enough money to live on you can jump out of the window or drown yourself." She told a New York *Post* reporter in 1958, "If I have stepped on some people at times because I am at the top, it couldn't be helped. What should I do if someone gets hurt. Retire?"

She may have been referring to the Enzo Sordello incident. He was a young baritone who sang with her in *Lucia* at the Metropolitan Opera. According to him, Callas went sour in the final note of a duet. "I picked it up," said Sordello, "and she grew furious. At the end of the act she said that she would never sing with me again. . . . It was not fair for her to do this to a younger singer who was making his first appearance in this country." Sordello was fired; the Metropolitan Opera blandly said that it was because of disagreements with Fausto Cleva, the conductor.

But Callas could take on bigger game than an unknown baritone. She and Renata Tebaldi had their sessions. Tebaldi, the Italian spinto soprano with the ravishing voice, was the toast of La Scala and the Metropolitan in the 1950's. She was a sweet, inoffensive woman, without malice, adored by all. She and Callas often had the same roles. Callas sneered at Tebaldi; she said that Tebaldi's voice was soda pop and hers champagne. Callas conceded that Tebaldi could sing. "What a lovely voice," she said, listening to a Tebaldi recording. "But who cares?" Their feud

Renata Tebaldi, the big rival of Callas at La Scala and elsewhere. There was no love lost between the two divas.

started in Rio de Janeiro. At a concert in which both appeared, they agreed that neither would sing an encore. But Tebaldi sang three, and Callas was enraged, all the more in that she had prepared only one encore. A few days later Callas sang Tosca and was booed. She accused Tebaldi of starting a campaign against her. She also eventually managed to get Tebaldi out of La Scala. When Callas carried a grudge, she planted it, nursed it, fostered it, watered it, and watched it grow to sequoia size. At a performance of *Aida* in Chicago, with Tebaldi in the title role, Callas was in the audience. She waited until the big aria, *O patria mia,* and then made a big fuss, saying that she had lost a piece of jewelry, calling for an usher with a flashlight, and in general disturbing the performance. Poor Tebaldi could no more handle this kind of behavior than Boris Spassky could against Bobby Fischer's carryings-on in their famous match in Reykjavík.

Maria Callas was born in New York on December 4, 1923. Her family's name was Kalogeropoulos. She started singing lessons at eight. Her mother took her to Greece when she was thirteen, and she was trained at the Royal Conservatory in Athens, working for seven years with the famous coloratura soprano Elvira de Hidalgo. A few weeks before her fifteenth birthday she sang Santuzza in *Cavalleria Rusticana* with a company in Athens. After the war she returned to the United States for two years. She had an audition at the Metropolitan Opera. Edward Johnson, the general manager, offered her a Butterfly, which Callas promptly turned down. She thought that a 210-pound woman trying to sing the petite Butterfly would only be making a fool of herself. There also was talk about a *Fidelio* in English and again Callas, already a woman with a strong mind, would not touch it. "Opera in English is so silly. Nobody takes it seriously," she said. Everybody told her she was foolish in turning down the Metropolitan. "I'm sure I'm right. My voices have told me so," she answered mysteriously. She also had discussions with the San Francisco Opera and was turned down. Gaetano Merola, the general manager, told her to go to Italy and get a reputation. "Thank you," said

Callas, "but once I have made my career in Italy I will no longer need you."

In those days Callas was aiming at dramatic soprano roles, and when she made her Verona debut in 1947 it was in a pretty hefty one, Gioconda. Later in life she bragged that she had never sung secondary roles in any opera house. "Either you've got the voice or you haven't, and if you've got it you begin singing the lead parts right away." Her conductor for the *Gioconda* was Tullio Serafin, the great veteran, a man of vast knowledge who knew everything about opera and singing. His advice and coaching helped ease the path for several generations of singers. He became interested in Callas, who after his death spoke glowingly about him in the *Saturday Review:*

> During rehearsals he was after every detail, but in performance he left you on your own. "When I am in the pit I am there to serve you because I have to save my performance," he would say. We would look down and feel we had a friend there, in the pit. He was helping you all the way. He would mouth all the words. If you were not well he would speed up the tempo, and if you were in top form he would slow it down to let you breathe, to give you room. He was breathing with you, loving it with you. It was elastic, growing, living.

Callas in the late 1940's sang the biggest roles in the repertory—Isolde, Aida, Norma—and even made a few appearances as Brünnhilde. In Venice she filled in for a singer in Bellini's *I Puritani,* learning the role of Elvira in five days. She may not have known it, but with this *Puritani* in 1949 she started a new age of opera as well as a new career for herself.

Bel canto opera lay pretty much in ruins in 1949. *Norma* was the only Bellini opera in the international repertory. Of Rossini's many operas, only *Il Barbiere di Siviglia* was a universal favorite. Donizetti, who composed about seventy operas, fared just a little better, with *Lucia, L'Elisir d'Amore,* and *Don Pasquale.* The singing traditions of bel canto opera had been given a death blow in the 1860's by the dramatic operas of Verdi, and they had vanished once the verismo and Wagnerian operas took hold. Everybody seemed to have forgotten that a hundred years previously the bel canto operas had been sung by such dramatic actresses as Pasta, Malibran, and Grisi. But when the bel canto operas were presented in the period after 1930, the heroines were generally sung by high, warbling sopranos of the Lily Pons type—even though so many bel canto soprano roles, Rosina in *Il Barbiere* included, had originally been created for mezzos.

The Callas *Puritani* hit the world of opera like a blast from the then-new atomic bomb. As Raymond Ericson was to write in *The New York Times,* her performance showed that bel canto opera was not merely canarylike warbling. "Miss Callas showed that they could be sung, that the melodies and all the embellishments that were thought to be for virtuoso display could be turned to genuine dramatic use. It opened up a whole new repertory for singers such as Joan Sutherland and Beverly Sills to follow the path set by Miss Callas." Sutherland and her husband Richard Bonynge, the conductor, pianist, and scholar of the bel canto tradition, freely admit that Callas had inspired them. Sutherland, like Callas, had started out as a dramatic soprano. She and Bonynge heard some Callas records, and he says that the music and singing "really got to us." Sutherland started working on the bel canto repertory and was even in a Covent Garden *Norma* cast singing Clotilde opposite Callas. She was impressed not only with Callas's musicality, but also with her capacity for work. Callas may have been bitchy and temperamental, but on one thing all her colleagues are agreed: when it came to rehearsals, Callas was strictly business.

Within fifteen years, thanks to the Callas *Puritani,* opera houses all over the world were reviving forgotten bel canto operas. Callas herself reintroduced many of them. Perhaps it was too much of a good thing; some of them were pretty feeble. Today the mania seems to have crested, but there was at least a great deal of vocal excitement while it lasted, with new singers making great reputations as exponents of the bel canto style. (The new era did

Joan Sutherland, the Australian soprano who took over the Callas repertory and, thanks to a secure vocal technique, was able to sing for decades.

not embrace tenors and baritones, who went along singing the way they always had done.) Among them were Teresa Berganza, Marilyn Horne, Beverly Sills, and Montserrat Caballé. For the first time since the days of Melba and Tetrazzini opera audiences were hearing singers who could really trill, who knew something about appoggiaturas and embellishments, who did not squeak out the roles but really sang them.

The big rival of Callas as a bel canto stylist was Joan Sutherland. Born in Sydney, Australia, on November 7, 1926, she became famous when she sang Lucia at Covent Garden in 1959. Callas, who had shown the way to the bel canto tradition, had the style and musicianship. But Sutherland had the voice—a big, golden, radiant instrument. Big, golden instruments can be unwieldy. Wagnerian sopranos are not normally expected to sing Rosina or Lucia. But Sutherland's big Wagnerian voice proved itself capable of the most demanding of coloratura feats, including (at the beginning of her career) ascents up to a high F with no hesitation or fear.

The trouble was that Sutherland concentrated on pure vocalism. It was not that she was musically insensitive. But to pour forth those unceasing floods of tone she neglected her diction, her enunciation was mushy, and critics complained of the lack of tension in her phrasing. In addition she was a very large woman who had nowhere near the dramatic impulse of Callas. Sutherland, *La Stupenda,* was set up against Callas, *La Divina.* Immediately the world of opera was divided into two camps. Sutherland admirers and the Callasites would have nothing to do with each other. To the Sutherland admirers, a voice like that came only once in fifty years, and they reveled in the singer's virtuosity coupled to the huge vocal dimensions of the instrument. They pointed out that not since the Golden Age of Lehmann, Nordica, and Sembrich had there been such a soprano—a soprano who could sing the Queen of the Night or Constanza one evening, and follow it up a few days later with Norma. They had never heard anything like it before. And it was true; they hadn't. The Callas admirers could not stand Sutherland. They derided her: to them she was uninteresting and unmusical; she abused the portamento (sliding from note to note), made all vowels sound the same, and was hopeless as an actress. And they too had a point. As it turned out, Sutherland, who had a secure singing method, was before the public as a superstar soprano for decades after the untimely retirement of Callas. Callas, incidentally, had a good opinion of Sutherland's talents. She told Walter Legge that Sutherland would make a big career if she kept up the good work. "But only we know how much greater I am," she added.

About the time that Callas discovered the bel canto repertory, she met and in 1949 married Giovanni Battista Meneghini, an Italian industrialist. He was twenty-seven years older than she. Callas, the most calculating of women, never did anything without a reason, and there always have been speculations about the marriage. Some believe it was never consummated. Some hold that Callas married him because he was wealthy and could further her career. Callas, in a 1971 interview, indicated that love was distant from that union. "Yes," she told the reporter, "I was married to Meneghini for ten years. Now I am divorced. Meneghini says he helped me. He did not help me. . . . He helped create problems for me."

In the 1950's Callas hit her full stride. She went on a diet and lost over sixty pounds. (One school of thought has it that Callas lost her voice so early because of the diet. But a comparison of her 1951 and 1959 *Gioconda* recordings does not show any significant differences.) She became a star at La Scala, got rid of her rival Tebaldi, opened the 1951–52 season at La Scala, and began to appear in major houses the world over. At La Scala she worked a great deal with the director Luchino Visconti, in such operas as *La Vestale* (by Spontini), *Traviata,* and *Sonnambula.* He gave her intensive coaching in acting. In the United States she sang at the Chicago Lyric in 1954 before going to the Metropolitan. Rudolf Bing went to Chicago in 1956 and negotiated a Metropolitan Opera contract with her. That same 1956 season a process server caught her backstage and thrust papers into her hands, with a resultant Callas explosion together with photographs that made her look like a combination of Medusa and one of the Erinyes. In 1947 Callas had signed an agreement with a lawyer named Edward Bagarozy. He was to support her and in return get 10 percent of all her future fees. Bagarozy was responsible for the process server. "I will not be sued!" she shrieked. "I have the voice of an angel! No man can sue me!" The episode made the international headlines. Later the case was settled out of court.

For her Metropolitan Opera debut, on the opening night of the 1956–57 season, Callas sang Norma with a strong cast that included Fedora Barbieri, Mario Del Monaco, and Cesare Siepi. During the season she was also heard as Tosca and Rosina. She returned to the Metropolitan for another two seasons. Bing was impressed with the woman as well as with the singer. "Maria Callas was the superstar of stars," he wrote in his *A Knight at the Opera*. "She needed no advice from any manager. She knew what parts to sing and what parts to avoid. She knew what fees to ask and what to refuse." If she had respect for a director, such as Franco Zeffirelli, she would cooperate to the utmost. If she didn't, she would ignore him and do exactly what she wanted.

Callas and Bing broke up in 1958 for a combination of reasons. He had offered her, for 1959, Norma, Lucia, and Rosina. She agreed but also wanted a new production of Donizetti's *Anna Bolena*. Bing flatly turned down the Donizetti request. He had also discussed with her the possibility of Lady Macbeth and Violetta, to which Callas said no. Her rationale was that she could not switch from one opera to the other in a short time. Lady Macbeth in the Verdi opera, she said in a *Life* interview, demanded a voice that was "heavy, thick and strong," with "an atmosphere of darkness." Violetta in *La Traviata*, on the other hand, was "fragile, weak and delicate . . . with sick pianissimi." She said that Bing was asking too much from her, both mentally and physically. She also attacked the Metropolitan for its lack of rehearsals and its "scenery and costumes from the Middle Ages." The notoriously thin-skinned Bing did not like that. Callas refused to be pinned down, and would not tell Bing what her plans for the Metropolitan were. Bing, after all, had a season to prepare and time was running out on him. He sent a telegram to Dallas, where she was singing, canceling her contract. Callas hit the ceiling. Bing was his usual urbane, razor-edged self: "I do not propose," he said, "to enter into a feud with Madame Callas since I am well aware that she has considerably greater competence and experience at that kind of thing than I have."

And so Callas went her own way without the Metropolitan Opera. And tempestuous it was. There was a major scandal in 1958, when she walked off the stage of the Rome Opera. Callas claimed that she had a sore throat. It was the opening night of the season and the President of Italy was there. A riot ensued. Callas brought suit against the Rome Opera and won the case. There were grand fights with the managements of the opera houses in San Francisco, Vienna, and Milan. At the Edinburgh Festival she canceled a performance, waving a doctor's certificate, and was seen the following evening at Elsa Maxwell's ball in Venice. She canceled her entire San Francisco season in 1957, claiming "nervous exhaustion." Such was her nervous exhaustion that she spent her "convalescence" recording *Medea.* Another 1958 scandal had Callas on the wrong end. She had been feuding with Antonio Ghiringhelli, the general manager of La Scala. During a performance of *Il Pirata* Callas started to lose her voice and Ghiringhelli unceremoniously dropped the curtain on her in the middle of an act. That was in all the papers, too.

In all, she sang forty-seven roles. Most of them were concentrated in the early part of her career. After 1954, when her voice started to go, she sang only eight roles up to her retirement in 1965, and in that entire span made only forty-two appearances. Lanfranco Rasponi, in *The Last Prima Donnas,* has analyzed her repertory, arriving at some interesting statistics. Callas took many new roles for only a few appearances. Thus in her entire career she sang Gilda in *Rigoletto* only twice; and he lists about twenty-five operas in which she sang only twelve times or less. Norma was the role she sang most, making eighty-four appearances as the vestal virgin. She also recorded four operas in which she never appeared on the stage—*Pagliacci, La Bohème, Manon Lescaut,* and *Carmen.*

Her Carmen is fascinating; in 1964, at a point in which she had little voice left, she sounds comfortable and relaxed; and the interpretation has the characteristic imagination and wordplay of Callas at her best. Can it be that Callas went through life with a voice that was improperly placed; that she was really a mezzo-soprano who ruined herself by singing soprano roles?

She found a new life in 1959, leaving her husband for the Greek shipping tycoon Aristotle Onassis, whom she had met two years previously. (Meneghini never gave her a divorce, and Callas in 1966 got one on her own by renouncing her United States citizenship. Up to then she had carried two passports—American and Greek. Greece did not recognize her marriage because it had not been in a Greek Orthodox church. Callas not only got rid of a husband. She also no longer had to pay United States income tax except for money she earned there.) For a year or so Callas had a honeymoon with Onassis, not singing in public. As 1960 approached, Callas was experiencing severe vocal problems and must have known that her voice was starting to go. When she made a comeback at the Theater of Epidaurus she was in a high state of nerves and had to have pills and injections every time she sang. After 1960 she kept only three operas in her repertory—*Norma*, *Medea*, and *Tosca*—and her appearances became increasingly rare. When she was heard as Tosca at the Metropolitan Opera in 1965, it was a vocal disaster. Her audiences loved her—Callas still had the aura—but it was a painful experience for those admirers who remembered her a decade before. On July 5, 1965, she sang her last operatic performance—in *Tosca* at Covent Garden.

Her relations with Onassis started to disintegrate in 1963 when Jacqueline Kennedy entered his life. Onassis is said to have told Callas, "What are you? Nothing. You just have a whistle in your voice that no longer works." Callas had found a man tougher and more ruthless than she herself. Their affair broke up after Onassis and Mrs. Kennedy got married in 1968, though they occasionally saw each other after that—a fact that did not please the new Mrs. Onassis very much.

Callas, though retired from the stage, was not yet through.

For eight years following her Covent Garden farewell she did not sing in public. She lived in Paris, very comfortably. Onassis had provided for her, she had made top fees in her singing days (her contract specified that she was to be the highest-paid member of any company in which she sang), and even after her retirement the income from her records alone was bringing her an estimated $100,000 a year. She made a film of *Medea,* directed by Paolo Pasolini, in 1971. She gave master classes in 1970 and 1971 at the Juilliard School and the Curtis Institute of Music in Philadelphia. Awed students and auditors thronged to these classes. They did not come away with very much. Callas seemed unable to explain the wonderful things she had done on stage, and her observations were never very stimulating. She would make such fatuous remarks as "I am proud and easily hurt, but I do not show it. You must suffer to be an artist. To live is to suffer . . ." and so on. She also told her students that most of Mozart's music was "dull." (In all her career, she sang only one Mozart role—Konstanze in the *Entführung aus dem Serail,* and that for just four performances.) In 1973 she started to give joint recitals with her old friend Giuseppe di Stefano, who in his short career had been a brilliant tenor—one of the most exciting ones in the world—but who now had as little voice left as Callas had. They then embarked on a worldwide tour in 1974. The result, even though the Callas admirers turned out en masse, was a travesty. She died on September 16, 1977, in her Paris apartment. Many, including Bing, believe that she took her own life. She left no will, and her belongings were auctioned. The value of the estate has been estimated at $10 million. Meneghini died in 1978 at the age of eighty-five.

For twenty-five years Callas had been in the news more than any other singer, conquering the world with the blazing personality that went into her characterizations. Where any other singer would have been defeated by so recalcitrant a vocal organ, Callas actually made it an asset. She let the world know that she represented more than merely "beautiful singing," and that "to convey the dramatic effect to the audience and to myself I must produce sounds that are not beautiful. I don't mind if they are ugly as long as they are true." This may have been a rationalization: artists and human beings in general who lack certain qualities defiantly assert that those qualities are not important anyway. But her remark does bring up the question of the very nature of opera. If drama in opera is the most important element, then Callas was indeed the greatest singer of her age. But if singing, pure singing, is the most important element, as many believe, then Callas can be found to be sorely wanting.

For listening to Callas was not always the most pleasant experience. Certain parts of her voice had a haunting beauty and richness; elsewhere she produced shrill, off-pitch sounds, and some of her high notes were little more than desperate shrieks. Her admirers rationalized her defects as well as she did. They had to admit, as John Ardoin did, that with so wide a repertory and so intense an involvement with her roles, "there is no doubt that Callas demanded more from her voice than she could comfortably deliver. Yet a parallel conclusion is equally clear: had she put herself in less peril, had she taken fewer chances or remained within safer limits, she would never have been Callas." Fair enough, but Ardoin seems to undercut his case when he describes her voice with its three distinct registers instead of a single seamless one: "a bottled, covered low voice; a reedy middle; and a top that was brilliant at times to the point of stridency and that would, without warning, threaten to wobble out of control." This is not exactly the description of a singer with any real kind of vocal equipment. Indeed, it is the description of a singer with a badly flawed voice. Ardoin, like all of the Callas fans, lamely concludes that "She conquered, and as much by her 'faults,' if you accept them as such, as by her virtues." Conquering by faults is a new critical concept. But few will disagree with one of Ardoin's statements: "It was a voice that once heard could not easily be forgotten. It haunted and disturbed as many as it thrilled and inspired."

29 *A Digression on Health and Ills*

JUST as the Industrial Revolution and the nineteenth century were the age of steam, so the period after World War II became the atomic age, the space age, the electronic age, and the scientific age in general. When the atom bomb was dropped, the thinking of mankind was irrevocably changed, and the greatest menace in history was presented to shuddering humanity. When man went into orbit, he was for the first time free from the bondage of gravity, and the planets and stars would be the next step. When the computer chip was developed, the storage and retrieval of information entered a new era. All this, and much more, in a forty-year period. The impact of the resulting convulsions in human thought and behavior has, of course, been discussed, but we are too close for a dispassionate assessment. That will have to be left for future generations.

In music the most significant change in long-term habits came in 1948, with the introduction of the LP disc. Within twenty years virtually the entire spectrum of music was available for the music lover. Previously the international field in classical recordings had been dominated by a few giant companies that were internationally linked, and they concentrated on standard repertory, performed by famous artists and organizations, that promised reasonably good sales. Now there were thousands of record companies, many of them small operations with a specialty—contemporary music, or ancient music, or the spoken word, or the reissue of the early recordings of great performers of the past (especially legendary singers), or the baroque, or whatever. The baroque explosion was one phenomenon of early LP records. Baroque music demanded small forces, was relatively inexpensive to record, and all of a sudden everybody was into Vivaldi, Corelli, Fasch, Albinoni, and dozens of names nobody had ever heard of. But the movement, of course, was not only toward the baroque. Where, on 78 r.p.m. discs, a complete symphony took from four to seven discs, and a complete opera twenty and more, now a symphony could be recorded on a single side of an LP disc and complete operas on three. Thus complete operas, many of them rarities, began to flood the market. There came a mania for discographic completeness—the complete chamber music and symphonies of Beethoven, Mozart and Haydn, the complete music of Webern, Stravinsky, Chopin, the complete plays of Shakespeare. As for the popular repertory pieces, they could boast of a multiplicity of available recorded performances—as many as thirty of the same item.

It was paralyzing. No one listener could begin to keep up with the output. But, in substance, whatever anybody would ever want to listen to was there. Listeners became much more sophisticated than they ever had been. Music lovers in provincial sections of the world could now be as musically literate as any of their big-city brethren. They not only had available to them the entire history of music in a wide variety of performance. They also could study and evaluate the work of artists who normally never would appear in their vicinity. The LP era in addition introduced many new artists whose careers were materially helped by the exposure they got through recordings. As technology improved, the records became much more faithful to the original source—at least, when honest recording engineers were at work.

But all of this glory was accompanied by dangers. In many instances the technology became more important than the artistic product. With tape recordings there could be splices and other electronic fakery that had no relation to the real life of the concert hall or opera house. After a while many listeners, used to the inhuman perfection of musicians on records, actually began to prefer it to the concert hall. On records there were no errors to remind the listener of human fallibility. If a passage did not go well during a recording session, it could later be done better and spliced in. Often told was the story of a young pianist and the conductor Artur Rodzinski. The pianist had been engaged for a disc containing both Chopin concertos. During the recording sessions he would break down time and again. The music was too difficult for him. At each breakdown the engineers would say, "Don't worry. We'll fix it." After a week or so of constant splicing a composite concerto was assembled. The pianist and Rodzinski went to the control room to listen, and the pianist was happy. "Not bad, eh?" he said to Rodzinski. "My boy," said Rodzinski, "it's very good. Don't you wish you could play like that?" Recording engineers were wonderful. They could take tiny voices and make them sound big. They could add a degree of color to a voice or piano that the artist simply did not have. They could add echo-chamber and time-delay effects to simulate hall acoustics. And often they ruined a work for many listeners.

The famous Decca-London recording of Wagner's *Rheingold* in 1959 was a case in point. John Culshaw, the producer, believed recordings should take full advantage of the then brand-new stereophonic process, even if it meant helping the composer along. So at the entrance of the gods into Valhalla, at the culminating point of Wagner's great orchestral crescendo, he and the conductor, Georg Solti, departed from the text. Wagner had scored a triangle amid the percussion to represent the mighty hammer of Donner. Tinkle, tinkle. But for the recording, the percussionist hit a section of steel railroad track. The effect was thrilling, even cataclysmic, and all who have experienced the recording find the equivalent measure in the opera house flat and somehow disappointing. Granted, Wagner should have had Culshaw at his side when composing the opera. But he didn't, and he has been misrepresented in this otherwise magnificent recording.

Recordings also gave a false idea of what singers could do. Many singers, among them some of the world's greatest, sang operas on records that they would never dare do in the flesh. They could do so because they could take their time, record the demanding arias out of sequence (later they would be inserted into the proper place in the score), get an assist from the engineers, and repeat a phrase or even a single note until it came out to their liking. Thus, to cite but two examples, Joan Sutherland recorded *Turandot* and Renata Tebaldi *Il Trovatore,* operas that they never sang in public.

Recordings were not the only area to be revolutionized after World War II. Culture suddenly became big business. In the 1960's there was much talk, especially in America, of the "cultural explosion." And in one way, at least, there really was one. There are two ways of looking at that particular phenomenon. One has to do with quality, the other with quantity. Qualitatively speaking, the cultural explosion was a dud. Standards did not appreciably improve, and the level of creative work did not impress many with its chance of permanence. There were, to be true, world leaders—Pierre Boulez in France, Karlheinz Stockhausen in Germany, Milton Babbitt and John Cage in America—but no matter how their music captured the intellectual flagbearers of the avant-garde, it was stubbornly rejected by the public, and it is hard to think of a single piece of serial or post-Webern music that has entered the international repertory. Between creator and public there was a chasm. In the 1970's this kind of music began to disappear; some thirty years of work along that line had failed to produce anything viable. Composers began to return to music of the past for their inspiration, and the neo-Romantic phase came into being.

But in terms of the "cultural explosion" there was no denying the tremendous increase in quantity—that is, the sheer volume of energy and money that went into the presentation of culture. Year after year it seemed to increase in exponential jumps. The 1960's in the United States saw performing arts centers springing up in many cities that previously had laid no claim to any kind of cultural activity. The centers went up at immense cost, often with no idea of what was going to be put into them. Yet once built they had to be used. So local orchestras and opera, ballet, and theater companies were beefed up. Most of this was done through private enterprise. This had its dangers, too. It led to highly conservative programming. Where a European manager with a large government subsidy behind him could present experimental works that almost always are death at the box office, American managers could not afford such luxuries.

Nevertheless the decades in America after 1960 were astonishing. Before 1950, for instance, the country had only four opera companies of any real size and season: the Metropolitan, the Chicago Lyric, the San Francisco, and the New York City Opera, which was founded in 1943. But in the 1980's opera houses, many of them using international casts, were all over: in Washington and Boston, Santa Fe and San Diego, St. Louis and Dallas, Houston and Miami, and many other localities. Where there were not big opera houses, there were regional operas and opera workshops. Ballet groups also enjoyed phenomenal growth. So did orchestras. Before World War II not one orchestra in America enjoyed a fifty-two-week season. Now all of the major orchestras, and many lesser ones, were signing contracts with their musicians for full employment. Chamber music came into its own, and here the universities of America were a major factor. Universities started to feel deprived without string quartets in residence. Summer festivals sprung up everywhere, in Europe as well as America; they were major tourist attractions, if nothing else, and they covered almost every aspect of music, from symphony and opera to chamber music.

The arts in America became a multibillion-dollar enterprise. Government money started to flow into them on a local, state, and federal level. Private enterprise, in the form of corporations, foundations, and industry, helped out, often lavishly. Nobody could have predicted this amazing state of affairs in 1945. If there was grumbling in some sophisticated circles that all this activity was doing nothing more than preserving the status quo, making American culture even more museumlike than it had ever been, there nevertheless could be no denying the vastly increased attention paid to the arts. It also could be that the sophisticates, who so often represent a kind of cultural snobbery, were dead wrong. If cultural health is to be measured by experimental work, there was avant-garde activity in all parts of America, and much more than in most European countries.

Jet travel arrived, and it proved to be another complicating factor in the artistic malaise of the times. Old Ignaz Moscheles was amazed that he could get to Manchester from Leeds in a few hours on that new invention, the railway. Now musicians took it for granted that they could cross the Atlantic in a few hours. Once again progress carried with it its inbuilt dangers. The expansion of concert and opera seasons, the vastly increased number of musical organizations and such facilities as cultural centers, the impossible demands on important artists—and their apparently insatiable desire to meet those demands and collect their imposing fees—led to a lowering of standards. Not only that. It actually threatened the death of singing.

In the 1980's the situation scared observers. In all the world there was not one Wagnerian tenor worthy of the name. There was not one Wagnerian soprano ready to replace the retired Birgit Nilsson. Big voices of any kind seemed to have been a thing of the past. Forget Wagner. Opera managers who wanted to cast even so popular and standard a work as *Aida* had trouble finding a singer for the title role, or for a tenor to sing Radames or a baritone for Amonasro. Dramatic sopranos, except for the few veterans still in action, seemed to be extinct, and those half dozen or so veterans could not be in more than one opera house at a time. Real contraltos of the Schumann-Heink variety had long vanished. Coloratura sopranos who could attack a role with the agility, security, and confidence of a Melba were nowhere available. In the 1970's and 80's, things got to a point where the few singers who could satisfactorily take on a role were in effect their own touring company; they would appear in an opera at La Scala, turn up again in Vienna a few weeks later, then play Covent Garden, the Metropolitan Opera, and San Francisco. In certain demanding operas the same principals would be appearing together at various times during a season in the major houses of the world. In short, there were not enough great singers to go around, and the few who were available were singing themselves to death.

What had happened? There was much worry about the problem, and many theories were advanced. Some of the theories were untenable. One school of thought maintained that singers started too soon. But, it was quickly pointed out, most of the great singers of the past, the women especially, had started before they were twenty. It also was being said that singers were being overworked. There was something in that, though singers of the past maintained schedules that were just as hectic as those of today. But at least they settled in for a season, not having to worry about jet lag or moving to another location within a very short time. Today's singers are constantly on the move. As Terence McEwen, the general manager of the San Francisco Opera, said in an *Opera News* interview, everybody—singers, conductors, directors—is busy rushing to get somewhere else. McEwen gave a representative example:

> Last winter in Munich . . . Wolfgang Brendel sang Papageno. He had sung Rodrigo in *Don Carlo* the night before there, and backstage he said that on Friday night he had sung *Ballo* in Hamburg, the *Don Carlo,* and this afternoon a concert and tonight Papageno.

McEwen mentions a famous tenor who was proud of the fact that he had sung an opera on Sunday in Vienna, a concert in another hall on Tuesday, a second opera in Vienna on Wednesday, a *Tosca* in another city on Friday, and a third opera on Sunday. It is true, concluded McEwen, that in those five days he made much more money than he would have while settled in an opera house. But he also was shortening his career.

When the supersonic airplane started to carry passengers on a regular run, a *New York Times* critic really started to worry. He was thinking of Nilsson, a notorious bear for work. Suppose, he said, Nilsson sang a Salome at a matinee in Vienna. She could then get into an SST and sing the evening performance at Covent Garden the same day. But more. The SST travels almost with the sun when headed west. After the Covent Garden *Salome,* which would end before 10 P.M., Nilsson could catch a waiting SST to get her to New York for an evening *Salome* performance—still the same day. And if Chicago had a double bill of, say, *Gianni Schicchi* and *Salome,* Nilsson could catch her waiting SST for Chicago and do her Salome there—still on the same day. She also, had she any voice left, could do still another *Salome* in San Francisco—again still on the same day.

Even more deleterious to a voice is the assumption of roles when the organ is not yet ready for them, but that is a way of life in the operatic world these days. Singers refuse to learn the lesson of Melba in *Siegfried,* when she almost ruined herself. When a really promising opera singer appears today, there is immediate competition, and managers who should know better thrust untrained or inexperienced artists into heavy roles that all but ensure the end of a career within a few years. It takes a peculiarly mature or intelligent young singer to turn down a flattering contract from the manager of the Vienna Opera or the Metropolitan; and in any case, it is the nature of youth to think that it is immortal. In his *The Last Prima Donnas* Lanfranco Rasponi discusses the Marcella Pobbé case. He describes her as a beautiful woman who was the best Desdemona and Tosca in Italy after Tebaldi had left for the United States. Pobbé later accepted a series of *Aida* performances at the open-air Terme di Caracalla in Rome. Rasponi asked her why she, a lyric soprano, would take a role so unsuited for her voice. "Her answer was significant; in a few words it depicted clearly, and put into tragic focus, what goes on in the operatic world today." This is what Pobbé said, around 1960:

> There are no dramatic or spinto sopranos left, and all we lyrics are forced, if we want to survive, to accept these offers. Look at Virginia Zeani and Gabriella Tucci, who are in the same boat. There are plenty of very small-voiced lyrics, and these directors think that we, with the experience of years, can cope with our little more know-how. It is crazy, I know—but I must pay my bills at the end of each month. If one wants to work in the summer, all the opera seasons [in Italy] are out of doors, and they only go in for spectacular works. Only rarely is there [for Pobbé] a Micaela or a Liù. Even Tosca is a far tougher proposition for me under the stars. But we must live.

"Shortly after," Rasponi says, "Pobbé fell into oblivion. As for Gabriella Tucci, a charming lyric, the dramatic roles she undertook caused her downfall too." The prima donnas of the past, Rasponi points out, "stated that they sang with the dividends of their vocal instrument and never with their capital. Today it's capital all the way, and in a period of galloping inflation the capital soon vanishes, leaving nothing."

Perhaps singers today impress the public more as executive types than as prima donnas and divas. Certainly very few of them have the kind of flaming personality that the Melbas, Carusos, Farrars, and Chaliapins had earlier in the century. They were constantly in the news; they fascinated the public, which was eager to know everything about them. Only Pavarotti today has become an equivalent household word, and he is the only one who has become a real media hero—in America, at least. Outside the opera world, most of the other major singers today are anonymous.

Stage directors these days get more attention than the singers in the cast. This is a recent development. In the nineteenth century the singer ruled the opera house. Then it became the turn of the conductor. After the middle 1950's it was the director. When the

Bayreuth Festival resumed after the war, Wolfgang and Wieland Wagner got all of the media attention because of their innovations in staging the *Ring* cycle. All over the world directors hastened to follow in their footsteps, and Wagner became the subject of murky psychological, sociological, archetypal reinterpretations. And not only Wagner. Such directors as Götz Friedrich, Jean-Pierre Ponnelle, Frank Corsaro, Peter Hall, Luca Ronconi, Patrice Chéreau, and Giorgio Strehler were the stars of any production in which they were participating. One got the feeling that they were in business to vie with each other in outrageous conceptions that flouted every concept of the composer. Cio-cio-san and Suzuki in *Madama Butterfly* were now lesbians in Nagasaki. How cute! The Rhine Maidens now cavorted at the bottom of a power plant. *Der fliegende Holländer* was nothing more than the dream of the Steersman. *Don Pasquale* and *Rigoletto* were pushed into the 1920's. The rationale often offered was that in this manner opera could be "brought into the twentieth century." Nobody seemed to ask why on earth any seventeenth-, eighteenth-, or nineteenth-century work *should* be brought into the twentieth century. Often the very same people who applauded these perversions would have been outraged at hearing a Mozart symphony played with the full 104 musicians of the modern symphony orchestra. That—they would be the first to point out—would be ignorant, unstylistic, all wrong in relation to what the composer had in his mind. But in opera equivalent distortions seemed to be perfectly admissible. What it comes down to is that the directors were—and continue to be—indulging in an ego trip at the expense of the composer; and it also is clear that they either do not know the music and its traditions or have no faith in them. Thus cynicism and show business triumph, and the result is opera for those who do not like opera or, even worse, opera for the tired businessman. For the more sophisticated listener, the modern reinterpretations of opera point up an esthetic dichotomy. The music and librettos of operas by Mozart, Bizet, Wagner, Puccini, and all the others have the vocabulary of a specific period. Listening to *Don Giovanni* involves coming into contact with an eighteenth-century artifact and identifying with it as such. To be saturated with that eighteenth-century experience in the opera house, and at the same time to be confronted with an interpretation that uses a twentieth-century frame of reference, leads to nothing less than esthetic schizophrenia.

The 1970's saw the emergence of another phenomenon new to musical history. For the first time classical performers other than singers, pianists, and violinists emerged as superstars. Mstislav Rostropovich became the first superstar cellist; Jean-Pierre Rampal and James Galway, though "merely" flutists, became concert heroes, receiving the kind of fees and media attention normally reserved for top violinists and tenors. Pablo Casals, the greatest cellist who ever lived, never became a superstar, no more than did Artur Schnabel, the pianist whose Beethoven, Mozart, and Schubert playing set the standard in the period before World War II. Casals and Schnabel were pure musicians, were internationally respected, and, of course, had splendid careers; but pure musicians generally lack the charisma and extroversion to be superstars. Rostropovich had both the mastery of his instrument and the necessary charisma. He had the charisma as a conductor, too, though there his work was not as universally admired by the critics.

Still another outburst of frenzy after World War II came with the musical competition. There was nothing new in competitions, of course; they have been with us since the ancient Greeks. In music, artists are always competing: they vie with each other for first prize at the Paris Conservatoire or in the various competitions at any conservatory anywhere; and that has been true since the early nineteenth century. At the turn of the twentieth century there were such major competitions as the Rubinstein prize, won by such immortals as Josef Lhévinne and Wilhelm Backhaus; and later there were such prestigious competitions as the Leventritt, the Naumburg, and the Queen Elizabeth in Brussels. But after World War II competitions became a mania. They proliferated with unchecked abandon on an international scale, and it was hard to think of a major instrumentalist who had not won one of the big competitions. Many serious observers had reservations about competitions and wondered if they were not more a cause for bad than good. The feeling was that competitions fostered correct rather than original playing. But, after all, nobody—in the West, anyway—ever put a gun to a young artist's head and ordered him to compete. And the fact remained that competitions launch major careers. Consider the important postwar pianists who won major competitions. Vladimir Ashkenazy, Leon Fleisher, Gary Graffman, Emanuel Ax, Murray Perahia, Alexis Weissenberg, Radu Lupu, Garrick Ohlsson, Van Cliburn, Christian Zimmerman, Maurizio Pollini, Malcolm Frager, and Martha Argerich are names that come instantly to mind.

And it very well could have been that "correct" playing was not the fault of competitions; rather it was the *Zeitgeist*. Young artists everywhere seemed to be cloned from the same cell.

Personality, daring, communication—the elements that always have been part of a superstar—were missing. A prevailing solemnity was substituted. Musical training for well over a generation had been centered on the correct translation of printed note into sound. Very few liberties were allowed. The result was an emphasis on form and content rather than on expression. Musicians today think in terms of structure, and all over the world they have been taught to get rid of their egos and concentrate on creating a structure in sound. As a result they all tend to sound alike. They approach the printed note with such trembling devotion that their interpretations are all but anonymous. To express that devotion, to avoid any hint of being accused of exhibitionism, they have amputated their personalities. They all want to be profound, and to show their profundity they use prevailingly lethargic tempos. Tempos today are much slower than they used to be; slowness is equated with profundity. It is all very noble, dedicated, honest—and, alas, somewhat boring. Charm, and the sheer joy in music-making as represented by a Caruso, a Kreisler, or a Rubinstein, have virtually disappeared. In its place is a gray uniformity of excellence without inspiration.

30 *Leonard Bernstein, Herbert von Karajan, and Georg Solti*

TIMEBEATERS THREE

IN the 1970's and 80's there could be no argument about the three superstar conductors of the day. They were Leonard Bernstein, Herbert von Karajan, and Georg Solti. Each was active on the symphonic and operatic circuit, though Bernstein was always breaking away to take time off to compose. Each commanded top fees, had an enthusiastic following, made many recordings (Karajan more than any conductor in history), was a supreme egoist, and was always in the papers. Anything they did made news, which is part of being a superstar.

Each has a markedly different style, in life as well as in music. Karajan represents the Apollonian side of music. Under his baton everything proceeds in a cool, objective, totally organized manner. One of the most polished technicians in history, he strives for a kind of tonal perfection (to which all conductors aspire) and achieves it (which not all conductors do). Clarity and precision are the hallmarks of his work, expressed in a luminous, transparent sound when he is at the helm of the Berlin Philharmonic. Solti and Bernstein are much more Dionysian. They worry less about details than about getting at the emotional meaning of the music. It is not that their conducting lacks polish. But both are essentially Romantics where Karajan is classic, and they get temperamentally and even physically involved in the music, while Karajan tends to stand outside it in an objective manner.

Karajan, the oldest of the three, was born in Salzburg on April 5, 1908. Solti was born in Budapest on October 21, 1912. Bernstein was born in Lawrence, Massachusetts, on August 25, 1918. All three started out as accomplished pianists, though Bernstein came to music unusually late. Where Karajan and Solti were at the piano well before the age of six, Bernstein did not start real training until he was a young adult. Karajan and Solti followed the usual European path for conductors. That means opera first, symphony second. It is hard to think of a European-trained conductor who did not serve his apprenticeship as a rehearsal pianist or coach at an opera house. It is equally hard to think of an American conductor who started in opera. Until recently, the United States had very few opera houses but many orchestras, and aspiring conductors first tangled with the symphonic repertory.

Yet of the three it was Bernstein who started at the top, even if he did not have the preparation that Karajan and Solti brought to their debut performances. Intensely musical and talented though Bernstein was, it was not until the age of ten that he began to discover that music was going to be his life. But he did not enter a conservatory. Instead he took private piano lessons, went to high school and then to Harvard. In 1939 he went to New York and shared a Greenwich Village apartment with Adolph Green, then a nightclub entertainer. Green was to be associated with Bernstein in various Broadway enterprises. Then Bernstein went to Philadelphia to study conducting with Fritz Reiner, piano with Isabelle Vengerova, and orchestration with Randall Thompson at the Curtis Institute of Music. He became an expert pianist and a phenomenal score reader. At the Tanglewood Music Festival in 1940, Serge Koussevitzky took an interest in Bernstein, who

Herbert von Karajan (above) at a recording session with the cellist Mstislav Rostropovich. Karajan made more records than any conductor who ever lived. In the 1940's his rival and great enemy was the celebrated German conductor Wilhelm Furtwängler (left).

became his protégé. But nothing immediately ensued. After 1942 Bernstein lived permanently in New York, did some work in jazz, and composed his *Jeremiah* Symphony. Artur Rodzinski took him on as assistant conductor of the New York Philharmonic in 1943. On Sunday afternoon, November 14, 1943, Bernstein conducted a major concert for the first time in his life, as a substitute for an indisposed Bruno Walter. He was young, handsome, charismatic, brilliantly talented, and—above all—American. No American those days was in charge of a major orchestra. The unexpected debut was front-page news in the New York newspapers. From that moment Bernstein never looked back.

Karajan's debut was more orthodox. After studying in Vienna he landed a job with the opera house in Ulm, and in 1934 moved to Aachen. To get those early appointments he had to join the Nazi party. Whether or not he was a committed Nazi is unknown. The consensus is that he was more an opportunist than an ideologist. Then in 1938 he conducted *Fidelio* and *Tristan und Isolde* at the Berlin State Opera and ran into Wilhelm Furtwängler. The two men hated each other, and Furtwängler did everything he could to stop his rising young colleague. There were political implications, too, with a pair of very important Nazi leaders using the conductors as pawns in a power struggle. Furtwängler was a protégé of Joseph Goebbels, the propaganda minister, while Karajan's sponsor was Air Marshal Hermann Goering. Karajan conducted in Italy and Occupied France as well as in Germany. One of Karajan's French concerts was at the Paris Opéra to celebrate the conquest of the country. But it was Furtwängler who finally won, and Berlin's doors were closed to Karajan while his eminent colleague still held power. He had to wait until Furtwängler was dead (1954) before getting a chance to conduct the Berlin Philharmonic. Elisabeth Schwarzkopf, who sang with both of them, has said that Furtwängler's hatred was absolutely irrational, "to the degree that he was unable to pronounce his name! ('This man K!')."

Solti's development also was traditional. At the Budapest Conservatory he studied piano with Bartók and Dohnányi and composition with Kodály. Then he worked at the Budapest Opera as a coach. At the Salzburg Festival in 1936 and 1937 he was one of Toscanini's assistants. Not until 1938 did he make his debut, in *Le Nozze di Figaro* at the Budapest Opera. He spent the war years in Switzerland, where he could not find a position as a conductor. So he resumed work at the piano, won the Geneva International Piano Competition in 1942, and supported himself at the keyboard. His chance came after the war, when he was invited by the American military authorities to conduct *Fidelio* in Munich. He had never studied conducting ("If you want to conduct, *conduct*!"). His success was such that he was appointed director of the State Opera in Munich, and he remained there from 1946 to 1952.

Karajan all but took over musical Europe after the war. He moved with incredible speed after he was de-Nazified. Had he really been a Nazi, or was he merely an apolitical opportunist ready to use any means to get what he wanted? The American military authorities had no doubt that he had been a Nazi. A document from the Zonal Offices of Information Services, dated August 16, 1949, presented a bill of particulars. It said that Karajan had joined the party on April 8, 1933, and had been called to the Berlin State Opera to take over as Generalmusikdirektor at the special request of Goering. "Karajan is an excellent conductor," the report stated, "but is known as an ardent Nazi. The fact that he married Anna Maria Sauest, née Gütermann, according to the Nazi terminology a 'Mischling Grades' (25% Jewish), in 1943, did not prove in any way detrimental to his splendid career during the Third Reich. The above information comes partly from the United States Documentary Centre, partly from the files of the former Reichskulturkammer, and from other reliable sources." Karajan had to wait until 1947 before he was permitted to conduct again. His return was at the Salzburg Festival. Gütermann, incidentally, was his second wife. His first, Elmy Holgerloef, was a soprano in his Aachen company. His third wife, to whom he is currently married, was Eliette Mouret, an ex-Dior model.

Within a few years he was everywhere. In London he was the

head of the Philharmonia, an orchestra created for recording purposes by Walter Legge, the Electrical and Musical Industries (EMI) executive. In 1948 he took over the leadership of the famous Gesellschaft der Musikfreunde concerts in Vienna. Furtwängler was furious and refused to conduct there after that. It worked both ways. At a Bayreuth *Meistersinger* conducted by Karajan in 1951 the curtain was delayed for half an hour because Furtwängler was in the audience and Karajan would not mount the podium until he left the hall. When Furtwängler died in 1954 Karajan became lifetime conductor of the Berlin Philharmonic, and soon made it one of the best orchestras in Europe—probably the very best. Nobody but a superior musician could enter its ranks. James Galway, the first flutist in Berlin under Karajan for some years, claimed that the last man in the second violin section of the Berlin Philharmonic was most likely the equal of the best violinist of any other orchestra in Europe. The Berlin Philharmonic musicians considered themselves the elite then, and consider themselves the elite now. At concerts, says Thomas Brandis, the concertmaster, "Every musician is playing for his life."

Karajan also took over the Vienna State Opera, was active at La Scala as producer as well as conductor, led the *Ring* cycle in Bayreuth in 1951, was (and still is) director of the Salzburg Festival, and became the principal conductor of the London Philharmonic. No wonder he was called "the Generalmusikdirektor of Europe." There were jokes about it. Karajan gets into a taxicab. "Where do you want to go?" asks the driver. "It makes no difference. They want me everywhere," answers Karajan. The Karajan mystique developed. He was handsome and aristocratic-looking, owned four luxurious houses, flew his own jet, had a big racing yacht, loved expensive cars, and was a high-speed driver. He had his hang-ups. Clearly he wanted to be taller than his five feet eight inches, and he could not bear to be around tall people unless they were seated or he was perched on a high stool. There was an air of mystery about him. With all of his activity he was a reserved person who kept his life very private. To the German-speaking peoples he became a legend, and John Culshaw saw something menacing about it. Karajan, he wrote in *Putting the Record Straight,* was more than a musician. He was something special to the Germans:

> Unwittingly he had filled the void left by the death of Hitler in that part of the German psyche which craves for a leader. His behavior conformed to pattern. He was unpredictable, ruthless and outspoken. He was exceptionally intelligent and took great care of his appearance: in other words there was an aura about him which, had it been a cultivated or calculated attribute, would have been repulsive.

But one thing was certain. Karajan was a good businessman who tied himself into records, television, and films. Often to work with Karajan was to be part of a package. For a *Ring* cycle he did in Salzburg he had his own orchestra, the Berlin Philharmonic. He had a recording contract for the *Ring* with Deutsche Grammophon. He selected all the singers. He had a deal with German television and films for the *Ring* and for his concerts. He also took his *Ring* production to other houses. Occasionally he was thwarted, though not very often. When he signed a contract for the *Ring* at the Metropolitan Opera, he demanded that his own soprano, rather than Birgit Nilsson, sing Brünnhilde. Here Rudolf Bing put his foot down. He told Karajan that the both of them would be tarred and feathered if they presented a *Ring* in New York without Nilsson. Karajan saw the light. He conducted the first opera of the projected Metropolitan Opera cycle in 1968. It was *Die Walküre,* and he also was the stage director. Bing was not enchanted with Karajan's production. "He told me," Bing said, "that he had taken fourteen technical rehearsals to get the lighting right. I said I could have got it that dark with one." Karajan's business ventures have posed problems to opera houses in which he is working. In 1977, at the opening of La Scala's 200th anniversary celebration, Karajan refused to allow a worldwide telecast of Verdi's *Don Carlo*. He said it would be prejudicial to his interests because many of the singers were under contract to him for a film version of the opera. Karajan got his way, as he almost always does. He can be ruthless when he feels he is crossed. In January 1983 he was in the news. After twenty-eight years with the Berlin Philharmonic his dignity had been ruffled when, after he hired a woman for the clarinet section, the orchestra voted against her. Karajan immediately canceled all of his Berlin Philharmonic appearances except for his eight stipulated ones. That would have cost the orchestra over $10 million in recording contracts alone. The orchestra thought it over and did not take much time before welcoming the clarinetist into the bosom of the family. Walter Legge had said of Karajan that "No other man has worked out so exactly the psychology of players, their needs, and what he must do to get exactly the results he wants." Karajan obviously could manage all that away from the concert hall, too.

Leonard Bernstein was completely different from the autocratic Karajan. He was extroverted, voluble, wanted to be loved, and ended up a star of Broadway as well as a superstar of the podium and even of television, a medium that normally does not produce classical music superstars. After his spectacular debut he was asked to guest-conduct all over the United States; and he did, giving about eighty concerts. He immediately was invited back to the New York Philharmonic as a guest conductor. In 1944 he was named conductor of the short-lived New York City Symphony Orchestra, and the city was a livelier place. Bernstein offered a repertory that the staid Philharmonic avoided; his programs contained music by Stravinsky, Hindemith, Milhaud, Bartók, Shostakovich, and Chávez. When he resigned in the spring of 1948 the orchestra went out of business. By this time he had written his first two popular successes—the ballet *Fancy Free,* which had its premiere in 1944 with the Ballet Theater; and its Broadway adaptation, *On the Town,* with book by Betty Comden and Adolph Green, directed by George Abbott. A film of the show promptly followed.

Bernstein became an American legend, insisting on being called "Lenny," appearing on popular television shows that explained music to the unsophisticated, and becoming a public figure. He continued his Broadway successes with *Wonderful Town* and *West Side Story*. *Candide* did not make an equal impression, though many thought it his best score. Years later, in 1982, it was to have a tremendously successful revival at the New York City Opera. He also composed much serious music, including an ambitious symphony for piano and orchestra, *The Age of Anxiety*. There was some film music, including an impressive score for *On the Waterfront*, starring Marlon Brando. For the 1971 opening of the Kennedy Center in Washington, D.C., he composed an evening's entertainment named, simply, *Mass*. Like many of Bernstein's serious attempts, it was not received with much warmth by many critics. They felt that Bernstein's talent was for sophisticated, entertaining music rather than attempts to grapple with the Infinite; that he should stick to Broadway, where he could have developed into the American Offenbach.

In the 1950's Bernstein started conducting in Europe. At La Scala in 1954 he was the conductor for Maria Callas in *Medea*, a nearly forgotten opera by Cherubini that became one of the soprano's legendary vehicles. He returned to the Philharmonic in 1956, as chief guest conductor, became co-conductor with Dimitri Mitropoulos in 1957, and took over the orchestra the following year. He remained there until 1969, after which he was named laureate conductor for life.

Solti did not come up as fast as Bernstein or Karajan. After his years at the Munich State Opera he went to Frankfurt in 1952 as Generalmusikdirektor. He made his American debut with the San Francisco Opera in 1953 and his Covent Garden debut in 1959. For a few years, between 1960 and 1965, he conducted at the Metropolitan Opera. He also was named conductor of the Los Angeles Philharmonic, in 1960, but never conducted a single concert. When he heard that the orchestra board had engaged Zubin Mehta as a guest conductor, Solti resigned before his first season started. He felt that as music director it was his prerogative to name the guest conductors. A prickly man, Solti often has been engaged in disputes. He had an argument with Jon Vickers during an *Aida* recording, and Vickers left the cast. He also had a public argument with Rudolf Bing over a soprano named for Britten's *Peter Grimes*. He felt she was unfit for the role.

In 1961 Solti was appointed music director of the Royal Opera in Covent Garden and he was there for ten years. He impressed the British musicians as Germanic in manner and temperament. Michael Langdon, the British bass, has written some amusing stories about Solti's first years in London. Solti always was a highly charged man, nervous and jittery, and he communicated that to the singers. If he felt one of them was too tense he would grab the singer's forearms with a hard grip and bark a command, "Relax!"—at which the singer would really go into a muscular spasm. His English was not very good then, but that did not stop him from correcting everybody's English during rehearsals of Britten's *A Midsummer Night's Dream*. "Voman. Cannot you say voman?" Later Solti was told the awful truth. "Vy did not somebody tell me? Ve make it 'woman' then." But Solti commanded respect for his musicianship. Langdon believes that Solti consolidated the work of all of his predecessors and established the Royal Opera as one of the finest in the world. Solti was a man of great strength, energy, and dynamism. "He was not," wrote Langdon, "a man to accept second best."

He became the conductor of the Chicago Symphony Orchestra in 1969. Like all major contemporary conductors, he has always held several jobs simultaneously. For a few years, concurrent with the Chicago Symphony, he was music director of Orchestre Nationale de Paris and the permanent conductor of the London Symphony. He also guest-conducted elsewhere and retained his association with the Royal Opera, Covent Garden. In Chicago he became one of the baton idols of America, and when he brought his orchestra to New York it was always one of the highlights of the season. There was some critical sniping—there always is critical sniping—but audiences responded wildly to Solti's supercharged dynamism. Solti's musical approach, which favored perfection of ensemble and wide dynamic contrasts, was felt in some quarters to be superficial—all gloss and little content, often with an unsettling tenseness. Yet the same charge about

Georg Solti, the exponent of supercharged dynamism. He made the Chicago Symphony one of the most responsive and richest-sounding orchestras in the world.

Leonard Bernstein, the multi-talented American conductor, composer, pianist, lecturer, author, television personality, and superstar.

gloss and overpolish had been leveled against the much more classical conducting of Karajan. But Solti annoyed some critics, who felt that he was using the music to exploit his own ego. All were agreed, however, that Solti had made the Chicago Symphony one of the most responsive and richest-sounding orchestras in the world, and some have compared it to Karajan's Berlin Philharmonic. Solti, never the most modest of men, has been quoted as saying that Chicago should erect a statue to him. "Eight years ago when I came, the orchestra was virtually unknown, nationally and internationally. We accomplished a small miracle."

Solti's beat is unusual. He resembles a shadow-boxing praying mantis, with hunched shoulders, jabs and hooks, exuding physical and nervous energy. He gets brilliant results, and one wonders how much his tense-looking style of conducting contributes to his reputation as a bundle of tense nervous energy. Karajan, on the other hand, uses the least movement of all the virtuoso conductors. He stands almost motionless before his orchestra, eyes closed, molding the music with a short curve of the baton. In fortissimo passages a mere flick of the wrist does the trick. It is Bernstein who is the most kinetic of the three. From the beginning his podium mannerisms have aroused incredulous or amused comment. Music seems aphrodisiacal to him. He crouches and levitates, dances and shakes, sometimes uses the baton and sometimes shapes phrases with his hands, and in general indulges in a kind of choreography unique in the annals of conducting. When a performance is over there is, more often than not, an orgy of crying and kissing. Bernstein is a highly emotional man, altogether different from the reserved Karajan and the sardonic, saturnine Solti.

Bernstein always was an audience favorite. In his New York Philharmonic tenure, however, he often had trouble getting a decent press. His brilliant talent was obvious; but where was Lenny going? What was his major interest? Conducting? Playing the piano? Composing serious music? Writing Broadway musicals? Becoming a media hero via his television music-appreciation shows? Mixing with the Beautiful People? The feeling was that he was spreading himself too thin. Critics also felt that the Bernstein ego was getting in the way of the music. He always seemed to be trying to prove something, and his interpretations could have a curious pedagogic element, as though he were lecturing in sound —underlining phrases, leaning heavily into melodies, overemphasizing, slowing up with an ecstatic look on his face as though to say, "Look how beautiful this is!" At the same time the inconsistent Bernstein could lead superb performances of Stravinsky, Copland, and Haydn. Identification with Stravinsky and Copland could have been expected; Haydn was something of a surprise. Bernstein seemed to have an affinity with Haydn, conducting him with none of the affectations he could bring to other music. His Mozart was nowhere near as convincing as his Haydn; the one he played simply and naturally, the other he "interpreted." Perhaps his major contribution was toward the cause of Gustav Mahler. Bernstein was almost single-handedly responsible for the Mahler renaissance. Here again some critics were uncomfortable with Bernstein's sentimental, lingering approach to Mahler. He would swoon over the melodic sections, indulge in all kinds of rubato effects, and was constantly breaking up the line. And yet there were moments of glory in his conceptions. In the theater he was much more natural. Bernstein, after all, was a child of the theater. When he conducted a *Falstaff* at the Metropolitan Opera it had grace, strength, and a wonderfully plastic line. With age came less necessity to be constantly proving something. In 1984, when he conducted the Vienna Philharmonic on an American tour, his performances of the familiar repertory pieces, especially the Brahms symphonies, were hailed for their warmth, bigness, and generosity. All of a sudden the erstwhile "Lenny"—"the Peter Pan of music," according to one critic—had become an old master.

Bernstein's stick technique owes a great deal to his mentor, Koussevitzky. Karajan admits a debt to Toscanini, and he agrees with Toscanini that if all of the details are right, the performance will take care of itself. At rehearsals Karajan is an anatomist, dissecting every phrase. "If I exert control," he told Bernard Holland of *The New York Times,* "it is in rehearsal. When I rehearse I am like a man with a microscope. I hear everything, every sound. But in the performance I let them be free. At least, they feel that they are free, though they remember the work that has gone on before." It has been a long haul for orchestra and conductor. "It took me twenty years of basic, basic work and relentless rehearsing to mold their personalities and my personality together," Karajan told *Newsweek* in 1982. "And now? We have something that you cannot find anywhere else." Karajan has said that he has tried in his own conducting to achieve a combination of Toscanini's precision and Furtwängler's fantasy. He also admired Victor de Sabata, the Italian epigone of Toscanini. De Sabata told Karajan of the importance of conducting from memory (which Karajan, like most conductors today, does). "If you *really* want to say something, you must forget the printed page" was a de Sabata maxim Karajan has always obeyed. It is interesting to learn that Karajan never tries to see the notes when he is conducting. "The moment you are tied to seeing the notes your mind has shifted away from the music. The Zen Buddhists speak of seeing the front page of the soul and the back page—but in *satori* the two sides are one. This applies exactly to the music."

Solti, like Karajan, came under the Toscanini influence. Very few conductors since then have impressed him—save one. That is Karajan, who is equally at home in opera and symphony. Solti discussed some conductors for a *New York Times* article in 1976. Bernstein, according to Solti, is strictly a symphony conductor. James Levine, who was then starting his brilliant career, was dismissed as "an extremely nice boy." Carlo Maria Giulini, then with the Los Angeles Philharmonic, no longer conducted opera. Karl Böhm was "too old to count." So, Solti concluded, "there were only two conductors equally good on both levels, and I have great admiration for Herbert von Karajan. He has always incorporated for me what a conductor should have: talent, taste, leadership." Solti, unlike Karajan, always has the score in front of him. He has memorized most of the repertory he conducts, but he believes that the presence of the printed note is an important prop: "I want the safety. Everybody makes mistakes. Musicians, especially singers, want the security that the conductor *always* knows. I get nervous myself when I sit in an audience and there is a concerto and the conductor doesn't have a score. I am so angry—it is such a stupidity to create a nervous atmosphere."

The period between 1960 and 1980 saw the emergence of a strong school of new conductors. Prominent among them were Bernard Haitink, Claudio Abbado, Riccardo Muti, James Levine, Carlos Kleiber, André Previn, Colin Davis, Zubin Mehta, and Seiji Ozawa. None of them seriously threatened any kind of coup d'etat. They were all talented, and in some cases were treated with real deference by the critics. Haitink and Davis gathered a very strong group of admirers, who responded to their unfussy, clean-cut, intelligent music-making. Abbado was a brilliant opera conductor, and began to achieve real success as a symphonic conductor. But to the international public, Karajan, Solti, and Bernstein provided something that no other conductors could match. Perhaps some of the youngsters snapping at their heels would eventually catch up with them and even take their places. But that would be a long time in the future.

31 *Luciano Pavarotti and Placido Domingo*

MANO A MANO

IN the 1970's the two best tenors in the world were, by common consent, Luciano Pavarotti and Placido Domingo. Pavarotti was unleashing the most ravishingly beautiful lyric sound since the days of Beniamino Gigli. Domingo, who had a bigger voice, was making connoisseurs talk in terms of Jussi Bjoerling, the great Swedish tenor who had died in 1960. In the first part of their careers, there was no real competition between Pavarotti and Domingo. Both had their areas clearly defined, even if their repertories did impinge in certain operas. But toward the end of the decade Pavarotti began to take on heavier roles, began to give concerts at unprecedented fees, and was the central figure in a media blitz that made his name a household word. To the Americans he became known as the World's Greatest Tenor.

Domingo did not like that at all.

One good reason was that *he* was the world's greatest tenor and, among professionals, generally accepted as such. He had always maintained a very high norm, going along year after year with no discernible deterioration in his powerful organ; whereas Pavarotti, in assuming such roles as Radames, was not doing his voice any good. The former lyric velvet was now being replaced with a frequently hard and even strained sound, and the exciting high notes were gone. In the minds of experts there was no doubt about the comparative merits of the two singers. Domingo was a much more valuable man to have around an opera house. In addition to being a splendid vocalist, he was a fine all-around musician—an expert pianist and a competent conductor. He had an immense repertory that ranged from lyric roles to such dramatic ones as Otello. He was a fast study and a complete professional who was seldom temperamental and got along very well with everybody. In addition he was tall, well-built, and very macho. It was true that nobody ever called him a great actor, but he had improved with experience and competently went through the motions. Placido Domingo was unique at the time. He would have been a valuable member of any house in history. In the 1970's, with so few major tenors around, he was a giant.

Yet it was Pavarotti who captured the public imagination. He had the talent to begin with, of course. He also had a kind of outgoing, generous personality that the more reserved Domingo lacked. Caruso had this kind of personality, and Pavarotti did become the most popular tenor after Caruso. And if Domingo was macho, Pavarotti was sexy. He obviously liked women, and they cooed over this gigantic teddy bear. Pavarotti was indeed gigantic—a six-foot, 300-plus-pounder who happily beamed upon the world and made the world beam back. As with the superstars of the past, whatever he did was automatically news, even when he tried to take off weight. All America followed his epic struggles when he went on a diet; there were interviews and articles in papers across the country. Domingo never could receive this kind of attention, no matter how hard he tried. There was one significant difference between Pavarotti and Domingo. When Domingo walked on stage, he demanded respect. When Pavarotti walked on stage, he demanded, and received, love and adoration. His accom-

Luciano Pavarotti in 1980, leading the Columbus Day parade on New York's Fifth Avenue. He is mounted on a horse. To the American public Pavarotti was The World's Greatest Tenor.

panist, John Wustman, described the phenomenon with astonishment:

> Something happens between Luciano and an audience that I've never seen with another artist. When he walks onto a stage to start a concert—even in a new city—I can feel waves of love for him sweeping up from the audience—before he has sung a note. It is so hard to explain, it borders on the mystical.

It was after the mid-1970's that Pavarotti moved out of the opera-singer category to become a public figure. An incredible media campaign was put together by Herbert Breslin, his shrewd public-relations counselor. All of a sudden the mountainous Pavarotti was to be seen everywhere. There he was on television, endorsing a credit card. There he was in the magazines, photographed in a swimming pool and spouting a whalelike spray. There he was on the back of a suffering horse, draped in a flag and wearing a cowboy hat, leading the Columbus Day parade in New York as grand marshal. Presidential candidate Jimmy Carter was in the parade, but he and all the other notables marched behind Pavarotti. There he was at Radio City Music Hall, singing with Frank Sinatra in a benefit for the Sloan-Kettering Cancer Center. There he was, the star of a Hollywood film, *Yes, Giorgio*. There he was on television as the star in a Christmas special, singing hymns and carols. (By coincidence, of course, a Pavarotti Christmas record of the same music had just been issued.) There he was, giving master classes at the Juilliard School (the classes were immediately seen on television). There he was, singing in the 20,000-seat Madison Square Garden, New York's sports arena. There he was, the recipient of an official biography that had enough syrup in it to float pancakes from here to the moon.

Those in the know claimed that Domingo seethed every time Pavarotti made the headlines. That meant a good deal of seething went on. On the surface the two men maintained a friendly relationship. Behind the scenes there could be hysteria. When the photographer Christian Steiner was preparing a book of his studies of musicians, the Domingo people heard that Pavarotti might be on the cover. They threatened a lawsuit and also warned London Records that Domingo might no longer record for them. It was Domingo who got on the cover. (As it turned out, Steiner had really wanted Callas for his cover.) When Domingo filmed a television show based on Caruso, Pavarotti sniped back by calling it "bad taste."

Their careers were more or less simultaneous. Pavarotti was the elder; he was born in Modena on October 12, 1935. Domingo was born in Madrid on January 21, 1941. Pavarotti's parents were music lovers. The father, a baker, had a fine, untrained voice and was delighted when Luciano showed promise as a singer. The youth's first teacher was Arrigo Pola; then he worked with Ettore Campogalliani. In 1961 he won a competition at the Teatro Reggio Emilia and made his debut there as Rodolfo. He was then getting about $50 a performance. The following year he sang in Amsterdam and at Covent Garden, where he substituted for Giuseppe di Stefano as Rodolfo. When he sang the title role of Mozart's *Idomeneo* at Glyndebourne in 1964 he attracted a good deal of attention. The American soprano Judith Raskin, who was singing in Glyndebourne at the time, remembered people coming to her and saying that she simply had to hear that "incredible" young Italian. At Covent Garden he sang opposite Joan Sutherland. Pavarotti called her "absolutely phenomenal—the fabulous resonance, the shading, such range, such security." He was the leading tenor in the *Lucia* touring company that Sutherland took to Australia in 1965, and he learned a great deal from her. "How is it possible," Pavarotti would ask himself, "that this woman's notes never seem to end? How does she produce this endless chain of sound? I gradually realized it was her breathing." He tried to imitate the Sutherland technique and has paid full tribute to her, saying it was she who taught him how to breathe correctly.

Pavarotti made his La Scala debut in 1965, his American debut with the San Francisco Opera in 1967, and his Metropolitan Opera debut in 1968. At the Metropolitan he sang only two *Bohème* performances; he had influenza. Yet enough came through for Peter Davis in the *Times* to hail the emergence of a major talent with a natural beauty of voice and easy top notes. When Pavarotti returned to the Metropolitan Opera in 1970 another *Times* critic heard his Rodolfo and started writing about him in terms of the Golden Age of Singing. Certainly his recording of Mascagni's *L'Amico Fritz,* made around that time, would uphold that judgment; no more fluent, lovely, elegant singing could be found anywhere in the world. And when, in 1972, he sang with Joan Sutherland in *La Fille du Régiment* at the Metropolitan Opera and snapped off those nine high C's in the famous second-act aria, New York went wild. It was not only the vocal feat; it was also the elegance and musicality with which the music was delivered, and also the presence of those two enormous figures on stage, having a good time and poking a little fun at themselves in a bit of self-parody. As Pavarotti grew older his voice thickened and deepened, all the more in that he started to sing roles not suited for his basically light, lyric organ. His first Radames, in San Francisco, was not a success, and he had trouble in *Lucia* a few months later at La Scala. Had he been content to remain a true lyric in the Tito Schipa tradition, he could have continued to produce beautiful sounds for years to come. Schipa was still singing beautifully in his sixties.

Pavarotti started giving concerts in 1973. That was where the big money was. At the opera he was restricted by the top fee of an opera house. In New York the top fee of the Metropolitan was $6,000 in the late 1970's. It was higher in Europe, where Pavarotti could command as much as $15,000 for a single performance. But in concerts the fees could be astronomical.

Pavarotti's concerts had their ritualistic aspects. The huge bearded man would come on stage with a smile. In his hand would be an unfurled white handkerchief that seemed as big as the flag outside the White House; he needed it the way Linus in the *Peanuts* comic strip needed his security blanket. He always would be accorded a standing ovation. His programs contained popular operatic arias in Italian and French, and there also would be a group of Italian songs. His singing was, on the whole, simple and tasteful. Above all, it was communicative. Pavarotti had the fortunate facility of making every member of the audience believe that the singing was addressed directly to him or her alone. When it was all over, Pavarotti would open his arms to the audience, give a few encores, and depart, leaving everybody with a warm feeling. Here was a man who enjoyed his work. His fees mounted. In 1980 he was able to get as much as $40,000 for a concert. In 1984 it had ascended to an incredible $100,000. Pavarotti boasted that nobody had ever lost money at one of his concert appearances. He was such a draw that every concert was an immediate sellout. Because of his fee, sponsors had to raise admission prices considerably. They would therefore make a Pavarotti appearance a special event, for the pension fund or whatever, and there was always a profit for the sponsoring organization. Pavarotti and Vladimir Horowitz were the two most highly paid classical musicians before the public. Horowitz's earnings were more of a secret, since he worked on a percentage basis, often with television and record tie-ins.

They were, however, not equivalent to Adelina Patti's in her day. Patti still remains the all-time champion regarding fees if the change in the value of money, workers' salaries, and taxes are taken into account. One way of approaching the equation is through salary levels. In the 1870's, when Patti was receiving $5,000 every time she stepped before the public, the average annual household income of a family was, according to the Phelps-Brown *A Century of Pay,* about $150 on the Continent, $220 in the United Kingdom, and $350 in the United States. (In 1910 the figures were, respectively, $250–300, $350, and $600.) Taking the $350 figure given for the 1870's, Patti was earning over fourteen times the *annual* income of an American worker every time she sang. On this she paid no taxes. In 1983, according to the United States Bureau of Labor Statistics, the average household income was $17,544. Assuming that Pavarotti in 1983 was making $100,000 a concert (which he wasn't at that time, unless he was working on a percentage of the gate), the single-appearance index of Pavarotti's fee against the average annual American income would be

5.69 against Patti's 14. Pavarotti also had to settle a huge income tax on his American earnings.

If Placido Domingo was not in Pavarotti's exalted class as a money machine, neither did he do badly. His early training took place in Mexico, where the family moved when Placido was a boy. Both parents were singers, and they encouraged his talent. In Mexico they appeared with a zarzuela (Spanish operetta) company, and it is said that Mrs. Domingo went from the theater after a performance to give birth to her son. As a boy Placido studied piano and later, at the conservatory, conducting with the eminent Igor Markevich. At sixteen he discovered that he had a voice. He started as a baritone, singing and playing the piano in nightclubs, and also appearing in zarzuelas. "I had no technique, just a natural voice," he later said. For a while he studied singing with Carlo Morelli, and then with Franco Iglesias, who concentrated on correct breathing. Domingo and his future wife, also a singer (he had been previously married, at sixteen, but a divorce soon followed), joined the Israeli Opera in Tel Aviv, and the young tenor had problems. He was constantly cracking on high notes, to a point where he was ready to give up singing. Iglesias, who had accompanied Domingo to Israel, worked on diaphragm support, and Domingo finally managed to free his voice. But at best he never was a high-note singer and was uncomfortable above a B flat, though he could and did sing B's when he had to.

In 1966 Domingo sang in the world premiere of Alberto Ginastera's *Don Rodrigo* at the New York City Opera and had a resounding success. Two years later he was at the Metropolitan Opera, and shortly after that all over the world. His voice may not have had the individual timbre of the young Pavarotti's, but it was strong, clear, well-focused, and dependable. He also was a musicianly singer who looked for something more than merely throwing his head back and emitting golden sounds. "Singers," he has said, "can be musicians and not know music. Conductors can know all the music in the world but have no feeling for music because they are intellectual, analytical." As for singers, "I do not like to hear a musically well-trained one who makes me feel they

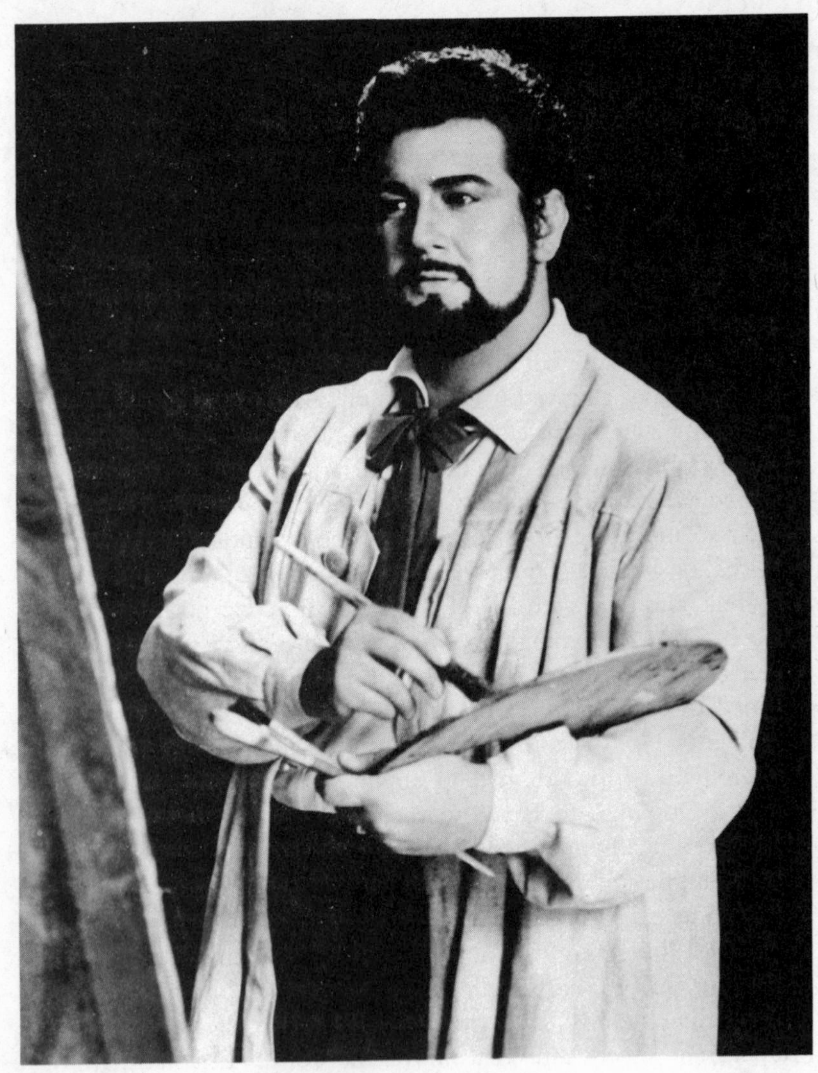

Placido Domingo as Rodolfo in La Bohème. *Year in and year out he maintained a high standard, despite a schedule that would kill most singers. Connoisseurs agreed that he was the best all-around singer in action. But the public never regarded him as The World's Greatest Tenor.*

are singing on a dotted note. It's the *line* of singing, with the dots and legato and staccato, but not making me feel those things are there. To make music you have to go beyond all these things."

When Domingo started moving, he broke all of the physical laws. Singers are supposed to rest, to avoid straining their vocal cords, to sing roles only within the natural compass of their voice. Domingo took everything that came his way. Critics solemnly pronounced his imminent vocal demise, giving him at most a few years before he burned himself out. It would have been true for anybody else, but not for Domingo. He took on a schedule that would have paralyzed any other singer, and he seemed to thrive on it. Most contemporary opera stars go through life without learning more than fifteen or twenty roles. Domingo learned over eighty. In the fall of 1981 he sang at the Metropolitan Opera, in Mexico, Munich, London, Monte Carlo, San Francisco, and Cologne—and that was only the fall. For the entire season of 1981–82 he sang seventy performances of fifteen roles in twenty-one cities in ten countries. When he was not singing opera he was making records and special appearances, and conducting. For some years every Italian opera on records seemed to have Domingo as the leading tenor. (At that, he did not make as many recordings as Dietrich Fischer-Dieskau, who probably made twice as many as any singer who ever lived, what with the song literature, opera, oratorio, and even contemporary music—which very few stars ever touch—at his command.) In the ten years until 1982 Domingo had sung about 1,600 performances of eighty-two roles. As of 1983 he had given close to 2,000 performances of opera, concerts, recordings, and television appearances. It averaged out to one appearance every three days for twenty years. He was the busiest singer in history, and he confounded his critics by going from strength to strength; the voice was as powerful and easily produced as ever.

Where Pavarotti was getting all the headlines and media attention, Domingo went quietly about his own business. But around 1980 he had had enough, and he started to make his move to become the kind of public figure that Pavarotti was. He en-

Domingo in a publicity photo for his LP disc of tangos.

gaged the Italian tenor in a publicity battle and started aiming at a popular market. His record, *Strictly Love,* a joint venture with the popular singer John Denver, was a big success, selling over a million copies. With Julie Andrews he made a Hollywood film of *The Merry Widow*. He hit the television circuit, appearing in guest shows and such spectaculars as the *Salute to Caruso,* in which he was the singing host. He was not beneath appearing with Miss Piggy, the star of The Muppets, on an Actors' Fund program, or endorsing watches, or serving as a disc jockey on a country and western station. Like Pavarotti, he too made a Christmas record; and, unlike him, a record of Argentine tangos. Robert Jacobson, in an *Opera News* interview, asked Domingo what his greatest ambition was. "To be known by many people in my own time," Domingo answered. Not to be the greatest singer; not to be the greatest vocal stylist; but to be the most famous. Apparently it had become an *idée fixe* with him.

It was a major attempt on Domingo's part, but there was almost unanimous agreement that he failed to beat Pavarotti in this area. Some have it and some don't. Domingo didn't. He never managed to twitch the American psyche as Pavarotti did; he lacked the cloud of bonhomie with which Pavarotti was enveloped. Because it was recognized that Domingo's media blitz was a rather desperate and even sad failure, the critics understood and even sympathized with his feelings. They never keelhauled him the way Pavarotti has been by some serious critics who resent his antics. Peter Davis in *The New York Times* wrote an article in 1981 in which he called Pavarotti no longer a singer, but rather a media phenomenon:

> Mr. Pavarotti has left the narrow confines of the opera world far behind and is appealing to a public with only a passing involvement with opera. . . . Mr. Pavarotti's undeniably superior vocal gifts are now only of marginal relevance in the over-all artistic context of the operas in which he performs—his extra-musical fascinations, carefully groomed by a slick publicity machine, have made him seem far more important than the art he is supposedly serving.

Pavarotti at the Scuola d'Italia in New York, congratulating a young artist who had drawn his portrait.

Pavarotti did not help his own cause by the self-serving excuses he made. He was asked by a reporter if he did not think he was overexposing himself, and his answer was a kind of portentous double-talk. Probably he was overexposed, he conceded. "But if you don't take risks, people don't like you." He did not explain what these "risks" were. "The reason I did the American Express card commercial," he continued, "was that Pelé also did one, and he's my favorite soccer player." In a final burst of tenorial logic, Pavarotti said, "The first people on the moon were overexposed. If you don't take risks you don't conquer." His wife helped out with fatuous inspirational remarks normally found only in the lower grade of women's magazines. She said that sometimes she wished she had married a bank clerk with regular hours, "but when I think about it for a minute I change my mind. Because of the wonderful gift that Luciano has given to the world I know it is all worth it." No wonder Pavarotti and the circle around him were not received as intellectual giants, and no wonder he was no longer taken seriously as an artist, even though on occasion he could put everything together and sing a beautiful performance—as he did in 1984 at the Metropolitan Opera's *Idomeneo.*

In the first half of the 1980's it seemed that Luciano Pavarotti would continue to hold his position as the vocal superstar of superstars, just as it was equally clear that Placido Domingo would continue to be the admired workhorse of opera singers and the best all-around performer in the business. Nobody of equal stature or audience appeal seemed to be coming up to challenge them. German, French, English, or American tenor stars seemed to be nonexistent; there were some good ones around; but good does not a superstar make, and none of them could dominate an audience as Pavarotti and Domingo could. The few popular tenors who specialized in the Italian repertory were either nearing the end of their careers (Nicolai Gedda, James McCracken, and Carlo Bergonzi), or unreliable (José Carreras), or lacking in charisma (Alfredo Kraus). Gone were the days when an entire galaxy of tenors could sparkle at the same time, such as the 1910–20 decade in which Caruso, McCormack, Bonci, Slezak, Martinelli, Pertile,

Chamlee, Fleta, Piccaver, Tauber, Schipa, Sobinov, Lazaro, and Zenatello were active. What had happened to the art of singing? Had the jet plane, television, and the overwork due to increased demand acted in a Darwinian manner to kill off an entire species? Concerned musical philosophers could only take comfort from history and patiently await the outcome.

Bibliography

Alda, Frances. *Men, Women and Tenors*. New York, 1937.

Aldrich, Richard. *Concert Life in New York*. New York, 1941.

Arditi, Luigi. *My Reminiscences*. New York, 1896.

Ardoin, John. *The Callas Legacy*. New York, 1982.

Arundell, Dennis. *The Critic at the Opera—Contemporary Comments on Opera in London over Three Centuries*. London, 1957.

Ashton, T. S. *Iron and Steel in the Industrial Revolution*. Manchester, 1921.

Auer, Leopold. *Violin Playing as I Teach It*. New York, 1980.

Baker, Janet. *Full Circle*. London, 1982.

Bauer, Harold. *Harold Bauer, His Book*. New York, 1948.

Berlioz, Hector. *Evenings with the Orchestra,* trans. Jacques Barzun. New York, 1956.

——. *New Letters,* trans. Jacques Barzun. New York, 1954.

Bertensson, Sergei, and Jay Leyda. *Sergei Rachmaninoff—A Lifetime in Music*. New York, 1956.

Bing, Sir Rudolf. *5000 Nights at the Opera*. New York, 1972.

——. *A Knight at the Opera*. New York, 1981.

Bowen, Catherine Drinker. *Free Artist—The Life of Anton and Nicholas Rubinstein*. New York, 1939.

Braddon, Russell. *Joan Sutherland*. New York, 1962.

Brahms, Johannes. *Letters of Clara Schumann and Johannes Brahms (1853–1896)*. New York, 1927.

Brombert, Beth Archer. *Portrait of a Princess—Cristina Belgiojoso*. New York, 1977.

Bulman, Joan. *Jenny Lind*. London, 1956.

Bülow, Hans von. *The Early Correspondence of Hans von Bülow*. London, 1896.

Burney, Charles. *Dr. Burney's Musical Tours in Europe,* ed. Percy A. Scholes. Two volumes. New York, 1959.

——. *A General History of Music*. Two volumes. New York, 1957.

Busby, Thomas. *Concert Hall and Orchestra Anecdotes of Music and Musicians, Ancient and Modern*. Three volumes. London, 1825.

Campbell, Margaret. *The Great Violinists*. London, 1980.

Chaliapin, Feodor. *An Autobiography, as Told to Maxim Gorky. With supplementary correspondence and notes, translated from the Russian, compiled and edited by Nina Froud and James Hanley*. New York, 1967.

——. *Man and Mask*. London, 1933.

Chapman, Guy. *Beckford*. London, 1952.

Chissell, Joan. *Clara Schumann: A Dedicated Spirit*. New York, 1983.

Chopin, Frédéric. *Letters,* trans. E. L. Voynich. London, 1932.

Chorley, Henry F. *Modern German Music*. London, 1854.

——. *Thirty Years' Musical Recollections*. New York, 1972.

Clapham, John. *An Economic History of Modern Britain*. New York, 1964.

Colson, Percy. *Melba—An Unconventional Biography*. London, 1932.

de Courcy, G.I.C. *Paganini the Genoese*. Two volumes. Norman (Oklahoma), 1957.

Crosten, William M. *French Grand Opera—An Art and a Business*. New York, 1948.

Culshaw, John. *Putting the Record Straight*. New York, 1982.

Davis, Ronald L. *Opera in Chicago*. New York, 1966.

Deutsch, Otto Erich. *Handel: A Documentary Biography*. New York, 1955.

——. *Mozart: A Documentary Biography*. Stanford (California), 1965.

Diehl, A. M. *Musical Memories*. London, 1897.

Duey, Philip A. *Bel Canto in Its Golden Age*. New York, 1980.

Dwight's Journal of Music (1852–1881). Twenty-one volumes. New York, 1968.

Eames, Emma. *Some Memories and Reflections*. New York, 1927.

Eaton, Quaintance. *The Miracle of the Met*. New York, 1968.

——. *Opera Caravan*. New York, 1957.

Edwards, Sutherland. *History of the Opera*. Two volumes. London, 1862.

——. *The Prima Donna*. Two volumes. London, 1888.

Elkin, Robert. *The Old Concert Halls of London*. London, 1955.

Farrar, Geraldine. *Such Sweet Compulsion*. New York, 1938.

Fay, Amy. *Music Study in Germany*. London, 1903.

Finck, Henry T. *My Adventures in the Golden Age of Music*. New York, 1926.

——. *Success in Music and How It Is Won*. New York, 1909.

Fitzlyon, April. *The Price of Genius—The Life of Pauline Viardot*. New York, 1964.

Flesch, Carl. *Memoirs*. New York, 1958.

Franca, Ida. *Manual of Bel Canto*. New York, 1959.

Friedheim, Arthur. *Life and Liszt*. New York, 1961.

Ganz, Wilhelm. *Memories of a Musician*. London, 1913.

Garden, Mary, and Louis Biancolli. *Mary Garden's Story*. New York, 1951.

Gatti-Casazza, Giulio. *Memories of the Opera*. New York, 1941.

Gerig, Reginald. *Famous Pianists and Their Technique*. New York, 1974.

Giffen, Robert. *The Progress of the Working Classes in the Last Half Century*. New York, 1885.

Ginsburg, Lev. *Ysaÿe*. Neptune City (New Jersey), 1980.

Gipson, Richard McCandless. *The Life of Emma Thursby*. New York, 1940.

Glackens, Ira. *Yankee Diva—Lillian Nordica in the Golden Days of Opera*. New York, 1963.

Goldin, Milton. *The Music Merchants*. New York, 1969.

Graydon, Nell S., and Margaret D. Sizemore. *The Amazing Marriage of Marie Eustis and Josef Hofmann*. Columbia (South Carolina), 1965.

Greenfield, Howard. *Caruso*. New York, 1983.

Hallé, Sir Charles. *Life and Letters*. London, 1896.

Hanslick, Eduard. *Vienna's Golden Years of Music*, trans. Henry Pleasants. New York, 1950.

Hauptmann, Moritz. *The Letters of a Leipzig Cantor*. London, 1892.

Haweis, Rev. H. R. *My Musical Life*. London, 1888.

Henschel, Sir George. *Musings and Memories of a Musician*. New York, 1919.

Heriot, Angus. *The Castrati in Opera*. New York, 1975.

Héritte-Viardot, Louise. *Memories and Adventures*. London, 1913.

Heron-Allen, Edward. *A Contribution Towards an Accurate Biography of Charles Auguste de Bériot and Marie Felicita Malibran-Garcia*. London, 1894.

Hetherington, John. *Melba*. New York, 1967.

Hoffman, Richard. *Some Musical Recollections of Fifty Years*. Detroit, 1976.

Hofmann, Josef. *Piano Playing, with Piano Questions Answered*. New York, 1976.

Huffer, Francis. *Half a Century of Music in England*. London, 1889.

Hughes, Jonathan. *Industrialization and Economic History: Theories and Conjectures*. New York, 1970.

Huneker, James. *Bedouins*. New York, 1920.

Joachim, Joseph. *Letters to and from Joseph Joachim,* collected and trans. Nora Bickley. New York, 1972.

Kellogg, Clara Louise. *Memories of an American Prima Donna*. New York, 1913.

Key, Pierre V. R., and Bruno Zirato. *Enrico Caruso*. New York, 1922.

Kirkaldy, Adam W., and Alfred Dudley Evans. *The History and Economics of Road Transport*. London, 1924.

Klein, Herman [Hermann]. *The Golden Age of Opera*. London, 1933.

——. *Musicians and Mummers*. London, 1925.

——. *The Reign of Patti*. New York, 1920.

——. *Thirty Years of Musical Life in London*. New York, 1903.

——. *Unmusical New York*. New York, 1910.

Kolodin, Irving. *The Metropolitan Opera*. New York, 1966.

Kotzebue, Augustus von. *Travels from Berlin Through Switzerland to Paris in the Year 1804*. Three volumes. London, 1804.

Krehbiel, H. E. *Chapters of Opera*. New York, 1908.

——. *More Chapters of Opera*. New York, 1919.

——. *Review of the New York Musical Season 1885–1890*. Five volumes. New York, 1886–90.

Langdon, Michael, with Richard Fawkes. *Notes of a Low Singer*. London, 1982.

Laughlin, J. Laurence. *Money and Prices*. New York, 1909.

Ledbetter, Gordon B. *The Great Irish Tenor*. New York, 1977.

Legge, Walter. *On and Off the Record*. New York, 1982.

Lehmann, Lilli. *My Path Through Life*. New York, 1914.

Leiser, Clara. *Jean de Reszke and the Great Days of Opera*. London, 1933.

Lochner, Louis P. *Fritz Kreisler*. New York, 1950.

Lumley, Benjamin. *Reminiscences of the Opera*. London, 1864.

MacKinlay, M. Sterling. *Garcia the Centenarian and His Times*. New York, 1908.

Mantoux, Paul. *The Industrial Revolution in the Eighteenth Century*. New York, 1961.

Mapleson, James H. *The Mapleson Memoirs—The Career of an Operatic Impresario 1858–1888,* ed. and annotated by Harold Rosenthal. New York, 1966.

Marchesi, Blanche. *Singer's Pilgrimage*. New York, 1978.

Marchesi, Mathilde. *Marchesi and Music*. New York, 1978.

Maretzek, Max. *Crotchets and Quavers*. New York, 1855.

——. *Sharps and Flats*. New York, 1890.

Margetson, Stella. *Journey by Stages*. London, 1967.

Marshall, Dorothy. *Industrial England*. New York, 1973.

Mason, William. *Memories of a Musical Life*. New York, 1901.

Mayer, Martin. *The Met—One Hundred Years of Grand Opera*. New York, 1983.

McPherson, Logan G. *Transportation in Europe*. New York, 1910.

Mead, William Edward. *The Grand Tour in the Eighteenth Century*. New York, 1914.

Mee, John H. *The Oldest Music Room in Europe*. London, 1911.

Melba, Nellie. *Melodies and Memories*. London, 1925.

Mendelssohn, Felix. *Letters,* trans. G. Selden-Goth. New York, 1945.

Merlin, Countess de. *Memoirs and Letters of Madame Malibran*. Two volumes. Philadelphia, 1840.

Moore, Gerald. *Am I Too Loud?* New York, 1962.

Moses, Montrose J. *The Life of Heinrich Conried*. New York, 1916.

Moscheles, Ignaz. *Recent Music and Musicians*. New York, 1873.

Mount-Edgcumbe, Richard. *Musical Reminiscences—Containing an Account of the Italian Opera in England from 1773 to 1834*. New York, 1973.

Napier-Tauber, D. *Richard Tauber*. New York, 1980.

Newman, Ernest. *The Man Liszt*. London, 1934.

Nugent, Thomas. *The Grand Tour; Or, a Journey Through the Netherlands, Germany, Italy and France. . .* Four volumes. London, 1766.

O'Connell, Charles. *The Other Side of the Record*. New York, 1947.

Owen, J. Goddard. *A Recollection of Marcella Sembrich*. New York, 1982.

Pallas, P. N. *Travels Through the Southern Province of the Russian Empire in the Years 1793 and 1794*. Two volumes. London, 1812.

Paterson, James. *The History and Development of Road Transport*. London, 1927.

Pavarotti, Luciano, with William Wright. *My Own Story*. New York, 1981.

Perenyi, Eleanor. *Liszt—The Artist as Romantic Hero*. Boston, 1974.

Phelps-Brown, E. H., with Margaret H. Browne. *A Century of Pay*. New York, 1968.

Pincherle, Marc. *The World of the Virtuoso*. New York, 1963.

Plaskin, Glenn. *Horowitz*. New York, 1983.

Pleasants, Henry. *The Great Singers*. New York, 1966.

Ponder, Winifred. *Clara Butt*. London, 1928.

Ponselle, Rosa, and James Drake. *A Singer's Life*. New York, 1982.

Rasponi, Lanfranco. *The Last Prima Donnas*. New York, 1982.

Reeve, Robin M. *The Industrial Revolution 1750–1850*. London, 1971.

Rimsky-Korsakov, Nicolai. *My Musical Life*. New York, 1972.

Rogers, Francis. *Some Famous Singers of the 19th Century*. New York, 1914.

Ronald, Landon. *Variations on a Personal Theme*. London, 1922.

Rubinstein, Anton. *Autobiography*. London, 1890.

Rubinstein, Arthur. *My Many Years*. New York, 1980.

——. *My Young Years*. New York, 1973.

Rudé, George. *Europe in the Eighteenth Century: Aristocracy and the Bourgeois Challenge*. New York, 1972.

Russell, Frank. *Queen of Song—The Life of Henrietta Sontag*. New York, 1964.

Russell, John. *A Tour in Germany . . . in 1820, 1821, 1822*. Two volumes. Edinburgh, 1828.

Sachs, Harvey. *Toscanini*. New York, 1978.

——. *Virtuoso*. New York, 1982.

Saint-Saëns, Camille. *Musical Memories*. New York, 1969.

Schoenhof, Jacob. *A History of Money and Prices*. New York, 1897.

Scholes, Percy. *The Mirror of Music*. Two volumes. London, 1947.

Schonberg, Harold C. *The Great Conductors*. New York, 1967.

——. *The Great Pianists*. New York, 1963.

Schultz, Gladys Denny. *Jenny Lind—The Swedish Nightingale*. New York, 1962.

Schumann, Robert. *Early Letters,* trans. May Herbert. London, 1888.

——. *Music and Musicians,* trans. Fanny Raymond Ritter. Two volumes. London, 1891.

Schwarz, Boris. *Great Masters of the Violin*. New York, 1983.

Scott, Michael. *The Record of Singing*. New York, 1977.

Seroff, Victor I. *Rachmaninoff*. New York, 1950.

Shaw, George Bernard. *How to Become a Musical Critic*. New York, 1961.

——. *London Music*. London, 1950.

——. *Music in London*. Three volumes. London, 1949.

Siloti, Alexander. *My Memories of Liszt*. London, 1913.

Slezak, Leo. *Song of Motley*. London, 1938.

Sommerfield, Vernon. *The Wheel*. London, 1938.

Spohr, Louis. *Autobiography*. London, 1878.

Stasov, Vladimir. *Selected Essays on Music*. London, 1968.

Stassinopoulos, Arianna. *Maria Callas—The Woman Behind Her Legend*. New York, 1981.

Steane, J. B. *The Grand Tradition—Seventy Years of Singing on Record*. New York, 1974.

Stearns, Peter N. *European Society in Upheaval*. New York, 1967.

——. *The Impact of the Industrial Revolution*. Englewood Cliffs (New Jersey), 1972.

Stendhal. *Life of Rossini*. New York, 1957.

Taubman, Howard. *The Maestro—The Life of Arturo Toscanini*. New York, 1951.

Thomson, Virgil. *The Musical Scene*. New York, 1945.

Tuggle, Robert. *The Golden Age of Opera*. New York, 1983.

Van Vechten, Carl. *Interpreters and Interpretations*. New York, 1916.

Verdi, Giuseppe. *Letters,* trans. Charles Osborne. New York, 1971.

Wagner, Cosima. *Cosima Wagner's Diaries, Volume I 1869–1877,* ed. and annotated Martin Gregor-Dellin and Dietrich Mack. Trans. and with an introduction by Geoffrey Skelton. New York, 1978.

——. *Volume II 1878–1883*. New York, 1980.

Walker, Alan. *Franz Liszt—The Virtuoso Years*. New York, 1983.

Walker, Bettina. *My Musical Experiences*. New York, 1893.

Wallace, Robert K. *A Century of Music-Making—The Lives of Josef and Rosina Lhévinne*. Bloomington (Indiana), 1976.

Weinstock, Herbert. *Rossini*. New York, 1968.

——. *Vincenzo Bellini*. New York, 1971.

Whitton, Kenneth. *Dietrich Fischer-Dieskau, Mastersinger*. New York, 1981.

Wineski, Henry. *Maria Callas—The Art Behind the Legend*. New York, 1975.

Woolridge, David. *Conductor's World*. New York, 1970.

Young, Percy M. *The Concert Tradition*. London, 1965.

Zamoyski, Adam. *Paderewski*. New York, 1982.

Index

Photos appearing on the following pages courtesy Music Division, The New York Public Library at Lincoln Center, Astor, Lenox and Tilden Foundations: 8 (top and bottom), 15 (top and bottom), 13, 22, 26, 34, 37, 40, 46, 52, 55, 60, 65, 69, 71, 73, 78, 82, 84 (top and bottom), 87, 98 (top), 106, 109 (top and bottom), 114, 125 (all), 136, 143, 149 (top), 152, 158, 162, 166, 171, 175, 178 (top and bottom), 187, 191, 193, 196 (upper right), 196 (middle left), 196 (lower left), 199, 202, 206, 209, 214, 219, 221, 233 (top and bottom), 236 (top and bottom), 239, 244, 247, 254, 258, 261 (top and bottom), 274 (top), 278 (top; photo by White Studio, New York), 278 (bottom; © Lumiere, New York), 297, 310, 320, 325 (bottom; drawing by LUPAS), 327 (International Newsreel Photo), 337, 341, 345 (by G. Maillard Kesslere, New York), 387 (© Kessler), 390, 393, 402.

Photos appearing on the following pages courtesy Billy Rose Theatre Collection, The New York Public Library at Lincoln Center, Astor, Lenox and Tilden Foundations: 149 (bottom), 272.

Photo appearing on page 270 (top) © Collection of Robert Tuggle.

Photo appearing on page 122 courtesy The Library of Congress.

Photos appearing on page 196 (top and bottom) from *Grosse Deutsche* (pp. 153, 186), reprinted by kind permission of Kindler Verlag, Munich.

Photos appearing on the following pages from *The Life and Times of Chopin* (pp. 70, 57, 45), reprinted by kind permission of Curtis Books and Mondadori, New York: 98 (bottom), 122 (bottom), 130.

Photos appearing on the following pages reprinted by kind courtesy of Angel/EMI Records: 429 (bottom), 457 (bottom).

Photo appearing on page 465 © Robert Lightfoot.

Photo appearing on page 352 © Boston Symphony Orchestra.

Photos appearing on the following pages © Rocco Galatioto: 472, 482.

Photos appearing on the following pages courtesy Culver Pictures: 316, 375.

Photo appearing on page 429 (top) © E. Piccagliani, Teatro Alla Scala.

Photo appearing on page 435: Photographer unknown; print courtesy London Records.

Photo appearing on page 270 (bottom) © A. Dupont.

Photos appearing on the following pages courtesy RCA Records: 364, 366, 371, 380, 384, 406, 409, 424, 478.

Photos appearing on the following pages courtesy Gregor Benko: 196 (upper left), 299, 306, 325 (top), 332, 360, 419, 431.

Photo appearing on page 465 courtesy Deutsche Grammophon/Henry Grossman.

Photo appearing on page 480 courtesy Deutsche Grammophon/Waring Abbott.

ABOUT THE AUTHOR

Harold C. Schonberg was awarded the Pulitzer Prize for Criticism in 1971. He joined *The New York Times* in 1950 as a music critic, was named senior music critic in 1960, and continued in that post until he became cultural correspondent in 1980. Mr. Schonberg is the author of twelve books, including *The Great Pianists, The Great Conductors,* and *The Lives of the Great Composers.* He lives with his wife in New York City and Shelter Island, New York.